LOTFI MANSOURI

LOTFI MANSOURI

{ *An Operatic Journey* }

LOTFI MANSOURI

WITH DONALD ARTHUR

Northeastern
University Press
Boston
Published by
University Press
of New England
Hanover and
London

NORTHEASTERN UNIVERSITY PRESS

Published by University Press of New England

One Court Street, Lebanon NH 03766

www.upne.com

© 2010 Northeastern University

All rights reserved

Manufactured in the United States of America

Designed by Eric M. Brooks

Typeset in Miller and Sveva by Passumpsic Publishing

University Press of New England is a member of the
Green Press Initiative. The paper used in this book meets
their minimum requirement for recycled paper.

For permission to reproduce any of the material in this book,
contact Permissions, University Press of New England, One Court
Street, Lebanon NH 03766; or visit www.upne.com

Library of Congress Cataloging-in-Publication Data

Mansouri, Lotfi.

Lotfi Mansouri: an operatic journey /

Lotfi Mansouri, with Donald Arthur.

p.   cm.

Includes index.

ISBN 978-1-55553-706-7 (cloth: alk. paper)

1. Mansouri, Lotfi. 2. Opera producers and directors—
Biography. I. Arthur, Donald. II. Title.

ML429.M28A3   2010

792.502'3092—dc22   2009044792

[B]

5 4 3 2 1

To
Midge
&
Shireen

CONTENTS

Acknowledgments ix

PROLOGUE } Staging My Own Funeral 1

1 } Paradoxes in Persia 13

2 } Lotfi in La-La Land 29

3 } Americans to the Rescue 52

4 } The Swiss Connection 61

5 } Iranian Intermezzo 81

6 } Back on Track 96

7 } North of the Border 108

8 } The Road Back to Tinsel Town 123

9 } From Provincial to World Class 130

10 } Open Your Golden Gate! 149

11 } Mother Nature Gives an Encore 165

12 } Leaving My Heart 200

13 } An Operatic Voice for North America 216

14 } Lords and Ladies of the Larynx, Potentates of the Podium

Mansouri's Gallery of Illustrious Colleagues 260

EPILOGUE } Still in Progress 294

APPENDIX A } Films and DVDs 297

APPENDIX B } Productions Directed by Mansouri 301

Index 309

ACKNOWLEDGMENTS

Usually after an opening night there is an after-party, when toasts are made to everyone who made a contribution to the production: singers, conductor, director, all the people who collaborated on it. Now I've come to my "opening" of *Lotfi Mansouri: An Operatic Journey* and I want to toast the stars of *this* production.

First and foremost, I propose a toast to Rüdiger Naumann-Etienne and Annette Campbell-White for making this production possible. Annette and Ruedi, I raise my glass to you in gratitude.

More toasts:

In Toronto, to Janet Stubbs and John Leberg, not only for the advice and assistance they've given me on this project, but most of all for their steadfast friendship and support.

In San Francisco, to Bill Godward, who was there at the beginning and without whom the San Francisco chapter couldn't have been written.

To Kip Cranna, whose unparalleled knowledge of the San Francisco Opera and loyalty to the company have been invaluable.

To Koraljka Lockhardt, archivist *par excellence*, who straightened me out when memory failed.

To Ann Farris, for her help with the illustrations.

And to Charles Barber, for putting this show on the road; to Mark Hernandez for continuing on that road; and last, but far from least, to Donald Arthur, who so brilliantly and deftly put the whole thing together—*my* stage director, who has brought me finally to the opening-night curtain.

I raise my glass to one and all.

I don't want realism,

I want magic! Yes, yes, magic.

I try to give that to people.

I do misrepresent things.

I don't tell the truth.

I tell what ought to be truth.

TENNESSEE WILLIAMS

A Streetcar Named Desire

Lotfi Mansouri

PROLOGUE

STAGING MY OWN FUNERAL

Clamori e canti di battaglia, addio!
Della gloria d'Otello è questo il fin!
ARRIGO BOITO
libretto to Verdi's *Otello*

Pride, pomp, and circumstance of glorious war! . . .
Farewell. Othello's occupation's gone!
WILLIAM SHAKESPEARE
Othello

It was one of those events that really trigger mixed feelings.

On the one hand, a gala evening at the San Francisco Opera is always a thrilling occasion for me, a reencounter with a number of talented friends from the profession, past and present, as well as the dignitaries who come to pay honor. While the planning of such an event is always a challenging exercise in logistics, the end result is invariably a stellar evening which everybody enjoys, and it generally commemorates a major event in an operatic career, such as Plácido Domingo's thirtieth anniversary of association with the company or Marilyn Horne's fortieth.

The Farewell Gala on September 8, 2000, however, would be a bittersweet one for me, because it marked my retirement from the San Francisco Opera, arguably the second most important opera company in the Western Hemisphere, after New York's Metropolitan Opera. It would bring down the curtain on an association of nearly forty years, fourteen of which I spent as general director while continuing to mount stage productions. I had been the only company head in the United States to serve this double function in a major house, although it often happens at theaters in Europe and Canada. Knowing the event would be an evening of heart-wrenching farewells, I was beginning to feel as if I were staging something akin to my own obsequies. To make matters more complicated, I was haunted by the premonition that I might be turning over the company to an uncertain future.

Uncertain?

From the beginning of my career, starting with student productions as both singer and stage director in California, ranging to master classes in Bayreuth and Berlin and positions at European and American opera houses, it had always gone without saying that the function of operatic production was to illuminate the meanings and values of the musical and verbal text, to search for and externalize hidden significance and subtexts, and, using intuition and a full armory of acquired skills, to bring the true meaning of each opera as close to the awareness of the audience as possible—in short, to read between the lines, without neglecting to read the lines. Now this approach was being challenged by a new wind sweeping in from Europe, Central Europe in particular, and given a wide variety of appellations, ranging from the rhapsodic to the vituperative. This new movement saw the actual work solely as a point of departure, to be enhanced—or obfuscated, depending on your outlook—by the subjective agenda of the stage director, and those approaches could take some fairly bizarre turns. To complicate matters, the kind of production my colleagues and I had always regarded as self-explanatory was now being ridiculed as old-fashioned or lightweight and—under the worst of circumstances—decried, with sociopolitical overtones, as "pandering to the rich." One of the cradles of this new school of thought was the Opera in Frankfurt, Germany, spearheaded by the general director of that house, conductor Michael Gielen, assisted by a native Californian named Pamela Rosenberg, whom I knew fairly well, having served with her on the jury of some vocal competitions in Europe. Meanwhile, she had moved up the ranks of various European theaters to a position as codirector of the Württemberg State Opera in Stuttgart, where she had been tapped as my successor at the San Francisco Opera. Whatever anyone's point of view might be about the function of staging, this succession would certainly represent a watershed in the history of operatic production in North America, and I frankly had my doubts.

For the time being, however, there was a gala to be planned and some wonderful accolades from high places to enjoy, including a Certificate of Commendation from the U.S. Senate issued by California's senior senator, Dianne Feinstein, a former mayor of San Francisco, and a letter of congratulations from President Bill Clinton. The Gala itself would be attended by celebrities and feature a grand parade of stars. It was meant to be my formal farewell to the house after all those years of direct association, beginning with my first six productions as guest director in 1963. It was also meant to promote the upcoming season, the last of my stewardship, along with its diverse repertoire and exceptional roster of artists. It was intended to be a gesture of thanks to my friends and, as always, an opportunity to raise money. It achieved all this, but the road was anything but smooth. Many things could have gone wrong—and several did.

Although I had the help of the company staff, and friends Bill Godward, the best board president I had ever worked with, and Dede Wilsey, an effective and supportive board member, who had donated a major gift for the event, I basically organized the Gala myself. I wanted to ensure that it would not turn into a gabfest. I wanted it focused on the great people with whom I had worked and on the great music they would sing. I did not want it to be taken over by self-congratulatory civic leaders (and board members), who would make it another sort of event altogether. My presence was the drawing card, but not the act. Although every singer had a personal connection with me, even more important, each one also had a significant connection with the San Francisco Opera. Among those were also the three musicians who would preside over the evening from the conductor's podium and with whom I had a highly varied relationship. First of all, there was the music director of the company, Donald Runnicles, with whom I was barely on speaking terms. Fortunately, I was on a cordial footing with the other two. My dear friend Patrick Summers had started out on the musical staff, advancing to concurrent positions as music director at the Houston Grand Opera and principal guest conductor in San Francisco. He, in turn, was joined by my longtime friend and colleague Richard Bonynge.

Throughout the Farewell Gala, I wanted humor to triumph over sentimentality, and art over artifice, an effort particularly important considering what had been going on behind the scenes. What the audience didn't know was that while a well-organized gala was being planned, the transition period from my administration to Pamela's was pure choas, thanks to a search process gone tragically wrong.

Coming from heavily subsidized theaters in two very wealthy German cities, Frankfurt, the home of Germany's prosperous banking industry, and Stuttgart, capital of a state that housed the world headquarters of several major corporations, Pamela Rosenberg was used to realizing her visions with confidence, calling her own shots and then sending the bill to the government. This would not be the case in San Francisco, also an up-market municipality, as well as a place where financial support was voluntary and to some degree contingent on public approval. Apparently, though, nobody had apprised her of the new circumstances.

Of course, I had been ready and willing to offer her all the help I could as the transition period ran its course, but in the six months she had been working in the house, she never talked to me about business. Not once. This extended period of overlap between the outgoing and incoming general directors was meant to allow for the smoothest possible transition. It was nothing of the sort.

I later learned secondhand that Pamela had canceled André Previn's commission to compose a new opera called *Silk* at a direct cost to the company of $300,000, all of which was siphoned off the budget of my final season, because I had initiated the commission in the first place. I also found out secondhand that she had abrogated the contracts of such major international artists as Olga Borodina, Franz Hawlata, Bo Skovhus, and many others, at a cost of nearly $1 million in cancellation fees. In her second year, her artist cancellations cost the company another $2 million of her own designated budget, while she simply discarded carefully planned productions of *Die Frau ohne Schatten* and *Le coq d'or* outright.

While all of this was going on, my loyal music director was intriguing behind my back, eager to score points with Pamela, a friend from his own European career, whom he had initially proposed as my successor, using some fairly underhanded tactics to push through the nomination with the current president of the board of directors. Having effectively pulled off this statagem, he probably thought of me as yesterday's news, to be cast off like table scraps—and I say that in the kindest possible way.

The planning of the Gala was proceeding amid the usual intrigues with the board, several of whose members had made it clear they wanted me gone as fast and as far as possible. Their lack of support for the Gala was, in that connection, an amusing surprise. In setting the agenda, I was eager to avoid cluttering the stage with local politicians, all of whose speeches could be counted on to run at least ten minutes overtime. To cite a single example, our charming but loquacious mayor, Willie Brown, one of the few San Franciscans besides myself to wear a hat, would probably claim twenty minutes for himself plus an additional three for the fedora. So I decided there wouldn't be any speeches. I wanted to serve the audience, and the audience wanted singers.

I wanted Dame Gwyneth Jones. We went back forty years to our early days at the Zurich Opera House, where we worked together while she was still a mezzo, and to her initial soprano years in Geneva, where I often directed her as well. Beyond that, she also sang many times in San Francisco. Everything about her radiates class, and in a most alluring way. However, when I phoned her, I never expected to have to start dancing like a hyperactive vaudevillian in a double-time tap number. The problem was that Gwyneth's best singing days were behind her and that she (or we) would have to select her repertoire very carefully to avoid exposing its weaknesses in upper registers that had once been glorious. But the only way she would sing for us was in exchange for the title role in a production of Puccini's *Turandot*, in which she regrettably could no longer cut the mustard. My darling Gwyneth just didn't know when to start winding down. She had built a wall, an alcazar, around the topic of her dwindling vocal ability, and I couldn't penetrate it. Singing is her life, so who was I to tell her to stop living? For Gwyneth's own sake and ours, we could not possibly have made such an offer. Dame Gwyneth did not appear at the Gala.

Other singers were less complicated.When I first asked Renée Fleming to sing for us, she said yes, but pointed out that she would have to travel from New York. The Met had agreed to release her from rehearsals so that she could fly out on Wednesday, rehearse with us on Thursday, perform on Friday, and be back East on Saturday. Renée was supposed to depart from midtown Manhattan at 1:00 P.M. on Wednesday, but the Met suddenly did an about-face and demanded that she stay until 6:00 P.M. on Thursday. The Met further insisted that she be back onstage by 11 A.M. on Saturday. This was all connected with a revival of *Don Giovanni*, which wasn't due to open for another three weeks anyway. It was maddening and totally needless. I couldn't help but wonder if it had anything to do with the fact that Sarah Billinghurst, then working for the Met, had not been appointed to take my place in San Francisco. Alberto Vilar had even offered a $20 million dollar donation to the company (money that turned out to be nonexistent) to get them to hire her, but they declined.

Not for the first time, San Francisco–based oil heir, composer, and opera patron Gordon Getty came to our rescue. Renée was transported from Lincoln Center to JFK Airport on Thursday, and we flew her first class to San Francisco. She rested that night, and we arranged a special noon rehearsal on Friday. I reorganized the Gala so that all of her work would take place in the first half, concluding that section with what proved to be the crowning glory of the evening, the sublime Act III trio from Richard Strauss's *Der Rosenkavalier* in the rarefied company of Susan Graham as Octavian and Anna Netrebko as Sophie. The audience was ecstatic. Then, at intermission, a limo sped Renée to San Francisco Airport, and Gordon's private jet raced her back to New York. Flying red-eye, she made the rehearsal at 11 A.M. the next morning. What a trouper!

Some rescues, though, proved impossible. The beautiful eighteen-page, full-color Gala program announced that soprano Patricia Racette was scheduled to appear. She joined us to run through her aria at the dress rehearsal on Thursday, but early Friday afternoon she sent a message saying that she would be unable to sing. She had decided to save her voice for Verdi's *Luisa Miller*, which was to open the following night. We had five hours to change the lineup.

Then came the Gala itself, given in our company's seventy-eighth season, and my thirty-eighth in San Francisco.

It began with the national anthem with the audience singing along. This was followed by the overture to *Ruslan and Lyudmila*, and then our master of ceremonies, the music administrator, Dr. Clifford Cranna, took over. "Kip" Cranna linked our groundbreaking collaboration with the Kirov Opera in Saint Petersburg to the first singer, the aforementioned Anna Netrebko. I had brought her from Russia when she was twenty-three to make her North American debut as Lyudmilla in Glinka's masterwork. At the Gala, she sang the "Wedding Aria" from *Ruslan*, and at that moment I knew we had a hit. The audience exploded.

Then I remembered that all of this was happening in the name of someone whose cultural roots could not have been farther from this place. As I sat with my wife, Midge, I could not stop my mind from returning to a childhood that had taken place in another culture, experienced in another language, and propelled by music totally unlike what the three thousand people at the Gala were hearing that evening. No matter how hard I tried to concentrate on the event before me, the sounds

With Anna Netrebko after the opening of Don Giovanni, *Spring 2000.*

of remote and ancient traditions kept flooding in. When the illustrious mezzo Judith Forst appeared with a very young Twyla Robinson, one of our Adler Fellows, in a duet from Donizetti's *Anna Bolena*, symbolizing my desire to inspire gifted up-and-coming artists through interaction with the top people in the craft, I was struck by how far I had traveled to be here, but here I was—responsible for creating such a partnership and such a moment. When Renée Fleming brought the house down with Blanche's final aria from *A Streetcar Named Desire*, "I can smell the sea air," I knew that a moment like this would have been inconceivable in my native culture. I had commissioned that opera and put together the artistic team that created it, and only in America would that have been possible.

And so the evening rolled on. For me, it whizzed past as an alternating current of excitement and memory, music and improbability.

My old friend, the great comedy star Carol Burnett, narrated a three-part presentation written by Kip Cranna and produced by Linda Schaller

With Carol Burnett in Santa Barbara, 2001. I was being honored as an "Illustrious Alumnus" of the Music Academy of the West.

and Kate Gaitley, telling my story. Good as it was, the tale it told defied credibility, and it didn't even hint at the fundamental preposterousness of my unlikely biography. Who was I, Lotfollah Mansouri, from a broken home in the capital city of Persia, to have had a hand in any of this? It was to laugh!

When operatic legend Dame Joan Sutherland—by then retired—came onstage with her husband, Richard Bonynge, she offered the kindest of words: "Richard and I are so happy to be here in San Francisco tonight to help honor our dear friend and longtime colleague, Lotfi Mansouri. He was always so well prepared and could sing all the roles. . . . I cannot thank him enough for the help he has given me in my career over the years."

I nearly wept. The first time Joan and I had worked together was in 1963 when, along with Richard, we did our first *La sonnambula* in San Francisco. Back then, it had also been my first production at the theater and my first collaboration with Joan, although she had frequently sung the role in the course of her illustrious European career. Now Richard was here to honor my wish to commemorate that first staging by leading a fine performance of an aria from the Bellini opera with the lovely Ruth Ann Swenson as soloist.

I kept shaking my head. Had I really done such a thing? Had someone who had started out on the dusty streets of Tehran really worked with La Stupenda? It was almost ridiculous. I felt so proud—and so inadequate.

Other artists made an appearance in the next three hours to remind one of the world's most sophisticated opera audiences of their great gifts: Susan Graham, Ruth Ann Swenson, and Patrick Summers, along with Richard Margison, Marcello Giordani, and Carol Vaness. I am proud to say that I had showcased them early in their careers. I believe they trusted me at those initial stages, and they have been rewarding audiences ever since. Dmitri Hvorostovsky was glorious that night, as much as he had been when I brought him to San Francisco early in his American career. So, too, was Olga Borodina, whom I had introduced to this country in one of our Opera in the Park concerts, years before. It was an evening of dazzling talent, and I marveled at my good fortune in having been able to intervene in their favor at one time or another.

I don't know if it enhanced my reputation when Carol Burnett trotted out an old film of me playing the legendary Enrico Caruso—at least it was a definitive display of chutzpah! There I was on the screen, emoting my hambone heart out back in the days when I thought I might have had a chance at a Hollywood career. The audience laughed, and so did I.

In fact, the Gala concluded with one long joke, a sly wink. For this comedy number I had nine Adler Fellows from the 2000 ensemble join us at the end of the evening. These nine, Suzanne Ramo, Twyla Robinson, Donita Volkwijn, Elena Bocharova, Katia Escalera, Todd Geer, Kyu Won Han, Philip Horst, and John Ames, are all examples of our hope and treasure. I have always wanted to communicate the visceral excitement of opera. These nine young people did just that, magnificently. Talent like theirs has been the heart and engine of my entire career. When I had those wonderful new artists close the show, it was my way of paraphrasing the line Al Jolson loved to use so many years ago: "You ain't heard nothin' yet!"

But I had another, more subtle purpose that night. I was not unaware of how certain circles looked down on me as a mere entertainer, congenitally incapable of comprehending the greater subtleties, the deeper purposes. For the closing number, I had selected a parody, which was good fun and which also expressed my personal response to that appraisal. It was called "Lotfi's Song," written by the brilliant Elaine and Norman Campbell in Canada in 1981.

Opera is educational.
Opera is so refined.
People who are seen at the opera
Have usually just recently dined
On duckling and champagne and pheasant . . .

When it was initially performed, it celebrated my first decade in Toronto. Now it commemorated my last four in San Francisco. Connecting them was the paradoxical theme "Opera is educational. Opera is so refined," turned on its head. I was determined to make a fundamental point: for opera to have a real impact on an audience—any audience—it must connect to listeners at an *emotional* level. It must entertain. It must tell the truth. It must be direct and exciting. Before the mind can be changed, the heart must be opened. Too many operas, or their interpretations, have failed because they have been more interested in speaking to the initiated than to all of humanity. "High concept" usually gets in the way of even higher communication, and I wanted one more opportunity to make that point—but in good humor.

Patrick Summers on the podium got the joke. So did our nine singers. I'm not absolutely certain that the audience did. The entire text was anathema to my successor, and to the world of *Hochkonzept* that she would soon be bringing to San Francisco. It was also a parody of transition, and of traditional roles. So long as I was staging my own funeral anyway, I couldn't resist the temptation to tell a few jokes at the service. The best, a visual one, was saved until the end.

"Lotfi's Song" began with a vamp as our young artists came onstage. In ensemble, in duet, trio, and solo, they took turns singing Norman Campbell's witty and mocking lyrics. Gradually, appearing backlit from upstage, they were joined by members of the San Francisco Opera Chorus, in motion but silent.

The soprano sang:

Who's the one who razzle-dazzles them,
The one to hit the highest "D,"
Stops the show with such vibrato?

Then the basso slyly interjected:

(You might think he was castrato.)

And the tenor resumed:

> It could only be the tenor
> Who is me!

He was followed by coloratura Suzanne Ramo as the prima donna:

> Well, someone has to hit the highest note
> With trills that outsing the nightingale
> With a voice so filled with power
> It can reach the CN Tower
> That's your basic coloratura—me!

By now, the whole chorus had moved downstage, and the company of singers was standing together.

Throughout the evening, I had been nowhere to be seen, watching the show from the penumbra of the general director's box. That's how I wanted it; in part, it was the best way to shield myself from Important Dignitaries, who might have demanded equal time. But it was also a setup. Nothing is ever what it seems. Every object has its secret side. At about 10:15 P.M., the audience saw a bald man wearing a tuxedo and thick black glasses walk briskly from upstage right to downstage center, waving to everybody in sight. They roared, thinking it was me. Then, to their surprise, he started singing. The audience was now thoroughly confused.

> ENOUGH! ENOUGH! ENOUGH!
> Attend, you stars and prima donnas.
> I'm sick of hearing all that jazz
> Though you take me for a rat
> Underneath I'm a Persian cat.
> I'll show you how to do it with pizzazz!

The bald tenor then merrily directed a kick line, with everyone singing:

> For whatever you think opera is
> It's simply good old-fashioned showbiz, showbiz.
> What do you get for your money?
> What do you get for your dough?
> You get the most spectacular extravaganza,

Sensational, magnifico!
What do you get for your money?
What do you get for your dough?
A really sensational show!

A minute later, to the laughter and bewilderment of the audience, the number ended in a blackout.

But the show wasn't over yet.

When the lights came back up, *two* bald men in tuxedos and black glasses came onstage, one from each side. They met in the middle, each startled by the appearance of the other. After a quick mutual examination, in a vaudeville gag that harked back to an old Marx Brothers mirror routine, and probably even beyond that, the first one bowed to the second and then took his place among the kids. The first bald gentleman was tenor Matthew Lord. The second one was me. The audience had been deceived and amused, and I had avoided subjecting them to the tedium of having myself introduced by some garrulous dignitary.

I was never the one they imagined me to be.

All my life, I have been an actor. The Gala, and this book, explain the who and why of a fifty-year career in the making of opera, and two of its greatest companies, and a number of its most important commissions.

"Please, let's welcome back our wonderful artists for tonight, " I said, and all of our soloists returned to center stage. I thanked the audience for their welcome and their support. I reminded them that "we are here for you, to bring beauty, joy and new ideas." I thanked the entire San Francisco Opera team, declaring that "I worship their friendship, their dedication and their talent."

On that magical evening, we were celebrating the very art of opera, and on that night, I was remembering the extraordinary chains of incident and personality that had taken me thousands of miles to this place and through so many wonderful times and people in between.

This is not work you see—this is not a profession. This is life. Here's mine!

1

PARADOXES IN PERSIA

My life began in contradiction.

It was a sweltering June day in 1929. At my parents' home in Tehran, my mother, Mehri, was undergoing a very difficult birth. It was so painful and bloody that the midwife thought both mother and baby would probably die. As soon as I emerged, they put me on a block of ice and turned all their attention toward saving my mother's life.

Fire and ice—what better way to begin? The life I have led and the terrain I have occupied have always been rich with contradiction. I was raised a Christian in a Muslim country. Throughout my career, I have felt the desire to make great art and faced the necessity to beg for money to do it. I had a need to work with great artists and tasted the agony of their insatiable egos. I knew the necessity of enriching the repertoire by commissioning new work and the cold reality of the obstacles that could prevent it. Above all, I needed to build wide audiences for the greatest of all art forms in a culture that exalts money and materialism above all values.

I was born into paradox.

As I lay on my ice block, my mother's life was saved. When I began gurgling, somebody finally looked at me. Apparently I was going to make it, too. It was considered a miracle that I had survived, so my grandmother named me "Lotfollah," Arabic for "kindness of God." When I was finally shown to my mother, she screamed with fear and pushed me away. She couldn't cope with having a baby. She was only fifteen.

I believe my father, Hassan Mansouri, was eighteen to twenty years older than my mother, but my parents' exact ages are a mystery to me. Much of what I think I know about my childhood is a mixture of experiences I recall, secrets that were spilled, and gossip that became half-truths I wanted to believe. I do know this: My father was a member of a conservative family of merchants and landowners. In addition to their rural holdings, they had an important presence in the bazaar of Tehran, where they controlled one of the largest intersections dealing in silver, artworks, and—even a hackneyed cliché is generally based on truth—carpets. The bazaar was a powerful engine of the Persian economy, and its masters were the leaders of society.

As Mohammad Reza Shah Pahlavi learned in 1979, the bazaar wielded political power, too. When the *bazaari* turned away from the tyrannical shah and shifted their support to the fundamentalist mullahs, Pahlavi's days were numbered.

My father led the family. Trained as a lawyer, he never practiced in the courts. He dealt only with the legal and financial interests of the family. His union with my mother was, like most marriages at the time, arranged. Her family was also prominent, and its elders knew my father's people. Even so, in outlook and attitude, the two clans could not have been more different.

My mother, Mehrangiz Jalili (nicknamed Mehri), came from an intellectual, avant-garde family. They were related to the Qajars, the dynasty that had controlled Persia from 1799 to 1921. Although my mother's family was ethnically Persian, it were considered Western by the standards of the day. Her relatives, including some of the women, traditionally studied in France. They spoke French as their second language, and they were imbued with the spirit of the Enlightenment. The women of my mother's generation did not wear the all-enveloping garment called the *chador*, preferring French fashion. In the 1930s and 1940s, the first shah made it illegal for women to be veiled. He was trying hard to move Persia toward the West. In fact, his policemen would rip the *chador* off of women on the street—just the opposite of today's religious police, who now summarily arrest and fine any woman they deem to be "immodestly dressed" or who gets caught wearing makeup.

My mother's family was different from my father's in another remarkable way: his was Muslim, hers Christian, having converted in the throes of historical developments that had come to a head back in the 1930s and early '40s.

At the beginning of the century, the Anglo-Persian Oil Company had made its first big strike, which began a period during which Great Britain took a proprietary interest in the government of the country, try-

Me at age ten with my mother, Mehrangiz Mansouri, outside of Tehran.

ing to protect its petroleum reserves from the Germans and Russians. Shortly after World War I, General Edmund Ironside made one of the greatest blunders in the history of the region by appointing a semiliterate thug by the name of Reza Khan, a six-foot, three-inch-tall former gunnery sergeant once singled out for valor in combat, as a kind of local front man for his army of occupation. It was a little like selecting Don Giovanni to run a convent.

Reza Khan wasted no time kicking all the foreigners out of the country and then led a coup against the ruling Qajars in 1921, adding the name Pahlavi to his own, renaming the country Iran, and declaring himself shah. His regime was an odd admixture of healthy Westernization and low-grade corruption, on the one hand modernizing the country by force, initiating women's rights, introducing a railroad, built for him by the Germans, from the Persian Gulf to the Russian border, and setting up a telegraph network, while on the other helping himself to other people's property and lavishly bestowing considerable largesse on his friends and supporters. Finally, in 1941, he decided to ally his regime with Nazi Germany, and the British government assumed control of the nation for twenty-four hours, then politely but firmly suggested that he abdicate in favor of his playboy son—or else!

Back in the 1930s, my mother's family had been among the victims of his usurpations, and her father vehemently protested these seizures, as a consequence of which he had to go into hiding. He ultimately sought and found protection with a group of Presbyterian missionaries from the United States, who fed and sheltered him for several months. He never forgot their decency and soon adopted their religion as well. In those days, although it was frowned upon, becoming Christian was still not illegal. Like many converts, my grandfather ardently believed in his new faith and began going from village to village proselytizing and urging the villagers to convert, not a very successful effort, which often found him leaving town precipitously to avoid being stoned by the outraged peasants. My grandfather was not intimidated, though, and actually built a Presbyterian church in Tehran as a token of his gratitude and faith. When I was five, my mother also formally converted to Christianity and began sending me to Bible classes at this church. My father seems to have tolerated it, although many of my contemporaries did not. I quickly learned to survive in two worlds. While reading about the disciples by night, I was studying Islam by day, memorizing long passages from the Koran. My gift for juggling conflicting demands came from those early days of living in competing cultures. I was never forced to choose between my parents or their religions. I didn't really take either faith very seriously, nor did I believe anyone had cornered the market on the truth. I still don't.

I loved to go to the Presbyterian Church because of the singing. I also enjoyed the festivity of Christmas, when we would put up a decorated tree and hold a Christmas party. On these occasions, my mother would serve French ham, but of course she gave it another name because pork is just as forbidden in Islam as it is in Judaism. My mother called it nightingales' tongues. Apparently Allah didn't notice.

In Islam, children do not celebrate a birthday. Instead, on the day of their birth, their parents choose a Prophet's Day, a day of the year marking the death of a prophet. On that day every year, they vow to give certain foods to the poor. I really like this part of Islamic tradition with its boundless hospitality. My Prophet's Day was in February, and the special food was a rice pudding prepared with saffron. Every year, we prepared dozens of plates of it. Some went to the poor, I suppose, but it was also misdirected to friends and relatives. In this sense, some Muslims would probably feel right at home with American televangelists.

My mother was different in other ways, too. She translated French literature, such as the stories of Alphonse Daudet, into Farsi, the Iranian national language. She loved music and played a traditional stringed instrument called the *tar*. She enjoyed singing traditional Persian songs, and on Fridays, the Persian equivalent of Sundays in the Western world, a day of rest, she presided over an afternoon salon. Many learned individuals, including men, would read poetry there, something that was virtually unknown in Tehran at the time.

Beyond adopting Christianity, her family had other unusual traits. My mother was one of five children. Her sister was a sweet, severely retarded woman, who came to live with us for a while. My mother also had three brothers, the eldest of whom was a doctor. He married a woman with a "bad" reputation, and they were often left out of family events. Her second brother taught French, and his students included the shah's family. He married a distant cousin, another woman who had been educated in France. They had a daughter, and years later I found out that I would one day be expected to marry her. This brother was not my favorite relative. When I was twelve, I played some sort of prank, and he announced to my mother that I would grow up to be a criminal. The uncle I preferred was my mother's youngest brother, a poet. He worked for the Ministry of Culture and traveled around the country giving lectures on women's rights and the importance of education for women. Today he would be imprisoned for this. I still have a photo of him lecturing before some two thousand women. He was witty and handsome and usually in love with someone who did not reciprocate his affections. He was also passionate and self-destructive. I remember waking up in the middle of one particular night. People were running around in a frenzy, and a doctor was called. The next morning, one of our servants told me that my uncle had tried to hang himself. Later he attempted suicide again with poison. He died quite young, probably from tuberculosis. In my childish innocence, I thought this was a romantic death. I had seen a movie about Chopin, in which Cornel Wilde coughed up blood, which fell on the piano keys.

Such was the romantic, dramatic, and enigmatic life of my mother and her family. I never understood what my father saw in her, although

*My uncle Jahangir Jalili, speaking to a group
including men and women, in the 1930s.*

that was a question nobody asked in those days or in that culture. My mother was passionate, questioning, and deeply alive. My father was distant and aloof, the sort of person who shook hands with his children when he dropped them off at school. I was aware of him at breakfast, the only meal where the three of us sat together. It was quite formal. My contribution consisted of answering questions: "Yes, sir," and "No, sir." Throughout my youth, I never had a single conversation with my father that could be regarded as intimate. For the first thirty years of my life, I believed that my father had no emotions at all. He had a collection of preconceived notions about life and our place in it, perhaps best illustrated by something that happened when I began getting keenly interested in music and expressed a desire to have a piano and learn how to play it. He suggested it would be more appropriate simply to buy the instrument and then hire somebody to play it for me. To this day, I find myself seeking his absent emotions throughout my work in opera.

Thus it is not hard to explain why my mother dominated my life and the lives of all those around her in both a positive and a negative way. She was a charming conversationalist and a renowned hostess, famous for the lively parties she gave at our house in Tehran. But she also had her dark side, which she artfully concealed. She had a hysterical, uncon-

LOTFI MANSOURI

trolled temper, which she often took out on me. She sometimes pinched me so hard she left bruises. Later, when I got smart and speedy enough to run away, she took to throwing things at me.

In her social circle, she was also a tireless matchmaker who loved to bring people together. She had a large and varied collection of admirers.

It would be unfair to describe my mother as a flagrantly promiscuous woman. She suffered greatly because she was way ahead of her time, intelligent and romantic, yet living in a stifling society in an arranged marriage. At fourteen, she had been taken by the hand into a room, where a curtain was opened and a man pointed out to her. Then she was told that he would be her husband. She craved affection, but she didn't get much from my reserved father. Many men were attracted to her because she was not like other Iranian women, but I believe her relationships with them never went beyond the flirtation stage. Nevertheless, that aspect of her life was hard for me to accept as a small child yearning for the warmth of an intact home life.

Years later, I found out how much my father really cared for her, but that is a story for later on.

Her love life was filled with bizarre events. One night a man came to the front door, carrying a package. Inside was an emerald necklace. My father answered the door, sent the package back, and said nothing. Another of her swains once arranged to have me kidnapped. My mother and I were walking near our house when a car pulled up and two thugs jumped out. They tried to grab me, but my mother screamed and tugged until they gave up and raced away. She had rejected the man, claiming she could not leave her son. Apparently he decided that getting rid of me would solve his problem.

On another occasion, we traveled to Mashad in eastern Iran and one of the holiest shrines for Shiite Muslims. While we were on this "pilgrimage," a samovar tipped over, and I was severely burned. We went to the hospital, where the attending physician was a handsome young man doing military service. He, too, became one of my mother's admirers and later was appointed minister of petroleum in the cabinet of Reza Shah Pahlavi. I ran into him again in the 1970s at a reception in Tehran. Although it was clearly apparent we both remembered his infatuation with my mother, we didn't talk about it.

My mother's romantic adventures were also painful because she used me as a confidant. For hours on end she would complain about her situation, telling me I was the only reason she stayed in her marriage—then she would burst into tears. I was ten years old.

Today we would call this emotional abuse. I believe, though, that she had no idea what she was doing to me. She was so unhappy, so frustrated, and so lonely, and apart from me, she had no one to talk to. She couldn't talk to her family, and it was probably too risky to talk to her friends. We were only fifteen years apart, which must have made it seem to her that she was talking more to a friend than to her own offspring. Those sessions must have made her feel better, because eventually she would stop crying and go off to her own bed. By the time she finally left, of course, I was the one sobbing desperately, unable to fall asleep. With no brothers, sisters, or friends to confide in, I felt like the loneliest child in the world. It was at this point that I began designing escapes. The first of them was school. The second was theater.

I was attending a coeducational kindergarten not far from our home in north Tehran. One of my classmates was the future shah's youngest sister, Fatemeh Pahlavi. Our teacher organized a class play, and she and I starred in the show. I was the Grand Vizier, while Fatemeh played the Queen. A new world was dawning. Unfortunately, the crown prince himself, along with his mother, the real queen, and his two sisters, decided to attend our little performance. I knew who he was and got so nervous that I wet my pants and started crying onstage. From that moment, I developed a lifelong sympathy for singers' nerves.

After this thespian venture, I went to a school run by Zoroastrians, members of one of the oldest religious sects in Iran. They had a reputation for being intellectual urbanites, firm in their honesty and principles, a bit like Muslim Jesuits. Our school was very strict, with excellent teachers, and known throughout the capital for the high quality of its academics. It was an all-boys' school.

Poetry was essential to my education. It was traditionally the most beloved art form in Persia, and I was raised in its embrace. My parents, like most educated Persians, were great reciters of poetry and could find a poem for every occasion. Edward Fitzgerald's superb translations may have made Omar Khayyam more popular in the West, but in our culture, a fourteenth-century mystic from Shiraz called Hafez is regarded as far superior. Much of what he wrote, such as this incredible verse with its haiku-like simplicity, has an enormous impact to this day:

Good
Poetry
Makes the universe admit a
Secret.

In Tehran we also used Hafez as a kind of fortune cookie. Like many Iranians, my mother used to consult his works whenever she faced a difficult decision. Her ritual was to let the book fall open at random, then skip back to the beginning of the poem and take the advice that was offered. It was remarkable how often the book opened to an appropriate passage.

For my friends and me, poetry became a kind of game. As a test of memory, one of us would toss a verse like a baton in a relay race, and then we would see who could continue the poem, using the last letter of the previous line as the first letter of his line, until someone was unable to continue.

I was a voracious reader. I found Western books, especially those in French, particularly influential. They helped me forge a lifetime appreciation for Western culture. But even as I was becoming European, I read as a Persian. I did most of my reading in my favorite room in the house. As in most Iranian homes, this room was centered around a corsi, a coal-burning stove covered by a rug and surrounded by sofas piled high with cushions. There was no central heating. Tehran can get bitterly cold in the winter, and the *corsi* is the cozy center of winter life. We took many of our meals there, and this is where I devoured many books, discovering the world beyond.

My grandmother's garden was also a major part of my world. Grandmother was a tiny woman with blue-green eyes, and I loved her unreservedly. Her garden was in an old part of Tehran, an immense tract, with a stream running along one end of it. The splash of fountains and the shade of the trees were extraordinary in a land that is mostly desert. Today, it is the strongest memory I have of my homeland. But my grandmother's garden was more than my playground. It was also my theater, the place where I could act out all my fantasies. It was there that I made up dramas and then played all the roles: men, women, or children. I borrowed grandmother's *chador* and transformed it into whatever I wanted to portray. If I was a prince, it became my robe; if a queen, it was a huge skirt. If I was an Arab nomad, I would wrap it around myself and ride speeding camels in the caravans of my mind.

All of this make-believe was fueled by movies. They had an immense influence on me, and continue to do so to this day. Because it was socially acceptable for a woman to go to the movies with her children, my mother began taking me when I was five or six. We once went to see *Anna Karenina* with Greta Garbo, Fredric March, and Basil Rathbone. In one scene, Anna is in Venice with Count Vronsky, and she sees a little tyke who reminds her of the son she left behind in Russia. My mother began to sob. Even at that age, I understood how much she identified with Anna's unhappy marriage and the even more disastrous alliance into which she had mistakenly thought she could escape.

If we watched Iranian movies, I can't remember them. We went to American, Egyptian, German, French, and Russian films, projected with translation cards that interrupted the action every few minutes. Because of the general illiteracy, a theater employee also walked up and down the aisles reading the dialogue out loud. In addition, the people who could read kept explaining the plots to their friends, evoking a constant chorus of elucidations along the lines of ". . . and then he said he loved her." It was completely chaotic, but I didn't care. I was falling in love with American movies and American movie idols. I was a tall, dark Iranian boy who wanted to be blond and all-American, like Alan Ladd. I was so crazy about Ladd that I sent him a fan letter and received an autographed photo, which I pinned up on my bedroom wall along with posters and movie magazines.

I also fell madly in love with Vivien Leigh. When *Gone with the Wind* came to Tehran, it was shown as a serial. The first half ended with the scene where the Yankee soldier walks up the steps of Tara. We had to wait three months to find out what happened next. I went to the first half at least twenty times and memorized the script. I did the same thing with the second half.

I was becoming a believer. I was convinced that Mr. and Mrs. Miniver should have been my parents. Although I was nuts about Carmen Miranda, with all that vegetation on her hat, my greatest crush was on Deanna Durbin. When she was seventeen, she starred in *First Love* and introduced me to opera. The final scene culminates in "Un bel dí" from *Madama Butterfly*, which she sang in English. It blew me away. I had never heard anything like that before. In those days, Hollywood used a

LOTFI MANSOURI

lot of operatic music, although rather peculiarly. In *His Butler's Sister*, my beloved Deanna actually sang "Nessun dorma." It was years before I discovered it was a tenor aria. And Risë Stevens, a real opera singer, sang some syrupy English lyrics to a baritone aria originally written for Wolfram von Eschenbach in Wagner's *Tannhäuser*, which had been selected for some reason to enhance the original score by Oscar Straus in a film version of *The Chocolate Soldier*, in which she starred beside Nelson Eddy.

It was all bizarre, but I didn't know that then. I even indulged in some feats of vocal transsexuality myself. Before my voice changed, I could imitate Jeanette MacDonald. I improvised on music I heard in her movies. I used to go out into our garden and sing so loud that the servant next door would come over and ask that I stop so his mistress could have a nap undisturbed. When she awoke, he would come back to announce that I could resume my performance.

I also heard my first symphonic music from the silver screen. We had no such tradition in Iran, and I owned no Western recordings. I heard Tchaikovsky and Wagner, Liszt and Chopin, and I loved it all. In part, this was because I could never develop any affection for Iranian music. I hated the mournful drone of its melodies and especially the vocalism of my mother's favorite singer, the portly Egyptian songstress Oum Khalsoum, whose records were adored everywhere in the Middle East. She may have appealed to millions, but she never did anything for me.

When I became a teenager, my cinemania started getting me in trouble. I was no longer picked up by the chauffeur after school, so I started fibbing to my mother that I was visiting friends. Instead, I rushed to a movie and then raced frantically through town to make it home by six. My mother smelled a rat, and she said she could tell from my eyes where I had been. Like a fool, I would rush into the bathroom as soon as I got home to wash my eyes out. This only made them red and instantly revealed what I had been up to. One morning, over family breakfast, she told my father what I was really doing after school. He didn't say a word. He just got up from his chair and slapped me. It was the only time he ever laid a finger on me, and I think it was more for the lie than the movies.

Most of my friends were foreigners, and many of them were Russian. There was Gary (real name: Igor), with whom I used to trade copies of *Photoplay* magazine. When we greeted one another, we would often whistle the themes from Bette Davis movies. There were also three charming Russian teenage girls living next door. Many of my friends were Armenian, including Ray Aghayan, who went to California around the same time I did and became an extremely successful costume designer. Another early friend was Harmik Gasparian, who subsequently metamorphosed into the well-known fashion designer named Harry Gasperian in New York City.

The Armenians were important to me. They were the closest you could get to Westerners. They were Christian, and girls danced with boys at their parties. The Armenian church was across the street from my school, and I envied them their Easter eggs and happy games. I joined a club of Armenian boys and girls and went with them on donkey rides in the Alborz Mountains north of Tehran. But I wasn't really all that interested in meeting donkeys. I wanted to meet Americans, and, of all people, it was the Russians who were about to make the introductions.

After the Allies had sent the abdicated Reza Shah into exile and catapulted his son to the Peacock Throne, they sent troops to occupy the country, to make sure the younger Pahlavi wouldn't get into the same kind of mischief his father had. They also used the German-built railroad to shuttle supplies to the Russians to hold off the German invaders in Stalingrad in a move that marked the beginning of the end for the Nazis. In the winter of 1943, a major conference was held in Tehran, at which President Roosevelt of the United States, British Prime Minister Churchill, and Premier Stalin from the Soviet Union met to agree on some significant policies for the future conduct of the war. During this conference, some seven different Stalins were sighted around the city, apparently doubles placed there to enhance his security.

The Russians, the British, the French, and the Americans established military camps on the four corners of Tehran, with the Russians and Americans as the predominant forces. Most Iranians shunned the Americans. Not me. I listened to broadcasts on the Armed Forces Network, moved to the rhythms of Artie Shaw and Glenn Miller, and tried to understand the zany wordplay of a takeoff on a quiz program called "It Pays to be Ignorant."

While I was delighting in the sounds coming over the radio, the Russian girls next door took American boyfriends, and I finally got to meet some authentic Yanks. My father was horrified that these girls were dating Americans, but he didn't prevent me from going with them to the movies at the base. The first time I did, it was a glorious evening. The movie was *Objective Burma* starring Errol Flynn. I will never forget the smells of the solders' soap, their aftershave, their food. That night I felt like a featured player in an American movie.

A few weeks later I went back. This time it was for *This Is the Army*, a touring musical review. The all-soldier production I saw featured comedy skits and a collection of Irving Berlin songs, including some evergreens like the title tune and "Oh, How I Hate to Get Up in the Morning." This was the first time I saw singers, dancers, actors, a chorus, and an orchestra—all performing together. Nothing else I had ever experienced made such a profound impression. The fact that it was an "American" experience made it all the more appealing. Visits with these foreigners and their free-and-easy way of living were changing me. At the same time, I was becoming totally negative about the Iranian lifestyle, which seemed to me devious and hypocritical. I hated the constant gossip. My mother and her cousin would get together and whisper behind their fans, gleefully ripping everyone's reputation to shreds. At the same time, these people would put up an elaborate front of exquisite manners. All of it served to disguise true feelings and true intent. If you were offered a piece of cake, you could never just say yes. You had to indulge in an odd formality called *taroaf*, in which you would be offered something and you would be expected to refuse it over and over again before finally relenting and accepting it. You were never allowed to take the direct approach. This extended to every transaction, and I thought it was a phony waste of time. I preferred the straightforward American way.

When I needed a new pair of shoes, my father would take me to the bazaar, where we headed down a street of shoe merchants to a shop owned by one of his friends. He would examine the stock very carefully, before saying, "That's a good pair of shoes for my son. How much are they?"

The merchant would quote the Persian equivalent of about a hundred U.S. dollars, whereupon my father would rise to his feet and say, "Okay, Lotfi, let's go." As a parting shot, he would offer one-quarter of that price, whereupon the shopkeeper would launch into a pathetic threnody, claiming his children would starve to death if he accepted that paltry sum. I sat there, mortified, while the two men haggled on and on, eventually meeting in the middle at about one-half the asking price, which was the figure they both had in mind in the first place. I found this downright humiliating, but they loved it. We always went to the same shops, and everybody knew everybody else. My father was play-acting, and so was the shopkeeper. If you are laid back about it, this little drama can be fun, but I despised it so much that it affected my ability to handle money later in life. I thought bargaining was so degrading I would pay people whatever they asked just to get it over with.

Clearly my life in Iran was one of privilege. Our family always maintained its links to the countryside. Like many other prosperous families, we owned entire villages in a system just one step away from feudalism. (In America, I knew everybody lived like kings.) The peasants worked the land and got to keep 20 percent of the harvest for themselves. The other 80 percent belonged to the landowners, so most of the food that we ate at home came from one of our own villages, or *deh*. One of my most exotic memories of those days is of a night when we rode back to Tehran from a *deh* on camels, forming part of a caravan delivering produce to the market in the capital. It was a moonlit summer night, and I romanticized the experience even further by pretending I was in a movie. I had visions of Ronald Colman, Victor McLaglen, and Sabu riding over the next sand dune.

Vacations were another matter altogether. They were an embarrassment. My father's family did not socialize with my mother's relatives, and vice versa, except on formal occasions like weddings and funerals. As I grew older, I began to see dissent, tension, and hypocrisy at every family event. Lavish displays of love and affection were nothing but a dumb show in which everyone was just role playing. No one cared, or even knew, what was going through my mind. I was far more comfortable with the American custom of telling it like it is. With the Americans, at least we all knew where we stood. I began to feel that I'd been born in the wrong country, in the wrong family.

Even though the Pahlavis were desperately pushing modernization, it wasn't really working. I grew up in a period of social upheaval, when the old world and the new reluctantly coexisted, cheek by jowl. Massive trucks and sleek limousines shared the highways and byways with camels and donkeys. Trains on the shah's railroad roared past villages where nothing had changed for a thousand years. International banks were opening subsidiaries to process the vast petroleum revenues, but the real hub of the Iranian economy was still hidden in the shadows of the bazaar. My father's mother was modern enough to sit at the dinner table with the male guests, but she still wore the *chador*. Everywhere I

LOTFI MANSOURI

looked, there were contradictions. Growing up in this tug of war, I was ineluctably drawn to the West. That was where I would study, and eventually live and work. Nothing bonded me to Iran.

Fortunately, it was a family tradition that its younger members study in Europe, especially France and Britain. Many of our relatives had done it, and a year before I graduated from high school, my father began to discuss—with others—where I would be sent for further education. He never asked me what I wanted to do. He thought the only respectable occupations were the law, medicine, architecture, and engineering. Soon enough, he made my choice. I was to study medicine in Scotland, at the University of Edinburgh.

Meanwhile, Ray Aghayan and I had been taking English lessons from an Armenian woman and dreaming of California. The thistles of Scotland held no appeal for us. I began to make my case for stateside studies, but my father's enthusiasm knew bounds. He had no respect for American education, which he believed was vapid and insubstantial. He held a very low opinion of American culture in general and saw no point in my wasting my time in it or being corrupted by its superficiality. The points of attraction I found so desirable were utterly lost on him, but I finally won out because my mother pleaded my case. After months of urging, he finally relented and agreed to allow me to study medicine in the United States. I chose the University of California at Los Angeles, overtly because a great many Iranians, as well as my Armenian friend Ray, had settled in southern California. In reality, though, I loved the idea of UCLA because it was so close to Beverly Hills and my beloved movie stars.

I graduated from high school in June 1947, and from that point until my departure in October, my life was a whirlwind of Western clothes, Western ways, and American English. All of this helped distract me from the fact that I would soon be leaving my family, perhaps forever. The eve of my departure finally arrived. My parents gave a farewell party, and our house was filled with some sixty or seventy chattering relatives crowding into my bedroom with questions and advice. An aunt would appear at the door to inquire, "Does he have enough underwear?" A cousin would saunter in to inspect my luggage. An uncle would fret about money, and my father actually showed up with a money belt. Somebody else asked to inspect my passport. The emotional pitch got so high that I suddenly began to weep. My mother saw this and slapped me hard across the face, screaming, "If you don't want to go, why are you putting me through this hell?" She did not understand that I was crying because of the stress and emotion of the moment. She was in the same state herself, crying because her only child was about to travel halfway around the world to live in a country she had never seen.

Finally the nightmare came to an end.

The next morning, I was taken to the airport for the first leg of my journey, a flight to Beirut. It was the first time I had ever flown, and the chaos at the terminal was unimaginable. All my relatives, the same ones who had histrionically taken their leave the previous evening, were present and accounted for. Mass farewells are part of Iranian tradition, and one reason that Tehran Airport is a beehive of crowds and confusion. Finally, after I had been hugged and kissed a million times, my flight was called, and I heaved a sigh of relief as I headed toward the gate to my plane.

I felt a tap on my shoulder. It was my father. He smiled sadly and asked, "Aren't you going to say good-bye to me?" It was the first time I had ever witnessed my father show *any* kind of emotion whatsoever. I was speechless. I gave him a hug; then, in a state of shock, I went aboard.

It took twenty-three years and another life in another world for me to discover my father. It took the same new world for me to discover myself. The price I paid was fearsome. Today, I regret more than anything that I succeeded in repressing my Iranian background to such a degree that today I have a hard time remembering it. All that wonderful literature, those poems and stories—they're all lost to me. I've forgotten most of my Farsi. The Koran is a closed book. Its beauty and musicality are gone. And the lushly festooned caravan that was my family's position in the world has vanished like morning mists above the desert.

The future was still just one big question mark.

2

LOTFI IN LA-LA LAND

I could not have asked for a better transitional threshold to my new life than Beirut, which back then, although still part of the Middle East, was very much like the south of France with its elegant boulevards, new Hollywood films, and American University. I arrived there and settled into a hotel, where I was to remain one week until the departure of the ship that would take me to America. My first night there was the first time I had ever been alone—and independent. With my perspiration-soaked money belt and traveler's checks hanging up to dry, I sat on my bed, exhausted from the flight and the excitement of the past six weeks, and started crying. It was the last time I ever felt homesick for Tehran or my family.

Then things started looking up. I boarded the SS *Marine Jumper*, a converted troop ship, along with a group of other students, all moving on to America to continue their education. During the three-week journey, we heard gunshots from Haifa and stopped at Alexandria, Athens, and Marseille, but nothing was as exciting as my first view of the Statue of Liberty and the Manhattan skyline.

Arriving in New York, I was taken with the mystical feeling that I was coming home. I recognized landmarks from movies I had seen, visited Radio City Music Hall (showing *Cass Timberlane*, starring Spencer Tracy and Lana Turner), and saw *Forever Amber* with Linda Darnell and Cornel Wilde at the Roxy, along with the remarkable stage shows that alternated with the film screenings. Dining at a local automat was a godsend for me; I had yet to learn the names of the foods in English, but I could look into the little compartments at the various dishes available and make my selection by dropping nickels in the slot.

After a few weeks in New York, during which I connected with my

Tehran friend Harmik, I started the long train ride that would transport me to Los Angeles, then sat glued to the window watching the huge country pass in review. When I arrived in California, I contacted Ray, with whom I was to room. I also got in touch with a Mr. and Mrs. Stevens. Mrs. Stevens was the sister of an American missionary my mother and I had come to know through my Christian grandfather. She became a kind of guardian for me, teaching me English and taking me to major local events like the Rose Parade on New Year's Day in Pasadena.

After the 1947 Christmas holidays, I registered at Los Angeles High School for one semester to learn better English and study the terminology I would need for my pre-med studies. For the first couple of weeks, I wore a suit and a tie to class, but little by little I began to go native. The formally dressed Persian must have seemed like quite an oddity amid the other seniors at L.A. High.

Six months after I got there, my mother unexpectedly showed up, saying she missed me. With the aid of the Stevenses, we found an apartment near the campus of the University of Southern California, where my mother had decided to perfect her English. The fact that I would be studying at UCLA, a one-and-a-half-hour commute by bus from USC, never occurred to anybody. But one of the advantages of this place was that the woman across the courtyard gave piano lessons, so at least I could learn how to play the instrument.

It didn't take long for our small apartment to become a kind of social center for a large group of Iranian students. My mother was Lady Bountiful, bestowing her largesse on them all, cooking familiar dishes, entertaining them, and often continuing her matchmaking activities. A couple of marriages actually resulted from her machinations. With our apartment bursting at the seams with Iranian visitors, the only place I could study in peace and quiet was the library at USC. Finally, fed up with the chaos I thought I'd left behind in Tehran, I moved closer to UCLA in Westwood, some eleven miles to the west, where I shared an apartment with a foreign student from France and an American from Wisconsin. This strained my relationship with my mother considerably. Nevertheless, after announcing that she would be visiting for only three weeks, she wound up staying for three years.

During my first semester at UCLA, in the fall of 1948, I had to carry a full course load: English for foreign students, chemistry, physics, and zoology. I seemed to be studying around the clock, because I was forced

LOTFI MANSOURI

to check the dictionary for the words I didn't know. My linguistic frustration was compounded by my total disinterest. When I expressed this to my student adviser, he suggested I take a class without homework, such as chorus. When I said I didn't know how to sing, he recommended a voice class for one semester and chorus thereafter. Talk about *kismet*!

At my first lesson, the teacher had me run up and down the scale, then stopped me and said, "You just sang a high C!" I had no idea what he was talking about. Then he handed me some music—one piece was an aria from *La Bohème* called "Che gelida manina." Later on, I took classes in piano, solfège, and music history. One member of the music faculty had a Dickensian surname: Irwin Windward. A tenor himself, he encouraged me to take private lessons with him. After only a couple of months in his care, I lost my natural high C and could only croak up to an F, a full five pitches below.

Meanwhile, my pre-med studies hit rock bottom. I managed to flunk Chemistry 1A four times. But I did get As and Bs in my music and acting classes. My adviser called me in and pointed out that I couldn't study just for the classes I liked.

Finally, after three years, my mother decided it was time to go back home. By this time, our relationship was virtually nonexistent, which caused me great guilt later on. On her way back to Iran, she stopped in Paris to visit a sick cousin and stuck around there for more than a year.

When she finally returned to Tehran, she reported to my father on all my musical activities—and the failure of my pre-med studies. His response to this intelligence was a typical Iranian tactic. I had been receiving a monthly stipend from him. Suddenly, the checks stopped. Presuming there had been a temporary breakdown in postal deliveries (at the height of the Korean War, with Europe still devastated), I borrowed money from the Foreign Student Department. Four months later, I received a letter from my father with a one-way ticket back to Tehran and a promise to settle all my debts if I used it.

The predicament I faced defined the old saying about being stuck between a rock and a hard place. Were I to go back to Iran, that would be it. I would never be able to live a life of my own. I would be isolated, unhappy, a stranger in the land of my birth, and permanently indentured to my father. But if I decided to ignore these instructions and venture out on my own, it would mean supporting myself, quite a challenge for somebody who had never even tied his own shoes until he left Iran.

The next morning, acting on the advice of some friends, I cashed in the ticket and paid off most of my debts. I never saw my mother again, and it would be another twenty years before I laid eyes on my father.

But I had no time to concern myself with family ties as I closed ranks with the work force. I cleaned houses, did gardening, guided tours of the homes of the stars in the snazzy suburbs, and packed chocolates at a candy company. Fortunately, I had acquired a driver's license in a vastly spread-out city where anyone without a car was fairly lost, and I spent hours tooling up and down the freeways from one odd job to another.

I also worked behind the checkout counter at various branches of a supermarket chain in Los Angeles. That job proved to be the venue for a number of incredible adventures in my life, ranging from the perilous to the exalted. One Christmas Eve, in a somewhat unsavory neighborhood in Hollywood, I found myself looking down the barrel of a gun in a holdup, but I managed to extricate myself intact. I was transferred to a more up-market branch in Beverly Hills, where I had the joy of waiting on some of the movie stars I had admired on the screen. Loretta Young and Eleanor Parker were among the regular clientele, and Zsá Zsá Gábor would show up to buy cases of frozen fish to nourish her large contingent of cats. I also got to meet Ezio Pinza, who was in Hollywood making his screen debut in a picture called *Mr. Imperium*, costarring Lana Turner. I couldn't help confessing to Mr. Pinza that I had ambitions of doing opera, and he graciously said he thought I had the right body for a singer.

The store had been selected as a model supermarket to show Queen Juliana of the Netherlands on her visit to the city, and the management singled me out to welcome her majesty by presenting her with a pineapple. I also had the privilege of waiting on Middle Eastern royalty, in the person of the exiled Queen Nazli of Egypt, the mother of King Farouk. I remembered the queen from a previous encounter in Tehran when I was ten years old. She had come for the wedding of her daughter, Farouk's sister Fawzia, to the shah. The wedding feast turned into a fiasco when the electricity went out and the rice never got cooked—perhaps a harbinger of the marriage to come, which ended in divorce and Fawzia's eventual exile to California. Recounting my memory of these events to her majesty in the store while her Rolls-Royce waited outside was a surreal experience, and she must have felt very uncomfortable—at least, she never came back.

In an attempt to do something a little more related to my studies than these menial tasks and to learn some skills that might more practically bring in an income, I decided to take an education course. Hoping to acquire a teaching certificate, I found myself practice-teaching at L.A. High School, where I had been a student only a couple of years before. I began getting occasional jobs singing solos at weddings and funerals, and at a sophisticated supper club called the Purple Onion, I introduced the audience to chamber opera in the form of Gian Carlo Menotti's early work, *The Telephone*.

As I was on a foreign student's visa, I had to carry a full load of academic subjects in order to remain in the country. That was when I shifted my major from pre-med to psychology, while continuing with my musical and theatrical activities. I auditioned for a student production of Benjamin Britten's *A Beggar's Opera*, and much to my amazement, I was put in the chorus. It was my first stage experience. The conductor was Dr. Jan Popper, with whom I would ultimately become closely associated.

Los Angeles in the 1940s and '50s was an amazing place, filled with brilliant artists who had managed to escape from the Nazis. There were composers, writers, conductors, musicians, people like Bertolt Brecht, Thomas and Heinrich Mann, Max Reinhardt, Franz Werfel, Bruno Walter, Otto Klemperer, and many others. There was also the father of twelve-tone music, Arnold Schoenberg, whose daughter Nuria was one of my classmates at UCLA. I wandered into this milieu without realizing its importance. Among this group were Dr. and Mrs. Fritz Zweig. I was lucky to connect with them, to study voice with her and coach with him.

Dr. Zweig had been a conductor in Germany and a member of Otto Klemperer's musical staff at the Krolloper in Berlin, the first opera company in the world to present truly provocative avant-garde stagings and introduce a remarkable collection of new works. He was a cousin of Stefan Zweig, the great Viennese author and librettist of Richard Strauss's opera *Die schweigsame Frau*. As Tilly de Garmo, Mrs. Zweig had been a lyric coloratura soprano, who sang Sophie in *Der Rosenkavalier* with Lotte Lehmann as the Marschallin at the Vienna State Opera. Mme. de Garmo slowly and patiently worked on my voice, and little by little, I got my high notes back, but I would never again have the natural freedom I started with. Dr. Zweig was a fantastic pianist, who could make eighty-eight keys sound like a full orchestra. Lawrence Foster, Johnny Green,

Henry Lewis, and many other conductors studied with him. Whatever taste in music I may have, I first gained from him.

One day, as I was practicing in one of the rehearsal rooms, the door opened and someone with a smiling face asked, "Are you a tenor?" The face belonged to a young man named Irving Beckman, an excellent coach, who would later have a lengthy European career. He explained that the tenor in a musical act they were preparing had been drafted into the Korean War and asked if I could take his place. My partner in this act was a young woman named Carol Burnett. We entertained at ladies' clubs and even sang at some rallies for a Republican officeholder aspiring to higher things by the name of Richard M. Nixon (beggars can't be choosers), all for the princely sum of five dollars a gig. Irv Beckman was also a coach at the UCLA Opera Workshop and encouraged me to join it as well, tenors being in short supply.

And so began my direct association with Dr. Jan Popper, the Workshop's director and one of the most important and influential people in my career. A Czech émigré, he had also been a pilot in his country's air force. His first position in California was at Stanford University in Palo Alto, where he conducted the first West Coast production of Benjamin Britten's *Peter Grimes*. Later he came to UCLA, eventually taking over the Opera Workshop. He gave mesmerizing lectures and sparked a great love for opera in the hearts of many students, myself included. He was the Pied Piper who drew me into opera, a truly seductive personality. It was not until later, when I got to know him better, that he came tumbling down from his pedestal. He proved to be a very complicated, narcissistic individual. He was a user—and incredibly insecure. Uncomfortable with other people's successes, he would often strategically plant stumbling blocks in their paths, but they didn't always trip them up.

I sang a number of roles with the Opera Workshop, with a widely varied palette ranging from the lyric Ferrando to the spinto Rodolfo and on to such heroic characterizations as Lohengrin and Otello. Young tenors rush in where experienced artists fear to tread. I also sang the title role in the West Coast premiere of Claudio Monteverdi's *Orfeo*, performed with period instruments long before it became fashionable, and I sang Laca in Leoš Janáček's *Jenůfa*, another West Coast premiere. What an education!

One day in the autumn of 1951, I saw a notice on the Student Union bulletin board recruiting supernumeraries for the San Francisco Opera,

*As Laca in a UCLA
Opera Workshop
production of* Jenůfa,
*with Page Swift in
the title role.*

which would be coming to the Shrine Auditorium in Los Angeles on its annual fall tour. My first professional operatic appearance and my first employment by the San Francisco Opera involved carrying a spear in a performance of *Otello* featuring the great Chilean tenor Ramón Vinay. My fee was one dollar, but I was becoming aware of the almighty power of make-believe. On my way to the stage, I saw a tall guy with blond hair whose face bore a remarkable resemblance to my own—I needed a second to realize I had been walking past a mirror.

I was also cast by the Workshop as the lead in Lukas Foss's one-acter, *The Jumping Frog of Calaveras County*, a musical setting of the Mark Twain story. The composer conducted. It was first performed at UCLA, and then we took it to the real Calaveras County, along Highway 49 in California's Gold Country about two hundred miles inland, where we presented it at the annual jumping frog contest. Because it was a short opera, we rounded out the evening with a Gay Nineties variety act, with a cast that included a young dancer by the name of Eva Rubinstein, the daughter of the legendary pianist Arthur Rubinstein.

Eva and I became friends and dated casually a few times. After the UCLA performance, her father came backstage. He was like a child, telling us how much he enjoyed it, which transported me straight to seventh heaven. Later, in August 1952, I was invited to Eva's birthday party. Her family's home in Beverly Hills had previously been owned by Ingrid Bergman. I arrived in my banged-up old coupé (purchased from the proceeds of a summer job with a storage and moving company) and parked it among all the fancy cars. It was a great party, attended by many

As Smiley in The Jumping Frog of Calaveras County, *1953.*

Hollywood offspring, including Candice Bergen and Joan Benny, among many others. Everywhere there were sculptures of Rubinstein's hands, which I found a bit disconcerting, and the walls were lined with original paintings by Marc Chagall and Pablo Picasso. (Eva's grandmother had covered the Chagalls to avoid exposing the young people to the sight of pubic hair.) Rubinstein was elegant and handsomely attired—and I was in awe of him. About two in the morning, after almost everyone had left, he came down in his robe, took a seat at the keyboard and played for us, while Eva did an impromptu dance. It was an extraordinary moment. Eva went on to become a prominent photographer and was married three times, once to the Reverend William Sloane Coffin, a distinguished liberal Christian clergyman and peace activist, who later became chaplain of Yale University.

I got a job as tenor soloist with the choir of the Beverly Hills Presbyterian Church, attended by a number of Hollywood stars. One of my all-time favorites, Eleanor Powell, taught Sunday school there, and from my perch in the choir loft, I could catch a glimpse of her husband, Glenn Ford, lapsing into a snooze during the sermon.

LOTFI MANSOURI

Summer jobs were a major source of revenue in those days, and one year I worked as a member of the "cabin crew" at Mount Lassen National Park in northern California. Another crew member was a girl named Martha, a student from Oregon, who was about to transfer to UCLA. When the following term started, she and I would have lunch with other students, including some fellow Iranians, on the lawn in front of the Student Union. One day, Martha brought along a friend, a young woman from Wisconsin, charming, intelligent, and a little shy. After a while, I worked up my courage to ask Martha's friend for a date, and together we attended a touring performance of *State of the Union* by Howard Lindsay and Russell Crouse. She still remembers that I treated her to a root beer float before the show.

My companion that night, Marjorie Anne Thompson, whom we all knew as Midge, was an only child like myself, the daughter of Leone Weber, who worked as a secretary, and Glenn Thompson, the assistant advertising manager of the Carnation Milk Company ("The milk from contented cows," a velvet-voiced announcer used to purr), headquartered in a small Midwestern town with the tongue-twisting name of Oconomowoc, Wisconsin. In 1949, the company moved its offices to Los Angeles, and the Thompsons moved with it. Here, Midge began attending Redlands University, transferring two years later to UCLA. As we began getting serious, her father was frankly less than thrilled about her going with a foreign student, and he complained that he didn't even know what my religion was. When I assured him that I could be any religion he wanted, his misgivings slowly evaporated. I dutifully began attending services at their church Sunday after Sunday, whereupon he accepted me, and in 1954, he gave us a wonderful wedding. Our marriage has brightened and enriched my life for more than fifty years.

My directorial career started as an accident. One of the Workshop productions I was involved in was a children's opera called *Tony Beaver*. The plot is too silly to recount, but I remember I was required to jump down from a rock. The rock wobbled, I fell, and I ended up with a dislocated elbow, temporarily forcing me to interrupt my singing career. Dr. Popper had a "magnificent remedy." He asked me to direct one of the Workshop scenes, the prologue to *Ariadne auf Naxos*, with Marni Nixon as Zerbinetta. Marni soon became a Hollywood legend when she supplied the dubbed-in singing voices for Deborah Kerr in *The King and I*, Natalie Wood in *West Side Story*, and Audrey Hepburn in *My Fair Lady*,

Midge and I at our wedding, September 1954.

while maintaining an operatic, concert, acting, and entertainment career that continues to this day.

This directing stint proved to be a watershed in my career. Once I had tasted the joys of directing, I was hooked for life, and perhaps the fact that it was a hard-won victory made my satisfaction all the sweeter. Dr. Popper had no intention of ever actually putting it onstage. He had assigned me the task on the presupposition that this complicated back-stage drama, with all kinds of characters wandering in and out of the scene, would be too much for me, and I would probably throw in the towel before it was ready, but I finished the job, and he was forced to put it on.

Around this time, I was approached by Dr. Hugo Strelitzer, who was then the director of the Opera Workshop at Los Angeles City College. He had discovered and encouraged many young singers, including George London. He knew the Zweigs and would come to UCLA performances, where he had observed me in a number of scenes. I think he realized my interest in the dramatic component of opera, the totality of it, rather than in single roles. He asked me to come to City College and direct a production of Mozart's *Così fan tutte* for him. It was an absurd proposition, so of course I accepted.

When asked to do *Così* today, I hesitate. It is so rich in humanity, and so astonishing in its depiction of intertwining lives and music, it represents a major challenge to any director, but back then I still had the sometimes deceptive ambition of youth. As I prepared to direct it, I tried to create backgrounds for the principal characters. For example, I thought, somewhat anachronistically, that Fiordiligi would probably read Proust, while Dorabella was more likely to be the *Jane Eyre* type. It was, as I look back, the core of my lifelong approach to directing opera. I didn't have it all figured out right from the start, but the germ was there. Even then, I would not direct one move without a motivation.

It soon became clear that *Così* has a bit of Oriental, even Persian, philosophy to it. In Persia, everything is based on *kismet*. Humans have very little to do with their destiny. Fate is the engine. I identified with Don Alfonso, the voice of reason, declaring, "Don't take things so seriously. Nothing in life makes any sense." I took all my cues from the cinema. One of my early idols was Ernst Lubitsch. His timing and style were brilliant, especially in light comedy. I also liked Billy Wilder's touch of madness. William Wyler was very good for his subtle gestures, especially in *The Little Foxes*. Although I never consciously copied any of them, I absorbed their approaches. I wanted perfection in a marriage of music and visuals, as in the very best films. This remains my ideal, and it's how I tried to realize my first *Così*. It ran four nights, and by the end of the run, I was thoroughly convinced that what I wanted to be was a stage director. The show was a pretty successful venture, and I went on to direct *Suor*

Angelica and *Boris Godunov* at City College, all with excellent young artists, some of whom, like Maralin Niska and Robert Peterson, went on to achieve international careers.

Among our most peculiar productions was *Il tabarro*, one of the three one-act operas in Puccini's *Trittico*. The story takes place on a barge moored on the Seine, so of course it was only natural to stage it in the swimming pool of the Ambassador Hotel on Wilshire Boulevard. Kurt Herbert Adler, the general director of the San Francisco Opera, attended, although nothing would come of that connection for years.

During the same period, I was also directing scenes and highlights at UCLA as a volunteer. It was only after seeing *Così* at City College that Dr. Popper realized that Dr. Strelitzer had given me a paying job, so he invited me to become an associate professor of dramatics at UCLA. This was in 1957. Popper never did like competition.

Around that time, I got a chance to direct a production of Jerome Kern's *Roberta* at Marymount College in Bel Air, with a full orchestra under the direction of Roger Wagner. Marymount was a school primarily for the offspring of rich and famous Catholics. For example, Bob Hope, who had been in the original Broadway cast, was our technical adviser on *Roberta*. When I did *The King and I* there, Irene Dunne helped (she had played Anna in *Anna and the King of Siam*), and the costumes came from 20th Century Fox, thanks to Dick Powell, who was then head of the studio, and his wife, June Allyson—all Marymount parents with kids in the productions. The backstage "crew" consisted largely of nuns, and the mother superior would bless each seat before a performance and pray that someone would be sitting there that evening. Naturally, the Lord provided, and we always had full houses.

I also did an opera workshop at Marymount with Fritz Zweig, where I both directed scenes and sang my usual diverse collection of tenor roles. It was in a public performance of a scene from the first act of Wagner's *Die Walküre*, in which I sang Siegmund to Dorothy Sandlin's Sieglinde with Dr. Zweig accompanying us on the piano, that I experienced one of those mishaps that live on ignominiously for generations as operatic anecdotes. In that scene, Sieglinde tells Siegmund about a mysterious visitor, actually their father, Wotan, who had once plunged a sword into a tree in the middle of the room. She goes on to relate that nobody has been able to extract the weapon, which allegedly has magical powers, whereupon the valorous Siegmund strides over to the tree and summarily removes the sword, thus proving his status as an authentic hero. In our performance, I must have tugged a bit too enthusiastically, or else the sword was too firmly embedded in the trunk. In any event, instead of drawing out the mighty blade, I found myself hoisting the entire tree on high. Fortunately this incident didn't prevent either of us from enjoying good careers.

The husband of one of the cellists teaching at UCLA was a Hollywood talent agent named Sam Adams. At one cast party, he asked if I realized that I looked a little like Enrico Caruso. I thought he was joking, but he then told me that the Hal Roach Studio was casting a television show based on a *Reader's Digest* story about the great tenor and having problems because the production had been intended for Mario Lanza, but apparently Lanza was eating himself to death in Rome. They had also tried Richard Tucker, an excellent tenor but a less than excellent actor, as his screen test had proven. Sam asked if I might be interested.

Me? Interested? In being in a movie? I would have accepted a walk-on.

Sam arranged an interview and screen test without costume or makeup. I was finally on a sound stage. I didn't think I'd get the part, and I didn't hear anything for days. When I was about to give up, I got a call requesting that I do a test, this time in costume and makeup. The test was directed by Ted Post, an excellent director of film and television, whose credits later included *Cagney and Lacey* and *Gunsmoke*. He was very kind and helped me relax. Again, I heard nothing until one night around 11:00 P.M., a messenger rang my doorbell and delivered the script of "The Day I Met Caruso" along with a copy of the shooting schedule.

This half-hour television show was being done for a series called *Screen Director's Playhouse*, which had originated on NBC Radio in 1949 and moved to television in the 1955–56 season. From the beginning, it attracted A-list directors, including Gower Champion and John Ford. William Saroyan was one of the writers, and its stars included Lew Ayres, Errol Flynn, Kim Hunter, Buster Keaton, Angela Lansbury, Peter Lawford, Sal Mineo, Rod Steiger, and John Wayne, to name just a few. I was in elevated company, and the elevator was going up—or so I thought.

The series was produced at Hal Roach Studios, which over the years changed from producing wacky comedies to colorizing black and white movies. "The Day I Met Caruso" was directed by Frank Borzage, a renowned Hollywood past master. The first director to win an Academy

Award, in 1929 for his 1927 production *Seventh Heaven*, Borzage had made a number of great movies. I guess that with a long string of successes, he thought our little television drama was beneath his dignity. I never received a bit of direction from him.

"Caruso" was written by Zoë Akins, a charming lady, who invited me to her home and helped me with the script, giving me some material from Dorothy Caruso, the singer's widow. The story line was simple enough: on a train ride from Boston to New York, a ten-year-old Quaker girl, played by Sandy Descher, meets Enrico Caruso. She takes him to task for his worldliness and extravagances, but is eventually won over by his voice when he sings arias from *Aida*, *La Bohème*, *Tosca*, and *Pagliacci*, as well as "Over There," the patriotic song George M. Cohan had written for Caruso during World War I. Although I could sing the arias myself, I lip-synched them to original Caruso recordings. This often proved to be an onerous task, as the great man occasionally took some Neapolitan liberties with the original music.

"The Day I Met Caruso" sank like a stone. Ours was Episode 34, telecast on September 5, 1956. After one more segment, the series was canceled. My timing couldn't have been worse.

Having always been captivated by the idea of Hollywood, I had a lot of publicity photos taken, all of them fairly hammy, in a vain attempt to look like Charles Boyer. I had hair in those days, which was more than M. Boyer himself did. I then arranged a meeting with Ruth Birch, who had cast the episode and asked her advice. She replied straightforwardly that my best bet would be to go for roles as a Mafioso, an Italian waiter, or a chauffeur. Such was Hollywood typecasting.

Nothing much came of this apart from a commercial for Rheingold Beer, in which I was cast as Canio in *Pagliacci*. After stabbing Nedda, I stepped in front of the curtain to tumultuous applause and sang the familiar Rheingold jingle ("My beer is Rheingold, the dry beer—think of Rheingold whenever you buy beer!"). This was also dubbed—by a bass! The residuals from that one commercial helped pay our bills for a couple of years.

The following year, my career took another turn toward the Greats. I met Lotte Lehmann. She had been one of the foremost opera stars and recitalists of the twentieth century. In addition to her interpretation of Leonore in *Fidelio* and her Mozart and Wagner characterizations, plus her work singing the music of her contemporaries like Erich Wolfgang

Publicity shot for "The Day I Met Caruso," 1957.

Korngold, she was a specialist in the works of Richard Strauss and one of his favorite interpreters. When he and Hugo von Hofmannsthal added the prologue to their *Ariadne auf Naxos*, Strauss selected her to sing the trouser role of the Composer in the first performance, and she sang leading roles in the world premieres of *Die Frau ohne Schatten* and *Intermezzo*. She also sang the title role in the first Vienna performance of *Arabella*. Beyond this, she virtually defined the role of Strauss's Marschallin in *Der Rosenkavalier* for future generations after scoring triumphs as both Sophie and Octavian in the same opera. Her portrait as the Marschallin was featured on the cover of *Time* magazine. She sang with conductors like Wilhelm Furtwängler, Arturo Toscanini, and Otto Klemperer. Bruno Walter conducted her in opera and concert and also served as accompanist in many of her recitals.

As renowned for her unshakable conscience as for her definitive performances, she renounced her German citizenship when the Nazis came to power in 1933 and went to live in Austria until the brownshirts annexed that country in 1938. She continued on to the United States, where she sang at the Metropolitan Opera, the San Francisco Opera, and other theaters, giving recitals all over the world until she retired in 1951. She moved to Santa Barbara, California, some one hundred miles north of Los Angeles, where, along with Otto Klemperer and a group of philanthropists, she created the Music Academy of the West in nearby Montecito. Her master classes were a major attraction for years, and artists like Benita Valente and Jeanine Altmeyer gained valuable knowledge there, as did Marilyn Horne, who is now the Academy's director of the Voice Program.

Lehmann died in Santa Barbara in 1976 at the age of eighty-eight, and the concert hall of the University of California at Santa Barbara is named for her.

The Zweigs arranged for me to audition for Mme. Lehmann, and I won a scholarship to the Academy in the summer of 1957. Mezzo-soprano Grace Bumbry was there, too, and our meeting began a long friendship. Mme. Lehmann kept me on over the following winter, and I commuted weekly from Los Angeles to sing with the twenty or so women in her class. Tenors were hard to come by, so I sang Manrico, Don José, Otello, Siegmund—you name it.

Lotte Lehmann was a very strong teacher, but I was never one of her favorites. She loved it when her students flattered her by imitating her singing style. I never did, although one day she caught me doing a parody of her mannerisms. The problem with trying to imitate her was that she sang from the inside out, while her acolytes did it strictly on the surface. I was a prop, a partner to her ladies. When she wanted to demonstrate, I became *her* partner, and that was a magnificent experience. She taught me to look deeper into the material, the atmosphere, the substance of the work. I was almost the only one who ever dared question anything she said. She confirmed the principles I had learned from the Zweigs, and that was also very helpful.

She was a grande dame, although she dressed quite modestly, in blacks and grays. We all learned that there were certain hours of the day when we were not allowed to telephone her because her favorite radio programs were on. For all her greatness, she was never a very precise musician. There is a story that Richard Strauss went backstage after Mme. Lehmann had sung gloriously in one of his operas. He kissed her hand and said, "Oh, Lotte, that was so beautiful. It wasn't *my* music, but it was beautiful anyway."

When Lotte Lehmann died, I wrote a tribute to her, recalling how she had demonstrated the Marschallin's monologue in Act I of *Der Rosenkavalier*. She used the mirror in an extraordinary way, and I always referred to her approach thereafter. She moved slowly and majestically to the mirror, one hand reaching up to her face, tracing the painful realization of lines on her face and neck, then turned away from the mirror impulsively, as if to shut out the reality. Then something miraculous happened. Her shoulders, first stooped with sadness and the onset of middle age, lifted, and you could see a flow of tremendous energy pulsing through her body. There stood a woman, beautiful in the full flower of her early maturity, resigned, yet strong, somehow at peace with herself—and, above all, unsentimental. Lotte Lehmann could act with an honesty that was deeply affecting.

In the summer of 1958, my friends and coaches, the Zweigs, decided to take a trip to Europe and asked me to come along as their driver. We had a fabulous tour, and I saw opera the way it should be seen. They introduced me to legendary figures. We had lunch with Otto Klemperer in Munich, where I also first met Hans Hotter, after having marveled at his majestic Cardinal Borromeo in Hans Pfitzner's *Palestrina*. At La Scala, I saw *Adriana Lecouvreur* with Magda Olivero, Giulietta Simionato, and Franco Corelli. And in Salzburg, I finally experienced opera as total music theater. One production I cannot forget was an *Arabella* with a dream cast featuring Lisa della Casa, Anneliese Rothenberger, and Dietrich Fischer-Dieskau, and directed by Rudolf Hartmann, who had worked intensively with the composer only a few years before. These revelatory productions opened my eyes to opera's possibilities.

The only unfortunate performance we attended was Samuel Barber's *Vanessa*. It had come from the Metropolitan Opera with most of the original cast and was directed by the librettist Gian Carlo Menotti, Barber's partner and a fine composer in his own right. For some reason, the performance struck the audience as a melodrama, and there was laughter in all the wrong places. This was a very valuable experience for me, as I would direct the first West Coast performance of the opera myself the following season at UCLA.

I also saw the premiere of Menotti's *Maria Golovin* at the Brussels World's Fair and walked up and down beside the waterways of Venice for the first time. I never wanted to sleep. Being able to visit museums in Venice, Munich, Milan, Vienna, and Paris was heaven, as was the luxury of Dr. Zweig giving me the history and background of every place we visited. I was a kid in a wonderland of art, music, and opera.

In the spring of 1959, I auditioned for the Music Tent in Sacramento. This was a major venue for summer performances of light opera. I had the impression the company wanted me to join them, but in May I got a call from someone saying, "Sorry, we don't need you after all." I was annoyed, because that was to have been my summer employment.

Out of the blue, later that month, the administrator of the Music Academy, Ruth Cowan, called me. She told me that Mme. Lehmann was going to be on sabbatical and would be replaced by a stage director from the Metropolitan Opera in New York, a gentleman by the name of Herbert Graf. She offered me a package in which I would prepare scenes for Dr. Graf's public master classes. I would act as his assistant on a production of *Die Zauberflöte*, to be conducted by Maurice Abravanel. I was also to sing the role of Monostatos and would be paid five hundred dollars for the whole summer. Though he had been directing at the Met for twenty-three years, I must shamefacedly admit that I had never heard of Herbert Graf, and I still had my heart set on doing musical comedy. But Fritz Zweig told me to accept, and I reluctantly said yes.

The first scene I staged, before Dr. Graf arrived, was the second act of *Tosca*. When Dr. Graf got there and the classes began, he stopped every

As Monostatos in Die Zauberflöte at the Music Academy of the West, 1959.

ten seconds, correcting this and that. I was mortified. The cast members started sticking up for me, and Dr. Graf, amused, very knowing, started smiling a bit out of the side of his mouth. I decided that he really didn't like me, and I was certainly intimidated—well, I was still pretty young. As the summer went on in Santa Barbara, I started to love Abravanel. He was so elegant, and his sense of humor magnificent. Little by little, I also become aware of what Dr. Graf was doing. I came to realize that he was understanding, enormously patient, and generous and knew everything about the music, including the dramatic impulses that came from specific sections of the orchestra. The change in my attitude toward him was gradual. I watched and learned as much as I could. We set lights until two in the morning and then went out for a beer. He would talk about Toscanini, Furtwängler, and all the others he had worked with, but he wasn't a flagrant name-dropper—just the opposite. People like him really *are* great; they do not feign greatness by basking in reflected glory—that's for second-raters.

The summer of 1959 marked a period of enormous growth in my life, without my really being aware of it. One day, I drove Dr. Graf to Los Angeles to visit Bruno Walter. He introduced me as his assistant, "who is also singing Monostatos." Dr. Walter looked me up and down and replied, "I always thought Monostatos *would* look like that." Ouch—Monostatos is a fairly nefarious character, and I wasn't wearing any makeup.

At the end of the summer, Dr. and Mrs. Graf were scheduled to fly out of Los Angeles, and he wanted to spend a day there before leaving. Midge and I offered to organize anything he wanted. His wish? Disneyland! So that's what we did, and he had a wonderful time. He even had a WANTED poster printed with his name on it.

I went back to work at UCLA. Now Dr. Popper was on sabbatical, so Natalie Limonick and I ran the Opera Workshop. I think we did some of our best work that year, including that production of *Vanessa*. Remembering the negative reaction of the Salzburg audience, I decided to fly to New York to meet with Barber and Menotti and seek their approval for some changes. Barber was elegant, kind, understanding, and accommodating. Though Menotti was defensive, he finally accepted my suggestions. At that meeting, they told me the title role in *Vanessa* had been conceived for Maria Callas. She, however, said she would never sing in English; she felt the principal character was actually the young woman, Erika, originally sung by Rosalind Elias, and the opera should be retitled with that character's name. For the record, it is perhaps worth noting that the New York–born Callas did record Rezia's big aria from Weber's *Oberon* using the original English words. In any event, she didn't do the Barber opera at the Metropolitan, and Eleanor Steber assumed the role on six weeks' notice.

The Los Angeles Opera is now the fourth-largest opera company in the United States, with Plácido Domingo as its general director. Today, it gives a hundred performances a year. As it happens, I was there for the birth of an earlier incarnation, in the spring of 1960, at the Wilshire Ebell Theater. In those days the saying went that Los Angeles was a collection of villages connected by gas stations. A true city center didn't exist, nor was there any kind of cultural center such as you find in New York or San

Francisco. In 1919, the Los Angeles Philharmonic had been founded, and it has prospered to this day. Opera in Los Angeles was a different story. In the early 1920s, a conductor from Naples by the name of Gaetano Merola—building on the success of his touring opera company, named for the San Carlo Opera in his native city—founded two companies, one each in San Francisco and Los Angeles. The one in San Francisco, starting in 1923, took hold. The one in Los Angeles never did, although numerous efforts were made to reestablish its place in the city. In 1948, the Los Angeles Civic Grand Opera came into being, an event that subsequently led to the founding of today's Los Angeles Opera in 1986.

In my student days, both the Metropolitan Opera and the San Francisco Opera came to Los Angeles on tour every year, performing at the Shrine Auditorium. With a capacity of six thousand, this barn was also used for sports events and circuses. The seasons were short but welcome, because the Auditorium presented major international stars in their best roles—not to mention my own debut as a super. There were some sporadic attempts to start opera groups in various L.A. communities, but nothing ever came of them. Meanwhile, UCLA initiated a great many ambitious opera projects, including the West Coast premieres of such relatively new works as *Vanessa*, *Jenůfa*, and *The Turn of the Screw*. At USC, the Opera Workshop under the direction of Walter Ducloux produced Carlisle Floyd's *Susannah*, Gian Carlo Menotti's *The Saint of Bleecker Street*, and—amazingly enough—Alban Berg's fiendishly difficult but devastatingly powerful masterwork, *Wozzeck*.

Finally, an Italian American named Francesco Pace managed, after seven years of arduous labor, to bring together a board of directors and groups of volunteers to launch the Los Angeles Grand Opera Company. During its first season in 1960, four operas were presented, *Tosca*, *Rigoletto*, *Le nozze di Figaro*, and *La traviata*, all new productions as nothing had been performed before. The Wilshire Ebell Theater was chosen as its home base. It seated 1,270 and was an intimate venue for concerts, recitals, plays, and other artistic programs.

Francesco Pace was a short, quiet man, a furniture maker by trade, who bore a slight resemblance to Edward G. Robinson. He was a passionate opera aficionado, highly motivated and tenacious. He had seen some of my work and invited me to be his resident director, staging three productions in that opening season. Our first production was *Tosca* with soprano Mariquita Moll in the title role. Our Cavaradossi was Robert

Thomas, who was later engaged by the Zurich Opera. In *Traviata*, our Violetta was Maralin Niska, who went on to sing at both the Metropolitan and the New York City Opera. The Susanna in *Figaro* was Marni Nixon, and our conductors were Anton Guadagno and Amerigo Marino. Pace had a carpentry shop, where we would hold our production meetings. I felt as though I were in one of those Judy Garland–Mickey Rooney movies in which some kid would say, "Hey, my dad's got a barn, let's put on a show!" and proceed to follow through on this initiative, but we didn't have the unlimited resources that were eventually made available to those alleged neophytes. Nevertheless, it was exciting to present all those productions, one performance each, in a single month.

At the same time as I was working with the nascent Los Angeles Opera, I directed a production of *Pelléas et Mélisande* at UCLA with a strong and experienced conductor named Wolfgang Martin. Our Mélisande was a very gifted lyric coloratura, Catherine Gayer, who soon established herself as a major artist in Europe, where she became a specialist in contemporary music, while also singing a full array of standard repertoire works. Her son, Danny Ashkenasi, is now a remarkable actor, director, and composer in two languages and on two continents.

During my last full production in 1950s America, I served as guest director for the University of California at Berkeley, doing Puccini's *Trittico* with two different casts and with Jan Popper on the podium.

In the autumn of 1959, Dr. Graf wrote from New York to say that he had been engaged as general director of the Zurich Opera House in Switzerland and would begin his duties there in the autumn of 1960. He wanted me to join him as a stage director.

Around the same time, I got a call from my friend Robert Herman at the Met. Rudolf Bing wanted to interview me for a position there. My head began spinning! I called Dr. Graf and told him I was terribly torn. I needed his advice. He told me to take the Bing interview, think it all over, then call him back. I flew to New York and was ushered into Mr. Bing's throne room. I told him about my background, and we talked. His offer was $350 a week to become an assistant stage director. I asked very politely what I had to do to be assigned a production of my own. Mr. Bing put on his cryptic Viennese smile and replied laconically, "Mr. Mansouri, you would be coming here only as an assistant."

Midge and I talked it over. Positions like that are comfortable, well paid, and secure, but you get stuck in a rut and never move on, certainly not under the administration of someone like Rudolf Bing, who had very clear, if somewhat odd, ideas about where people belonged in the scheme of things, which sent many artists seeking—and finding—their fortunes elsewhere.

The most Dr. Graf could offer me in Zurich would be 12,000 Swiss francs, a little less than 3,000 U.S. dollars a year, as compared with Bing's proffered annual earnings of $16,800. At the time, Midge was working as an assistant editor at *Westways*, the magazine of the Auto Club of Southern California. Her salary and mine combined to make a grand total of $35,000 a year.

I called Dr. Graf back and told him that I would love to come—for $3,000.

3

AMERICANS TO THE RESCUE

When Europe beckoned, I did what any aspiring young professional would have done: I packed my bags without looking back. I had meanwhile become a U.S. citizen, and I truly loved my adopted country, but Europe was the birthplace of opera, after all, and I needed the experience of working at the source to give me the proper seasoning for the road ahead. What I didn't anticipate at the time was that Europe would transform me personally as much as it did professionally. In fact, I was entering a crucible where I could be refined, tested, and proven. When I emerged, I was quite a different person, both on- and offstage.

Though I hadn't really considered the matter at the time, having responded spontaneously to Herbert Graf's offer, Europe could not have been a more fertile field for talent from other places than it was at the time I arrived there. Accustomed to having a permanent resident opera company in just about every reasonably sized city on the Continent, especially the major cultural capitals of Central Europe, and supplying them with a generous government subsidy to cover the costs of entertaining and enlightening their citizens and visitors, these municipalities found themselves faced with shortfalls on every front. While many of the great opera houses—Vienna, Munich, Frankfurt, Dresden—had been destroyed in bombing raids, the personnel required to staff the theaters, either the ones still standing or others in transitional quarters, were sadly lacking. World War II had taken an enormous human toll that didn't stop at the doors of the opera house. Many singers and instrumentalists had fallen in battle, and quite a few younger people would face permanent health problems as a consequence of general food shortages and long periods of undernourishment. On top of this, many of the great teachers had been forced into exile to escape certain extermination by the ruthless regime that had dominated the Continent for much of the twelve-year period that the Nazis had touted as the "thousand-year Reich"; as a result, the kind of training that had previously been par for the course was no longer available.

Help would have to come from somewhere, and it did. Just as the Allies helped the war-torn nations of Europe rebuild, and even faced food shortages themselves to bolster the health of the citizenry on the other side of the ocean, so, too, they sent human resources to replenish the staffs of the many European operatic theaters, many of them polished to a high gloss by those very instructors the Nazis had considered dispensable. Some artists had already begun building careers at home, but the pickings in America were still pretty slim. For reasons best known to him, Rudolf Bing at the Metropolitan Opera, the only theater with anything like a full season, chose to divest himself of many of his best artists or used their services well below their capacity. This was the case with Astrid Varnay, a stellar dramatic soprano, who had spent a large part of her career rescuing performances by stepping in at the last minute for indisposed colleagues. As European sopranos became available, Bing even suggested that she might take a leave of absence, and so she took him at his word and became a household name on the European continent, as did Regina Resnik, who was taken seriously at the Metropolitan only after some triumphal performances, especially a definitive Carmen, overseas. James McCracken was vastly underemployed at the Metropolitan, singing miniscule tenor roles like the one-line character Parpignol in *La Bohème*, a part often entrusted to a chorister. Venturing away from his native land, he reestablished himself as a leading tenor in Europe.

Other artists were fresh from North American college campuses or had received initial impulses from some of the smaller opera theaters there. Soon theaters large and small all over Europe began swelling their solo rosters with such major talents in the offing as Marilyn Horne, James King, Teresa Stich-Randall, Thomas Stewart, Claire Watson, Jess Thomas, Grace Hoffman, George London, Evelyn Lear, and countless others. Beyond this, many first-rate African American artists on the same level, still often faced with discrimination in the United States, found fertile fields for their exceptional talents on the Continent: soon European audiences were thrilling to the performances of artists like Reri Grist, Margaret Tynes, Olive Moorefield, Debria Brown, Eugene

Holmes, Felicia Weathers, Annabelle Bernard, Grace Bumbry, Ella Lee, and Lawrence Winters, to mention but a few.

At this point, it was largely North American singers who were being welcomed to the Continent. Conductors and stage directors had yet to establish much of a foothold there, but the challenge was a risk I was more than willing to take, and fortunately I had the backup of a practical helpmate like Midge, willing to share the sacrifices right down the line.

As we prepared to depart for unknown horizons, there was one last surprise for me. I received a communication from Friedelind Wagner, the granddaughter of Richard Wagner and the only member of the family to go public in her opposition to the Nazis by leaving the country and throwing in her lot with the Allies, even doing propaganda broadcasts to Germany during the war. She said she had been referred to me by the Zweigs and Lotte Lehmann, and that she would be coming to Los Angeles shortly; she needed assistance in auditioning local talent for a summer master class program in Bayreuth, the site of her grandfather's "Temple of Sacred Art." To be honest, I wasn't all that surprised by this request. Thanks to the Zweigs, I had come into contact with Otto Klemperer, Arnold Schoenberg, and Alma Mahler. Now I would find myself working with a Wagner. She proved to be quite a personality, cordial and effusive, on the one hand, cryptic and even deceptive, on the other, but we managed to strike up a good professional relationship. I thought it would end there, but a couple of weeks later she sent me a letter inviting me to Bayreuth for the summer, all expenses paid. It would give me a golden opportunity to bridge the period before the start of the season in Zurich, watch the great Wieland Wagner in action, and polish my German before going to work for Dr. Graf. The ever-practical Midge would continue working in California before joining me in Switzerland.

In June 1960, I boarded a plane. I don't think I slept for more than a few seconds at a time during the long trip from Los Angeles to Vancouver to Shannon to Amsterdam to Bayreuth. This journey marked the outset of a significant chapter in my life, and I could feel a new day dawning. Mixed emotions—excitement, fear, above all loneliness—coursed through my mind. I couldn't help wondering if I was up to the challenge of that festival. But my time in Bayreuth would prove exhilarating and stimulating—but also frustrating as hell.

Friedelind had assembled an impressive group of singers, accompanists, and designers, with me as the only stage director. The season in

Bayreuth was a real eye-opener: I loved Wieland Wagner's production of *Parsifal* with Régine Crespin and Thomas Stewart—the best I have ever seen or heard. Day after day, the chorus and orchestra blew me away with their powerful, expressive, and tightly knit sound. No wonder—most of them were recruited from the solo rosters of smaller theaters and first-chair players from major symphony and opera orchestras all over Europe, including many from Eastern Europe, all accepting a cut in their usual pay just to take part in this festival of festivals. I relished the intensive discussions in the canteen that often lasted well into the night. Thanks to my language classes, my German improved by leaps and bounds. But there were also obligations that had me wondering if I had walked into a hackneyed operetta.

We were occasionally rounded up and marched over to Wagner's tomb; this was a pilgrimage, not sightseeing. I often wondered if we were expected to kneel. Much was made of being invited to the Master's home of Wahnfried for tea and coffee with Friedelind's mother, Winifred, the widow of Richard Wagner's son Siegfried and an unrepentant supporter of Adolf Hitler long after the truth was undeniable. She staunchly took her relentless support of the dictator to her deathbed. Behind her back, we called her "the Dragon Lady."

Then there were the "lectures," the worst of which were given by a gentleman named Robert Guttman, who had written a book that I remember chiefly for its sheer length. Professor Guttman was touted as a bona fide expert, but you couldn't tell it from those lectures. He would prance around in tight Levis and a shirt unbuttoned down to the navel, shove his thumbs into his waistband in a cowboy pose, and strut around like a rooster on speed. He delighted in referring to the great composer as "little Dickie" and describing his life as if it were a soap opera. He didn't delve very deeply, and it soon became obvious that he was patronizing us. I had learned a great deal about Wagner from classes at UCLA, and now here I was, at the shrine, being treated to *The Adventures of Little Dickie*. And I was expected to take this nonsense seriously? We all did whatever we could to avoid these surreal wastes of time, but whenever Friedelind found out, she would punish us by withholding tickets to the dress rehearsals; these were our only chance to witness productions, because, then as now, the actual performances were sold out years in advance. Instead of toeing the line, I got creative. I discovered I could climb to the top of one of the lighting towers, where I could enjoy an excellent view of the stage. Unfortunately, while clandestinely attending a *Ring* performance, I heard someone climbing the ladder. There was no place to hide—I could only watch as two hands came into view, followed by the stocky figure of Wolfgang Wagner, the Dragon Lady's younger son and administrative head of the festival, where he also staged some fine productions. He promptly banished me from my perch.

Diplomatic relations between Friedelind and her brothers were none too cordial, so I had to go to greater lengths to watch stage rehearsals, as Wieland tolerated no visitors, especially none from his sister's classes. For me, the most important reason for being in Bayreuth was to study Wieland's incisive approach to his grandfather's works, not to be regaled by the Dragon Lady or watch the professor flounce around. But the rules of the place were inviolate, forcing me to go outlaw. During staging rehearsals, they would lock the doors and even pull out the handles to prevent anyone from coming in, but I managed to "liberate" a handle for my own use, which helped me penetrate the holy of holies, where I watched and learned.

One of my colleagues got wind of this and asked me to sneak her in as well. I was feeling pretty confident by then and agreed. Unfortunately, as we inched our way through the darkened auditorium, she brushed against one of the rickety seats and it dropped open with a resounding clatter. Wieland jumped up and shouted, "Who's there?" Suddenly the aisles were filled with lackeys, shining flashlights all over the place. Visions of old war movies came to mind, but finally Wieland called off the dragnet and went back to rehearsing. As I lurked in the darkness, I promised myself that, were I to be captured, I would divulge only my name, rank, and serial number.

The highlight of that summer took place a couple of hundred miles to the north of Bayreuth, on a field trip to Berlin, where, after traveling from the grungy Zoo Station in the western part of the city to the Friedrichstrasse fortress on the other side of the Wall, and being scrutinized up and down by the stone-faced border guards, we would be admitted to the gloom of East Berlin. It was there that I met the great Austrian director Walter Felsenstein, the head of the Komische Oper, a pioneering man of the theater, and also a card-carrying tyrant. He was the founding father of opera as total theater, a master of externalizing the inner core of the musical drama and renowned for working through a production down to the minutest details. For *The Cunning Little Vixen*—one of the most

LOTFI MANSOURI

brilliant productions I have ever seen—he prepared for nine months, even spending two weeks in a screening room to get what he called the "choral soloists" ready for their roles in the barnyard, by showing them slow-motion films of prancing chickens. He'd rehearse his principals for hours, never allowing them to "mark" their parts by singing half-voice or an octave lower, as is generally the practice in staging rehearsals. He demanded full dramatic and vocal commitment every second. Was it any wonder the international stars avoided him like the plague?

The things I had heard about him had to be exaggerations, I thought. I would soon see for myself. Friedelind had arranged for him to work some scenes with her singers. There were no tenors on her roster, though, so she asked if I would do double duty and partner one of her sopranos in a scene from *Die Zauberflöte*, singing Monostatos to her Pamina. At our first session, Felsenstein spent four hours talking about the backstory: the life histories of Pamina and Monostatos, and how they came to be who they are. I was spellbound. Felsenstein related a thousand details I had never heard before. I couldn't help but ask where he had acquired all this material, to which he replied, dumfounded by my ignorance, "It's all in the score." I tried to cover my embarrassment by suggesting in jest that I had perhaps been shortchanged by a score printed in the United States, where publishers had a reputation, in Europe at any rate, for not putting out very scholarly material, but the great man was not amused. In all honesty, I was forced to admit to myself that I had yet to fathom the aspects of delving into the music and words combined to flesh out the characters, but I was learning fast.

We moved on to staging the scene. I made what I thought was a menacing entrance, dragging Pamina along and snarling my first line: "Du feines Täubchen, nur herein! [In you go, my little dove!]." I'll never forget those words, probably not even in my grave, because I had to repeat them about a thousand times. "No, no, no!" Felsenstein expostulated. "You don't understand, Mansouri! You want to RAPE her! Do it again." One more try, one more "No, no, no!" One day turned into two, and I still got no further. Now I no longer wondered why it had taken him so long to stage *Vixen*. Time after time, I hurled myself into the scene in a pitch of frenzy so intense I thought I was going to become delirious. He still wasn't satisfied. Finally, he barked, "Mansouri, take off your trousers!" I turned to our interpreter to make sure I had understood this command. Finally, I said, "Even with the biggest erection in the world, nothing would happen in this cold room." Felsenstein simply snarled, "You will never have a career." He was right: I never did get very far as a tenor.

During our visit, we also got to watch him put the finishing touches on his new production of Verdi's *Otello*. He prepared the chorus for the storm scene by putting them in an industrial wind tunnel and making them stand in nearly overpowering blasts of air. Onstage, the scene played so realistically I thought I was going to get soaked just watching it. There were a thousand other fascinating details, some of which struck to the heart and others of which mystified me. Otello started his heartbreaking aria "Dio mi potevi scagliar . . . [Had it pleased heaven to try me with affliction . . .]" with a guttural tone, more growling than singing. It certainly communicated his seething state of mind, but it must have been murder on his voice. At the end of the aria, the tenor has to sing a ringing high B-flat. I expected him to run downstage, face the audience, and let fly, as I had always seen when this opera was performed. In this production, however, he ran upstage, grabbed some of the fluttering flags, and kissed them as he sang, hiding his face during the climactic note. I wracked my brain and finally asked Felsenstein, "Why would Otello do this?"

I anticipated a psychologically well grounded explanation, but instead he just grumbled, "He can't hit the note. I don't know why, but he can't!" "I know why," I shot back, regretting it almost before the words were out of my mouth, "because he spent the first part of the aria growling. No singer can do that kind of damage to his voice and then be expected to sing out a ringing high B-flat." Felsenstein mumbled something about the music getting in the way of his concept, and I innocently asked, "If you have problems with Verdi's music, why don't you just stage the Shakespeare play?"

If looks could kill.

He then predicted once again to all and sundry, including Friedelind, that I would never have a career. Like everyone else, I ran into in Friedelind's aegis: Felsenstein did not want to be questioned about anything. Still I learned an enormous amount from him about how to motivate, how to use musical impulses to dictate movement, how to communicate characters' states of mind. But I also learned how important it was to trust the singers to act with their voices—something Felsenstein didn't always do.

It should be noted here that this turned out to be a legendary production, which was ultimately filmed by East German television and can now be viewed in a DVD collection of Felsenstein's best work, which is well worth seeing.

The whole master class experience, in both Bayreuth and Berlin, was beginning to get to me—and it wasn't all positive. I regarded the theater as a never-ending quest for human truth, not as a sanctuary for worshippers, and this did not align at all with the kind of atmosphere Ms. Wagner was trying to create.

Finally Dr. Graf came to my rescue, calling me from Venice to tell me he was about to begin rehearsals for his *Otello* production with Mario Del Monaco in the title role and Tito Gobbi as Jago—two of the most impressive singing actors in the history of the craft. He invited me to come down there as his assistant. Friedelind kindly allowed me to leave her program early to join him. From Bayreuth to Venice—what a change! As the train whisked me southward, I found myself moving from Stygian gloom to radiant sunshine, both literally and figuratively. I had tasted the pleasures of the city on the lagoons during my short stay there in 1958, and now I was returning to participate in a once-in-a-lifetime project.

Dr. Graf had a knack for staging operas in natural settings. He had created a *Walküre* for the Red Rocks Amphitheater in Colorado with Brünnhilde riding in on a white horse and an *Orfeo* for the Boboli Gardens in Florence with Eurydice making her entrance swimming across the lake. This *Otello* was set outdoors in the Doge's palace courtyard. The only added set pieces were a platform and a throne. The arrival of Otello on the *scala del gigante*, the giant's staircase before the palace, surrounded by his soldiers and burning torches, attended by the salty breezes blowing in from the Adriatic, was simply breathtaking. There was no fuss over Del Monaco's rendition of "Dio mi potevi scagliar!" He simply stepped forward and let loose with a commanding B-flat that reverberated off the walls of the fabled city. It's probably still echoing in one corner or another to this day. The audience was stunned, and when it was over, crowds lingered on the piazza. Nobody wanted such a special evening to end. Offstage, I became acquainted with Gobbi—the start of a lifelong friendship and prelude to numerous future collaborations. All in all, it couldn't have been more magical.

What a summer! For three months, I had wandered like Alice through an operatic Wonderland. Two very different productions of *Otello* had given me a lot to think about. I loved how Dr. Graf largely let the singing and setting stand on their own. I also loved the dramatic profundities

Felsenstein had plumbed. Vocal performance or theatrical incisiveness—was there a choice? I wanted both.

The day after the opening of *Otello* in Venice, I boarded a train for Switzerland along with Dr. and Mrs. Graf. It was time to launch my transition to new responsibilities in a new country with a new language. I had no idea what to expect or how I would be received. I didn't even know where we were going to live.

4

THE SWISS CONNECTION

D r. Herbert Graf, who had brought me to Zurich, was one of the seminal figures in twentieth-century opera. His father, Dr. Max Graf, a pupil of Eduard Hanslick and Anton Bruckner, was a distinguished musicologist and educator, as well as one of the leading music critics in Vienna. Herbert Graf grew up surrounded by the most distinguished musicians and scholars of that halcyon era in the Austrian capital, including one contact that came in very handy early on in his life. At the age of four, Herbert was walking in the park with the family's maid when he witnessed a horse collapse while trying to pull a heavy load. He ultimately developed a terrible fear of leaving the house, convinced that one of the thousands of horses transporting people and goods up and down the streets of the city would do him harm. His worried father approached a member of his social circle, Dr. Sigmund Freud, who suggested the child see him once and then have analytic sessions with his own father, these to be reported to the doctor for therapeutic consultation. The results of the successful therapy were eventually written up in a famous paper entitled "Analysis of a Phobia in a Five-year-old Boy," in which young Herbert made scientific history under the pseudonym "Hänschen" (Little Hans).

Clearly, Dr. Freud knew his stuff, because the child was completely cured and while still a very young man was selected to serve as assistant to the eminent theatrical director Max Reinhardt. After early engagements, he joined the staff at the opera in Frankfurt, where, at the age of only twenty-seven, he staged the world premiere of *Von heute auf morgen*, by Arnold Schoenberg, a composer his father had championed. Forced to leave Germany, he directed opera in Philadelphia in 1934 and 1935. In 1936, after a brief sojourn in Austria, where he worked at the Salzburg Festival, he joined the production staff at the Metropolitan Opera. He remained there until 1960, with frequent forays to other places, among them, the revivified Salzburg Festival, where he staged legendary all-star productions of *Otello* and *Don Giovanni* in the early 1950s, while helping the postwar Vienna State Opera get back on its feet. Also a distinguished pedagogue, he taught on the faculty of the Curtis Institute of Music in Philadelphia from 1950 to 1960.

On November 29, 1948, his *Otello* production at the Metropolitan, conducted by Fritz Busch and starring Ramón Vinay, Licia Albanese, and Leonard Warren, opened the 1948–49 season at that theater, while concurrently becoming the first live opera performance ever televised in the United States.

In the course of his long career, he worked with just about everybody who was anybody in the opera world, including conductors like Busch, Wilhelm Furtwängler, and Arturo Toscanini, with direct links to the great artists of the past. In this sense, he was something like a bridge: heir to traditions passed down from century to century, then mentor to new generations. Because of his contributions, many ideas about style and practice so central to making opera what it is, and what it can be, have survived to this day to be passed along to future generations. For all of this, the man had not an iota of egotism. Unlike so many others in this profession, he was kind and unpretentious. I knew him about as well as anyone, and yet I learned many of the impressive details of his life only after his death. In fact, it wasn't until 2008 that I found out that his godfather had been Gustav Mahler. Many of the artists who worked with him recall the universality of his background and knowledge, a fact Hans Hotter once summed up by saying simply, "Graf—there was a stage director who could read and understand music!"

I could not begin a chapter about my professional career in Europe without saying something about the remarkable man who made it all possible. Someday, somebody should write a full-scale biography of him.

In the 1960s, the Zurich Opera was a repertory house with a resident ensemble: orchestra, chorus, and ballet, along with the necessary technical departments. The season began in September and concluded at the end of June—something still unheard of the in United States, even in New York. For all of this, the company had an aura of provincialism. As in the regional houses in the rest of Central Europe at the time, with the exception of Vienna under Herbert von Karajan, all the operas were

With Dr. Herbert Graf, Zurich, 1960.

sung in German, regardless of the original language. Occasionally, international singers would show up and sing their roles, while the others would continue doing their parts in German, which could lead to some odd confusion. Such was the atmosphere in Zurich back then. Like many theaters in that part of the world, it largely churned out performances day in and day out, cutting corners wherever necessary to get the curtain up, and most of the evenings were predictably modest in quality, despite the fact that this was the largest city in the richest country in the world.

Enter Dr. Graf. He set out to raise the standards by infusing the company with fresh young international talent, a roster made up mostly of gifted young Americans, casting many of them in major productions. Among the first seventeen artists he brought in that initial season for major roles were sopranos Reri Grist, Jean Cook, and Virginia Gordoni; mezzo-sopranos Regina Sarfaty and Sandra Warfield; tenors Glade Peterson and Robert Thomas; baritone Robert Kerns; conductor Samuel Krachmalnik; and yours truly on the production staff.

To prove the high quality of these new artists, Dr. Graf launched his first season with James McCracken, the tenor who had been wasted on so many minuscule assignments at Rudolf Bing's Metropolitan, in the title role of an original-language production of Verdi's *Otello*, which soon had

The group of young American artists at Zurich, 1960. Rear, left to right:
*Glade Peterson, Robert Kerns, James McCracken, Robert Thomas, me,
unknown dancer.* Front: *Sandra Warfield, Reri Grist, Dr. Graf,
Virginia Gordoni, Mary Davenport, Jean Cook.*

the whole city buzzing and quickly sparked a skyrocketing international
career for the singer. Reri Grist had been known in her native city of
New York primarily as the haunting offstage voice singing "Somewhere"
in the original Broadway production of *West Side Story*. In Switzerland
she dazzled everyone with appearances as Zerbinetta and Titania, and
audiences discovered that *La traviata*, when presented by such incisive
artists as Virginia Gordoni, Glade Peterson, and Robert Kerns, could be
something quite out of the ordinary.

All of this newness shook up the rather sleepy, provincial status quo
of the company. While audiences loved it, many of the old-timers at the
opera house grew envious and resentful. Rather than embracing the
fresh winds blowing through the house and interacting creatively with
the new people, they sat around moaning and groaning, "The Americans

LOTFI MANSOURI

At the Metropolitan Opera, James McCracken was consigned to small roles such as the one-line character Parpignol in La Bohème. *In Europe he was a star who excelled in major dramatic tenor characterizations. I had the pleasure of directing him in* Otello. © *Metropolitan Opera Archives.*

are taking over." To some degree, I sympathized. I learned that when Dr. Graf offered me the position of resident stage director, there was no actual vacancy. He just snuck me into the roster. This was quite a vote of confidence in my abilities, but it caused bad feelings with the Swiss director already on staff, especially when I was assigned so many new productions.

Still, I was more readily accepted than some of the other American imports like conductor Samuel Krachmalnik. A native of St. Louis, he had an impressive musical background, having earned a scholarship to the prestigious Eastman School of Music, where he studied French horn and piano as well as conducting, and having continued on to graduate studies with the eminent Jean Morel at New York's equally prestigious Juilliard School, where he later joined the faculty for two years as Maestro Morel's conducting fellow. He had won the inaugural Koussevitzky Memorial Prize in Conducting at Tanglewood, where his teacher was Leonard Bernstein, and gone on to excel largely as a conductor of stage works in opera, ballet, and the Broadway theater, where he had been nominated for a coveted Antoinette Perry Award for his musical direction of Bernstein's fiendishly difficult score for *Candide*. In the course of his Broadway activities, Sam had become a streetwise Manhattanite with a sense of humor like a sewer lid. In a backhanded tribute to his often volcanic volume level at rehearsals, members of the orchestra satirically abbreviated his surname, referring to him jokingly as "Herr Krach" (Mr. Noise).

Despite his impressive background, for the implacably straitlaced citizenry of mid-twentieth-century Zurich, he was the ultimate square peg in a round hole. In all fairness, this was not an easy atmosphere to adjust to after the freewheeling tolerance of Manhattan. In Zurich, if anyone sullied the sacrosanct repose of a Sunday by mowing the lawn or running the washing machine, some neighbor was more than likely to call the police, and anyone who drove one kilometer over the speed limit could expect to be confronted by a cacophony of honking horns calling the miscreant to order. In this astringent atmosphere, anybody as unabashedly in-your-face as Sam didn't stand a chance.

Initially, I wondered why I was having an easier time of it. Slowly it dawned on me: when the Swiss looked at me, they didn't see an American; they saw an Iranian. In the patchwork civilization of California, nobody could find Iran on a map, nor did people care where you came from. I could pretend to be whatever I wanted to be and get away with it. But Zurich was a lot closer to Iran than it was to California. Here, my name and appearance told quite another story. I thought I was at peace with the person I had become, but the Swiss scrutinized my persona in quest of my native culture, my heritage—things I had spent years repressing. A quandary began to form in my head: who exactly is Lotfi Mansouri? In those first months in Zurich, though, I put those thoughts on hold. I had to. My brain was in overdrive with the tasks of learning a new job and trying to earn a living.

My first year's salary was 12,000 Swiss francs, or about $3,000 at the exchange rate of the time, roughly one-tenth of what I had earned during my last season in Los Angeles. Dr. Graf was aware of my financial situation and helped me out by casting me in small parts. I happily resuscitated my singing career for such assignments as the Dancing Master in *Manon Lescaut*, Valzacchi in *Der Rosenkavalier*, and other secondary roles. My efforts were respectable, and the performance fees added a sorely needed supplement to the family exchequer.

But my very first production in one of those secondary roles almost proved my undoing when I ran into an irascible conductor by the name of Nello Santi. The opera was *Rigoletto*, and I had been given the role of Borsa, one of the Duke of Mantua's courtiers. The part is almost over before it begins: Borsa exchanges a little banter with the Duke about a recent romantic exploit, leading into the aria "Questa o quella," then sticks around for the occasional one-liner and joins in on some chorus entrances. But one false move in that initial dialogue can throw the beginning of the opera completely out of kilter, and this was exactly what happened in one performance. I had discovered that the house director was resentful of my having been given so many good assignments, so in an effort to mend fences, I went to him and asked if he had any advice to give me on my interpretation of the minor role. He simply said that everything would be fine if I would just stay close to the tenor singing the role of the Duke. Fortunately the tenor in question was more than cooperative, and all went well, until, at one matinee another tenor showed up, and nobody bothered to tell me he would be singing Italian, not the German translation I had learned.

When I got my first cue in the opera's original language, I was so taken by surprise I fluffed the next line, which sent Maestro Santi into spasms. Howling "questo cretino!" he swore a solemn oath that he would never allow me to set foot onstage again.

We almost came to blows again when I started rehearsals for my own production of *La traviata*. In Act II, when Alfredo's father, Giorgio Germont, comes to confront the heroine, regarding her as little more than a tart, I told Robert Kerns, as a sign of disrespect, to leave on his hat, setting it down on a table later in their exchange when he realizes that she is a more substantial human being than he had been led to believe. When Bob did this in dress rehearsal, Maestro Santi stopped the rehearsal and told me in no uncertain terms that nobody in Italy would ever put a hat on a table. In the hope of lowering the volume, I courteously reminded the maestro that this scene takes place in France, which set the orchestra laughing and promptly moved Santi from fury to hysteria.

It was important for me to maintain good relations with Maestro Santi. After all, he was the resident conductor for the Italian repertoire in Zurich at the time, and beyond that, he was a first-rate musician from whom I could and did learn a lot. He carries every score he conducts in his head and can sing all the roles. As a matter of fact, he actually enjoyed it when a singer was incapacitated at a rehearsal, so he could sing the part. He knows every note each instrument in the orchestra plays and usually conducts without a score. He can recognize almost any Italian musical work after hearing just a couple of notes. He is also is a straight shooter, without an ounce of hypocrisy in his sizable frame. Fortunately for our relationship, in the dozen or so productions on which we worked together, I tried to be as well prepared as he always was, and when he realized that I did my homework as assiduously as he did, his heart opened to me, and we got along fine from then on.

But he could be horribly blunt and direct. Joan Sutherland once walked out on him at a rehearsal at La Fenice in Venice because he kept laughing at her. That was when she insisted she could be conducted only by her husband, Richard Bonynge. In Munich, somebody in the audience booed, and Santi stormed out of the pit to punch the perpetrator in the nose.

Midge joined me shortly after my arrival and went to work doing English correspondence for a Swiss printing company, her wages supplementing my salary and occasional performance fees for small roles to help us make ends meet. We first found an apartment in the nearby town of Meilen. It was unfurnished when we moved in, and considering our straitened circumstances, that's pretty much how it remained. Shortly afterward, I became acquainted with a local aristocrat, who made me an offer I couldn't refuse; in fact, I fairly jumped at the chance: if I would direct a summer attraction for the garden theater at his château, he would rent us one of the apartments he owned, cut-rate. Midge and I promptly moved into a glorious two-bedroom flat in a handsome modern apartment house overlooking Lake Zurich.

My first directorial assignment, just in time for the holidays, was Gian Carlo Menotti's Christmas one-acter *Amahl and the Night Visitors*, sung in German, with Sandra Warfield as the Mother. It was the first European performance of the piece, and I got fairly good write-ups—all in all, a promising debut. Now other productions came fast and furious: standards like *La traviata, Il trovatore, Carmen, Il barbiere di Siviglia*, and *Don Pasquale*; lesser performed and modern works like *Wozzeck, Ernani, Samson et Dalila*, and *Le prophète*, the latter two starring the husband-and-wife combination of James McCracken and Sandra Warfield; and lighter fare like Otto Nicolai's *Die lustigen Weiber von Windsor* and *Carnival!*, a short-lived Broadway musical based on the 1953 movie *Lili*. Then there were works that defied categorization, such as the world premiere of Hermann Schiebler's *Blackwood und Co.*, a sat-

LOTFI MANSOURI

ire on American consumerism, and *Cleopatra*, a new piece with a score borrowed from Johann and Josef Strauss, which asked the audience to overstress its willing suspension of disbelief as the legendary Egyptian queen went waltzing down the Nile.

Over the years, Dr. Graf had launched several training programs for young artists, considering this kind of on-the-job training essential to the future of the art form. When he arrived in Zurich, he promptly enlisted the aid of leading families and philanthropists to found the International Opera Studio, to this day one of the most outstanding programs of its kind anywhere in the world. He appointed me director of drama classes and stage director of productions. The first year, the Studio boasted some fine young professionals on the threshold of international careers. These included a promising young mezzo-soprano from Wales named Gwyneth Jones, who moved up during her stay in Zurich to soprano, then went on to conquer the world. Following a spectacular win at the International Singing Competition in Sofia, an Indiana University graduate named Felicia Weathers was invited to join the Studio, moving on rapidly to international stardom. Others in the blue-ribbon class included Joanna Simon, the gifted daughter of Richard Simon, cofounder of the American publishing house Simon & Schuster and also father of Carly, still a pop music icon. A number of fine European singers and pianists also studied there. The Studio productions I directed included Bernstein's *Trouble in Tahiti*, with Gwyneth Jones as Dinah, *Albert Herring*, and *L'incoronazione di Poppea*.

From 1960 to 1966, I directed a total of eighteen productions for the theater and several other productions for the Studio. I was finally experiencing the comprehensive, high-level challenge for which I had always strived. My repertoire ran the gamut from grippingly dramatic to utterly silly. I was becoming a specialist in everything—period pieces, modern, abstract, whatever suited the work—and in a number of languages. My casts and conductors were uniformly top level. I was plunged into the crazy quilt of backstage society, dealing personally and professionally with performers, designers, members of the stage crew, board members, and the people who swept up after all of us. Never before had I experienced such a volume or variety of work. Each day brought fresh demands. I had to grow—and I did.

In many ways, the Zurich experience represented my coming of age as a director. I used it to establish my aesthetic footing. My productions were as theatrical as possible without distracting from the music—my answer to the question that arose during my summer in Bayreuth and Venice of how to balance theatricality and musicality. I had become clearly aware of how the drama of any great composer's opera is propelled as much by the musical text as by the words of the drama, if not more so, and I saw to it that my staging reflected that, never getting in the way of the singing. I sought to give the unseen motivation of the musical impulse a meaningful visual form.

German and Italian agents began getting interested in representing me in their countries. My first job in Italy took place in 1961 at the Teatro San Carlo in Naples. I was grateful to have been assigned François-Esprit Auber's *Fra Diavolo*, a relatively unknown, untraditional *opera comique*, which was a lucky choice because Italian audiences could be merciless when it came to the standard repertoire. The cast, including the revered veteran Giuseppe Valdengo, singing a relatively small role as one of the bandits, was strong on comedy and waited to see what I would do with the piece. After all, I was an unknown quantity, making my Italian debut with a work I had never done before, and I had to prove myself. I decided to go for broke and incorporated gags from the cornball Laurel and Hardy film of the same name I had seen when I was a teenager. As I envisioned, these transferred well to the stage. The performances came off without a hitch, and the experience gave me a lot of fuel for the next time I mounted the piece, seven years later in San Francisco, with the magnificent Nicolai Gedda in the title role. Invitations then followed from theaters in Genoa, Turin, Venice, Rome, and other Italian cities. Virtually at the same time, I started juggling assignments in Germany for companies in Heidelberg, Kassel, Nuremberg, Freiburg, and Dortmund.

One reason for this rich collection of assignments was my versatility. Just as most American singers were in demand because they could perform in several languages and styles, I was getting work because my directing skills were applicable to a variety of works. What fascinated me was that I became known as a director of the French and German repertoire in Italy, while the Germans generally brought me in for Italian and French opera. I should have been flattered to be regarded as multifaceted, but this circumstance just brought my identity dilemma to the fore. Traveling from city to city, I became more and more aware that I was never really *from* any of those places.

So where was I from? And just exactly who was I?

My professional life was right on track, but my personal life was falling apart. For months, something had been dogging me. It was like a black cloud over my head, and it wouldn't go away. Eventually I felt as if I were being pursued and had to keep running faster and faster. I was wearing down.

My few years in opera had been hyperactive, filled with work and an extended odyssey from one place to another, from one culture to another, from one language to another. Just crossing the border from Switzerland to Germany brought me into conctact with another language. Although the Swiss all understood what they called *Schriftdeutsch* (standard "written" German), their own spoken language was so unfamiliar in other German-speaking areas that Swiss films were traditionally subtitled there, or the same actors came to Germany to dub in their own voices so the Germans and Austrians would understand them. To this, add Italian and French, English, and memories of my native Farsi. Everywhere I went, I had to adjust to new colleagues and a new social milieu. I found myself continually struggling to win acceptance. As if this weren't rough enough, I was plagued by all the insecurities that come with the territory in any artistic career. Each production found me feeling as though I were auditioning for yet another new cast, new chorus, new critics, new audiences. Like a puppy wagging its tail nonstop, I desperately tried to curry favor everywhere I went. Compounding the problem was the fact that I had spent so many years in the United States trying to assimilate, trying to become American, that I had repressed all my childhood experiences of Iran, working furiously to expunge anything Persian from my being: the language, the attitudes, the behavior patterns. All this helped me cope with a grim thought: if my family didn't want me, I didn't want them. I was someone else now. At least, so I thought.

The move to Europe shook up the superficial individual I had created in the same way I might have staged a character in a performance. I had been putting on an act for so long that I had lost touch with who the real Lotfi was. The less I knew of myself, the more insecure and self-conscious I became. I began to question all my work: if I was a phony, then everything I did had to be phony. Slowly and inextricably, I sank into an ever-deeper depression. Somehow, I managed to keep on working. During rehearsals I was all high energy, laughing, joking—essentially role-playing. The minute the rehearsal ended, while driving home,

I would break down and cry. The more this depression took hold of me, the more I began to fantasize about ending my life.

Thank God for Midge and Dr. Graf. They witnessed and empathized with everything that was happening to me, and they urged me to seek professional help. A physician prescribed antidepressants, but they did nothing for me. In my lowest moment, I just gave up and threw out all the pills. Finally the doctor suggested psychoanalysis, recommending a prominent psychiatrist. As my German wasn't strong enough to profit from the experience, he referred me to a colleague who was proficient in English, a Dr. Fritz Morgenthaler, a highly regarded Jungian, who had recently returned from a period of ethno-psychoanalytic research in West Africa. It was a truly serendipitous encounter: Dr. Morgenthaler could relate directly to the travails of someone involved in the arts. The son of a distinguished painter named Ernst Morgenthaler, he also did some painting himself and had even performed professionally as a juggler. He would certainly have his hands full juggling my various personality manifestations.

The treatment would be expensive, adding further stress to our already precarious finances, but I was at the end of my rope. Midge, who had briefly quit her job, went back to work to enable us to pay for the sessions.

Conveniently, Dr. Morgenthaler's office was right around the corner from the opera house. My sessions began at 9:00 A.M., so I could make it to 10:00 rehearsals. The first few months were brutal. Dr. Morgenthaler seemed merciless, targeting all the guises and defenses I had fabricated over the course of fifteen years. Some sessions left me lacerated and drained, and yet ten minutes later, I was expected to be onstage to direct a comic opera like *Il barbiere di Siviglia* or a frothy musical like *Carnival!*

Eventually, Dr. Morgenthaler helped me reach the bottom of my problems by getting me to admit I was never satisfied with myself, never good enough. In fact, I was intensifying these feelings by setting impossibly high goals, falling short of them, and then using this as graphic evidence of my inadequacy. My desire to "be the best" had propelled me from Iran to California and now to Europe. But why was I feeling so driven in the first place? It had to do with the expectations forced on me as a child— expectations I couldn't live up to, indeed didn't want to live up to. I had always been drawn more to Western than to Persian culture, and this had brought on feelings of resentment and guilt. My own birthplace was like alien territory. My father would ask, "Why aren't you more like your cousin?" I was like a stranger at gatherings of my own family. I coped by driving myself to excel when all I really wanted to do was escape. My relentless striving to excel was in fact an inexorable desire to be liked, because "if I wasn't good enough," then I had no value as a human being.

"You must realize," Dr. Morgenthaler told me, "you are not a flag on the altar of a cathedral."

My analysis lasted two and a half years. It was one of the most important and constructive periods in my life. With Dr. Morgenthaler's help, I gained a clearer, more objective understanding of myself, both my strengths and my shortcomings. I found that my increased self-knowledge gave me a better grounding for assuming various professional roles in a variety of settings. Following Shakespeare's cannily simple observation that "each man in his time plays many parts," I could act one way as a stage director with artists and another way as a general director with volunteer board members. I could be a chameleon, changing colors to suit the surroundings, without ever losing the core of who I really was.

Dr. Graf began relying on me more and more. When Luchino Visconti withdrew from a production of Donizetti's *Poliuto* at La Scala, Dr. Graf stepped in at the last minute and brought me along. In the summer of 1961, I assisted him with *Simon Boccanegra* at the Salzburg Festival, returning in 1962 to direct the revival. I was working with singers like Maria Callas, Franco Corelli, and Ettore Bastianini, with me as the proverbial kid testing everything in sight.

Back in Zurich, I was getting more prestigious assignments, one daunting task in particular. Otto Klemperer was having trouble finding a stage director to meet his exacting stipulations for a production of *Fidelio* he wanted to mount. Remembering me from the time I had visited him with the Zweigs, he asked Dr. Graf, "What about that Turkish guy?"

"Do you mean Mansouri? He's Persian."

"Yes, that's the one, the *Turk*," Klemperer replied.

I was directing *La traviata* at the time, and Dr. Graf arranged for Klemperer to observe the dress rehearsal. This threw me into a panic. Dr. Graf thought I was being ungrateful in the face of such an opportunity, but while I was more than appreciative, I told him that Klemperer had behaved atrociously toward me at an earlier visit when the Zweigs introduced us at lunch in Munich's Vier Jahreszeiten hotel. Admittedly, at the time of that first encounter, I had been unaware of some of his health problems, and I just thought he was an abusive boor. Whatever the cause of his odd behavior then, there was no escaping it now: I would have to put up with having him right beside me at the rehearsal. The instant the soft introductory music began, the great musician dozed off, his head reclining on my shoulder. No amount of training can prepare anyone for a situation like that. I sat stock-still, whispering my notes to my assistant. At the conclusion of Act I, with the buoyant postlude to "Sempre libera" playing full throttle, Virginia Gordoni as Violetta hurled her champagne glass at the wall with a loud crash, which suddenly woke up the maestro. Klemperer sat bolt upright and called out, "Very good, very good! We will work together on *Fidelio*!"

Still unaware of his mammoth reputation, I reacted to this vote of confidence with stark terror. For me, he was an excessively demanding nut job who would drive me bananas by confronting me with one frustration after another. I begged Dr. Graf to assign somebody else—*anybody* else—to this *Fidelio* production. My boss was baffled by my reluctance, explaining that, yes, he was somewhat eccentric ("Somewhat?" I thought to myself) but he was one of the great figures of musical history, a man who had discovered and introduced some of the finest contemporary works of his generation, compositions by such titans as Janáček, Schoenberg, Stravinsky, and Hindemith, to mention but a few, when he presided over the Krolloper in Berlin. Dr. Graf insisted that a collaboration with the great Klemperer would do wonders for my career and promptly shipped me off to London so I could witness his greatness by attending the final rehearsals of his *Fidelio* production at Covent Garden.

I still remember an episode at that *Fidelio* rehearsal that proved a harbinger of things to come. In the heartrending moment during the final scene, Don Fernando, the government minister, who has come to set things aright, is told of Leonore's enormous sacrifices in her successful effort to obtain the release of her innocent husband, Florestan, and in a beautifully noble musical utterance, tells Rocco the jailer to allow her to unlock the shackles confining Florestan. Sena Jurinac as Leonore stepped over to Jon Vickers as Florestan, their eyes met, she inserted the key into the padlock and started to turn it when a cry of "Nein, nein, nein!" exploded from the pit.

Klemperer had been permanently disabled by the effects of a stroke, followed by a botched brain operation, but he still insisted on struggling

LOTFI MANSOURI

out of the pit and up the steps to the stage level, where he proceeded to tell poor Jurinac in no uncertain terms that the key must be turned clockwise, not counterclockwise. Then, having delivered this bit of wisdom, he took what seemed like forever to hobble back down to the pit on his cane to resume the rehearsal.

I could see that there were rough waters ahead for me.

Dr. Graf had no sympathy with my misgivings whatsoever, calling me "an ungrateful child" (I was twenty-nine). He said he had been so eager to acquire Dr. Klemperer's services for this opera that he had willingly given in to one nonnegotiable demand after another. Normally conductors were accorded two to three stage rehearsals with orchestra to coordinate the production. Klemperer wanted eleven; he got all of them, including the big-name artists engaged for the premiere, Sena Jurinac, repeating her London performance as Leonore, along with James McCracken as Florestan, Dezső Ernster as Rocco and Gustav Neidlinger as Pizarro. Hardly anyone does *Fidelio* without making massive cuts in the long passages of spoken dialogue, much of it fairly brainless. Klemperer wanted every word of it uttered onstage, and every word was uttered. He had his reasons for that demand, as implausible as it was. He respected the text, because it had inspired Beethoven and because he was obsessed with the quest for the ideal woman, as expressed throughout the opera, a quest, he claimed, that dominated his life. Apparently, he never realized that to find an ideal woman you had to be an ideal man, but that didn't stop him from womanizing notoriously right into his advanced years.

This led to yet another manifestation of odd behavior that almost shipwrecked the production. His fascination with the opposite sex took precedence over everything else, and just such a fascination came about when the soprano singing Marzelline in our production, a very pretty American singer named Jean Cook, caught his fancy, prompting him to hurl a major monkey wrench into the work of preparing the opera with the lamest of excuses. In his erotic zeal, he simply interrupted one rehearsal and walked out of the theatre muttering angrily, then "casually" asking Jean to join him at the Lyrique Restaurant across the street from the theatre. All of a sudden, I was appointed the peacemaker and dispatched across the street to find out what was the problem. Without taking his eyes off Jean on the other side of the table, he whined: "They don't love me. They don't love me. I'm not coming back," whereupon I rushed back to the theater to confront the musicians. Explaining that they had done something, nobody knew what, to offend the great Klemperer, I added that he was no longer a young man and this might perhaps be his final *Fidelio*. A meeting was called, and the chairman of the orchestra committee was charged with making a declaration of love to the conductor in the hope of getting him to return. I was sent back to the restaurant to advise Dr. Klemperer of the imminent declaration. Somehow he managed to extricate himself from his tête-à-tête with Jean and work his way across the street, into the theater, and down to his accustomed place in the pit, at which point the chairman formally implored him to return to the rehearsal, declaring the musicians' undying support, admiration, and affection for him. The chairman made this declaration in generally understandable German, albeit with a thick Swiss accent. When he finished, Klemperer looked down contemptuously and muttered, "Would you repeat that in German? I didn't understand a word you said."

At the end of the run, after being subjected to even more conductorial tomfoolery, the orchestra members told Dr. Graf that they had put up with Klemperer long enough and were not prepared to play for him if he came back. Dr. Graf had already contracted him for further performances in the subsequent season, and other prominent conductors like Rudolf Kempe sprang to their colleague's defense, declaring publicly that they would not conduct in Zurich until diplomatic relations with Dr. Klemperer were restored. Of course, he returned.

Much of the shaky stability he still possessed was the product of the tender loving care he received from his adoring daughter Lotte and the unwavering support he got from the famous record producer Walter Legge, who, more than anyone else, had put his career back on track with prestigious engagements on the highest level after the war. One afternoon, Mr. Legge called the theater and asked if he might attend a rehearsal with a conductor friend, and knowing of the close relationship between Dr. Klemperer and Mr. Legge, Dr. Graf saw no reason to object. I arranged everything meticulously; I met Mr. Legge at the door with his friend and snuck them into the back of the house, where they sat in respectful silence. Apparently they weren't silent enough, or Klemperer had eyes in the back of his head, because the minute he sensed their presence in the hall, he turned around and snarled, "This isn't a conducting school!" whereupon Mr. Legge quickly and quietly departed the scene, taking Herbert von Karajan with him.

LOTFI MANSOURI

On balance, the Klemperer collaboration was more than worth the travails the conductor put us through. The production was an enormous success; the house was packed every night, as if Beethoven himself were on the podium, and the audiences went crazy. More important, Otto Klemperer brought a dignity and truth to the music I have never seen surpassed. And yes, Dr. Graf was right—it did give a major boost to my career.

I had become Dr. Graf's righthand man. He was my artistic father, and I was his artistic son. It was an exhilarating time, but it did have one bittersweet side. The Grafs had only one child, a son named Werner, and they had hoped he would follow in his father's footsteps. Thanks to his father, Werner had enjoyed some excellent directing opportunities, including one involving a terrific cast for *Don Giovanni* with Josef Krips on the conductor's podium, but he never lived up to his parents' expectations. It might have been in his DNA, but he didn't have it in his heart, and he ultimately became a teacher. The effect of this disappointment on the Grafs became abundantly clear to me after the opening of my *Amahl and the Night Visitors* when Mrs. Graf made her way through the throng of well-wishers around me and said, with tears in her eyes, "This might have been my son." I froze, overwhelmed with equal measures of joy and sorrow—emotions I'm sure the Grafs shared. Recalling my own early experiences, I couldn't help but reflect that living with "what you see is what you get" is also a good guideline for parents.

Meanwhile there was trouble brewing. In the 1960s, Zurich was fairly insular. Anything foreign triggered suspicions. It wasn't uncommon to read a letter to the editor of a local paper from some irate dowager complaining that her luncheon by the lake had been ruined by the presence of a *Gastarbeiter* (guest worker). All foreign workers and other hired help, of whatever nationality other than Swiss, were referred to as guest workers. All the changes at the opera house—the new and ambitious productions, the influx of foreign artists, even appearances by such living legends as George Balanchine and Igor Stravinsky—had unsettled the locals. In the short space of three years, a sleepy provincial company had been transformed. The talent-challenged began to see the end of their careers. Rumors and gossip abounded. Eyebrows were raised. Although the country had saved many lives and priceless careers during the war years, excoriating foreigners was unfortunately still a hallowed tradition in some influential circles, and so the outcry of "too many

Americans" began to filter from the corridors of the opera house out onto the streets.

The Zurich Opera's board of directors, composed of upscale citizens with long pedigrees, heard the rumblings and saw the budgets inching upward. The board members became apprehensive that they might be losing control. Too many changes too soon, they said. Things came to a head in 1962. Dr. Graf took a stand: if his plans were not approved, he would resign. It was a tactical error. The board stood firm, and Dr. Graf had no alternative but to make good on his threat. I watched it all unfold, and it proved to be a painful if instructive first lesson in working with boards.

After Dr. Graf's departure, a German-Swiss agent by the name of Emil Jucker slithered in from the middle distance and appointed himself interim director. Actually, he was part of a cooperative management, but he simply took it upon himself to run the show. Jucker had all the integrity of the average viper. A smile from him was like a death sentence. I ended up using him as a model for Scarpia and other stage heavies. The scams and intrigues began, with everyone jockeying for position. Downhearted and disgusted, I buried myself in work and tried to stay away from the nonsensical political maneuvering that now began in earnest.

Mr. Jucker's nefarious administration was blessedly short lived. A few years later, after being given the heave-ho from Zurich, Jucker was hired as a kind of general factotum by Herbert von Karajan, but when it was discovered that he was continuing his wastrel ways by shaking down artists for kickbacks on the fees for their engagements, he was summarily sacked from that job as well.

After a lot of dickering, the board of directors finally appointed Hermann Juch from Austria as general director. Austrians adore titles—Herr Doktor, Herr Geheimrat, Herr Professor, and so on—and Juch was equipped with a double-barreled title. Professor Doktor Juch was frigid and formal, more of a functionary than an artist. Still, at our first meeting, he said he liked my work and looked forward to our collaboration. He assigned me one of the first operas in the 1964–65 season, a new German-language production of *Carmen*.

In another production he gave me, Juch's dogged insistence on following the flock by inserting a far-fetched contemporary reference into the production, along with his ill-concealed racial bias, had him locking horns with just about the wittiest member of the profession, an encoun-

LOTFI MANSOURI

Martina Arroyo bristled at the suggestion that her Leonora in Il trovatore *should resemble Jacqueline Kennedy, and true to form, she had the last word.* © *Metropolitan Opera Archives.*

ter that left him with a healthy portion of egg on his face. The opera was *Il trovatore*, featuring the colossally talented, rhetorically irrepressible Martina Arroyo in the leading soprano role of Leonora. Shortly before we went into rehearsal, I received a memo from the general director instructing me in no uncertain terms that in the first act finale, when Leonora is about to enter a convent, she was to bear a striking resemblance to Mrs. Jacqueline Kennedy visiting the pope. For all her versatility, there was no way that resemblance could be concocted, and this suggestion was so preposterous that, rather than insult Martina by even mentioning it, I decided I would simply consign it to the dead-letter office of my memory.

Unfortunately, however, this crackpot memo had already made the rounds, and when Martina went in for a costume fitting, she was apprised of it by the wardrobe mistress, whereupon she did an about-face and marched resolutely into Juch's office, demanding a meeting.

Fixing him with a steely glance, she said, "I understand that when I take the veil in the convent, you think I should look like Jackie Kennedy."

A little sheepishly, Juch admitted to having made the suggestion.

"There is no way I can look like Mrs. Kennedy, sir, no matter what I do," she replied, "and while we're on the subject, there's no way Mrs. Kennedy can sing Leonora."

Rather than admit that he had made a clumsy mistake, Juch decided to compound the felony with a backhanded racial retort, "Ms. Arroyo, there are some people who don't think you have any business singing Leonora in the first place."

Unshaken by this cheap shot, Martina laconically replied, "Professor Juch, there are a *whole lot* of people who don't think you have any business running an opera house."

The story of that well-aimed zinger became a legend in the theater, and Juch finally had the wisdom not to come up with any more ridiculous suggestions.

Nevertheless, one glance at Juch's plans for the rest of the season made it clear to me that he was hell-bent on restoring Zurich to its position as a somnolent provincial house. The number of foreigners on the roster, apart from the Austrians, began to dwindle, and many of the remaining artists were well past their prime. Before long, the Zurich Opera acquired the nickname of Juchheim, which in local parlance was the description of an old folk's home.

Fortunately, by this time, I had plenty of other options. I was now known throughout Europe and had made recent debuts at both San Francisco Opera and Santa Fe Opera. Once again Dr. Graf called—this time from Geneva—with yet another offer. I was about to embark on another adventure, an adventure that would be abruptly bifurcated by a singularly bizarre intermezzo.

5

Iranian Intermezzo

In 1965, Dr. Graf was appointed general director of the Geneva Opera, and he immediately asked me to join him as principal stage director. Needless to say, I was happy to accept. I expected Professor Doktor Juch to react angrily, but to my surprise, he asked me to continue my association with the Zurich theater as guest director both with the main company and with the Opera Studio, so I agreed to commute back to Zurich occasionally. Then Midge and I packed up and departed.

The Grand-Théâtre de Genève was an exquisite fusion of old and new. In the 1950s, the nineteenth-century house burned down during a *Walküre* rehearsal. Obviously somebody got carried away with the magic fire in Act III. When the city rebuilt the edifice, it retained the ornate façade and foyer, while adding a modern 1,400-seat auditorium with cutting-edge backstage facilities and machinery. The sight lines and acoustics were the best in my experience, and the orchestra pit accommodated up to 110 musicians, half of them underneath the stage. Geneva used the *stagione* system, producing one work at a time with a company of soloists brought in especially for each production rather than casting from a resident company. The production would then be presented seven or more times before the next one was staged. The theater availed itself of the services of the magnificent Orchestre de la Suisse Romande, with superb forces in the chorus, the scenic and costume studios, and the ballet company. Casts and conductors were first rate, some of the best to be found in the world. My first production in the house, for example, was an *Otello* starring James McCracken and Gwyneth Jones, with Tito Gobbi alternating his definitive Jago with Ramón Vinay, with whom I had appeared as a super in Los Angeles, when he was still singing the title role. Now he was back singing baritone at the end of his superb career. Even the relatively small role of Lodovico was cast from strength with bass-baritone José van Dam, and Maestro Santi presided on the podium.

Continuing his commitment to the future of the craft, Dr. Graf founded another artist development program, the Centre Lyrique.

If Zurich was the launching pad for Lotfi Mansouri's career, Geneva was the stratosphere where it finally took wing. I was assigned every type of opera in larger-scale productions with uniformly superb casts and conductors. In my ten years with the company, I directed virtually every standard-repertoire opera, several obscure works and a couple of musicals: all in all, thirty-four productions. I collaborated with some of the greatest conductors of their generation, including such legendary figures as Ernest Ansermet, Lamberto Gardelli, and Sir John Pritchard. Even the audience contained some all-star names. I had the privilege of having one performance of my *Albert Herring* production given in the presence of the composer Benjamin Britten, who had come to Geneva with his partner, Peter Pears, to hear his *War Requiem*. The great choreographer George Balanchine was a good friend of Dr. Graf, who had worked with him in New York, and soon the Grand-Théâtre de Genève became Balanchine's "farm," where members of his New York City Ballet came to learn and try out new roles. Balanchine also directed a couple of productions at the theater. I had the pleasure of working with him on a beautiful French-language production of *Evgeny Onegin* with Elisabeth Söderström as Tatiana. He had a unique take on the final act, placing the scene between Onegin and Tatiana at the ball and book-ending it with the Polonaise—as if to say, the dance of life keeps going on.

Offstage, things were better than ever. Thanks to my sessions with Dr. Morgenthaler, I felt totally comfortable with my identity, both as a person and as a professional. It never occurred to me that this new psychological grounding would be put to the acid test when I came face to face with the juxtaposition of my past and present lives, but I soon found out.

In all my years outside of Iran, I had succeeded in consigning the land of my birth to an antechamber in my mind. Childhood memories surfaced only once, when Princess Ashraf Pahlavi, the shah's twin sister, visited Geneva and I was invited to a reception in her honor at the Iranian Embassy. We had a polite conversation, during which, of course, I did not remind her of that ignominious occasion when I wet my pants while costarring with her sister Fatemeh in a kindergarten play.

Although I had pretty much eliminated Iran from my thoughts, in 1970 Iran began thinking about me. The U.S. State Department had issued a book about cultural activities that included a photo of me in action at the Santa Fe Opera, captioned: "Iranian-born Lotfi Mansouri directs a scene from. . . ." Somehow, this book landed on the desk of the man who had been appointed to organize an opera company in Iran, and one day, out of the blue, I got a phone call from an associate of his inviting me to direct a production of *Carmen* in Tehran. The occasion was the so-called 2,500th anniversary of the Persian monarchy under Cyrus the Great. Of course, the country was well over four thousand years old, and the implication that the Pahlavis were even remotely descended from the mighty Cyrus was absurd on the face of it, but it did give the shah and his empress, Farah Diba, a golden opportunity to throw an enormous party and invite several dozen heads of state, ranging from the sublime, in the persons of reigning monarchs from around the world, all the way to the ridiculous: soon-to-be-ousted Vice President Spiro Agnew heading the U.S. delegation and Imelda Marcos representing the Philippines. One wonders if Imelda needed a separate plane to transport her shoes.

By this point in my career, I had directed productions in what I thought was every imaginable set of circumstances, but this would be one for the books. My first reaction was to accept and treat the whole affair as a lark. Then I realized this would also be a magnificent opportunity to reunite with my family, especially my father, whom I had not seen in twenty-three years. My initial enthusiasm, however, soon waned. In Iran, my profession was still regarded as irregular at best and disreputable at worst, and having embraced a Western way of life, I might be looked upon as an outsider, if not a traitor.

Iran's political climate at that time was volatile. It was the kind of place where people "disappeared." And I had to give some serious thought to whether a reunion with a family I had had no contact with whatsoever, not so much as a postcard, let alone a letter, for more than two decades might overturn all the security I had gained in the arduous years of psychoanalysis. Perhaps my family would want nothing to do with me. The more I thought about the situation, the more nervous I got. There was too much to lose, and so I declined the offer, but for the Iranians my "no, thanks" was regarded as a ploy, like saying no to a proffered piece of cake before finally accepting it.

The Iranian culture minister, not incidentally a brother-in-law of the shah, promptly dispatched an emissary to Geneva with a first-class, round-trip plane ticket, a beautiful silver tray, and a box of pistachios, along with the message "The Shah wishes you to reconsider. . . ." This was not the kind of contract negotiation to which I had become accustomed. I stared at the open box decorated with a delicate inlay, desperately wanting to shut it. As I saw it, it was a Pandora's box, and the longer it remained open, the more hell would break loose. As formally as possible, I explained that I would regrettably be unable to accept his majesty's kind offer. I said that my boss, Dr. Herbert Graf, general director of the Geneva Opera, had given me a number of important assignments, and there was no way he would allow me to take a leave of absence.

Apparently the emissary had been outfitted with a packing case full of lavish gifts, because he promptly approached Dr. Graf without advising me and also presented him with another first-class round-trip ticket, silver tray, and inlaid box of pistachios. As it had never occurred to me that anyone would try that stratagem, I hadn't warned Dr. Graf, as a consequence of which he graciously told the emissary he saw no reason why I couldn't have a short hiatus to return to my birthplace. The minute he okayed the deal, word went back to Tehran, and a day or two after that, it was in the newspapers. There was no escape. I wired my family, advising them of my imminent arrival.

I got aboard the aircraft in a quandary. To compound my agitated mental state, I realized that I could remember very little of my native language. By now, I was fluent in English, French, German, and Italian, but I had no occasion to converse with anybody in Farsi. The moment the plane touched down in Tehran in the middle of the night, my heart began pounding violently. I was about to disembark in a place I barely remembered, a place I had never really understood, and one that seemed replete with all kinds of dangers. As I approached the immigration desk, I saw a man I recognized instantly. My father had come to meet me, surrounded on all sides by a cascade of milling relatives—at two o'clock in the morning! Seeing all of them, but unable to talk to them from my place in line behind the glass barrier, I was a bundle of confusion. When I finally cleared the entry formalities, what would I say? And how would they react? When I reached the head of the line, I was abruptly thrust back into reality. The immigration officer took one look at my U.S. passport and called over two uniformed men, who escorted me into a little room. The two of them exchanged a volley of words, but I couldn't understand a thing they said. Finally, one of them told me in English, "We do not accept your American passport. You were born in Iran, and therefore you must have an Iranian passport." With that, they confiscated my travel document and told me it would be returned only when I had an Iranian one. Robbed of this proof of my new, hard-won identity, I was naked and defenseless. It was a nightmare come to life. The two uniformed men then hustled me out of the room and into the arms of my waiting tribe. My father, who had never done this before in all the years when I was growing up, started hugging and kissing me. My relatives burst into tears and took turns embracing me, saying over and over again, "Oh, Lotfi, dear, dear Lotfi!" I didn't recognize a single one of them. I later discovered that one of the girl cousins embracing me fervently at the airport was the one who been singled out more than twenty years ago to be my wife. Faces, gestures, words—all were familiar, yet unfamiliar. A different lifetime came crashing back over me, and I was getting dizzy. On reflection, I realize I must have been going through the final phase of my analysis without any medical counsel to guide me. Either this experience would finally fill the blank spaces in my identity, or I would emerge a total basket case. I determined to get through it as best I could, but it wasn't easy.

My father drove me to the family home, followed by a caravan of aunts, uncles, and cousins with all their families. By the time we arrived, I was punch-drunk. Then I laid eyes on a beautiful face, which I recognized immediately, that of my precious grandmother, whom I had loved as a child and whom I immediately loved again. I was dying for a drink, but my father, a devout Muslim, did not have a drop of anything alcoholic beneath his roof. Fortunately, I had presciently stashed a bottle of Chivas Regal in my luggage, and under some pretext or other, I went to my room for a giant slug.

The following morning, I sat down to breakfast with my father. My uncle, who spoke English, sat next to me, ready for my steady stream of "How do you say this in Farsi?" questions. Words and phrases had already begun coming back to me, but we still had a hell of a time communicating. After breakfast, I was driven in a chauffeured car to the shiny new opera house for a tour. I could not help but be impressed. Designed by Fritz Bornemann, the architect who had built the Deutsche Oper in West Berlin, it had everything: a turntable, modern rigging and lighting equipment, spacious backstage areas, a breathtaking foyer, mosaics, chandeliers, lush gardens. It was a dream of a building in a sleek, modern district flanked by glamorous corporate headquarters, hotels, and arts and entertainment palaces. The whole area was constructed with Westerners in mind. But all I could think about was my confiscated passport.

As soon as the tour ended, I rushed to the U.S. Embassy and stated that I, as a United States citizen, had had my passport seized at the airport. The young official gave me a skeptical look. How long, I asked, would it take to get an Iranian passport? He answered airily, "Oh, about three to six months." I felt sick to my stomach. All my worst fears about returning to Iran were coming true. When I told him I had to be back in Geneva in four weeks, he replied that there was absolutely nothing the embassy could do. With a condescending smile, he leaned over toward me and said, "Really, Mr. Mansouri, you have to remember you're in the *Middle East.*"

"You snot-nosed creep," I thought to myself. I fantasized about wiping that smug grin off his face, but that did little to dispel the terrible realization that I was in a country that was not exactly renowned for rule of law, and I had no proof of my U.S. citizenship. The chaos and filth of Tehran became even more sinister. I wanted to get out of there as soon as possible.

Fortunately, I was able to pull a few strings. I went to see the petroleum minister, who had been one of my late mother's admirers, although we wisely kept that fact out of the conversation. He personally escorted me to the Foreign Ministry, and forty-eight hours later, I had my Iranian passport. I was still scared, because at that time a U.S. citizen was not permitted to hold dual citizenship, and I might be in danger of losing my claim to my U.S. passport. The minister, however, reassured me, "Don't worry. We've all got two passports. Just put one in your right pocket and the other one in your left pocket, and don't forget which is which." I rushed to the U.S. Embassy and slapped my Iranian passport down in front of the same smug official. His jaw dropped. "How on earth did you manage this so quickly?" I smiled sweetly and said, "Don't forget we're in the *Middle East.*"

I was high as a kite. I had my Iranian passport. I had my U.S. passport. I then rushed off to get my international driver's license. The passports gave me security, and the driver's license gave me mobility. I could get rid of the chauffeurs and have a little privacy. I promptly rented a car, but in my zeal to get started I neglected to check the fuel gauge. The tank was almost empty, and before I knew it I found myself stalled in the middle of the most impenetrable gridlock I have ever encountered. My car was instantly surrounded by shouting, gesticulating, gawking rubberneckers. I was still so euphoric about getting those passports and being able to drive that I just didn't care. In fact, I began to laugh. The onlookers must have thought I was crazy. A man leaned through my open window and asked me if I needed help. I could sense hands going through my pockets, and in a flash, I realized what was happening. I threw up my arms at just the right moment, locking on to the would-be thief's hands, which were holding my two precious passports. "Thief!" I screamed. More Farsi came leaping back into my brain, mostly curses, and I swore a blue streak. I wrestled with the man as if my life depended on it, and finally he let go and went running off. I clutched my two passports to my chest as the crowd began chasing the man, yelling. I stuck my head out of the window and shouted, "Let him go!" The last thing I needed was to have to file a complaint at a Tehran police station; I had experienced all the run-ins I wanted with Iranian law, and I was still in a quandary as to how I was going to get out of this situation with an empty fuel tank. Fortunately, a taxi driver came by and provided me with enough gasoline to do it. By now, I was dizzy with relief and overwhelmed with nervous tension. When I got home, I broke out the hidden bottle of scotch. This time a single swig wouldn't do. I really tied one on.

I had been back for only three days.

Western opera tradition did not exist in Iran. The shah's remedy— instant opera: just add money and stir. My arrival at the opera house was greeted like a rather shiny penny from heaven. The technical director was German, and the orchestra members were largely from Eastern Europe, but virtually all the others were Iranian, and few of them had the vaguest notion of what they had to do. I hurled myself into my new assignment. Money wasn't an issue; as a matter of fact, there was no budget. I was simply told I could have whatever I wanted. Still, after so many years at major international opera houses, flagrant extravagance simply wasn't in my blood. I set about confronting my primary challenges: organizing, moving my staff along a steep learning curve, and putting together our *Carmen* production. However, things didn't come off as planned, for reasons I could not possibly have anticipated.

Literally days before an important dress rehearsal, I received a message informing me that it had been canceled. The crown prince, it appeared, wanted to see a performance of the ballet *Giselle* with some friends that day. My rehearsal disappeared—poof—and the theater was readied for the ballet. The prince, incidentally, was all of eleven years old. I was too flabbergasted to be upset. In fact, I was so curious I hid in the hall to watch. Apart from the royal box, the auditorium was empty, while a lavish production filled the stage. I had never seen anything like this. It made no difference that it was a fine performance; the situation was too bizarre for it to be anything other than sad. I found out this was actually a common event. A year or two later, I was told that an entire opera performance had been delayed because the empress had flown in a French *chansonnier*, Sacha Distel, if memory serves, and she wanted to hear him first. Performers, stagehands, production artists, the audience, all waited patiently until the empress enjoyed her private concert. An hour and a half later, the theater opened its doors, the audience filed in, and the curtain went up on the opera. Having been trained in the West to regard time as money, I was totally befuddled by this extravagance.

I was becoming attuned to a thousand cultural subtleties, but there was nothing subtle about one thing. The chorus was composed largely of ethnic Armenians, and I was quickly reminded that there was an enormous prejudice against them in Iran. Their forebears had emigrated here years, even centuries, earlier only to find themselves marginalized, partly because they were Christians in a Muslim environment and partly because of their affinity for Western culture, which aroused suspicion in the dominant circles. The Armenians remained, understandably, a tight-knit group with strong ties to Western values, including music. That was the reason practically all the choristers were Armenian: they had trained voices, they could read Western notation, and they understood musical styles. The average Iranian didn't have an inkling about any of these things. That meant very little in Tehran, though. Armenians were regarded as servants and treated accordingly. The members of our chorus received the equivalent of a paltry $90 a month and had no medical care, no time off, no security, nothing. They approached me asking for help, and I immediately set out to remedy the situation, mandating that they be given breaks and predictable working hours. For the first time, I began to sense some resistance.

LOTFI MANSOURI

The gifted young soprano I wanted to cast as Micaëla happened to be Armenian. She was an attractive lady, who had already sung in some small regional German companies along with her husband, who was cast as Remendado in our production. Unfortunately, the finance minister's wife, who came from an old aristocratic family, also wanted to sing the role. She, too, was good-looking and had studied singing in France, where she had sung professionally, while making some appearances in Tehran as well, but she was a bit past her prime. She installed herself in a three-level dressing room at the opera house that was larger and more ornate than the director's accommodations, and was attended to by two servants and a full-time chauffeur. She insisted on singing Micaëla on opening night, and there was no way I could tell the finance minister's wife she couldn't do it. I did, however, manage to manipulate her into graciously giving the opening night to the Armenian soprano by telling her she would be regarded as the soul of generosity if she withdrew in favor of the younger artist. I even staged a radio and television interview in which I thanked her profusely for her generosity. When he saw this, the Armenian soprano's father thought I was trying to humiliate her, so on opening night he walked irately up to me and spat in my face. Shocked as I was, I found it hard to blame him. In his eyes, I was just another upper-class Iranian trying to exploit the Armenian population. He couldn't appreciate that I wanted to promote his daughter's talents.

Apart from that incident, opening night went pretty well. I was pushed downstage to take a curtain call, which I normally don't do, and the audience showered me with flowers and applause. At that moment, my father realized that his son's chosen profession might not be so bad after all. He may have forgone a medical career in favor of going into this odd trade, but he had clearly made a name for himself. I was dying to know his reaction to all of this, and I couldn't wait to get home to ask him.

"Very interesting," he replied, "very interesting." Then he reflected for a minute and asked, "Do you like the lady who sang Carmen?" I told him that I both liked and respected her. He was clearly troubled, so I asked him what had prompted him to ask, to which he replied, "Well, if you like her so much, why do you make her work so hard? You might have hired her to do some of it, then used somebody else to do the rest. She's been standing in the middle of the stage working all evening. You should have employed somebody to help her out." My father's frame of reference for everything, opera included, was colored by his concept of propriety and good manners. In its way, it was very sweet. I never completely won him over, though. Until his dying day, he honestly believed that my operatic activities were a kind of phase I would get over at some point.

My father lived in Shemiran, at the time a quiet suburb north of Tehran; today it is a district of the sprawling metropolis. His home, built in the typical style of the region, was a square, two-story structure around a central courtyard with gardens and a cooling pool. This edifice housed my father and my grandmother, along with an uncle, aunt, and cousins. On any given day, several other relatives might come to visit. To get from Shemiran to the opera house, I had to take a fiercely congested, six-lane highway. I had lived for several years in Los Angeles, but nothing could have prepared me for this. I never did adjust to the antics of the Tehran drivers on that road, and I kept muttering to myself, "I can't believe this. Oh, my God! No, don't do that!" Midge was so skeptical of my tales of highway horror that I actually filmed a bit of it, capturing, among other things, the sight of cars hurtling down the shoulders of the road, cars making U-turns over the median, and a donkey cart filled with cucumbers lazily competing with the endless stream of motor traffic. In a way, I didn't mind. Between work and family, I had little time to myself, and being in the car, even in this endless traffic jam, was about the only privacy I ever got.

The opera house demanded most of my attention. As a professional, I understood this. My relatives, however, didn't. I was expected to live at home and fall into the rhythm of family life. Lunch was served promptly at noon, dinner at 7:00 P.M., each meal lasting about two hours. Unfortunately, on more than a few occasions, I was unable to make it home on time, rushing in anywhere from one to three hours late to find the entire family sitting around the table, their food untouched, waiting for me. Over and over, I pleaded with them to start without me, but to no avail. Thankfully, my aunt, who oversaw the preparation and serving of the meals, proved to be practical about the whole thing. She learned to get everyone started, then saved a plate for me.

It was all worth it for the opportunity to spend so much time with my father. If I left the house or went to sleep without hugging him, his feelings would be hurt. This was the same man who used to shake hands with me when he brought me to school! I was touched beyond words. Then there was my darling grandmother. Just seeing her every day was a gift. In future years, I would stay in a European hotel just a block

My grandmother,
Saltnat Mansouri.

from the opera house. My father was never happy about my not residing under his roof. He even went to the trouble and expense of having a third story constructed above the family home as an apartment suite for me, but I never got the chance to live in it. My family smothered me with parties. Everyone had to give me a separate one. Moreover, my social schedule was subdivided into get-togethers hosted by my maternal relatives and the ones hosted by my father's family. The two families did not mix, but my father was invited on all these occasions, and he invariably attended.

The first gathering was a special reception he gave for me. "Lotfi," he told me one morning, "you have to give me a day when you can sit."

"Sit? What do you mean 'sit'?"

I found out soon enough: I had to sit in the middle of my father's salon surrounded by flowers and sweetmeats, with my grandmother, my aunt, my father, and my uncle beside me. Then everybody came in, bringing me the most stunning floral arrangements. Marie Antoinette would have blushed at the lavishness. Then some strange lady "of a certain age" would come over, hug me, and sob: "Oh, Lotfi, Lotfi, remember when . . . ?"

I didn't remember any of that stuff. After about fifteen minutes of this, she would move to one of the chairs lining the walls, and somebody else would take her place to continue the interrogation, but I had successfully repressed every memory of my early years. In the course of the coming years, some recollections would surface, but this first visit was a real drill. Every once in a while, I would excuse myself, go to my room, and take out the scotch bottle—it was the only way I could cope with this ritual.

Whether hosted by maternal or paternal relatives, every party was a gargantuan affair often attended by a hundred guests. Apart from that, they couldn't have been more different. My mother's family was completely Westernized. People smoked and drank, and the ladies came dressed in the latest fashions from London, Paris, or Milan. The conversation was loud and boisterous, with endless joking and clowning. My father's family was strictly religious. Conversations were formal and festooned with flowery phrases, and downright solemn. Needless to say, tobacco and alcohol were nowhere to be seen. This called for all my acting skills, my ability to transmute myself chameleon-like from one set of circumstances to another, but the effort to adapt often had me mixing up one relative with another. On one occasion I expressed my condolences to one cousin on the passing of his father, and he replied, "You idiot! You just hugged him!"

But this little slip of the tongue was nothing compared with the blooper I made a few days later in a radio interview that was broadcast live nationwide. By this point, I was feeling more confident about my Farsi and did the interview without an interpreter. Things were going swimmingly, or so I thought, with the interviewer dropping names and asking if I had worked with this one or that one, to which I replied in the affirmative, but I didn't get the syntax quite right.

The host would ask me if I knew, say, Renata Tebaldi, to which I casually responded with the Farsi equivalent of "Oh, yes, I did it with her." Then I'd gild the lily even more with some other names: "Beverly Sills? Did it with her several times." "Renata Scotto? Loved doing it with her." Thank goodness he didn't ask me about any tenors or baritones. Then I looked up and saw the people in the control room cracking up, red-faced and doubled over with laughter. Nobody told me what was so funny.

Shortly after *Carmen* opened, the shah summoned me to an audience. I had first seen him in person when, at the age of ten, I attended his wedding to the Egyptian princess Fawzia Binte Fuad, whose mother I later waited on in the supermarket in Beverly Hills, but that had been

*My "audience" with the shah of Iran, 1974. Man at right
is the prime minister at the time, Amir Abbas Hoveda.*

a long time ago for both of us. Meanwhile, he had already cast off Fawzia
and his second wife, Soraya Esfandiary, and married Farah Diba, with
whom he ultimately went into exile. At this meeting, I tried to converse
with him in Farsi, but noticing my discomfort with my native language,
he switched to English, promptly snarling, "You people who go away are
all the same—you forget your language, your heritage, you forget that
Iran is one of the leading nations in the world." His imprecations had
the same effect on me as water on a duck's back. I wanted to say, "Look,
Shah, I have no allegiance to you or Iran. When I went to the United
States, I cleaned toilets, moved furniture, worked my way from nothing
to make a career in opera. Did you ever have to do that—or anything at
all, for that matter—to get where you are?"

Needless to say, I kept those inquiries to myself. If I hadn't, my hordes
of relatives would be lining up now to water the flowers on my grave.
Then the shah took me totally by surprise by telling me he expected me
to remain in Iran, to settle down and continue my career in Tehran. That
sent cold shivers down my spine. This monarch was not used to being
denied anything, and I remember wanting nothing more fervently than
to get out of this palace and this country.

I didn't have to wait long for this imperial audience to have repercussions. The finance minister's wife began a campaign to have me appointed director of the Tehran Opera House. The culture minister invited me for negotiations and offered me a house, a chauffeured car, an unlimited expense account, a lavish salary, the whole nine yards. While he thought he was offering me the world, I felt that I had been backed up against a wall. I loathed the idea, but I couldn't come up with any effective way to turn it down. It was all straight out of a Kafka story: they could have confiscated my passport or subjected my family to all kinds of repressions. Extricating myself would take every ounce of diplomacy I possessed. Well, I had cut my teeth negotiating with divas; now, I hoped my teeth would be sharp enough. I replied that I was terribly flattered, but unfortunately I had a binding contract in Geneva. I did offer to return on a part-time basis as an artistic adviser, coming back for good when I could see my way clear to do so—to which, of course, there was not a grain of truth. I made a mental note to ask Dr. Graf on my return to advise Tehran that I was tied up in Switzerland indefinitely.

In those days, Tehran was booming, loaded with petrodollars. Foreigners were everywhere, crowding the hotels to such a degree they even found themselves sleeping in the lobby. Prices were skyrocketing, and even though Iran was an agricultural country, the fancy restaurants thought nothing of importing meat from Australia and Argentina, eggs and butter from Europe, flour from the Americas, everything. The shah's delusions of grandeur were boundless. There was nobody to call him to order; he was surrounded on all sides by yes-men, and he considered himself infallible. I was duly warned by the culture minister never to contradict him on any point. "Come to me instead," the minister urged me.

The 2,500th anniversary was intended to be a showcase for the nation, but instead of highlighting the country's accomplishments, it simply highlighted its flagrancy. The shah had built 2,500 schools, one for each year in the history of the monarchy, but overlooked the necessity of staffing them with teachers. Empress Farah Diba established a chain of government-owned shops to sell local handicrafts, but nobody apart from a couple of puzzled tourists set foot in those places. A parade was held in Persepolis with troops of soldiers clad in historical uniforms, and the distinguished guests from all over the world were luxuriously accommodated in specially constructed apartment tents that looked like something out of the *Arabian Nights*, and the caterer for the banquets was no less a culinary all-star than Maxim's of Paris.

Then there were the arts festivals. A film festival was attended by major Hollywood stars such as Raquel Welch, and there was a children's film festival and a modern theater festival, for which Peter Brook had been given an enormous grant to research the "roots of theater" in small villages. Maurice Béjart received $250,000 to create a ballet based on works by some Persian poet, and as if this were not ludicrous enough, somebody came up with the harebrained idea of inviting the ultra-avant-garde composer Karl-Heinz Stockhausen to present a full evening of his works. With all respect, apart from the usual initiates, it is almost impossible to attract even a European audience to a program featuring one of his works, and these people expected an Iranian audience with no background whatsoever in new music to sit through a whole evening of it. When I asked the director of the festival if it might not perhaps be wiser to ease audiences into this kind of thing with a little Mozart or Beethoven on the program, he replied curtly, "Oh, they wouldn't know the difference!"

Not everybody was overjoyed by this extravagant display and the corrupt regime it celebrated. Not only were the dispossessed landowners, including my own father, totally disgusted, a collection of mullahs, whose property had been confiscated as well, were beginning to plot and plan against the regime from communities of exiled Iranians in Europe. One of them—the Ayatollah Khomeini—swore vengeance, but he had not yet appeared on the world's radar screens.

Finally, I managed to negotiate my departure from this forced sojourn in a golden cage. It wasn't easy. Until I was actually out of the country, I dreaded the thought that one of the shah's bureaucrats might suddenly revoke my exit visa, and as I prepared to board the plane, I followed the petroleum minister's advice to keep my Iranian passport in one pocket and my U.S. passport in another. I was escorted to the airport by the same crowd of relatives who had greeted me on my arrival. Fortunately, the shiny new Iranian passport enabled me to breeze onto the aircraft, where I sat trembling throughout the flight until the plane set down in Athens.

Once I was back in Geneva, it took me six weeks to recover.

6

BACK ON TRACK

I returned to Iran once or twice a year for five years as artistic adviser to the company, although I stipulated that I would fly there only on Swissair. One flight on Iranian Airlines in those days, complete with people lounging in the aisles smoking their pipes, was enough. After looking down on the Swiss sense of order, I was beginning to appreciate it more and more with every flight.

Every time I got back to Switzerland, very much the worse for wear, Midge would implore me not to go back, but having established such a solid relationship with my father, I felt I owed it to him to keep the contact alive. In the course of those five years, I directed quite a few new productions in Tehran, including Verdi's *Aida* and *Falstaff*, Offenbach's *Les contes d'Hoffmann*, Bartók's *A Kékszakállú Herceg vára* (*Duke Bluebeard's Castle*), and Ravel's *L'heure espagnole*, all featuring many leading international artists like Giuseppe Taddei, Beverly Sills, and Tito Gobbi.

The theater housed five different companies, ranging from a symphony orchestra to a folk ensemble, and all of them were egregiously mismanaged. In the opera house, I had to vie with a former tenor who had returned to his native land after failing to make a career abroad and, having been appointed operatic administrator with the aid of the finance minister's wife, seemed hell-bent on pulling the theater down to his level of ineptitude, while he took time off whenever he felt like it to run off to Paris and London to buy shirts and underwear. The conductor of the symphony orchestra had a reasonable reputation, having allegedly trained with Herbert von Karajan, but the members of the European cast I had brought in for the Bartók–Ravel double bill thought I was playing a joke on them with this loser and that a real conductor would ultimately show up. When I suggested that he study the score and stop flailing the air like a hopeless parody of his hero, Leonard Bernstein, he took it personally and began spreading all sorts of evil rumors about me.

While I used the unlimited budgets to put handsome productions on the stage, mounting an *Aida* unequaled for elaborate trappings by any theater in the Western world, other members of the staff were busy telling the financial authorities they needed more money for materials I had ordered, then promptly stuffing that largesse in their own pockets. Nepotism had become a driving force at the theater, with everybody's friends and relatives on the take. Fortunately, very few of them ever actually showed up to do anything. The nepotism grew so rampant I began to wonder if there weren't perhaps a couple of overpaid camels on the payroll.

I never knew where I stood with anybody. Any number of barnacles on the hull of the opera company took it amiss when I tried to teach them some discipline and responsibility. They were determined to undermine my position wherever they could. To my face, people would lavish blessings on my head, in an exercise of the ancient Persian practice of *taroaf*, being exaggeratedly courteous, then they would casually plunge a stiletto in my back. I was beginning to feel like an oversized pincushion.

Were my best efforts raising the cultural level of the average Iranian? Hardly. The local citizenry, apart from a couple of conspicuous consumers, never showed up at a performance, so our audiences were populated largely by foreigners, who generally responded with ill-disguised condescension. "Isn't that cute?" they would snigger, "the natives are doing Bartók—how very funny!"

But my being there was totally justified by the restoration of relations with my father, bolstered by the self-knowledge I had acquired both from the intensive therapy I had undergone and from the simple fact of my having grown up. With this newfound knowledge, I began to realize how much my perception of my father had been colored by the way my mother regarded this man she had been forced to marry. Now I no longer saw him through that filter and began to realize what a warm, decent human being he was, how different from the mysterious and magisterial individual I had perceived him to be when I was small. My father hadn't changed—I had.

With his snow-white hair, patrician physiognomy, and walnut skin, my father was the very model of a true patriarch. He did right by his young and difficult wife, he worked hard, he supported a large, extended family, and not only did he never complain, he conducted himself with exquisite manners. Even at his advanced age, he was supporting his brother, sister, and mother and his sister's adopted daughter. At the same time, he walked a political tightrope—something people in the West have a hard time understanding. For example, he put himself at great personal risk to get a relative, who had been accused of denouncing members of the imperial family, out of prison and bring him back to the bosom of our family.

In 1957, while we were still living in Los Angeles, I received the news that my mother had been diagnosed with cancer and she was going to be sent to London for treatment. Sadly, however, she didn't survive to make the trip, dying at the age of only forty-two.

I wanted to discuss my parents' relationship with my father, but I was at a loss for a way to broach the subject. One day, while driving with him, I tried as delicately as possible to say that it couldn't have been easy to live with her, to which he reacted with shock, saying he considered himself lucky to have been married to such a wonderful woman, and he really meant it. Though I no longer regarded him as a statue on a pedestal, he was still a bit larger than life in my eyes. He might have objected to my earlier life choices and tried to guide me down a different path, but only because he felt it would be better for me and the family. Once I had established myself, everything was forgiven and forgotten. Opera might have driven us apart, but now it was bonding us.

But Tehran was going from bad to worse, and I found myself in the middle of a political situation that was slowly but surely coming to a boil. As a native son with a Western lifestyle, I found myself constantly approached by people eager to share their experiences with me, and many of those experiences were harrowing. A lady invited me to lunch and tried to recruit me to the cause of communism. Other critics of the regime tried to enlist my aid, believing I might have influential connections in the West. Then they would discover I had lunched with the finance minister, or they would see me on television with one of the shah's cousins, and promptly denounce me as a turncoat. It was a roller-coaster ride: on one side, I was being courted by the aristocracy and, on the other, approached by suppressed individuals, especially artists and other progressives. Eventually, the culture minister warned me I was spending too much time with "the wrong kind of people." It was clearly an impossible predicament.

As if this weren't rough enough, the pressure for me to resettle in Iran was unrelenting. The culture minister told me how necessary my services were for my homeland, both as an opera director and as a television producer. Everywhere I went, people were constantly telling me how ungrateful I was for not having long since accepted this generous offer. Every time I went back to Geneva, I was a nervous wreck, and it was taking more and more time for me to recover.

Finally, the shah personally summoned me one last time. The culture minister told me to dress appropriately and meet him in his office, and from there I would be driven to our special meeting. As we left the outskirts of the city and wound our way through a wasteland of hills, dirt, and sand, my stomach began forming into a knot. What kind of meeting would take place out in the middle of nowhere? It turned out that the shah was opening a museum underneath the Shahyad, a triumphal arch designed as a stunning fusion of ancient and modern Persian architecture. When I arrived, the cabinet was already lined up to receive the shah: the prime minister, the ministers of finance and petroleum, and the other high officials in serried ranks on the edge of a huge red carpet. Uniformed guards with machine guns could be seen in the distance standing around the perimeter of the monument. It was a surreal sight. I was just an insignificant speck in this vast setting, and it was beginning to look more and more like I was about to be presented with a nonnegotiable demand.

At last, the rattle of the shah's helicopter was heard in the distance, and it swooped in for a landing. The imperial couple moved to a waiting limousine to be driven a few yards to the monument and finally set foot on the red carpet, whereupon all and sundry bowed to the ground, except me. I just couldn't match the low bow the others were making. Well, they'd had years to practice. Apart from the participants in this ceremony, there wasn't a soul around. The silence was deafening. Until that moment, I didn't believe anything like that ever happened in the modern world.

The culture minister escorted me to the empress, beautiful as ever, who smiled charmingly and said, "We know you talented people have many things to do in the world, but we would be so grateful if you could stay here for just a little while." She couldn't have expressed herself more graciously, but the last thing I wanted to hear was imperial flattery. It would have been music to my ears if I were in the West, but here in

Iran it scared the living daylights out of me. For a moment, I hoped against hope that the shah might have forgotten me, but that hope was short-lived.

Somebody ran up to say that the shah was waiting to speak to me. I raced down the line, carelessly allowing one toe to touch that red carpet, an act I later discovered could have had dire consequences, but his imperial majesty had another agenda in store for me. "When are you resettling here permanently, Mansouri?" he wanted to know. I tried to say something noncommittal, but he continued. "You know that opera house you're working in now? It is nothing. We'll have a new theater for you in three or four years. And we're also going to build a new subway. We've studied the Toronto subway system, and ours will be even grander!" He went on to describe his vision of a new Tehran. He was going to build a new opera house, as if I didn't have enough trouble with the present one.

Fortunately, I could always refer to my binding contract in Geneva, and that would get me out for a while until a propitious turn of events liberated me from this obligation for good.

Back in Geneva, things were going better than ever, both on- and off-stage. The positive results of my therapy, fortified by the beautiful new relationship I'd established with my father, had given my regained identity, both as a person and as a professional, greater stability. I was directing at more important companies, many in the United States, including those in Chicago, Dallas, and Houston. Virtually every production I now directed included top-ranking performers and production artists.

As if on cue, our family expanded. All our married years, Midge and I had longed for a child, but to no avail. Just as we were considering adoption, Midge became pregnant. Nine months later, our beautiful daughter, Shireen, arrived in, of all places, Santa Fe, where I was scheduled to direct *Carmen* and *Salome*. She appeared ten days early, though, just as I had gone off to Vancouver for a production of *La fanciulla del West*. The birth of our daughter was one of the greatest moments of my life. I loved every minute of watching Shireen learn to crawl, stand up, walk, and talk. That's why our stay in Geneva became the happiest time in my personal life.

Tragically, the same was not true for Dr. Graf. While in Zurich, the Grafs had lived next door to a German-Swiss divorcée, who befriended Mrs. Graf, a petite and incredibly sweet woman. Because of her husband's professional commitments, Mrs. Graf was alone much of the time, and she must have been pleased to make this new friend. Ms. Divorcée, however, was a calculating woman. After becoming welcome in the Graf home, she turned to Dr. Graf, telling him the sad story of her marriage to a "horrible man who had abandoned her." Dr. Graf couldn't help but offer a sympathetic ear and a shoulder for her to cry on. At the same time, he was undergoing all the *Sturm und Drang* at the Zurich Opera, and he fell into an increasingly weak and vulnerable emotional state. Slowly but surely, Ms. Divorcée worked her wiles on him, finally seducing him. She then casually announced that she was expecting his child and began to pressure Dr. Graf to leave his wife for her. The drama followed him to Geneva. On many an evening, Dr. Graf and I would sit over a glass of wine, and he'd pour out his heart over his guilt and pain. It was an untenable situation, but he desperately wanted to do the right thing. Ultimately, the pregnancy tipped the scales: the new child, he felt, should have a father. Dr. Graf quietly divorced his wife and married Ms. Divorcée. Mrs. Graf had devoted her entire life to her husband, supporting him while he built a career, sharing the ups and downs, and being a mother to their only son. She couldn't continue without him. A few months after the divorce, Mrs. Graf, as lovely a woman as I have ever known, drowned herself in Lake Lugano outside their summer home.

This devastating event brought Dr. Graf and me even closer. By this time, Midge and I had bought our first home, a lovely house in the village of Genolier, between Geneva and Lausanne, with a commanding view of Lake Geneva and the Alps. Dr. Graf decided to buy the house next door. By this time, he had a young daughter named Ann-Kathrin. Now that she had solidified her position, the new Mrs. Graf dropped all pretensions, revealing herself to be scheming and ravenous for money and prestige. We treated her with all due respect, but made sure we kept our distance.

Toward the end of 1970, Dr. Graf was diagnosed with cancer. This was shocking news, but it wasn't immediately clear what impact it would have on his duties, so we continued as if all would be well. Later, his condition was discovered to be terminal, and only then did the governing board of the Grand-Théâtre de Genève move to cancel his contract.

By this point in my career, I had learned a few things about boards: how to play their political games and, more important, how to pay attention to potentially useful information whenever I came across it. I invited the chairman of the board, a prominent lawyer named Jean-Flavin Lalive, to lunch. He was an insufferably arrogant gentleman, who had a notorious reputation as a womanizer, and I had heard some juicy bits of gossip about him.

During the luncheon, I played the role of the concerned friend, saying I had heard that some of his colleagues on the board had considered canceling Dr. Graf's contract. What would happen if the Geneva papers, let alone the international press, were to get wind of that news? What a terrible light it would shed on Geneva and its civic leaders. Questions about those leaders might be asked, and what if, heaven forfend, any . . . sensitive information were to surface? I stared straight into Maître Lalive's eyes. He maintained a poker face and even thanked me for my concern. Still, a formal search for a new theater director had to begin.

Dr. Graf refused to accept his condition. When I visited him in the hospital, he wanted only to talk about future work. He preoccupied himself with his next production at the Verona Arena, and I spent hours at his bedside helping him with costume and prop lists, never alluding to what we both knew: that he was going to have to cancel. At the Grand-Théâtre, the intrigues and political games began, as everyone jockeyed for position in anticipation of Dr. Graf's successor. I tried to protect Dr. Graf from the gossip and rumors. The new Mrs. Graf, however, brought all of it to his hospital room, along with a sheaf of documents for him to sign, eager to make sure everything would be turned over to her when he died. Above all, she wanted to make absolutely certain that Dr. Graf's son, or anyone else who might be able to make a legitimate claim, would be completely cut off.

One day, I arrived as usual during lunchtime to find a great deal of commotion. Dr. Graf was agitated and refusing to stay in his bed. His doctors and nurses were trying to calm him down, but he was using all his strength to fight them off. When they surrounded his bed, he jumped up and stood on it, demanding over and over to be told when he could go home. Finally, they managed to give him an injection to calm him down. I sat by the bed, holding his hand and trying to distract him with funny stories from my morning's *Così fan tutte* rehearsal, a production that featured a number of his favorite artists. He smiled faintly at one of the stories and then slowly drifted off, still holding my hand. I don't know how long I sat there. After a while, a nurse came to check on him. She immediately called for a doctor, who pronounced Dr. Graf dead, with his hand still in mine. My artistic father and mentor—a great man, a giant in his field, a warm and generous human being—was gone.

There was a tawdry epilogue. On the day of the funeral, I served as an escort for the new Mrs. Graf. I rode with her in a limousine. It was an unbearably sad day for me, and I was lost in thought when I felt a hand on mine. I thought Mrs. Graf was comforting me, but I turned to find her eyes filled not with sympathy, but with something quite different: she was actually hitting on me! At least, she was making it easier for me to have nothing further to do with her in the future.

I later learned that her own end had not been a pleasant one. As it happened, a friend of mine became something of a surrogate mother to Ann-Kathrin, and I was able to ask after her over the years. When she became an adult, she tried to establish herself in the theater, as a singer, writer, or director. Like Dr. Graf's son, Werner, she had trouble trying to follow in her father's footsteps. She was rudderless and seemed to need guidance or a helping hand. Dr. Graf had done so much for me that I wanted to do something for her. I made my friend promise that the next time I visited Geneva, she would arrange a meeting between Ann-Kathrin and me. This turned out to be in the early 2000s. I resolved to offer her anything I had: contacts, introductions, advice, financial assistance—anything. When we met, I recited the grand speech that had formed in my head: how much her father had meant to me and how, without him, I never would have had a career. I ended by saying, "My wife and I are here for you. Is there anything we can do?" She looked at me with a dry expression, extended both hands, as if in supplication, and made the one request I couldn't fulfill: "Can you give me talent?" Our meeting ended with me at a loss for words, trying to hold back the tears.

Dr. Graf's successor as director of the Grand-Théâtre de Genève was a Frenchman from Alsace-Lorraine by the name of Jean-Claude Riber. Apparently the board passed over me because I wasn't French enough, or perhaps because I was too close to Dr. Graf. Like most incoming directors, Riber let it be known in no uncertain terms that everything before him had been garbage and that under his direction the Grand-Théâtre would finally assume its place among the greatest opera companies in the world. I could feel the negative vibes the minute we met. I think my closeness to his predecessor made him feel insecure, and it clearly seemed that he was jealous of my experience at so many major opera houses. I was apprised of my demoted status at the Grand-Théâtre in a number of unusual ways. The theater had two elevators, one for the orchestra, chorus, and stage crew, and another for top brass. Anyone wishing to use the latter had to have a key. One of the first orders from Riber's office was for me to hand in my key and use the other elevator. Next, he took away the long-distance telephone in my office, obliging me to go through the switchboard for the countless calls I had to place in the line of work. At least, he let me keep my private toilet. These were minor infractions in my book, though. They didn't bother me much. What I couldn't abide were the major atrocities that were not long in coming.

Thanks to Dr. Graf, the theater had established a fine collaboration with the town of Divonne-les-Bains, just across the French border, which boasted one of the largest casinos in the country. Divonne was a favorite of the super-rich, especially wealthy Arabs, who loved to fly their private jets into nearby Geneva, speed across the border in a limo, and place million-dollar bets on the table—all in the space of minutes. In accordance with French law, the casinos allocated a percentage of their annual profits to cultural activities. The most important of these was the two-week Divonne Festival every summer. Most of the events took place in the ornate two-hundred-seat Théâtre André Dussolier, where international superstars like Christa Ludwig gave intimate recitals. The luxury was mind-boggling. Divonne approached the Centre Lyrique about the possibility of presenting chamber operas during the Festival, and Dr. Graf put me in charge of the project. I organized and directed productions of Haydn's *La cantarina*, Bernstein's *Trouble in Tahiti*, Weill's *Das kleine Mahagonny*, and other works. The budgets I prepared were simplicity itself: after production costs were subtracted, whatever money was left over was divided among all the participants.

Soon after his arrival, Riber got wind of this and took exclusive charge of the budget. Although I still organized and directed the performances, I was to have no knowledge of either expenses or payments. The money was to go to him, and he would make the disbursements. This seemed more than odd to me, as budgeting was a fairly pedestrian task for a chief executive. I never did get an answer to the question of why he was doing it, and when I brought up the subject of the Divonne Festival budget with him, he simply evaded the issue. All the significant productions were taken away from me. Instead, I got dusty revivals of tired chestnuts like a French version of Johann Strauss's *Der Zigeunerbaron*. Meanwhile, Riber gave himself grand new productions of the *Ring* and *Les Troyens*.

With fewer responsibilities, I accepted more guest directing assignments, commuting from Iran all the way to California. I was away from home for eight or nine months of the year. My daughter's childhood was happening in my absence, and there was a strain in my private life. As much as I loved our life in Geneva—our beautiful home in its bucolic setting and the benefits of raising our child in Europe—I realized that the Geneva Opera had become a dead end for me. It was time to move on.

My final production was Franz Lehár's eminently forgettable bit of ham-handed chinoiserie, *The Land of Smiles*, in a French version entitled *Le pays du sourire*. I jokingly referred to it as *Le pays du Mansouri*, and I had every reason to smile as I mounted it. Sixteen years earlier, I had arrived in Europe as an eager but inexperienced director. Now I was a seasoned and well-known professional, with a mile-long list of credits at major opera houses on three continents. In Dr. Graf I had found the mentor of a lifetime. With Dr. Morgenthaler's help, I had come to grips with my true self. I was blessed with a beautiful family. Whatever came next, I was solidly equipped to handle it, and an offer to head a major North American opera company was not long in coming.

By an ironic twist of fate, that offer lifted a sword of Damocles from its perilous position directly over my head. In 1975, the Iranian newspapers picked up an Associated Press dispatch that I had signed a contract to lead the Canadian Opera Company in Toronto. They immediately ran editorials asking why I had accepted an offer from a foreign country when my native land needed me. A short while later, I received a curt note from the culture minister stating that, since my loyalties lay elsewhere, my services would no longer be needed. He was especially incensed by my claim that my contract bound me to Geneva for years to come. Instead of my terminating my relationship with them, they terminated theirs with me. When I put down that letter, I felt as though a ten-ton load had been lifted from my shoulders.

In 1979, the Ayatollah Ruholla Khomeini returned to Iran after fourteen years in exile and removed the shah from power. Under Khomeini's doctrinaire regime, there was no room in the culture for opera or other frivolities of that nature, and so the opera house was converted into a venue for religious plays. I imagine it's probably still rife with intrigue and corruption, and doubtless, to this day, somebody's camel has its name on the payroll.

With my father,
Hassan Mansouri,
and Shireen
at our home in
Switzerland,
1973.

My father visited us in 1975 in Geneva, getting to know his grand-daughter, to whom he was a doting grandparent, and then came to see us again in 1979 in Toronto. That was our final meeting. He died from a heart attack shortly after Khomeini seized power. I was happy that we had been able to reconnect, but sad that he didn't live to see his grand-daughter succeed where I had failed, by becoming a doctor. Happily married, she is now a successful family physician, living and practicing in Canada.

My father's family, although privileged, is not political. Under the rule of the Islamic state, they have chosen to lead quiet lives. Most of my mother's relatives fled to the United States and Europe.

I still see the former finance minister from time to time. His granddaugh-ter is now an aspiring pop singer. Incredibly enough, I still occasion-ally find myself surrounded by intrigue, only now it's being perpetrated not by Iranians but by Iranian Americans in the United States. I am often asked to serve on boards devoted to one cause or another. Early on, I accepted several offers, wanting to make some sort of contribu-tion to my ethnic community, but I quickly resigned when I discovered that what these people really wanted was my presumed Rolodex of rich people, who could be cajoled into making donations, or my contacts at city hall. I recently joined a group that promoted Iranian performing arts. I took part in all kinds of meetings, helping with plans and budgets. Ultimately we met with Mayor Gavin Newsom of San Francisco, allegedly to discuss possible performances. The instant we sat down, the group leader began talking about political issues, making thinly veiled references to the clout of the Iranian American community. The mayor motioned toward the group, myself included, as if to say, "What's all this about?" Being on good terms with Mayor Newsom, I immediately stood up, shook his hand, and said, "Gavin, you don't need me for this," then walked out without a word to the others.

In the years to come, I would manage to expunge Jean-Claude Riber from my memory, but he did make one odd reappearance in my life. Some time in the mid-1980s, I saw him out of the corner of my eye, lingering in the back of the lobby after a performance at the Théâtre du Châtelet in Paris. With no appetite whatsoever for another encounter, I raced for the door, hoping he might pretend that he hadn't seen me, but he stopped me in my tracks and was effusive in congratulating me on my recent appointment as general director of the San Francisco Opera. I put on my Persian cat smile and told him that I owed it all to him: after all, without him, I might still be stuck in Geneva. He took it as a compliment.

7

NORTH OF THE BORDER

In early 1974, I was contacted by Dr. Herman Geiger-Torel, general director of the Canadian Opera Company in Toronto, Ontario. Although I had already directed two productions in Vancouver, in 1967 and 1968, I wasn't quite sure where Toronto was, what people did there, or what it might be good for. It had never shown up on my operatic radar screen. I thought Canada was populated by colorfully uniformed Mounties, intrepid hockey players, and peacekeepers. Somebody told me Canadians kept beavers as house pets, but that was about it.

I was in San Francisco, directing a production, and after a long rehearsal and a pleasant cocktail evening, I didn't get to bed until two or three in the morning. The phone rang around 7:00 A.M. Pacific time. Through my grogginess, I heard someone with a slight German accent introduce himself as Dr. Geiger-Torel. I couldn't quite place him until he said we had met at various operatic events. He paid me a couple of compliments, then he got to the point.

"I have something very confidential to ask you."

He told me he was getting ready to retire in Toronto, and the company was looking for a successor. He felt I would be a suitable candidate. He was very formal, very European, and I was so sleepy I could have agreed to anything just to get back to bed, so I said yes, and later I received formal notice that I had been added to the list.

Hermann Berthold Gustav Geiger was a remarkable gentleman with an amazing background. Like Dr. Graf, he had been raised in an art-loving Jewish home, the son of pianist-composer Rosy Geiger-Kullmann, a pupil of Carl Schuricht. At an early age, despite the usual family objections, he decided he would make music, in one form or another, his life. Being fond of theater as well, he thought perhaps stage direction was his thing. At the age of eighteen, he made the acquaintance of one of the giants of our craft, the Austrian director Lothar Wallerstein, who at the time was codirector of the Frankfurt Opera. Wallerstein brought him as his assistant to the Salzburg Festival, helping put artists like Lotte Lehmann through their paces. When the Nazis took over Germany, he was able to secure an engagement at the Teatro Colón in Buenos Aires, where he worked with the great Erich Kleiber. After a couple of further European engagements in Czechoslovakia and France, where he changed his name to Herman Geiger-Torel, he was able to get out of Europe and resettle in South America, first continuing his work at the Colón, then founding an opera company in Uruguay, eventually moving on as principal stage director in Rio de Janeiro.

He first came to Canada in 1948, where plans were under way to form an opera company in Toronto as an adjunct to the Royal Conservatory. He would have enjoyed sticking around, but commitments in South America drew him back to the continent on the other side of the Equator. He then continued on to New York, where he again worked with Dr. Wallerstein, now both a stage director and drama teacher at the Metropolitan Opera.

In 1949, Felix Brentano, another Austrian émigré based in New York, was directing a production of *Orfeo ed Euridice* in Toronto and needed somebody to stage the dances. He asked Geiger-Torel if he would act as choreographer. Geiger-Torel had never done any dance staging in his life, but he saw no reason why he shouldn't add another arrow to his quiver, and so he tripped the light fantastic back to Canada.

The following year, Felix Brentano had so many commitments in the United States directing opera that he resigned from his Canadian activities, and Geiger-Torel was brought back as stage director.

A festival in 1950 marked the company's coming of age. The opera organization separated from the Conservatory, and nine years later, the Canadian Opera Company appointed Geiger-Torel general director. His company began national tours, traveling some ten thousand miles a year and pioneering operatic productions over the length and breadth of the world's second-largest country. The productions' strength and reputation increased from season to season, while Dr. Geiger-Torel's operating deficits grew along with them. Unlike the few companies in the United States in those days, opera in Canada did receive some government aid, but nothing to match the kind of financing its managers had been used to in their earlier years in Europe.

The consequence was that, after putting the company on its feet, Dr. Geiger-Torel was regrettably beginning to wear out his welcome. His financial shortfalls struck panic in the hearts of his board members, especially Douglas Sloan, the chairman of the Finance and Operating Committee. The board moved to cut productions from an annual total of six to four, all of them bunched up in the scant space of five weeks, from September to early October, which some people felt led to a kind of operatic indigestion.

What I didn't know at the time was that Doug Sloan was also working to get rid of Dr. Geiger-Torel, who by now had run up a current deficit of $60,000 along with an accumulated deficit of $700,000. Though his services in the cause of art were appreciated, the board told him, the director would do the company a big favor if he would quietly step down from his administrative position, for which Sloan was willing to compensate him with an annual pension of $12,000 plus an additional $3,000 fee for directing one production a year. Considering that they had been paying him $33,000 a year, this was a fairly paltry thank you gift, but on January 29, 1975, he agreed to step down in favor of a change of leadership at the Canadian Opera Company. He would leave a significant company to his successor, and the more he told me, the more I began to realize that this could represent an extraordinary opportunity for me.

Dr. Geiger-Torel made it quite clear that he was not personally in a position to offer me the job, especially in view of his less than cordial relations with the aforementioned Mr. Sloan, who had been named president of the Opera Association, but he promised to work behind the scenes to guarantee that I would be given every possible consideration. The rest would be up to me. Midge and I had been looking for some way to reestablish America as our home base, and Toronto was a lot closer to the United States than Geneva was. Soon afterward, I received a formal notification from the search committee. They had begun with more than 120 candidates and had gradually whittled the list down to 9.

For my first interview, I was booked into an $18 room at a rather run-down hotel. I realized the search committee was getting serious when, for the last interview, I was housed in a $250 room at the Four Seasons. Later, the chairman of the committee, Rod Anderson, flew to Houston and San Francisco to watch me work with the companies there. Soon enough, there were only two candidates left: Peter Hemmings, at the time managing the Scottish National Opera, and myself. At that stage, I

L O T F I   M A N S O U R I

was flown back to Toronto, where Dr. Geiger-Torel picked me up personally at the airport. He had an enormous car, but he was a little ungainly behind the wheel. Having recently given up smoking, he constantly munched on candies.

"If Mr. Sloan were to find out you were my candidate, you wouldn't stand a chance of getting the job. He is so against me, he would oppose anyone I favored—just on principle—so if I look at you somewhat negatively at those meetings, please understand why."

President Sloan treated his long-standing general director miserably, which made me very angry. After the last meeting, I had my only private interview with Sloan. Rod Anderson drove Midge and me to Stratford to see *Ariadne* and meet more board members. I had come to the conclusion that Sloan was a bit of a tyrant, and I wondered if I wanted to leave Geneva to work with him. In the back seat of the car, Midge was very eager to find out how everything had gone, and what we were going to do. Trying to be subtle, I turned to her and mouthed the words "I don't want this."

Rod, who could apparently read lips backward in a rear-view mirror, said, "Oh, by the way, I forgot to tell you. Mr. Sloan has only six more months to go as president." Clever man. Later that summer, Rod phoned and asked me to stand by the following evening. The board, he said, would be making its decision, and he wanted me to hear it—yea or nay— directly from him. I deeply respected his integrity in this delicate situation and waited impatiently for his call. He was as good as his word; the following evening, he phoned to tell me the job was mine and that contractual terms and a public announcement would soon follow. Then he phoned Peter Hemmings; he was very upset and warned the committee that I would sink the company. I was offered a salary of $50,000 a year with an additional $5,000 annually for the first five years of the contract. I was amazed and delighted, as was Midge, who had already fallen in love with Toronto because it reminded her of her native Wisconsin.

In August 1976, I came to a company with artistic goals well beyond the limits of its material resources. Many of the fundamentals other companies take for granted were unknown in Toronto. There was no marketing department at all. The fund-raising department was primeval. In my first year, its goal was a paltry $220,000; six years later we raised $1.25 million. When I joined the team, the company enjoyed an endowment of zero; in my first six years, we created our first endowment and filled it with 2 million dollars. In 1958, the federal government had created the Canada Council, modeled after the Arts Council in England, with the objective of subsidizing the arts across the nation. It was a tremendous success, but soon the law of unintended consequences kicked in. Before long, many of the arts organizations were almost wholly dependent on government largesse. They never developed an independent means of fund-raising, nor did they see the need for it. "Ottawa will pick up the check" was the mantra. However, it soon became clear that Ottawa neither could cover all of any organization's expenses, nor would it ever be able to do so. As that became undeniably clear, many organizations found themselves in serious trouble; new ways had to be found to make the arts more self-sustaining.

When I arrived in Toronto, a membership in the Canadian Opera Association cost $10. My proposal that this be raised to a more realistic $100 was castigated as undemocratic. Canada had long been built along European lines with a Scandinavian sense of social equality and an Anglo-Saxon concept of fairness. In this context, resistance to my proposal for a $100 membership fee was not irrational, but it certainly wasn't helpful either.

Like many people in the arts, our board members functioned as a sort of family council, but they genuinely aspired to greatness for their opera company and were prepared to make changes to achieve it. Even so, the board had a lot to learn about how to become a modern and powerful organization. Before I could educate the members, I had to educate myself. I attended several seminars on leadership, fund-raising, and marketing. I went to the strongest people I knew for advice, and I read books and journals. None of these matters were familiar to me with my European background. The result of our efforts in researching the North American artistic and economic model led to a reconstruction of the entire company.

In the same period, I set out on a strategic, cross-country exploration of Canadian musical resources. I wanted to visit the great schools, meet the great teachers, and hear the most promising voices. I wanted to do this personally and give our company a face and a voice to which musicians throughout the world could relate. In time, I wanted to create a meaningful apprentice and training program for the best young Canadian singers and make it the "national" opera. My tour proved immensely valuable, and nine provinces showed a great interest in our ambitions.

We had very little impact, however, in Quebec, although we were able to help such artists as soprano Christiane Riel and baritone Gaetan Laperrière and composers like Richard Désilets and Michel-Georges Brégent. During my thirteen years at the Canadian Opera Company, La Belle Province was undergoing wrenching changes, and we could do little more than watch. In 1976, my first year in Toronto, Quebec had 6.2 million residents, 80 percent of whom were Roman Catholic and 82 percent of whom spoke French. Then as now, Montreal was the second-largest French-speaking city in the world. In many ways, Quebec is a separate nation, built on lost wars, memory, regret, and uniqueness. It never quite fit into the pattern of the rest of the country.

We were luckier elsewhere. In October 1979, with the aid of a considerable grant from a company aptly named Imperial Oil, we were able to announce the creation of Canada's first professional opera ensemble. A year later, we were in business. Establishing an ensemble was one of many changes I wanted to make at the company.

To form a first-class international opera company, drawing from the diversity of the Canadian population to offer authentic productions from a number of operatic cultures, we set out by building a tremendous team in Toronto. The project began with the appointment of John Leberg as our first director of operations. He had studied composition at the University of Toronto and worked in an administrative capacity at Canadian Opera. No one could have been better organized, more efficient, practical, or helpful. A man of unquenchable energy and inspiration, he had an unassailable personal integrity. For many years, John was the company's greatest asset. He was soon joined by others.

On one of my directing jobs in San Francisco, I made the acquaintance of Philip Boswell and ultimately brought him to the company in Toronto as artistic administrator. Philip is one of the most knowledgeable, intelligent, and honorable people I have ever had the privilege of working with. The son of an American diplomat and his French wife, he grew up in Rome, eventually acquiring almost native fluency in some five languages. In the course of our collaboration in Canada, he became like a member of the family for Midge and me. When I moved on to San Francisco, I invited him to join me, but he was committed to his work at the Canadian Opera Company and decided to stay in Canada. He continues to be associated with the company.

I hired Margaret Genovese to create a modern marketing department, and she was brilliant, developing a compelling face and voice for our company. On one occasion, to promote a production of Puccini's *La fanciulla del West*, she collaborated with John Leberg and our PR director to organize a horse-drawn stagecoach parade, based on the Calgary Stampede, down Yonge Street, the Broadway of this northern metropolis. Margaret was full of bold and vivid ideas. Because of her, we became a living presence even in the eyes of those millions who had never attended an opera.

A young American named Dory Vanderhoof, whom I appointed to take on fund-raising as a full-time responsibility, also brought that department into the twentieth century, applying all the best techniques for identifying, soliciting, and rewarding the corporations and foundations that chose to support us. Several years later, he and Margaret left the Canadian Opera Company to form Genovese Vanderhoof Associates in Toronto, one of North America's leading arts and cultural management consulting firms.

Within months, our board began to see the results of our team's efforts. The board was now led by Rod Anderson, and he was a superb president. Walter Stothers, whom I met as a member of the operating and audit committees later became president and was also an excellent asset. Between Rod's endless fount of ideas and Walt's relentlessly tough-minded analyses of budgets and planning, we very quickly assembled a management team as strong as any on the North American continent.

As we were strengthening the organizational capacity of our administration, we set out to improve our presence in the Greater Toronto market. By 1977, after studying our company's limitations, our audience's purchasing patterns, the seasons of related arts organizations, and historically troublesome marketing issues, I decided we had to move the company's season from the autumn-only orientation where it had always been anchored. If we wanted to rise to the level of major companies, we were going to have to operate at least eight months out of the year. We went about this in stages. The first of them was made possible by one of the most unusual men I have ever met.

His name was Edwin Mirvish, but everyone called him "Honest Ed"— without any irony. He was born in 1914 in Virginia and was introduced to show business, as he puts it, when Rabbi Moshe Reuben Yoelson, the father of Al Jolson, performed his bris, or ritual circumcision. In 1923, the family moved to Toronto and ran a small grocery store. After a series of failures, Ed opened a "bargain emporium" in 1948, and it flourished, soon occupying an entire city block and generating millions of dollars a year. It also gave him the means to get involved in show business. In 1960, he bought a derelict theater called the Royal Alexandra on King Street for $250,000. He later built the Prince of Wales Theatre up the road, took over the old Pantages Theatre a few blocks away on Yonge Street, and eventually purchased the Old Vic in London. Ed and his son had this venerable house completely refurbished, and I had the pleasure of being present in the British capital for the grand opening, when Ed escorted the elegantly attired queen mother into the theater.

The Royal Alex, as it was called, seats fifteen hundred, and by virtue of an ice pit underneath the orchestra seats, it ranks as having been North America's first air-conditioned theater. It had been a jewel, with an Italian marble lobby, Venetian mosaic floors, elaborately carved walnut and cherry wood stairs and railings, silk wallpaper, and an enormous mural entitled *Venus and Attendants Discover the Sleeping Adonis*. Ed spent a small fortune bringing it back to life, operating it as a venue for touring companies, and selling a whole season of plays and musicals. It was a very smart business model. By the time we were introduced, he wanted to expand his theater's subscription base and made us an offer nobody could possibly have refused.

At the same time our planning staff and I were starting to create a spring season, Ed Mirvish came along. He had a theater, a plan, and a cash offer. He wanted the Canadian Opera Company to join him at the Royal Alex. He offered us his subscription list for four weeks at the theater, in effect providing an audience for anything we produced. He also guaranteed an income of $100,000 a week for four weeks. In addition, he supplied the theater for free, including the services of his box office, front of house operations, and marketing machinery—all at no charge. We became part of his season, and he enabled us to create a new season of our own. It was the perfect *quid pro quo*. He needed a product for his theater, and we needed a theater for our product.

This wasn't all philanthropy, of course. Ed Mirvish was an enormously creative businessman, and he was not exactly losing money on this arrangement. He kept his subscription series ticket prices low but provided an internal subsidy by opening up several restaurants in the immediate vicinity of the Royal Alex, and just as he had predicted, the restaurants were packed with theatergoers.

We planned three productions for 1978—*Il barbiere di Siviglia*, *Le nozze di Figaro*, and *La traviata*—all with wonderful young Canadian artists. The productions were site specific for the Royal Alex, a house with almost no backstage and a very small orchestra pit. The emphasis throughout was on the young artists. Curiously, the predecessor of the Canadian Opera Company, back in the days when it was an outgrowth of the Royal Conservatory, had also given its first performance at this theater almost thirty years before. In fact, the company had performed at the Royal Alex until its move to the O'Keefe Centre for the Performing Arts on Front Street in 1961.

The public and critical response could not have been better. Although one or two regular patrons of more popular forms of entertainment at this venue walked out of our opera performances, there was also a good deal of crossover from that same subscriber base to our regular audience, which in the long run balanced out in favor of our company. Almost every production at the Royal Alex was a success, and we enjoyed an average 90 percent attendance at every show. It was a family enterprise. Ed's wife, Anne, even helped with the makeup and appeared as a supernumerary in our *Carmen* production.

Ed Mirvish provided tremendous financial security, a terrific house, and comfort to our board. Thanks to him, we were not going naked into the night. Years later, in 1986, Ed and his son David paid the company a $650,000 fee to stage the musical *Kismet* by Forrest and Wright, with a lot of help from Alexander Borodin. It was a huge hit.

In our second year at the Royal Alex, we did two operas, *Carmen* and *Cenerentola*, but without the $100,000 weekly guarantee. The rest of Ed's offer remained intact and made our success financially feasible. We gave sixteen performances of each opera, and both of them had three casts.

Our agreement with Ed lasted only two years, but its spirit has endured for thirty. Thanks to him, we expanded our repertoire base to eight productions a season, gave the company a year-round identity, and were able to showcase the finest young Canadian talent we could assemble.

The following year, we made a deal with the National Ballet to use the O'Keefe Centre while the ballet was out on tour. Within three years, we were able to do four operas in the autumn and another four in the spring as well as the tour in the autumn. We built an audience and a proper season. This task took me three years in Toronto—and thirteen in San Francisco.

We also decided to enter the world of opera on film and television. During my Toronto years, we shot our first commercial film releases and did our first telecasts. These were an essential element of our plan to raise the company's profile but, much more important, to bring opera to people across the country. All of our films and telecasts were produced by Norman Campbell. In 1978, our first film, Tchaikovsky's *Orleanskaya dyeva (Joan of Arc)*, starring Lyn Vernon, Carol Wyatt, Pierre Duval, and Bernard Turgeon, was presented at the National Arts Centre in Ottawa. This was followed by *Norma* in 1981 with Joan Sutherland and Tatiana Troyanos, *Anna Bolena* in 1984 with Sutherland and Judith Forst, *The Rake's Progress* in 1986 with Costanzo Cuccaro and John Stewart, designed by David Hockney, and *Les dialogues des Carmélites* in 1986 with Carol Vaness, Irena Welhasch, Janet Stubbs, and Maureen Forrester.

I was determined to extend the presence of the Canadian Opera Company into the life of every part of Toronto. We would have no future if we were to continue to rely on a diminishing demographic. In Toronto, a unique experiment in multiculturalism was under way, and we decided to join it and bring opera under its umbrella.

In the United States, we talk about a melting pot. The Canadians refer to the same phenomenon more appropriately as a mosaic. The "Metro International Caravan" was a summer festival organized by and for Toronto's numerous dynamic ethnic communities. Every community offered a wide-ranging program with restaurants, entertainment, dancing, and shopping. For ten days in June, people bought a "passport" allowing them access to all fifty pavilions throughout the city. It was wonderful. Our team decided to become a part of the Metro Caravan. In 1978, we took over the Ontario College of Art. Dean Paul Fleck made it possible. We called ourselves the Toronto Pavilion and declared the world of opera our ethnicity. People entered rooms that demonstrated the development of opera from the Camerata of Florence to the present day, with pictures, costumes, programs, and a sound track. We told the whole story of the craft. The menu in our restaurant featured specialties like "Zucchini Puccini," "Maestro's Meat Pie," and "Isolde's Potion," all with operatic seasoning. Then in the auditorium we presented capsule versions of famous works such as *Il barbiere di Siviglia*. Finally, our audience entered the Falstaff Beer Garden, where anyone could give a dollar to a waiter or waitress and he or she would sing. Of course, they were all our kids.

We also managed to offer a Canadian premiere at the Metro Caravan: Douglas Moore's charming parody of daytime television drama, *Gallantry*, first presented in New York in March of 1958. A "soap opera" in the most literal sense, this little gem was better received than anything else we did. The budget was actually rather small because we relied so heavily on volunteers. Everybody loved the idea. I was determined to eliminate the phony elitist mystique of opera. It had started as a people's art form, and we took it back to its roots. After two years of this, we shifted to the Harbourfront Festival. That was where the world first heard Ben Heppner and many other wonderful singers. By doing all of this, and much more, we developed audiences, made friends, raised our profile, and had people talking about opera in Toronto. Our participation in this Festival made a meaningful contribution to our success, and our board members loved it. They enjoyed having their friends tell them how popular opera was becoming in Toronto—so did I.

We also wanted to inaugurate new programs for the development of young artists in Canada. With the founding of the Canadian Opera Company Ensemble in 1979, we envisioned offering first-rate training and real-time experience. Our goal was to keep the best young singers in Canada so that they would not find themselves forced to relocate to Europe in quest of careers. On our national tours, we had found—repeatedly— that the finest rising singers uniformly believed their own country offered them nothing beyond college and conservatory. I had worked with several young-artist programs in the United States and Europe, including workshops at the San Francisco Opera and the Santa Fe Opera, along with my collaborations with Dr. Graf in Zurich and Geneva, and, of course, I myself had benefited from my work at UCLA, Santa Barbara, Bayreuth, and Berlin. It was time for Canada to launch a similar system.

We offered two-year contracts (later extended to three) and an annual salary of $15,000 to eight singers, plus extra fees for major roles, and allowed them to devote their full time to learning and building their careers. The only analogous programs in those days were in San Francisco and at the Metropolitan. This was the kind of training no classroom situation could ever offer, providing financial security, collegiality, a unique opportunity to watch world-class artists up close, and a chance to work with a full complement of professional staff members: music and drama coaches, advisers in stage movement and dance, fencing trainers, and specialists in various languages, diction, and vocal technique.

I appointed Stuart Hamilton the first music director of the Canadian Opera Company Ensemble. He proved an excellent choice and gave leadership and identity to a vital part of the company. Stuart had studied piano with Alberto Guererro, Glenn Gould's teacher, and had made his recital debut at New York's Town Hall in 1967. With a natural facility for languages and diction, he ultimately migrated to coaching. In the course of his long, distinguished career, which continues to this day, his students have included Maureen Forrester, Ben Heppner, Rosemary Landry, Richard Margison, Lois Marshall, and Isabel Bayrakdarian. At the time he came to my attention, he was already one of Canada's most accomplished coaches, and he led our Ensemble for the crucial first three seasons. Four years later, he was awarded the Order of Canada, the nation's highest civilian recognition. His successor at the Ensemble was Stephen Lord.

After creating the Ensemble, I continued my annual cross-country audition tours, where one fact stood out. Many talented singers demonstrated significant potential but little technique. In 1983, we added a preliminary class for those who were not ready to enter the Ensemble but were clearly destined to get there in due course. This pre-training paid rich dividends, especially in a nation as large and disparate as Canada. We called these singers our apprentices, which brought the total number of Ensemble artists to twenty-one by 1987.

Just one of our discoveries was the great tenor Ben Heppner. Born in 1956 in Murrayville, British Columbia, Ben sang in choruses and church choirs before beginning his formal studies at the University of British Columbia. He won the CBC Talent Festival at the age of twenty-three and sang in the Ensemble from 1980 to 1984. I believe his first professional role was with us, when I cast him as Kunz Vogelgesang in Wagner's *Meistersinger*. Today he travels the world, makes definitive recordings for major labels, and earns standing ovations and rave reviews wherever he appears. The opera world rightfully regards him as one of the great dramatic tenors of his generation. I remember him as a strapping young man eager to learn, determined to succeed and driven by a rare devotion to family, friends, and home. The Canadian Opera Company made some of Ben's early success possible, and his outstanding talent did the rest.

The Canadian Opera Company Ensemble was more than self-serving. From the beginning, its members also served as operatic ambassadors to the community at large. They took productions on tour in Ontario and about the city. They took part in numerous outreach and educational programs, and thousands of schoolchildren first met Mimì and Rodolfo, Pinkerton and Cio-Cio San thanks to the Ensemble. They appeared as part of the Metro International Caravan and in a tent at Harbourfront, and they presented *Das kleine Mahagonny* by Bertolt Brecht and Kurt Weill as part of a larger citywide Brecht Festival. Beyond any conceivable call of duty, they actually sold bricks for the subsequent development of the Tanenbaum Centre, the evolution of which is a remarkable story of the interaction between an arts organization, a helpful government, and some remarkable philanthropists, one of whom put us on the map.

When I came to Toronto, our offices were diminutive warrens that would have put rabbits to shame. They were located over a steakhouse on Front Street, which was sometimes so noisy I had to send my assistant to ask that the loudspeakers be turned down. And these cramped quarters cost us a fortune in rent. Our set and costume workshops were all over town. The company rehearsed in the time-dishonored way so many amateur organizations are forced to do: in churches, community centers, schools, and various basements. All these circumstances made it hard for the Canadian Opera Company to be taken seriously by the general public. Shortly thereafter, we moved to Harbourfront, which wasn't much better, although the rent was only one dollar, because the group wanted to attract arts organizations. Then Harbourfront became a for-profit organization, which jerked us right back to square one, looking for overpriced quarters. We needed everything—offices, studios, a small theater, workshops, archives, rehearsal rooms, set and costume workshops—all under a single roof.

Then one day, we found that roof.

There was another building on Front Street in downtown Toronto, a former gasworks that had become a fruit cannery. It dated back to the nineteenth century, and having been closed down for years, it was in fairly disastrous shape and shrouded in some fairly acrid odors. But I realized the facility could be ours if we were to organize our resources correctly and marshal new ones. Our planning committee was essential for that process, and so was Joey Tanenbaum.

Ann Moore, our most seasoned fund-raiser, told me about Mr. Tanenbaum, a wealthy patron of the arts and a tremendously successful builder. She suggested we meet for luncheon and set up a date. I had heard that he had never once attended an opera performance. His grandfather was an immigrant from Eastern Europe, who arrived in Canada with some needles and threads. He later got into surplus lands and goods, and his grandson Joey built much of Toronto. There was no time for opera.

Mr. Tanenbaum arrived at the Italian restaurant we had chosen. I had prepared an elaborate scenario for him. When he walked in, smiling pleasantly, I started to launch into my presentation, but he interrupted me, saying, "Look, Lotfi, all I can give you is a million dollars."

My jaw dropped. I had been banking on a hundred thousand at the most. I said, "But Mr. Tanenbaum, I haven't even done my act for you— I'm still putting on my tap shoes!"

I then took him to his first opera, a semi-staged performance of Richard Strauss's *Capriccio* at the brand-new Roy Thomson Symphony Hall. We had produced it as our contribution to the opening-week gala there. What an introduction—a rather long-winded, idea-driven conversation piece, albeit with a masterfully crafted musical score. He came with his wife, Toby, and that marked the outset of our relationship. He wound up on our board, as well as the board of the Ballet/Opera House Corporation.

Joey's philanthropy comes from the heart, and from his love for Canada. His generosity isn't pretentious—he profoundly believes in it. His greatest interest has always been the visual arts. Over the course of thirty-five years, he and Toby have donated $90 million to the Art Gallery of Ontario and made equally generous gifts to the Royal Ontario Museum and the Art Gallery of Hamilton at the western end of Lake Ontario. When I left for San Francisco, Toby, knowing my fondness for caviar, made a caviar pie for me as a going-away present. Just looking at it could clog your arteries, but I ate it, and many more pies thereafter.

After a two-year planning and development phase, in which I must have spoken with hundreds of supporters across the city and province, we purchased the first Front Street structures in 1985 and embarked on a comprehensive program of gutting, restoration, renovation, and reconfiguration. The building complex was renovated at a cost of $10 million by Bregman + Hamann Architects and Arcop Associates, an architectural cooperative that has done yeoman service in the field of architectural design and renovation. They did a brilliant job.

Major funding was provided by the federal and provincial levels of government. Federal cabinet minister Paul Hellyer was a great help, as was entrepreneur Hal Jackman, but the seeds were planted by Toby and

Joey. In addition to their investment toward the restoration of the buildings, the mosaic in the box office lobby honoring Joey's mother, and the new Max Tanenbaum Courtyard Gardens in memory of his father, were also gifts for the people and opera of Toronto.

Phase I of the renovation of what we were now calling the Tanenbaum Opera Centre was devoted to converting the old gas purifying house. It was completed in November 1985. It now houses the 450-seat Imperial Oil Opera Theatre and rehearsal, coaching, workshop, and reception facilities. Phase II, renovating an old woolen mill, gave us administrative offices, a box office, a wig and makeup department, a music library, an archive, and props and costume workshops. The ribbon was cut on December 2, 1987. During this period, we also purchased a former watermelon storage building on Melita Street for $600,000 and converted it to a set construction shop for another $100,000. By the usual standard in the arts world, that was an incredibly short period and the envy of opera companies everywhere.

As we continued to elevate the Canadian Opera Company to world standards and recognition, we now had our own offices and workshops, as well as rehearsal spaces for our singers, the orchestra, and the Opera Ensemble. Then as now, it was the finest opera administrative and rehearsal space in Canada and as fine as anything in the United States. But the Canadian Opera Company's contribution to the advancement of opera as a cultural force was only beginning.

8

THE ROAD BACK TO TINSEL TOWN

In so many ways, my life was like a four-ring circus, with the main three rings anchored in my various home theaters: they involved planning and logistics, artistic administration, and staging my own productions. In the fourth ring were my far-flung assignments, directing opera as a freelancer in other places. In 1981, a fifth ring was added when my agent at Columbia Artists received a lucrative offer for me to come back to Hollywood as operatic adviser to a film production.

It had all begun with a producer by the name of Alain Bernheim, who, like millions of other opera enthusiasts, had understandably fallen head over heels in love with the exceptional artistry of Luciano Pavarotti. He was determined to make the great tenor the star of a motion picture, despite the fact that the recycling bins of Hollywood are littered with films featuring opera singers, almost all of which barely raised a ripple of response from the filmgoing public. But all that was no impediment to Pavarotti. Anything that flattered his vanity appealed to him, and so he plunged headlong into this project, regardless of the fact that he had no training and precious little skill in acting. What did that matter, he thought, when you had one of the most beautiful voices of all time, which he certainly did, as well as an instantly recognizable profile? How could a film built around him possibly fail?

Read on.

The project did have a lot going for it. If there was one studio that specialized in putting successful musicals on the screen it was MGM, and that was where we would be shooting. In addition, the director, Franklin J. Schaffner, was one of the top-ranking professionals in the field. He had a sterling career, he was a charming gentleman, and I enjoyed working with him very much.

My involvement in the project, which was later released under the title *Yes, Giorgio*, began when somebody saw a documentary on our production of *La Gioconda* at San Francisco Opera and sent out feelers to see if I might be interested in playing the part of the opera director in the movie. This person had seen how I interacted with Pavarotti, Renata Scotto, and the rest of the cast and thought I could manage effectively as the stage director on an opera set built on a motion picture sound stage. The only problem was that the job would require me to be in Los Angeles for three months, and the time was simply not available: I would be away from Toronto rehearsing a production in San Francisco right in the middle of the shooting, and I would need what little time off I might have to concern myself with my Canadian duties. Franklin then offered me a job as "opera consultant" for the filming of the *Turandot* sequence, saying that he had no experience staging opera, although one would have thought that his famous cult film, *Planet of the Apes*, would have familiarized him with operatic monkeyshines. In any event, he really wanted me to come along, and when we sorted out our scheduling issues, I agreed to the deal.

The problems with the film began with the story, which gave new meaning to the word "trivia." It concerned a renowned opera singer by the name of Giorgio Fini who loses his voice during an American tour. He goes to see Dr. Faye Kennedy, a throat specialist, and promptly falls passionately in love with her across the laryngoscope. Joy abounds, as do a lot of songs, and that was about it.

Franklin's problems continued with casting. Just about everybody he wanted turned him down. The handwriting was on the wall for all to see, but I must have been looking in the other direction. The role of the ENT specialist was offered to Meryl Streep, Jill Clayburgh, and Jacqueline Bisset, all of whom took one look at the screenplay and consigned it to the nearest dumpster. Then it was offered to Kate Jackson, previously one of Charley's Angels, and she actually accepted the part, but when it came to the scene where she was supposed to kiss Pavarotti, she pulled out a copy of her contract stating clearly that she would not be required to advance to that level of intimacy, whereupon they parted company. The part finally went to a petite, attractive B-picture actress named Katherine Harrold. Standing beside Luciano, she looked like a Lilliputian from *Gulliver's Travels*.

Rushing in where angels fear to tread, Franklin offered the part of the prima donna to Joan Sutherland. She read the screenplay until she got to a food fight, then promptly went back to her knitting. It finally went to a fine soprano named Leona Mitchell, who sang the role of Turandot on the screen and dubbed it on the sound track—then dubbed in the part of Liù as well. It was absurd on the face of it, but when I called attention to this, I was told that Hollywood had its own laws. The technicians just made Liù sound lighter by fiddling with some knobs on the recording equipment.

The screen credits list a Madelyn Renée as "dialogue coach." Heaven knows, Luciano could have used that kind of assistance, but Madelyn was hardly able to supply it. At the time, she was serving as his secretary, an attractive young woman with vocal aspirations who was a regular member of Mr. Pavarotti's traveling circus. I explained to Luciano that he was in Hollywood, a city with the finest dialogue coaches in the world, but he wouldn't listen. He wanted things to happen his way, and common sense was no argument.

Then things got even worse. Schaffner also had problems with one of his executive producers, Herbert H. Breslin, who just happened to be Luciano's personal manager. Breslin had basically come along for the usual ride, but he decided to add the role of producer to his résumé. For Mr. Breslin, motion picture production was a book with seven seals and a large contingent of walruses. He didn't know his elbow from a sprocket hole, but he did know a lot about Luciano. As the tenor's antics began taking on even more unlikely proportions, Breslin could be counted on to feed all of that foolishness, much to the glee of his client. Having dealt with other nut jobs in his distinguished Hollywood career, Franklin Schaffner knew something would have to be done with Breslin, and it was. The other producers got together and hired a secretary whose sole duty was to deal with the errant manager. Whenever he showed up in Hollywood, especially when "Giorgio" was shooting, the secretary's job was to get him out of there—anywhere else would do—on one pretext or another. I witnessed this happening several times and developed an enormous admiration for this lady's resourcefulness.

There were other personnel problems. The role of the conductor was offered to Kurt Herbert Adler, general director of the San Francisco Opera and my boss when I guest-directed there. It would have been a done deal had Mr. Adler not been Mr. Adler. He made a series of demands for money, a chauffeured car, and all the other goodies he felt came with a Hollywood role. They turned him down, apart from a brief appearance in a cameo part, and the role went to Emerson Buckley. A highly competent conductor with a vast repertoire, Maestro Buckley was a jovial New Yorker who often toured with Pavarotti, but he had a vocabulary that made even Sam Krachmalnik look a bit like a Trappist by comparison. Fortunately, his participation was limited, but I paid a high price for the presence of Emerson Buckley, which in all fairness was not Buckley's fault.

Mr. Adler was upset about losing the role, which led to his making my life difficult while I was trying to commute between the four-week filming in Los Angeles and my directing duties in San Francisco.

My assignment was to stage the *Turandot* sequence, the opening chorus scene, the riddle scene, and the beginning of Act II, including the famous tenor aria, "Nessun dorma." I prepared about fifteen minutes of action, just as I had done for a stage production many times. I provided the palette, and Franklin chose the camera angles. A fabulous set was built on MGM's biggest sound stage in Culver City, where all the great musicals had been filmed. The set alone—complete with a duplicate of the Metropolitan's pit—cost more than a million dollars. As the *pièce de résistance* it included a giant dragon's head, which appeared to be regurgitating an enormous red carpet. I told Franklin this was so outrageous that the audience would probably be waiting for Harpo to show up with one of his ooga-ooga bulb horns.

It didn't take long for Franklin to become tremendously frustrated with Luciano. Franklin was totally disciplined, and Luciano, away from an operatic scenario, had all the self-control of a raging musk ox. Conflict was inevitable. Finally Franklin started saying to me, "Tell your fat friend . . ." and so on. I had to remind the director that he was the one who had hired Luciano in the first place and that I had to keep working with him in the "real" world of opera. Pavarotti was never a problem with me. In fact, I had a calming influence on him because I was a member in good standing of the world he knew, which was why Franklin kept asking me to intervene. I guess I provided a familiar comfort, which put him at ease. Even so, his performance was sadly farcical.

One example speaks for many. A big selling point of the film was to be "Nessun dorma," the aria that had justifiably become Pavarotti's personal calling card. On his original recording, Luciano held the high note in the final word "vinceró" for four seconds, which is quite long enough.

Yes, Giorgio,
*1981, with Luciano
Pavarotti and
Franklin J.
Schaffner.*

In the film, it became *ten* seconds, which went way beyond the bounds of likelihood, apart from being hopelessly unmusical. I complained to Franklin that nobody would believe he could do this, and he consolingly told me, "Oh, come on, Lotfi, this is Hollywood. People will be so busy looking at the credits, they won't even notice." Unfortunately, they did notice everything, and nobody noticed better than Janet Maslin, the star film reviewer of the *New York Times.* She began her write-up with an outline of the "plot":

> Giorgio sings at a friend's wedding and is then given a rousing send-off by the townsfolk, who gather adoringly around his Rolls-Royce. From there, he is off to America, where a concert tour is scheduled. En route to the airport, he stops to help some nuns who have a flat tire. He doesn't change the tire, but he offers a little serenade.

After Giorgio loses his voice, he meets the throat doctor, who

> gives him a shot in the derrière. Giorgio screams, regains his voice and decides to pursue her. "Pamela," he tells her, "you are a thirsty plant. Fini can water you." Who could resist such an offer?
>
> Mr. Pavarotti marches happily through "Yes, Giorgio" with an air of utter confidence. The story seems to strike him as a perfectly plausible one, and to some slight extent his opinion rubs off on the other players. . . . "Giorgio" is rated PG. Its sexual innuendoes will not disturb children, although adults may find them alarming.*

*Copyright The New York Times, September 24, 1982.

I was paid $10,000 for four weeks' work and given superb hotel accommodations. What's to complain? We did the Canadian opening in Toronto as a benefit for the Canadian Opera Company. Franklin and his wife attended and were extremely gracious, elegant, and helpful. I loved my experience with this film, even though it turned out to be such a dud. Working on that famous MGM stage was like a dream come true for a movie buff like myself. After it was all over, I was offered the actual set, if I would tow it to Toronto. But that was more than we could begin to afford, and I had to decline.

The reviews ranged from scornful to unabashedly incredulous, but the Canadian Opera crowd loved it because they were able to chuckle their way through the screening. They would have cringed if they had known this flop had cost $19 million to make and grossed a scant $1million in the United States.

I paid a professional price for working on this movie. Whereas some people asked, "How did he ever land this plum job?" colleagues took umbrage at my having been involved in such cinematic dross. In some ways, my choice may have been a poor one, but it did impress my board in Toronto; it impressed Mr. Adler and many others. But Hollywood has always wielded a two-edged sword. My willingness to take the job reinforced my reputation for range and flexibility, while also reinforcing my reputation as a lightweight. I have had to fight the latter all my life.

The next film I worked on at least had the merit of success. In my tenth year at Toronto, Hollywood came calling again. Canadian director Norman Jewison was making a new film, originally called *The Bride and the Wolf* and slated to star Sally Field. Today, we know it as *Moonstruck*, starring Cher. Many things changed in the development of this property, but one factor remained constant: the big set piece was fixed in an opera house, and Norman wanted it authentic.

He had originally planned to film the scene at the new Met in Lincoln Center, but the Met wanted a million dollars for the privilege. That was prohibitive, so Norman decided to film the scene instead in a rather small theater in a Toronto suburb. He asked me to stage the opera sequences, which would be taken from Puccini's *La Bohème*. He also told me what he wanted, which was a re-creation of the third act as he had seen it in Franco Zeffirelli's famous production. After he gave me his general ideas, he let me realize them on my own. He was particularly eager to reproduce the eloquent hand gesture Zeffirelli had devised for Teresa Stratas at the end of Mimì's aria "Addio senza rancor." I didn't storyboard it, but once we had finished preparations, we did a walk-through for Norman with the sound track. He was satisfied and then filmed it from various angles. It went very well. His designer, Philip Rosenberg, made a small stage look very big.

Norman had managed to acquire the rights to the recording with Renata Tebaldi and Carlo Bergonzi but asked me to find good-looking singers who would lip-synch to the sound track for the filmed sequences. I showed him some photos of young singers in our Ensemble program at the Canadian Opera. He especially liked the baritone John Fanning, whom he chose as the tenor Rodolfo, allowing soprano Martha Collins to remain in her own voice category as Mimì. It was an odd vocal choice, but it made visual sense.

The grandfather was played by Feodor Chaliapin, Jr., the son of the great Russian basso. He was eighty-seven at the time, and rather poignantly, two people are listed in the film credits as his "assistants," one each in New York and Toronto. In actual fact, they were his caregivers.

Thanks to Norman, we did the Canadian premiere as a joint benefit for the Canadian Opera Company and his film institute in Toronto. He and his wife were absolutely charming, and he was a professional through and through. He is very musical and extremely sophisticated. Although Norman was fined by the Screen Actors Guild for not allowing his actors to take lunch until they had perfected the moods of their characters before filming the big scene in the kitchen, it got him the scene that he wanted, and the film as a whole was very well received. It grossed more than $80 million in the United States and Canada alone, and it was nominated for best picture and best director. Cher won an Academy Award as best actress, Olympia Dukakis received an Oscar as best supporting actress, and John Patrick Shanley got his Oscar for best screenplay. Receiving a credit in a major motion picture also lent a certain glamour to the Canadian Opera Company. It was fun for me to do, but I got the biggest kick out of impressing the board. They were starstruck by *Moonstruck*, and it sustained us in our mission to turn the Canadian Opera Company into an exciting place to work, to see, and to be seen.

9

FROM PROVINCIAL TO
WORLD CLASS

The Canadian Opera Company's orchestra began as a student ensemble. As the company became more proficient, professional musicians were also hired. In 1968, the board signed an agreement with the distinguished Toronto Symphony Orchestra, and that ensemble played in our pit for the next eight years.

The orchestra's executive director was a man named Walter Homburger. He was meticulous, an elegant dresser, and a very smooth operator. In the course of his career, he had managed Donald Bell, Victor Braun, and Glenn Gould. From 1951 to 1955 he managed the National Ballet, and he had also brought a huge number of world-class artists to Toronto, ranging from Lotte Lehmann, Kathleen Ferrier, David Oistrakh, and Victoria de los Angeles to Duke Ellington and Victor Borge. Walter took over the Toronto Symphony in 1962 and ran it brilliantly. He was a fabulous negotiator and presented a great challenge to me. People like that always do.

When I arrived on the scene, I was not particularly impressed by the sound of the orchestra. Andrew Davis had just taken over from the Czech maestro Karel Ančerl, whose long bout with diabetes had unfortunately led to a certain drop in the orchestra's discipline and standards.

I discovered that the procedure was to have an annual meeting with the bigwigs of both the Canadian Opera Company and the Toronto Symphony in a lawyer's office to renew contracts and establish schedules. I went into my first meeting trying to be diplomatic and explaining to the others that Canadian Opera needed more time with its orchestra. We were getting ready to mount a production of *Wozzeck*, which would require a large number of rehearsals. Mr. Homburger countered that the orchestra wanted to give us *less* time, and made some highly condescending remarks about opera in general, and the Canadian Opera Company in particular.

"At the end of each season," he said disparagingly, "we have to take at least a week or two for the musicians to correct their mistakes and bad habits." In all fairness, it must be admitted that the Canadian Opera Company at that time had some fairly routine conductors. This fact, combined with the problems engendered by Maestro Ančerl's health, had led to a situation in which the orchestra had become rather unimpressive. A more serious problem for our future was Mr. Homburger's contention that the orchestra's work with us was somehow "incompatible" with its concert function. I replied by saying, "Excuse me. You are from Europe. Would you make that statement about the Vienna Philharmonic? All of its members come from the Vienna State Opera pit, and many of them continue to do double duty in both orchestras, one evening in the opera house, the next on the concert stage. Are your musicians too weak to handle that challenge?"

The members of both boards watched us joust. They had never witnessed anything like this, and it soon became clear that neither Walter nor I was about to back down. I must admit, we were both enjoying the show we were putting on for our respective board members. Later on, we became good friends and shared a lot of mutual respect.

After this highly unproductive meeting, I asked John Leberg to undertake a study of our current orchestra costs and our options. John told me that our annual Toronto Symphony bill came to just a little more than a million dollars. Worse than that, we were contractually obligated to employ all one hundred or so members of the orchestra, even when we were doing Mozart. As if this weren't bad enough, the pit at the O'Keefe Centre could seat only sixty-five players. That meant that every time we gave a performance, we were paying at least thirty-five musicians to stay at home. The arrangement was completely untenable and more than a little ridiculous. I asked John to draw up a budget for the option of contracting our own orchestra. He is a wizard with numbers and came back with a figure closer to $500,000. The Toronto Symphony, it appeared, was charging us for a great deal of its overhead. I took the problem to our board, we terminated our agreement with the orchestra, and that was how we started the Canadian Opera Company Orchestra. We made up a diplomatic story for the media.

Although many major opera house orchestras also do a symphony season, there are some differences to be considered in the mind-set of the musicians. In the opera house, rehearsal periods and performance times are generally longer than in the concert hall, and the orchestra creates a different universe of sound, largely attuned to accompanying the human voice and breathing along with the singers.

I hired an Egyptian-born Canadian conductor named Raffi Armenian to recruit the new ensemble. He did a first-class job, and I rewarded him in part by assigning him the much-anticipated *Wozzeck* production. We were able to select specialists in operatic accompaniment, and our tactic paid off. However, we were never able to attract a major international music director. I tried almost every conductor of any stature, but no one would come—even as a guest. I kept hearing that the problems at the O'Keefe Centre were frightening some away, and our relatively low profile deterred the rest. As far as I was concerned, age was immaterial. Knowledge and confidence were everything. I heard a very young Simon Rattle at Glyndebourne. He was in his twenties at the time, and I adored his artistry. I tried desperately to get him to come to Toronto, but he turned us down. It was the same story with Calvin Simmons. Sensitivity and musicality poured out of him, but he also declined every invitation. I even offered what I thought was surefire conductor bait. Most conductors would sacrifice anything to do a rare and challenging repertoire. This includes the music of Arnold Schoenberg, which is as difficult and demanding as it comes. I went to hear Pierre Boulez lead *Pelléas et Mélisande* at the Welsh National Opera, invited him to dinner, and said, "Maestro, I hope you understand this is the highest compliment I can pay you. You are the *only* conductor apart from Ansermet to do this work with such passion." He appreciated the compliment, but when I asked him to come to Toronto to do Schoenberg's *Moses und Aron*, he just smiled.

I also tried my best to get Sir Charles Mackerras, but he politely declined. It was more than frustrating to be criticized for never bringing the best conductors to Toronto. I didn't want to break confidence with the conductors and managers I had approached, and I could hardly tell the press that we had been regarded as unworthy by just about every podium superstar I had asked. I remain convinced that the Canadian Opera Company could have gone much farther had we been able to bring world-class talent to our podium.

There were also two B-level conductors from whom I hoped great things and to whom I offered a special relationship. One of them was the Irish conductor Kenneth Montgomery, who I thought would make a good music director for our company. I had done a lot of work with him in the Netherlands, but his career never went where his talent should have taken him. He did a number of productions for us at Canadian Opera, and I tried to build him up, but he lacked ambition and preferred a comfortable lifestyle. There was never any fire in his performances.

The other conductor was a Canadian named Mario Bernardi. After I was appointed general director in Toronto but before actually moving there from Geneva, an elegant and intelligent man by the name of G. Hamilton Southam asked to meet with me. Mr. Southam was independently wealthy and had been largely responsible for building the National Arts Centre (NAC) in Ottawa and creating the NAC Orchestra. We met in Geneva, and I found him entrancing. He was sophisticated, witty, and stylish. Of course, it didn't hurt that he was an heir to a publishing fortune, but he was much more than that. Hamilton felt that all the leading Canadian companies should collaborate more closely, and he asked if I would serve as an artistic adviser to the NAC. Of course I agreed.

Mario Bernardi had founded the NAC Orchestra in 1969 and later became its music director. From that year to 1982, he was also artistic director of the NAC summer opera series, and during that period he led more than twenty operas. They were well received. Mario had a background in opera, having served in the mid-1960s as a resident conductor and music director at Sadler's Wells Opera in London. He had a better reputation as a pianist than he did as a maestro. I felt he had a somewhat exaggerated idea of his talent. Even so, he wanted a career and seemed willing to work for it, and he was far more ambitious than Montgomery.

I was asked to help with the NAC summer opera series, bringing in major stars and collaborating with Bernardi. I worked there for two seasons, directing a *Nozze di Figaro* with Mario conducting and a *Figlia del reggimento* with Norma Burrowes in the title role and featuring Maureen Forrester. As I moved back and forth from Toronto, I began to sense a terrible tension on Mario's part. We had done two productions together in San Francisco, and I thought I knew him, but he quickly became sarcastic, nervous, and rude around me. Although I tried all my Persian wiles on him, it was just no go. Nevertheless, I was eager to build real collaboration between Toronto and Ottawa, and I wanted to "hire Canadian." I offered him the position of music director of the Canadian Opera Company, telling him I wanted a partner in the creation of a first-class orchestra, such as he had built at the NAC. He replied by telling me we weren't ready to take on anyone of his eminence. To make matters worse, he was not happy over my assigning Raffi Armenian to conduct *Wozzeck*. It was a no-win situation with Mario.

After a couple of years of this, I sat down with him and said, "I want to help you. I'm not interested in taking away your position in Ottawa. In fact, I even offered you the second position with us here in Toronto, and you turned me down." Whatever the cause of our problems, they were creating a tense and unproductive situation for all parties concerned. Finally I said, "If you feel we cannot have a partnership, I will resign." I withdrew from a paying contract and stopped going to Ottawa. I regretted losing my contact with Hamilton, but Mario was so afraid of losing his own hold that he stood in the way of whatever I tried to do.

Incidentally, my confidence in Raffi proved highly justified. He has enjoyed a very distinguished career as a musician and educator, and a theater in Ontario is named for him, as well it should be, as he contributed decisively to its design.

One conductor in Toronto was a total disaster. Years later, he was actually arrested as an accessory in a murder charge. The story began with a 1983 production of *Lohengrin*, one destined to be superb, at least on paper. We had been able to secure the services of Siegfried Jerusalem for the title role, and this was a great coup for us. Our *Lohengrin* was to be a re-creation of Götz Friedrich's glorious staging in Bayreuth, and I had hoped Götz might be available to stage it for us; he was not, so we secured the services of his assistant, a Dutch director named Nando Schellen. Unfortunately, rather than basing his production on Götz's, Nando had his own ideas, and they weren't all that good. In fact, he annoyed Siegfried no end, and after several serious conflicts, I finally had to ask him to drop out of the production, which I then took over myself.

To make matters appreciably worse, I brought in a Swiss conductor named Michel Tabachnik, a bizarre character who held some peculiar views about things. Although he came highly recommended, he had become associated with something called the Order of the Solar Temple, a crackpot doomsday cult founded by a Frenchman named Joseph di Mambro. This prophet relieved the faithful of their money by promising they would be reborn on the star Sirius after committing a ritual suicide.

Sixty-eight people, including Canadians, willingly were duped—and promptly did themselves in. Tabachnik was accused of "participation in a criminal association" in 2001, acquitted, then charged and acquitted again in 2006. He continues to deny all the charges against him.

Our company was also turned down by others with a more normal frame of mind. The magnificent Canadian dramatic tenor Jon Vickers was a unique talent. Every year I was in Toronto I would offer him a role in his repertoire, including his signature role of Peter Grimes, and every year his agent would turn me down. I always felt he was permanently angry with Toronto itself, and in a certain sense, he had cause.

In 1974, he and his brother David had organized and financed "the Dream Concert of the Decade" at the venerable 2,752-seat Massey Hall on Victoria Street in the old downtown entertainment district. It featured Vickers and Birgit Nilsson singing Act I of Wagner's *Die Walküre* with the Toronto Symphony Orchestra conducted by Zubin Mehta. From all appearances, this should have been a huge success, but the event, on November 17 of that year, proved less than that. Jon had overreached. He had decided to give two performances of the same work on the same evening. Neither one sold out, and he and his brother lost $30,000 in this venture. He took it as a personal insult.

We were also turned down by Bernardo Bertolucci. I had always been interested in having certain motion picture directors do opera for us. When we were planning *Lulu*, I approached him. His film *Last Tango in Paris* was right in that mood, but he just wasn't interested.

Although we had problems acquiring some superstars, we had much greater success elsewhere. As well as building up our Opera Ensemble and the opera orchestra, I wanted to create an ongoing mechanism for identifying future opera composers. As the Canadian Opera Company, I felt we had an obligation to undertake such a project, and our team spent many hours and a great deal of money on it. During my tenure at Canadian Opera, we commissioned three operas for public performance. In March 1986, the Music Office of the Canada Council asked us to participate in "the Year of Canadian Music" and offered us financial incentives to encourage us. We decided to produce R. Murray Schafer's non-opera *Patria II: Characteristics of Man* and assigned Christopher Newton to direct it. The project cost us about $640,000. Starting on November 21, 1987, we gave six sold-out performances with Robert Aitken conducting. We finally calculated the cost to us per seat at an amazing $222.

Schafer lives high on the hog from government subsidies and certainly doesn't suffer from an overabundance of modesty. On his own Web site, he describes himself as "Canada's pre-eminent composer," going on to state that he is "known throughout the world." In our collaboration, he never let us forget this self-anointed status. Not only did he prove impossible to deal with, complaining about everything we did, he even attacked us in the *Journal of Canadian Studies*. I solemnly resolved never to work with him again.

From the beginning, I believed that Canada's national company should take the lead in developing Canadian opera with young composers, and so in 1987, with the financial backing of TransCanada Pipelines Ltd., we announced the Canadian Composer's Program, leading to a mentored residency with the company. Thirty composers submitted samples of their work. Canadian composer Lou Appelbaum and U.S. composer Carlisle Floyd served as advisers and adjudicators. They selected three finalists: Richard Désilets and his *Zoé*, Michel-Georges Brégent and his *Realitillusion*, and Timothy Sullivan for *Dreamplay* based on the drama by August Strindberg. We paid each composer $15,000 and budgeted $152,000 for the entire project. Every work had to be for six or seven singers and a chamber ensemble, and it could run no longer than sixty minutes. All three works were given public workshop performances at our Tanenbaum Opera Centre in May 1988.

In late June of that year, we sponsored a long weekend for interested composers and librettists to participate in a kind of shotgun marriage. On each of the three days, a composer would be matched with a librettist. There were two sessions of three hours every day, and each team was to prepare and write a scene. In the succeeding session, the composer would be matched with another librettist and asked to write a different scene. This way, over the course of the weekend, every composer and librettist would write six different scenes.

The measure of success in this unique approach was determined by how well composer and librettist interacted with one another and by how much the panel was attracted to the musical and dramatic content of the scenes. Once selected, these three composers and librettists were to sketch a one-act opera during the summer. In October, sessions began with the singers, the dramaturge, and the music director analyzing the creative efforts of the collaborators. Although this textbook example of hothouse Canadian content got off to a brilliant start, in 1989 Brian Dickie, my successor as general director, canceled the program.

The Canadian Opera Company's national tours dated back to November 1958 and had been preceded by regional tours in Ontario. They were an extremely important aspect of the company's mission and spearheaded the development of opera across the country. During the first decade, these tours were undertaken with minimal sets and costumes, young singers, and a dauntless pianist. The first tour covered five thousand miles, the next more than ten thousand. These tours went on for many years and eventually also included Alaska and Seattle, with additional appearances in Oregon, Montana, Michigan, Ohio, New York, and all the way south to Albuquerque. They were all underwritten by the Canada Council. In 1986, a sixteen-piece orchestra joined the touring company and significantly elevated the experience of opera for our listeners.

By the time I came aboard, Canadian Opera Company tours were a fixture of cultural life in Canada and, to some extent, in the United States as well. They proved very successful, and sometimes very odd. Once or twice, our singers were arrested for vagrancy (this happened to Victor Braun and Cornelius Opthof in Kenora, Ontario). They froze in temperatures that hit fifty below and were delayed by the rigors of Canadian winters. But our young artists learned their craft, and new audiences became acquainted with the repertoire and the traditions of opera. When we expanded into a spring season, we also expanded our touring activities. In one of my first seasons, we gave thirty-nine performances of *La traviata* and *Il barbiere di Siviglia* across Ontario and another thirty in the United States. But it was all getting a good deal more expensive. By the early 1980s, it became clear that our days as a national touring company were coming to an end. Together with operatic Johnny Appleseeds such as Irving Guttman in Winnipeg, Edmonton, and Vancouver, we had succeeded in helping give opera a presence in just about every province in the country. We decided to replace the power of these tours in making our presence felt by entering the world of public broadcasting. In 1983, we initiated another first for the Canadian Opera Company: broadcasting on the national network of the Canadian Broadcasting Corporation, then soon thereafter on some two hundred National Public Radio stations in the United States. Our ambitious claim to be "the" Canadian company at last had a touch of credibility.

In contrast to my reaction to having the Composers' Program dispensed with, I wasn't at all surprised when my successor discontinued touring in 1991, but while the tours flourished, we made friends among thousands of people who never imagined they would enjoy such an art, much less feel so at home with it.

When we invited some major, internationally recognized artists to appear in special benefit events, the mixed reaction was a classic example of the old adage "damned if you do, and damned if you don't."

Snobbery takes many forms, and reverse snobbery can be just as tiresome as the usual manifestation. I was criticized by some for importing stars and castigated by others for not importing enough of them. I took the view that stars attract larger audiences, which in turn creates a greater appetite for opera, and this, in the final analysis, can only benefit the local talent. Authentic opera stars create excitement, cachet, and legitimacy. If Joan Sutherland comes to town, then the town must be a pretty good place to sing. And when a local girl like Teresa Stratas returns to her hometown, she appears under the auspices of a company that has established a very good name and has proved itself worthy of showcasing her unique talents. The tricky part is to strike a balance between the two impulses, and here we did not always succeed.

It is important to know how to make the best use of star appeal. When I was in Toronto, we organized special concerts with great stars to raise money for the company. In late 1978, Renata Scotto and Carlo Bergonzi appeared under our auspices on the pretext of commemorating the 200th anniversary of the opening of La Scala. The event was a huge success. One year later, we brought one of the most luminous artists of the century, the great Birgit Nilsson. To my embarrassment, the concert didn't do as well as we had expected.

Sometime earlier, Mme. Nilsson had run into problems with the U.S. Internal Revenue Service through no fault of her own. She wanted to sing for us, but she was terribly frightened of what might happen to her if she were to land inadvertently in the United States and find herself arrested for tax evasion. She finally agreed to risk it, and her appearance at the O'Keefe Centre in October 1979 was magnificent. She gave an all-Wagnerian program; Kenneth Montgomery conducted, and the evening concluded with the majestic immolation scene from *Götterdämmerung*. Because we hadn't sold out, Birgit kept apologizing. It was the city of Toronto that should have apologized to her. The people simply didn't recognize what a coup it was to have her—Nilsson's first North American appearance in years!

Later in my tenure, I arranged with one of our big donors to sponsor a special fund-raising dinner if I could get Plácido Domingo to come to Toronto. For this, we would charge $1,000 a plate, an unheard of sum in Canada back then. He agreed to be our guest of honor, and that night we raised close to $50,000. Later we organized a concert featuring Plácido, this time singing for thousands. This event was to be held at Maple Leaf Gardens, a hockey arena seating 15,837 spectators, and was scheduled for January 1986. Luciano Pavarotti had done a hugely successful benefit concert there for the Toronto Symphony a year before. Thanks to my prescient director of finance, Anca Ghitescu-Mohnbatt, we wisely decided to insure the concert with Lloyd's of London for the full amount of a sold-out house, $750,000. The policy cost us $50,000, and some of our board members were vehemently opposed, saying it was a total waste of money.

On September 19, 1985, a devastating earthquake measuring 8.1 on the Richter scale struck Mexico City. Three days later, Plácido, who had been raised and educated there, flew down to help. He lost an aunt, an uncle, and a cousin to the natural disaster; nine thousand others were killed and a hundred thousand homes were destroyed. Over the next several months, he spent a great deal of time in Mexico, raising more than $2 million for earthquake relief. He was forced to cancel his Canadian appearance, and we wound up collecting the $750,000 on our Lloyd's policy, which, incidentally, was the last time Lloyd's ever agreed to issue a policy like that. When Plácido was finally able to join us on March 1, 1987, almost twenty thousand people attended his performace, and we cleared $200,000.

Nilsson, Bergonzi, Scotto, and Domingo were just a few of the operatic luminaries we brought to Toronto for an audience that would otherwise never have heard them in our city. I was especially proud to welcome the renowned Joan Sutherland and her conductor-husband, Richard Bonynge. Their musical eloquence, the lush sound of her voice, and the conductor's impeccable taste made it a matchless combination. They did *Norma* for us in 1981, Joan's first *Anna Bolena* in 1984, and *Adriana Lecouvreur* in 1987, as well as her only stage performance of Ophélie in Ambroise Thomas's *Hamlet* in 1984—all of which put Canadian Opera firmly on the world map.

Joan Sutherland as
The Merry Widow,
Australian Opera,
1979.

We devoted a lot of attention to introducing great masterworks to Toronto audiences. We presented Canada's first *Meistersinger* during a mini-Wagner festival. We also premiered Shostakovich's *Lady Macbeth of Mtsensk*, Janáček's *Jenůfa*, and Berg's *Wozzeck* and gave the first Canadian performance of his *Lulu* in the three-act version prepared by Friedrich Cerha. We also presented local premieres of Verdi's *Don Carlos* in the original French in 1977 and again in 1988, Britten's *Death in Venice* in 1984, and Poulenc's *Les dialogues des Carmélites* two years later. At the time I was roundly criticized for bringing such a "radical" repertoire to crusty old Toronto.

When I announced our first *Wozzeck* for 1977, the critic at Toronto's *Globe and Mail* wrote, "Mansouri smiles at the brink of disaster." Alban Berg's masterpiece had premiered in 1925 with a libretto taken almost verbatim from Georg Büchner's incredibly future-anticipating play, written some ninety years previously. Like the play, the opera tells a horrific story with one of the most compelling musical scores ever devised. It is not an easy sell, to be sure, but I believe deeply in this work and wanted our audience to share in its stirring compassion. I had scheduled six performances of *Wozzeck* rather than the two everyone had recommended. I may not have known the city, but I do have a reasonable familiarity with the operatic repertoire. It was a tremendous success, and its triumph gave me a free hand in years to come.

It also made me proud to attract artists from somewhat outside the operatic mainstream to our stage. One of these artists was a magnificent Canadian mezzo-soprano named Maureen Forrester, who was better known in concert than in opera. As the Marquise de Berkenfeld in our 1977 production of *The Daughter of the Regiment*, this singer could finally put her infectious sense of humor to telling use in Donizetti's comic opera. To up the ante, we paired her with the hilarious Anna Russell in the speaking role of the gossipy Duchess of Crackenthorp. Their comic scenes together stole the show every night.

If there was a single reason some major artists avoided us, it may have been that the Canadian Opera Company performed in a cave. The O'Keefe Centre, later called the Hummingbird Centre, seats 3,165 in a room better suited for artillery practice. It was built in 1960 and is a huge venue with booming acoustics. Its stage area, an astonishing fifty-nine feet wide and fifty feet deep with a thirty-foot high proscenium, would provide sufficient room for two parallel productions of *Aida* with enough space left over for a Cimarosa work. It was also a costly place to perform: in 1979, for example, our grant from the city of Toronto came to $56,953, and the rent was $278,691—payable to the city of Toronto! Mounting intimate works like *Albert Herring* or *Così fan tutte* meant decreasing the playing area, but nothing could mask the size of the auditorium, which consequently dictated many of our repertoire choices. It would have been infeasible to play two houses, but something would ultimately have to be done. We needed our own opera house with seating, sight lines, acoustics, and technical equipment equal to the requirements of Canada's finest company.

Long after my departure, in September 2006, the Canadian Opera Company's wish finally came true and, thanks to the inspired leadership of the late general director Richard Bradshaw, entered its own home, a handsome facility that also contains an elegant amphitheater bearing his name. The Four Seasons Centre for the Performing Arts was designed by Toronto architect Jack Diamond. From the beginning, it was hailed as "nothing short of triumphant" and "among the world's great opera houses." The acoustics are state-of-the-art, and the auditorium seats a sensible 2,144. They got it right, and they have earned the respect and admiration of everyone, including yours truly.

Thirty years earlier, we had tried to do the same thing. That we failed was my bitterest disappointment in Toronto. It had all begun years before my arrival, when the board explored the possibility of building the company's own opera house, knowing the company would never move beyond its provincial status without one. When I joined the company,

I went all out for it, and we gave it our best shot. In 1977, the Canadian Opera Company and the National Ballet of Canada agreed—at my insistence—to cooperate as equal partners in the construction of the building. We hired the consulting firm of Woods Gordon to guide us. Within five years we had a workable plan, and in November 1983 we created the Ballet/Opera House Corporation to manage our mutual affairs, increase public interest, and start lobbying for government support. We received numerous reports on possible sites, on the feasibility of renovating existing theaters, and on management options.

Relations with the National Ballet, however, were always touchy. Our old friend and benefactor Joey Tanenbaum understood the basic incompatibility of the partnership and offered the National Ballet a million dollars to acquire its own facility, but the ballet turned him down. Its demands were completely unreasonable. It asked for seven ballet studios the size of the main stage. Seven! Plus every extra room it could dream up.

The ballet's artistic director, the Danish *premier danseur* and choreographer Erik Bruhn, was good to work with on a personal basis. He led the company from 1983 to 1986 and achieved a great deal, but he became severely ill and died partway through the process. It was a tragedy, and his successors were so insecure it was impossible to deal with them.

As part of the plan to secure the highest possible level of cooperation between the ballet and the opera, I recommended that we combine our orchestras, but the ballet turned that proposal down, too. We even proposed calling our projected venue the Ballet/Opera House, but it didn't make any difference. No matter what concessions we made, the ballet was never satisfied.

Finally, in January 1985 a breakthrough came about—or so we thought. The provincial government announced the gift of a superb site at Bay and Wellesley Streets, one that would meet all our requirements. We calculated that $40 million would be needed from private sources and that we might be able to open in three years, but a provincial election put the quietus on that plan. Out went the Conservatives, in came the Liberals, and the new premier declared on March 5, 1986, that he would prefer to support a domed sports stadium rather than an opera house. We advanced our planned opening to 1991 and continued work. Singer-attorney Janet Stubbs, an exceptionally talented and canny woman, agreed to be my personal representative to the Ballet/Opera House Corporation, and planning moved on apace. In March 1988, amid great controversy, the distinguished Canadian Israeli architect Moshe Safdie was chosen to design the new theater. He had created the remarkably successful Habitat for Montreal's Expo in 1967. After a great deal of lobbying, in July 1988 the new provincial government agreed to restate the former land grant. Better yet, it offered us $65 million, but that was conditional on securing matching funds from the federal government. We were facing a hurdle we had no way of surmounting. Even with this working cash infusion available, we basically ran out of money to continue. We had already spent more than $20 million.

Municipal and provincial squabbles broke out, and when Safdie's final design came in at $320 million, we lost control of it, and the project failed. Although I was already in San Francisco by then, I always took it as a bitter personal loss. But our vision back then was confirmed when Richard Bradshaw took the reins and brought the project to reality.

Of all the Canadian Opera Company's remarkable achievements in its relatively short history, possibly one stands out as the most important. The issue of accessibility has always been a major point of concern in every art form, but nowhere has it played a more important role than in the international production of grand opera. Although it is clear that the original language sung by an international cast of artists familiar with that language is invariably the most authentic means of conveying the intentions of the work's creators, the elitist nature of a large-scale theatrical production in a language unfamiliar to the audience has always been a stumbling block to attracting audiences. Consequently, while one or two major opera centers offered original-language productions with international casts, companies in just about every other city in the world presented opera in translation with local artists onstage, and some of those translations could backfire hilariously.

In one provincial American production of *La traviata*, the heartbreaking last act turned into a laugh riot when the dying Violetta asked her maid Annina, "How much have I got left in my drawers?" and Annina replied, "Twenty louis," to which the expiring courtesan sighed, "Distribute them among the poor."

But even in major international capitals, the sudden indisposition of one artist and the unavailability of a replacement who knew the role in the same language could lead to some remarkably crazy-quilted evenings in the theater. At one 1951 *Aida* performance in London, Edith Coates sang Amneris in English; the performers of the secondary roles also sang in English, as did the chorus, while the Radames, Hans Hopf, sang his part in German. Astrid Varnay sang the title role in Italian, and Jess Walters as Amonasro switched from one language to another depending on who else was onstage.

In the course of time, more and more singers were arriving on the scene with greater language skills, but they were not all that eager to have to learn the same role in more than one language and switch-hit from one theater to another. The advent of the jet age had made it possible for artists to be brought in at the last minute from almost anywhere to take the place of a colleague who might have to drop out of a performance, but in what language? Slowly but surely, original-language performances became the most sensible and practical way to go, but accessibility continued to remain an issue.

The introduction of supertitles (originally called surtitles) in Toronto may have been our most important accomplishment. For millions of people, they have made opera a comprehensible art form. Supertitles are the most democratic and liberating tool we can employ in the modern era. They are as important as radio and television, shellac and vinyl, and DVDs in touching and raising the consciousness of every operagoer. In a post-literate society, they have enabled a new audience to understand languages they cannot read and to engage emotions they have always understood. Supertitles launched the modern operatic renaissance, and they began in Toronto in 1983.

My wife, Midge, is not a great fan of Richard Wagner, but her reaction to a Wagnerian experience marked the beginning of supertitles, and she has never received the credit she deserves for the idea. We were watching Patrice Chéreau's Bayreuth production of *Die Walküre* on television one night at home, and as the subtitles flashed by, Midge said, "You know, Lotfi, this isn't as dumb as I thought it was." And the idea was born.

We were planning Monteverdi's 1642 masterwork, *L'incoronazione di Poppea*, which has as complicated a story line as has ever been offered in opera. I was concerned about how to convey its intricacies to a modern audience that would be highly unlikely to have read the libretto first. Coming to a performance personally prepared was how it may have worked a century ago, but in our high-speed age, who has time? Before taking their seats, 95 percent of our audience would not have a

*For the first time, North American audiences could visually
follow a convoluted foreign-language opera plot in English, thanks
to the "surtitles" (later known as supertitles) projected over the stage,
in the Canadian Opera Company's 1983 production of* Elektra.
Robert C. Ragsdale, photographer; courtesy Canadian Opera Company.

clue about the story they were going to witness. At one point, because
basically *Poppea* is essentially nothing but dialogue, conductor Kenneth
Montgomery suggested we bring the house lights only down to half, so
that the audience could read the text. I appreciated the thought, but that
would basically turn the event into a concert.

Instead, I took Midge's idea to John Leberg and Bruce MacMullen,
our technical director. Why not find a way to display titles as in foreign-
language films? John and Bruce put together a kind of slide show, and
that's how it all began. As it turned out, we first used titles in our production of Richard Strauss's *Elektra*, with translations provided by Sonya
Friedman.

John restructured the *Elektra* budget and committed $15,000 to our
experiment. He paid Sonya $4,000 for the use of the text she had already
prepared for the Met telecast. Together with his friend, Jim Fuller, John

researched the technical options then available and purchased three Kodak Carousel projectors with high-powered bulbs at a cost of $2,500. After consulting with Bruce and lighting designer Michael Whitfield, John settled on a brownish gray screen onto which amber fonts could be projected. The screen cost $800, leaving $2,700 for the slides and nothing for the technician who operated them.

When our audiences entered the O'Keefe Centre on that historic opening night, January 21, 1983, they expected to see Olivia Stapp, Maureen Forrester, Viviane Thomas, and a very young Ben Heppner telling a very old story. What they did not expect to see was a screen above the proscenium, sixty-five feet wide and four and a half feet high. But the thing that came next was what really astonished them. There, using more than eight hundred title slides, we projected the heart of the story, the poetry of Sophocles, on whose drama Hugo von Hofmannsthal's libretto is based. The audience response was overwhelming. "At last I could understand everything!" was a typical response. It was an electrifying event and one from which we never retreated. When we presented *Poppea* two months later, our audience now expected—and demanded—to see supertitles.

They caught on fast.

John later said he had hoped that would be the end of this adventure, but the undertaking turned out to be such a success that he was presented with the challenge of finding the additional funds to pay for the *Poppea* titles.

Beverly Sills came from New York to see our titles and immediately took the idea back to City Opera. She understood their power, and very soon so did her audience. Unfortunately, proper credit was not immediately given to the Canadian Opera Company, and that led to bad feelings for a while. Beverly settled the matter forever when I went down to direct *La rondine* for her. She declared on television, "Lotfi, let's set the record straight. You started titles in Canada, and I came up to see them. Are you satisfied now?" I said I was. In the autumn of 1983, the San Francisco Opera was the next company to adopt this liberating technology.

We were quickly deluged with requests from other opera companies for information. To avoid drowning in them, we accepted an invitation from Opera America to give a demonstration of our new system at its annual meeting in 1983. John and Bruce traveled to Syracuse, New York, home of the General Electric Research Division, and examined the company's brand-new "Telaria" projector. This appears to have been the first effort to combine a computer with a projector. However, the machines cost $65,000 each—there was no way we could have afforded one of them—but GE did us a big favor and let us borrow the Telaria to use at Opera America. Meanwhile, John and Jim Fuller flew to Los Angeles to examine similar systems being used in the motion picture industry.

Unfortunately, the presentation at the annual meeting was a disaster. Scaffolding was erected. Kodak Carousels and GE Telaria machines were installed, and the sound systems were wired—or so we thought. The staff at the hotel where the meeting was being held went on strike. There was talk of sabotage, and nothing worked properly, if it worked at all. It was more than embarrassing. After that debacle, we slunk off to the nearest cocktail lounge and tied one on.

Along with our lawyer, John Carson, we applied to register a copyright for the name "surtitles," in contrast to "subtitles" in foreign-language films, but our application was rejected. The authorities said we had simply harnessed an existing technology for a new purpose, and that was not eligible for legal protection. In a way, this was not such a bad development. Had we been able to protect this innovation, it probably wouldn't have spread so quickly throughout the world to the point where even provincial opera houses present operas with international casts singing the texts the composers had in their minds when setting them to music—and ever larger and more broadly based audiences understand every word.

Of course, the titles must be well written, accurate, idiomatic, and suitable to the period of the story, and they need to be cued in at the right point in the stage action, an especially important factor in comic opera, where they mustn't telegraph punch lines.

Everybody has his or her favorite anecdote about a misbegotten title, possibly the most popular of which concerns the title that supposedly showed up onscreen at a *Tosca* performance in Texas, at the spot where the heroine tells her lover, the painter Cavaradossi, to change the blue eyes on his portrait of St. Mary Magdalene to match her own dark eyes. When a title came up reading, "Give her two black eyes," the audience exploded in hilarity, and the indignant soprano, thinking this was a reflection on her performance, angrily walked off the stage and refused to return. But this is an exception, not the rule. Titles work. They satisfy and inform. They raise the level of understanding and open up opera to everyone, which has been a fundamental mission of mine throughout my artistic life.

For all of that, the usual prophets of purism checked in with their voluble misgivings. In their opinion, we were vulgarizing opera and debasing the experience. London's *Opera* magazine decried titles as "the plague from Canada," which was mild criticism compared with some of the other abuse we were taking. My old friend, critic Martin Bernheimer, who was the godfather of our daughter, denounced me in print, listing all kinds of reasons why titles in the opera house made no sense and merely cheapened the operatic experience, averting the audience's eyes from the stage to wherever the titles were running.

Times change. I recently found myself sitting beside Martin at the Metropolitan, where the titles are displayed on small screens on the back of each seat, and patrons can switch them off if they would rather not see them, which is fine by me. The performance that evening was Tchaikovsky's *Pikovaya dama* (*The Queen of Spades*) starring Plácido Domingo, and the cast was singing in Russian, one of the few languages Martin does not speak. I couldn't help but notice that shortly after the house lights went down, he clandestinely turned his titles on.

I was pleased to note that, after we introduced titles in Toronto, our attendance increased by an average of 20 percent. One out of every five people in the audience a new patron? That's not bad.

My experience as general director of the Canadian Opera Company in Toronto was wonderful. For all of its ups and downs, it was one of the best experiences of my professional life. When I arrived, Toronto was a relatively provincial, purely Anglo-Saxon city. While I was there, thanks to a wave of immigration, a diverse population began arriving, and right before my eyes, Toronto became the first truly cosmopolitan city in Canada. And parallel to this, the Canadian Opera Company continued to grow and make new things happen. My time in Toronto was exciting, joyous, and highly collaborative. Not without reason did my Ontario license plates read "OPERA."

I didn't realize until long after I left that I had really been spoiled. We had a *wonderful* team at the Canadian Opera Company. We could get excited and collaborate, and we could even disagree with one another, but when the meetings were over, we came together as friends for a pleasant evening and enjoyed a drink together. We never took our disagreements personally. We all had the same vision and the same goal, and over the years, I have retained my friendships with everyone.

Things would turn out differently in San Francisco.

10

OPEN YOUR GOLDEN GATE!

first directed a production at the San Francisco Opera in 1963. You might say it was love at first sight. I was invited back, season after season, and I always looked forward to my time in the City by the Bay and its jewel of an opera house. In 1988, to mark the twenty-fifth anniversary of that first production, I heard I was going to be given a silver tray. Instead I was given the company.

My relationship with San Francisco Opera actually began in the early 1950s, when I worked as a dollar-per-show supernumerary at the company's Los Angeles tour performances. In those days, the company used to come to Los Angeles after the home season, bringing along all its productions, sometimes with different casts, and perform in the Shrine Auditorium, a barn of a place with more than six thousand seats. When I wasn't carrying a spear or marching in a procession onstage, Midge and I would buy the cheapest seats and attend performances under the rafters, watching carefully for empty seats lower down, which we could run to after intermission.

Gaetano Merola, the founding general director, was running things back then. He died in 1953, baton in hand, during an outdoor concert in one of those bizarre operatic ironies that so often befall conductors. He was nearing the end of the aria "Un bel dì" from *Madama Butterfly* when the soprano says she will keep her distance for a bit during Pinkerton's return, to keep from dying of excitement. When she got to the word "morire," Maestro Merola simply expired.

He was succeeded by Kurt Herbert Adler, completing an unlikely ascent from chorus director to general director. Adler was born in Vienna and had gone to school with Dr. Graf. As young men, they had both enjoyed a fruitful collaboration with the eminent director and teacher Max

Reinhardt. Adler entered the operatic world at the age of twenty-three, then worked his way up to the chorus director's position at the theater in Kaiserslautern, conducting performances in Italy and at the Vienna Volksoper. He then joined the equally young Georg Solti and Erich Leinsdorf as assistants to Arturo Toscanini at the Salzburg Festival. When he fled Austria following the Nazi annexation in 1938, he was engaged as chorus director at the Chicago Opera, where he served until 1943, when Dr. Graf recommended him to Maestro Merola, who offered him the same post in San Francisco over the phone. When he took over the company ten years later, it was expected he might invite Dr. Graf to direct, but he never did, although Dr. Graf had worked there with Merola.

Adler attended a performance of my production of *Il tabarro* at the Ambassador Hotel swimming pool in Los Angeles, and I followed up with a letter asking to apprentice for him, but he didn't answer it. When our paths crossed again, in 1961, he was on his annual European tour to scout talent, an enterprise at which he was superbly successful, introducing dozens of great artists, including Giulietta Simionato, Birgit Nilsson, Giuseppe Taddei, Elisabeth Schwarzkopf, Sándor Kónya, and Margaret Price, to name but a few, to the United States, while launching U.S. careers for such major American artists as Claire Watson and Leontyne Price. On this visit, he stopped in Zurich, where he came to the theater to observe one of my rehearsals of Meyerbeer's *Le prophète*. Following the rehearsal, he offered me three productions for his 1962 season in California. I was dumbfounded and barely stuttered that I would request a release from Dr. Graf. Adler brusquely informed me that he was giving me ten days to get back to him. The following morning, still flying high, I went to see Dr. Graf, naively expecting him to let me out of my duties in Switzerland. Graf, looking rather puzzled, said, "But Lotfi, you are already scheduled for three productions here during that period." The reality of this hit me like a bucket of ice water. I argued the importance of the San Francisco Opera, as if he didn't know. In retrospect, I have to admit that I was immature, and his Mona Lisa smile only increased my frustration. That night, at home with Midge, I continued to vent my rage, to the point of vowing to resign were I not granted that release. A few days later, I saw Dr. Graf again. I was still behaving petulantly, but he continued to remain his placid self. As San Francisco Opera seemed so important to me, he stated matter-of-factly that he would work around my schedule and release me for the required period. I couldn't believe my ears. Thanking him profusely, I left his office to call Adler, who said, in his usual aloof manner, that I could expect to receive a contract.

Weeks went by—still no contract. Finally I received a telegram: "Your services no longer required for 1962 season. Adler." I've never been clubbed by a baseball bat, but that telegram gave me an idea of what it must feel like. It was probably my first major lesson in the workings of international opera. As always, Midge was a comfort, working hard to lift my spirits. Then I had to face Dr. Graf. The next day I slinked into his office to break the news. Smiling amiably, he simply said, "All right, you're back on your assignments." Just like that. What a gracious, under-standing *gentle*man he was!

The following year, Paul Hager, a longtime member of the San Fran-cisco Opera team and a close friend of Adler's, came to Zurich to direct a new production. He invited me to join him for lunch, and we made lots of small talk until he got his coffee, at which point he abruptly said, "Kurt is wondering if you hold a grudge." After a slight hesitation, I put on my best Persian smile and replied, "Please tell Mr. Adler that at this point in my career, I can't afford any grudges." A few months later, I re-ceived an invitation to direct six productions for the 1963 season, and this time I didn't celebrate until the contract was signed. Thus began my association with San Francisco Opera. Over the next twenty-five years, I directed forty-one productions spanning the repertoire from Auber to Wagner. Not quite A to Z, but close!

Kurt Herbert Adler was one of the last of the Old World impresa-rios. In many ways, he ran San Francisco Opera like a personal fiefdom, oozing disdain for anyone he considered inferior in judgment or experi-ence, and his list was a long one. We were never close. I never called him anything but "Mr. Adler." Ours was a strictly professional relationship, and even that was a hit-or-miss proposition. He would often promise me a production and then forget about it. The only compliment I ever got from him came after the opening of my *Samson et Dalila* production in 1963 when he came backstage and said it was "a good musical perfor-mance." When I replied, "Maestro Prêtre is over there," he didn't smile. I soon came to realize that the only compliment he ever gave people was to rehire them.

He didn't meddle nearly as much in my stagings as he wanted to (or did with others). Nevertheless, I'll never lose the sound of his voice over my shoulder peppering me with such helpful insights as "Lotfi, the soprano onstage right—she needs gloves." After a while, I asked him to give all his notes to his assistant. I would be summoned to Adler's office and go over them item by item, and the adjustments were rarely more than cosmetic.

When it came to travel, Adler could be incredibly tightfisted. He booked steerage for me whenever possible. If I wanted a stopover in New York, say, it might cost an extra $15, which he would then deduct from my fee. I got a bit of revenge. When I engaged him to conduct in Tehran, I arranged first-class travel all the way, but I added a note, "If you stop off in New York, there will be a small deduction." I was often playful with him, but for a serious purpose: I wanted it quite clear that I was not his fool. If you let him push you too far, he would step all over you forever. I could be flexible, but only to a point. When he got to the end of his rope, things would end with him moaning, "Ghastly, ghastly!" to no one in particular and everyone in general. He never trusted anyone completely, with a single exception: Otto Guth, a superb coach, on whom he relied when it came to musical matters.

Adler could be arrogant, aggressive, rude, and insulting—and this was just on an average day. He once singled out a chorister and said, "You were flat!" only to be told, "Sir, he wasn't singing in that scene," to which he curtly responded, "He was flat anyway!" He could yell and scream like a banshee, and he burned through staff members, especially women, at an alarming rate. His parade of former secretaries even included a woman who lasted only four hours, allegedly because she neglected to peel his grapes. His attitude toward women colleagues was legendary. When he hired thirty-one-year-old Laurie Feldman to direct a production of the *Ring*, he sternly warned her not to chew gum at rehearsals, and when Reri Grist came to the theater in 1963, he greeted her by telling her not to bother him and referring her to his assistant, Ulf Thomson, if she needed anything, a cavalier gesture that backfired when Reri married Thomson.

When he wanted something from someone, such as a concession of some kind from a major star like Renata Tebaldi or Luciano Pavarotti, he could pour on the Viennese charm big-time, with a healthy dollop of *Schlagobers*. It was as much a lesson to watch him schmooze as it was to witness one of his frequent combustions.

Both his ire and his amiability often extended to the critics, especially Martin Bernheimer, the reviewer at the time for the *Los Angeles Times*.

Martin remembered him as someone who "had no reason to love critics in general and this one in particular," yet went on to say that "unlike some of his impresario-colleagues on the West Coast, he was inevitably thoughtful, kind and courteous when our paths would cross." While acknowledging that Mr. Adler "maintained generally lofty standards against the odds," he added, "Some of his productions were musically uneven (costly established stars cast with inexpensive would-be's), and some looked bargain-basement shoddy." Possibly the most acerbic assessment was made by Martin in a private conversation, when he remarked that it was a pity Adler had been born a Jew, adding, "Think what a Nazi he would have made!"

An inveterate womanizer, Adler went through women like some people go through socks. But that was before he met Nancy, who would become his last wife. Nancy was a wonderful mother and a loving spouse, and Adler's affection for her was genuine. Thanks to her, he became a better dresser, more gracious, and more courteous. He married well, and consequently everyone else could breathe a little easier.

Under Adler, San Francisco Opera rose to become the second house in America and on many nights the first. The repertoire and artists he brought to the opera were often superior. He did *Les Troyens* with Jon Vickers and Régine Crespin years before anyone on this side of the Atlantic knew what it was, and he presented the U.S. premieres of works like *Die Frau ohne Schatten* and the revised version of *Lady Macbeth of Mtsensk*. Not only did he introduce Leontyne Price to operatic audiences in *Les dialogues des Carmélites*, he also provided her with opportunities no one else would give her, and he fostered a production of *Carmen* that featured the first outings of Marilyn Horne and James King in roles with which they would later become identified. At a time when Rudolf Bing on the East Coast was defending his rigidly traditionalistic repertoire and production policies by equating a first-line opera house with a museum with old masters on display, Adler was famously quoted as saying, "Tradition is what you resort to when you don't have the time and money to do it right."

He also had brilliant marketing ideas: when the King Tut exhibition came to town in 1978, for example, there were long lines of people waiting to see it, so he hired a pickup truck and put a piano and singers in the back of it to entertain the ones standing in line; it was terrifically effective. He initiated "Opera in the Park," a free concert in Golden Gate Park

*With Shireen at an outdoor San Francisco Opera performance
at Yerba Buena Gardens, San Francisco, 1997.*

on the Sunday afternoon following the opening night of the autumn season, which introduced the enjoyment of opera to thousands. The Merola Program, which he inaugurated in memory of his predecessor, has done excellent work over the years in the training of young professionals. He also started Spring Opera Theater as a separate affiliate to produce opera in smaller venues, often showcasing young artists and new presentation methods.

His one blind spot was conducting, because although he did bring some good people to the San Francisco podium, his first choice was often himself—and, at best, he was a very good second-rate conductor. The first rank seldom came to San Francisco because he offered so few rehearsals. One exception was the great Karl Böhm, who came in 1976 to conduct a production of *Die Frau ohne Schatten*, an opera composed by his friend and close associate Richard Strauss. Böhm's appearance was made possible by a major gift from Cynthia Wood, an old friend from my Music Academy of the West days who ended up trading the life of a singer for the life of a philanthropist.

Inevitably, the end came. After twenty-eight years of ironfisted rule, Adler had probably made too many enemies. His final mistake was threatening to leave unless the board of directors acquiesced to certain demands. Instead, they accepted his resignation. Even then, he went out with a big bang. What he wanted more than anything was to have Leontyne Price and Luciano Pavarotti do one—just one—*Aida* together. In 1981, Adler's final year, both singers were in town: Luciano was doing his first Radames in *Aida* with Margaret Price, and I was directing Leontyne in *Il trovatore*. By this point in her career, Leontyne had retired Aida from her repertoire, but Adler was not to be denied. He hovered over my rehearsals like a hawk, schmoozing Leontyne relentlessly. I often saw the two of them in the wings with the exasperated Leontyne shaking her head and mouthing "no," while Adler went on beaming and gesturing. One day she told me, "Don't ever show that man a chink in your armor, because he's going to get right in it." Finally he did. Leontyne agreed, but only, according to legend, on one condition: that she be paid one dollar more than Luciano. That *Aida* performance was the one and only time the two artists did the masterwork together. When the smoke signals rose, the city went wild. The opera house was besieged with hordes of people desperate to get in. After the endless curtain calls, Leontyne took Adler's face in her hands, kissed him on the forehead, and said, "That's your going-away present."

During the search for a successor, my name came up, but Adler preferred to champion Terence A. McEwen, a Canadian recording executive. I wasn't offended in the least, as I was happily settled in Toronto.

On Adler's last night in the opera house, there were two parties: one for Adler and his cronies on one side of the house, with another in Terry's offices very conspicuously celebrating Adler's departure. I was one of a very few people invited to both. Terry's party was a bacchanal. Adler's was funereal, like an Ingmar Bergman film set in a half-empty hotel with the only guests over the age of ninety.

Terry McEwen came to San Francisco Opera after thirty years in the record business. Almost single-handedly, he had turned London Records, the U.S. outlet of the British Decca company, into the premier classic label, producing recordings with such artists as Sutherland, Tebaldi, Horne, and Pavarotti, not to mention Georg Solti's legendary first studio production of the *Ring*. Terry knew voices probably better than anyone of his generation. After hearing just a few notes of a record, he could not only identify the singer but also name the studio and recording date. When Terry died, philanthropists Bernard and Barbro Osher financed the acquisition of his large and unique recording collection and donated it to San Francisco Opera. I made sure we created a space in the renovated opera house where the collection could be preserved, and to this day the company's artists, especially its young Opera Center artists, can avail themselves of this remarkable legacy.

Immense personal charm and good taste were Terry's hallmarks. And no one loved the finer things in life more than he did. His cast parties were legendary: he could party on until dawn, long past the point where most of us were yearning for bed. While there was nothing Terry would not do to bring the best artists to San Francisco, he was an indifferent administrator, rarely entering the office before noon.

Terry and I regrettably got off on the wrong foot. One of his favorite London artists was Franco Corelli, and Terry dreamed of featuring Corelli in a recording of Verdi's *Otello*. At the same time, James McCracken was enjoying a great success with the role. To keep McCracken from recording *Otello* with another company before Corelli did one for London, Terry signed Jimmy to a contract that, in effect, kept him on ice. When Jimmy realized what had happened, he sued, and he asked me to be one of his expert witnesses. Thankfully, the matter was settled out of court, and Jimmy went on to make a superb *Otello* recording for EMI. Terry was, of course, aware of the sticky situation, but he never held it against me. He continued to hire me, giving me fine productions and excellent casts. I was never perceived as part of the Adler regime, so I never paid a price.

Sometimes when I met with him, he'd get kind of conspiratorial and tell me that he had a piece of paper in his safe with the name of the person he wanted to succeed him—mine. I always took this as nothing more than a playful compliment. Terry's safe was opened sooner rather than later, as it turned out. He loved life, opera, and voices, but he never

Plácido Domingo and James Morris in Les contes d'Hoffmann.
David Powers, photographer; courtesy San Francisco Opera.

took care of himself, eating rich food, smoking, drinking, and staying up all night. Eventually all of this took its toll, and as a result he planned to retire after only six years on the job.

Ironically, on the day after Terry announced his resignation, February 8, 1988, Kurt Herbert Adler passed away. The same day, Terry called me in Toronto and said irately, "That bastard upstaged my exit!" The news of Adler's death was on the front page of the newspaper, and Terry's resignation was on page 9.

Once again, San Francisco Opera was looking for a general director, and once again my name surfaced. True to his word, Terry pushed for me to take over. The search committee, though, had other ideas, adding my name to a list that included David Gockley, then general director of the Houston Grand Opera, and Ernest Fleischmann, then general manager of the Los Angeles Philharmonic. Coincidentally, I was a particularly hot commodity at the time: in 1987, I had a tremendously successful San Francisco production of *Les contes d'Hoffmann* with Plácido Domingo and James Morris. Even the incurably acerbic local critic Allan Ulrich not only liked it, but called it the "production of the year."

I was flattered to be considered, but I didn't take it too seriously, at least not initially. My name had been bandied about often in recent years, and I'd received several inquiries, mostly from European houses. To be quite honest, I had it pretty good in Toronto. My management team was excellent, our board provided superb support, and the level of artistry had steadily risen. The only shortcoming was our cavernous venue, the O'Keefe Centre. It was the sole reason I might ever consider leaving.

San Francisco had been like a second home to me for years. I would have consistently better productions and casts there, a longer season, and more programming flexibility. And then there was the War Memorial Opera House, a picture postcard of a venue with glorious acoustics. I flew to San Francisco to meet with the search committee, which was headed by the president of the San Francisco Opera Association, Tully M. Friedman, a prominent local investment company executive and philanthropist. Our initial meeting went well, but if I was going to be seriously considered, I had to make certain they knew what they were getting. I told Tully, "I can't audition for you like a singer. You'll only ever know so much through interviews. The best way to learn about me is to see my company. Come to Toronto. Poke around. Ask questions, talk to anyone you want—I'll give you carte blanche. See if I'm what you're looking for." Tully did just that, for two days. At the end of his stay, I didn't take him to some fancy restaurant to pour on the *Schlag*. Instead, I asked Midge to prepare a simple meal, which we ate in our kitchen—exactly the same approach I had used when I interviewed for the job with the Canadian Opera Company.

While the search committee deliberated, I met with David Peterson, premier of the Province of Ontario, one last time. I begged him for a straight answer to one question: was there any chance I might live to see a new opera house in Toronto? Like a true politician, he talked for an hour without saying much of anything. I took that as a no. I had always trusted in my *kismet*, and now I felt it was calling to me. The moment it became clear that I'd never see a new Toronto opera house in my professional lifetime was the same moment I was being considered for the leadership post in San Francisco. Then there was the challenge. I had gone as far as I could artistically in Toronto because of the venue. San Francisco would bring fresh demands. I would have one last opportunity to grow.

I went back to San Francisco for a final round of meetings and threw my hat into the ring in earnest. Maybe I could enter the last stage of my career at a company I knew and loved. The possibilities sparkled in front of me like the lights of San Francisco visible from the handsome hotel suite the search committee had provided. The next morning I was offered the position of general director.

My love affair with San Francisco Opera had been going on now for twenty-five years. Our relationship had been like one of those idyllic same-time-next-year situations you see in the movies. I thought the company was perfect, and the company had smothered me with hugs and kisses. All that changed when I took over as general director. The ideal in my head gave way to stark reality.

I didn't see this right away. Frankly, I didn't have the time, as my first six months in San Francisco overlapped with my last six months in Toronto. I was doing two full-time jobs simultaneously, on opposite ends of the continent to boot. And then there was the learning curve. When Terry took over from Mr. Adler, their tenures overlapped for a full two years. I got exactly three days with Terry; then, on medical advice, he went into retirement in Hawaii.

Any administrator faces a period of adjustment. But no one could have anticipated what I would have to face in my first few years. An unbelievably dysfunctional staff, a protracted strike, and a terrifying natural disaster were just the beginning. Add to that an inert board of trustees, a national economic downturn, and the self-inflicted wound that was my music director, and you might have some idea of what went wrong—and right—during my tenure in San Francisco.

The desk should have tipped me off. It was like some kind of prehistoric fossil. In fact, it was the very same desk Adler had used during his tenure. Terry had inexplicably decided to keep it. Absurdly large—which perhaps explains why Adler, a rather short man, favored it—the thing sprawled over most of the office. I am all for maintaining meaningful traditions, but this one deserved to be jettisoned. One of my first orders of business was to arrange for practical office furniture, something that would enable me to get some work done. Other needed adjustments wouldn't be that easy.

When Kurt Herbert Adler was general director, the entire company revolved around him. No decisions, no matter how trivial, could be made without his approval. He even exerted full control over the rehearsal schedule; often he wouldn't make decisions until late in the day, obliging staffers to make 11:00 P.M. phone calls to let artists know whether their services would be needed the following morning. No other company worked like that. This was hardly an atmosphere in which managers could develop individual initiative.

Under Terry's leadership things actually got worse. Accustomed to blindly following orders, no matter how arbitrary, the staff was suddenly faced with a hands-off boss. A power vacuum developed. Each department more or less pulled up its drawbridge and began operating as an autonomous unit behind its own barricades. All of a sudden, ten senior managers began ruling over their own domains, squabbling with one another and competing for resources and power. Instead of cooperation and teamwork, we were faced with intrigue and suspicion. To add to the chaos, there were no senior manager meetings, as incredible as that may sound. Terry refused to call any, and at the same time he prohibited them from happening in his absence. "All you'll do is talk behind my back," he said. As a result, senior managers never sat in the same room to discuss what was needed and how they could cooperate to get it done. Eventually Tully assumed many of the CEO responsibilities. He even hired a development director and had her report directly to him, all without any input from Terry. Unthinkable. This was the state of affairs I inherited.

I may not be as nefarious as Baron Scarpia, but I'm not Hans Sachs either. In my career, I had been through five changes of administration, and I knew they were difficult, but I'd never seen such a fractured and fractious staff. It took a while for me to fathom the degree of dysfunction. Thank heaven I insisted on having exclusive CEO rights and responsibilities anchored in my contract. The last thing I needed was to compete with another chief executive. Tully came from the tradition of running corporations and serving on committees for conservative think tanks like the American Enterprise Institute, and he was attuned to calling his own shots. When he saw that I was just as determined to do the job I had been hired to do, he grumbled. But he didn't put up much of a fuss. Perhaps he thought he could pull strings from behind the scenes.

The first lesson I ever learned as general director was that if you want a good management team, you need smart and strong people, not yes-men and -women. You also want people who can be persuaded to share a healthy artistic vision. I set about changing the managerial culture of San Francisco Opera, and it turned out to be a long and torturous road.

I immediately instituted weekly senior staff meetings, but these didn't translate into instant cooperation. For three years, the scene had been more than a little like downtown Kabul, with warring factions taking potshots at everyone else. I had my hands full just refereeing all this conflict.

Terry had left me a list of "people to watch out for." He referred to one senior manager as "Lucrezia Borgia," and sure enough, she proved to be remarkably two-faced. She barely knew me, but she would spend the mornings showering me with compliments, then spread vicious rumors behind my back after lunch. Then there was my first assistant, a lady I also inherited from Terry. Although I never found out what I had done to her, she could barely contain her contempt for me. When she finally left, I found a full three months of unopened correspondence addressed to me buried in the nether regions of her desk. My production director had been around for many years—perhaps too many—and seemed shell-shocked. If I needed a yes or no, he'd do an imitation of a tortoise and take refuge inside his shell. After bungling some negotiations, my union guy went off to the Sacramento Philharmonic, which promptly went out of business. The only senior staffers I could relate to were Jenny Green, whom Terry had brought from Covent Garden to run the costume shop, and our extraordinary and selfless music administrator, Dr. Clifford ("Kip") Cranna. For them, the company came first. I began to wonder if I could have them cloned.

Tully acknowledged that management had broken down. His solution was to bring in a consultant from a service organization called Opera America—at great expense, I might add. She had some useful suggestions, but just as many odd ones. A lot of what she proposed didn't take into account the prevalent reality in the various offices. And the people she brought in laid more eggs than an industrial chicken battery. A great deal of money was spent, but not much changed. I thought back to my time in Toronto—the excellent team we had, the environment of cooperation, and teamwork—and decided to bring in John Leberg, one of the key players there, as a consultant. It didn't take long for John to see how things were being done in San Francisco.

Early on, he went to the stage to observe what was supposed to be a technical rehearsal of *La Bohème*. What he found was a troupe of carpenters feverishly cutting a large hole into one of the side walls of the Act I and IV garret set. Aghast, he asked why this vandalism was taking place. He was told that it was "because of Pavarotti." The original entrance came from under the stage, since the garret had been conceived of as an artists' loft overlooking the rooftops of Paris, as clearly stated in the libretto. As a matter of fact, the view of the smoking chimney tops is the first thing Luciano's character mentions, but the tenor refused to climb the few steps involved. The solution, reached without anyone having been consulted upstairs, was to mangle a perfectly good set to provide the famous singer with a generously proportioned ingress to what had apparently become a ground floor apartment. This little episode perfectly captured the bizarre state of the company.

Next John interviewed all the staff members to compile a report on management conditions. With only a few exceptions, the common theme concerned the protection of individual turf, raising the question of whether everybody worked for the same company. So there it was: the report portrayed a group of experienced but aging prima donnas who had no idea where they fit into the structure of San Francisco Opera.

This challenge might have been reduced if I had had a supportive board. Sadly, for the most part the board members were fixated in an upstairs–downstairs mentality. Few of them had the foggiest notion of how opera was produced, but they were totally informed on antiquated notions of class and privilege. I got a jarring lesson early on when I brought my senior managers to a board meeting. They presented various reports, following which Reid Dennis, the chairman of the Opera Association, proclaimed, "And now will the *staff*"—no one could utter the word "staff" with greater entitlement than he did—"leave the room. We have important issues to discuss." I couldn't believe my ears. Virtually every issue up for discussion would ultimately be tasked to these managers. Moreover, having everyone in the same room would certainly facilitate the process of finding solutions. Instead of voicing my objections, I decided to let my feet do the talking. I stood up and began walking out with my managers.

"No, no! Not you, Lotfi," Reid called out, beckoning me to return as if he were calling for more coffee.

"Excuse me," I said, "you asked the staff to leave the room, and I am staff."

It took a lot of wrangling, but eventually our senior managers were allowed to remain at board meetings. Many of the board members found this scandalous; to them, it was like asking the scullery maids and foot-men to sit at the same table with the gentry. As for me, I don't remember how many times I accompanied board members on major solicitations, only to be treated like a glorified porter. Not all the time, of course. There were a few splendid board members who treated me as a professional and a partner. But others merely wanted me to schlep their luggage and hold my tongue. Victorian England would remain alive and well in the San Francisco Opera board room long after it fizzled out in the British Isles, casting a glum shadow on much of my tenure.

The board didn't understand the state of the company and couldn't grasp a vision of its future. There were more than eighty members, but power was concentrated in the hands of just a few—a kind of kitchen cabinet—with Tully wielding the festooned wooden spoon of authority. Tully had no interest in an artistic vision. The name of his game was power. His real desire was to become president of the board of trustees at Stanford University, and he saw San Francisco Opera as little more than a stepping-stone toward that goal.

By this point, I had amassed a fair amount of experience with boards. And I was fresh from a very productive experience in Toronto, where the board had undergone a sea change from inert to dedicated. If that could be made to happen in Toronto, it could be done in San Francisco, I reasoned. I was wrong. In Toronto, the board had made an honest self-appraisal and changed accordingly; some members left, new ones came aboard, and we created a rotation system to make sure that nobody got complacent. I tried to get the San Francisco board to undertake the same self-appraisal and met with nothing but indifference or resistance.

Things came to a head at a retreat I organized at the Clift Hotel. No one took it seriously. I tried to focus on the good of the company, but the board talked only about petty considerations. None of the members would even entertain the notion of asking a peer to resign, even if that peer had done nothing for years. When I raised the possibility of rotation, Reid Dennis said flat out, "If I'm rotated, I'm never coming back." At the end, Tully remarked, "Well, this has been a big flat flop." It couldn't have been clearer that I wasn't going to have much help from the very group that was supposed to be my primary ally.

In fairness, some of the fault lay with me. In retrospect, I see that I should have taken things slower at the beginning. My mistake may have been in pushing the board too hard, and I might have been more diplomatic in my pushing. Enthusiasm and optimism were my undoing, scaring off many trustees. Or maybe I should have been more devious.

Incidentally, John Leberg, the man who was instrumental in helping me get a grip on the state of the company's management, burned out after two years. I sympathized.

LOTFI MANSOURI

❧ 11 ❧

MOTHER NATURE GIVES
AN ENCORE

Everybody wants to be a critic, including, apparently Mother Nature. And nowhere has she vented her critical spleen more devastatingly than she did twice during opera seasons in that beautiful City by the Bay.

In April 1906, the Metropolitan Opera Company took some of its biggest stars on a lavish spring tour across the United States, finally landing at the westernmost point of the route on April 16, where it opened a season of guest performances at the Tivoli Theater in San Francisco. It presented Karl Goldmark's *Die Königin von Saba*, featuring some of the top artists of the company's German wing, including sopranos Edyth Walker and Marie Rappold, along with tenor Andreas Dippel and baritone Anton van Rooy under the musical direction of Alfred Hertz. This was followed by an all-star performance of *Carmen* the following evening, featuring Olive Fremstad, taking a little holiday from her Wagnerian characterizations in the title role, partnered by Enrico Caruso and Marcel Journet as Don José and Escamillo.

The audience response to this performance was tempestuous, but it was nothing to compare with what happened the following morning when, at about a quarter past five, a catastrophic earthquake, measuring 7.8 on the Richter scale, shook the city, destroying one building after another and ultimately sparking a conflagration that consumed everything in its wake, including the sets and costumes for the entire Metropolitan tour repertoire, not to mention the theater in which they were stored, along with the elegant Palace Hotel, where many members of the company were staying.

The stories of what happened to some of the most famous operatic artists of the day would fill a book, and those singers who wrote memoirs invariably chronicled what they had experienced during this natural disaster. Possibly the best-known story was Caruso's exit down the fire escape of the Palace as he clutched his most prized treasure, an autographed picture of President Theodore Roosevelt. Once out of the building, Caruso managed to borrow a car and drove to Lafayette Park in Pacific Heights, where soldiers guarding the entrance would not allow him in until they noticed the Roosevelt picture in his hand. After spending the night on the grass, he made his way to the Oakland ferry, then boarded a train east, vowing solemnly never to return to the city, and he never did.

Eighty-three years later, the ever cantankerous Mother Nature decided to give an encore. I thought all the man-made challenges I had confronted in this idyllic city had steeled me for any event, but nothing could have prepared me for what happened on October 17, 1989, when the Loma Prieta earthquake—a 7.1-surface-magnitude monster, the largest since the 1906 disaster—ripped through the Bay Area, collapsing buildings, freeways, and part of the Bay Bridge to Oakland, starting massive fires, killing sixty-three people, and injuring or displacing fifteen thousand.

I was in my office at the opera house late that afternoon, interviewing a candidate for the position of director of development—a mature and proper woman—when the quake struck. As the floor began to ripple beneath us and things started flying off the shelves, I yelled for her to run to the doorjamb, while I dove underneath my desk. When the dust settled, I slowly poked my head up to see her standing in the doorway, still the picture of propriety.

"Mr. Mansouri," she intoned, "I was told that my interview with you would be exciting, but I didn't imagine it would be *this* exciting."

We evacuated to the open space called the "Ellipse," joined by everyone else from the opera house, including Karita Mattila, Nancy Gustafson, and Wiesław Ochman, who were scheduled to perform *Idomeneo* that evening. We were all shaking, and for the first time in years, I actually lit a cigarette. As we wandered around, trying to collect ourselves, two couples nonchalantly strolled up in tuxedos and elegant gowns. It was a Series A evening, and they had arrived early for the performance, blissfully unaware of the magnitude of what had happened and utterly baffled that there would be no opera that night.

The next day, we began to live out the credo of performers everywhere: "The show must go on!" The opera house was closed and would remain so to anyone for five days, but we had performances scheduled, performers under contract, and audiences who had purchased tickets, so we all needed to find some way to process the jolt we had just experienced. We combed the city, looking for a suitable temporary venue, and seventy-two hours later we were doing *Idomeneo* at the Masonic Auditorium on Nob Hill. Before the performance, I made a short speech, concluding with, "The king is dead! Long live the king!" Life goes on—I felt it, the audience felt it, and our performances celebrated it. On subsequent days, we presented *Aida* and *Otello*. We had to make do with stripped-down sets and basic staging, and we had to perch the orchestra at the back of the stage behind the singers, but we made opera. Each performance was sold out, once again proving how flexible opera can be and how desperately needed this art—indeed any art—is in time of crisis.

The War Memorial Opera House, our jewel of a theater, and one of the main reasons I had wanted the job in the first place, was wounded, perhaps mortally. If it was to survive—and the company with it—it would need structural repairs, seismic upgrading, and more. Oh, God, I thought, the staff is inbred, the board is cloistered in an ivory tower, the budget is iffy, and now this?

The San Francisco War Memorial and Performing Arts Center is a massive complex in the heart of the downtown area, built to honor the men and women of San Francisco who served in World War I. The 3,146-seat War Memorial Opera House, constructed in 1932, originally housed the San Francisco Opera, the San Francisco Ballet, and the San Francisco Symphony, as well as serving as home away from home for myriad visiting performing arts organizations from all over the world. In 1980, the symphony moved to the newly constructed Louise M. Davies Symphony Hall, leaving the opera and the ballet at the opera house. None of the arts organizations permanently installed in the complex actually owns its performance venues; they rent them from the city, and oddly, the city has been something of an absentee landlord over the years, leaving it up to the tenants to maintain their facilities.

When the quake hit, the opera company had just begun its autumn season, with the ballet waiting in the wings to take the stage as soon as our time onstage was concluded. For a while, things were up in the air as to when and how this gem of a building might be usable again.

Fortunately for us, the building complex had become a community treasure, and the population as a whole took a keen interest in restoring it to its former glory. Regrettably, however, many community organizations with the noblest of intentions began forming factions, and the contentiousness that occasionally built up slammed down the brake on progress. With these problems, as well as the more immediate concerns of assessing the damage, planning the restoration, and raising the necessary funds to pay for it, it took some eight years before the opera company was able to return fully to its rebuilt home.

Even before the quake hit, the financing of the opera company had developed into a fairly delicate situation. Initially, the company's short season had been funded by ticket sales with some help from private donations. But over the years, with the growth of ambition and financial developments in general, an ever greater discrepancy came about between box office revenues and the budget needed to operate the company. Added to this difficulty, the educational efforts of many opera companies had resulted in a huge interest in making opera available in a number of cities throughout the nation, not to mention the rest of the world. With the consequent launching of new companies, there was an international competition for top artists and a need to nail their services down at a much earlier point in time, as well as to have the money available to cover those commitments two to five years in advance. As ticket prices went up and general ticket revenues increased, there was still no way these revenues could begin to keep pace with production costs—and this was without the need for major repairs after a natural disaster.

At the time we moved into the Masonic Auditorium, there was still no real news as to the extent of the damage to the opera house; we didn't know whether it could be rectified immediately or whether major renovations might be required to enable the company to use the premises at all. The hope was that the damaged opera house could still be used for performances—at least for the remainder of the current season—becoming more fully available thereafter while decisions were made on what to do with the building. As long as these problems remained unresolved, a sword of Damocles hung over the future of the company and of other organizations that used the facilities. They could be resolved only on a group basis, and so a restoration committee was formed, including representatives of the owner, the city of San Francisco, the opera, the ballet, tenants, and other interested parties, to enact the measures that would be needed and then find the money to finance the effort.

From the outset, it became clear that the city was in no position to assume full responsibility for the restoration or its funding, yet it continued to hold veto power over all the plans under consideration by its tenants. Meanwhile, it had finally been determined that the house could be utilized on a limited basis until all of the problems had been resolved, and then the building would be shut down on January 1, 1996, to undergo major restoration operations.

My tenure was not starting off peacefully, and there were more challenges ahead.

Opening night is typically one of the happiest occasions in the season, but 1990 was anything but typical. Our contract with the American Federation of Musicians (AFM), the union that represented the orchestra, was expiring, and with the start of the season rapidly approaching, we had to reach an agreement. The orchestra members proposed starting the season without a contract while continuing negotiations.

This same strategy had been employed in 1987. Back then, however, the idea of "continuing negotiations" evaporated on opening night, literally a half-hour before curtain time. At that point, the orchestra refused to go into the pit unless certain demands were met, whereupon Tully stepped in and agreed to everything. Now, three years later, I couldn't risk the same thing happening. For the good of the company I simply had to put my foot down. My intention wasn't to play hardball: I honestly believed that a clear mutual agreement was the best one for the orchestra and the company. Beginning a season without that matter settled would have doomed us to a long chain of misunderstandings—as had been the case in the 1987 debacle. So I pushed for the completion of a new binding contract before the start of the season, only to be stalled at every turn. When the orchestra advertised that it had been "locked out," implying that it had not been offered a contract, I moved to settle things as quickly as possible.

During my tenure in Toronto, labor negotiations had been a gentlemanly affair. They usually took one day, unless there were contentions to be resolved, in which case they might be extended to two days. This was a far cry from the situation in San Francisco. The orchestra was musically excellent, but its attitude toward management had been poisoned by a cabal of disgruntled members. Early on, I made a mistake: I attended the negotiations naively thinking this was a show of goodwill. Instead, it set off a lot of yelling and screaming, I left further negotiations to my team. The orchestra shot its first salvo when it presented demands for increased wages and benefits. The musicians wanted parity with the salary scale of the Metropolitan Opera, which is one of the highest-paid opera orchestras in the world. The San Francisco contract was for twenty-three weeks, and it included four weeks of paid vacation and complete full-year health care for the musicians and their families. These were better conditions than I had as general director. When we analyzed the demands, the total increase *over the existing rates* exceeded $18 million for the duration of the three-year contract. Bluntly stated, it would rapidly have bankrupted the company, even without the aforementioned sword hanging over our heads.

The AFM expected us to knuckle under the threat of losing opening night—after all, that strategy had worked in 1987—but we stood our ground. When things came to an impasse, I asked for a professional mediator. The AFM responded by sending additional "representatives" into the fray, including a plumber. For the first time in the history of San Francisco Opera, opening night was canceled. There were no rehearsals or performances for the next five weeks. The company lost approximately $5 million in revenues, although we did realize some savings from the unpaid salaries. Finally, we reached an agreement with an acceptable financial arrangement. More important from our perspective, we advocated and achieved unambiguous language in almost every article to prevent further misunderstanding. These clarifications gave the orchestra a clear knowledge of working conditions. There were fewer causes for anger because everything was spelled out. It was an extraordinary episode, and while arduous, it resulted in a frank exchange of ideas and a document that could serve as an effective foundation for years to come. It was also an important step toward the overall improvement of administrative culture in the company. Little by little, it was becoming easier to get things done.

Although San Francisco Opera might not have lived up to my expectations in those early years in terms of management, it certainly did in terms of artistry. In fact, the stage became something of a refuge where I could escape the slings and arrows of life behind the scenes and remind myself what had made me fall in love with this company in the first place.

Like any newly arrived general director, I had a long list of things I wanted to do. I knew I would have to implement the big, difficult stuff during the honeymoon period of my tenure or I would never have another chance, and at the top of my list was Prokofiev's titanic *Voina i mir* (*War and Peace*). I wanted to make sure we had a first-class, preferably Russian, conductor. He didn't have to be famous, just an outstanding musician. The first thing I did was to get in touch with Ronald A. Wilford, then the president of the prestigious Columbia Artists Management and the world's preeminent manager of conductors, hoping for a recommendation. He proved to be decidedly unhelpful and more than a little condescending. Next I asked Mstislav Rostropovich, but that didn't work out, which was just as well, because he would have insisted the production be staged by his wife, Galina Visnevskaya, a glorious soprano in her day but an indifferent director. Finally, I contacted Ron Wilford's associate at Columbia Artists, Judy Janovsky, who assists Ron with the agency's stable of conductors. Judy had arranged for Christian Thielemann to make his U.S. debut at San Francisco Opera conducting *Elektra*. When I asked her about a conductor for the Prokofiev work, she recommended an unknown Russian and arranged for us to meet over dinner at the Savoy Grill in London.

From the moment we shook hands, I felt as if I were caught up in a whirlwind. This young man, just thirty-seven years old, spoke impeccable English and talked with boundless passion, his eyes blazing with a mesmerizing intensity. After ten minutes, I was totally captivated. I engaged him on the spot. His name was Valery Gergiev. The production was nothing short of a triumph.

But there was just as much drama offstage as onstage. Gergiev brought along thirteen singers from his Maryinsky Theater, home of the prestigious Kirov Ballet and Kirov Opera companies in Saint Petersburg. On August 19, 1991, we were rehearsing the burning of Moscow in the Napoleonic Wars. The same day, a group of unregenerate old Soviet Communist leaders staged a coup d'état, sending troops and tanks into Moscow in an attempt to remove reformist leader Mikhail Gorbachev from power. In a way, Moscow was again burning. It was an unbelievable coincidence. Reality was imitating art. Our Russians were understandably unnerved, and we brought television monitors into the rehearsal hall so they could watch the news from their homeland. I'll never forget the raw emotion rushing over the stage that day: we were sharing a watershed

With Valery Gergiev, 2006.

moment with a group of people who had become like family to us. Later in the rehearsal period, one of the Kirov mezzos had a gallbladder attack and needed hospitalization. She received a bill for $35,000 and had no way of paying it. We organized a "Gall Bladder Gala" at the Russian Community Center on Sutter Street to raise funds. (When we called the Russian consul general for support, he sent us five cases of vodka—that was it!) Paul Plishka, Ann Panagulias, and many others contributed their talents, and Gergiev accompanied them on the piano. It was a lovely evening, and we raised $26,000, which I sent to the hospital along with a note asking them to write off the rest. They did.

While working on *War and Peace*, Gergiev and I spent a lot of time talking shop. I had always loved the Russian repertoire, and I felt it was underrepresented in American opera houses, largely because artists really familiar with the music were generally unavailable. When I mentioned my affection for Glinka's *Ruslan and Lyudmila*, Gergiev got animated as only he can. We looked at each other and instantly thought of a coproduction. Incredibly, the Kirov still had some of the original drops from a legendary 1904 production built to celebrate the centenary of Glinka's birth. We decided to have those re-created by the great designer and painter Thierry Bosquet along with more than seven hundred exquisite costumes, all handmade. The work was done at the Kirov's production shops, and we covered the entire $300,000 cost. If this sounds like an odd arrangement, consider that if the same work had been done in the United States, it would have cost more than $4 million.

I directed both the Saint Petersburg and the San Francisco productions, and the experiences in the two cities were as different as night and day. Since the fall of the Soviet Union, the Kirov had become notoriously chaotic. Organization was poor, and rehearsal routine was nonexistent. A number of my colleagues had lost their professional minds working there—enough for me to take notice. Going in, I was determined to hold mine together. In my wildest fantasies, I could not have begun to anticipate what I was in for. The sheer logistics were mind-boggling. I had to stage 175 choristers, 160 supers, and 65 dancers. Even under ideal circumstances, this would have been a monumental challenge, but these conditions were anything but ideal. As a matter of fact, it was wall-to-wall bedlam, with people coming and going as they pleased, all talking simultaneously at the top of their lungs. The only way I could communicate any staging instructions to this crowd was to match the volume level—and then yell out each direction at least thirty times. Thank God I had six weeks, because it took me two weeks just to stage the chorus for Act I. One day, things finally spiraled totally out of control. The stage was a complete madhouse, with hundreds of people milling around, doing everything but listen to me. I had promised myself that I wasn't going to fall apart, but all of a sudden I began giggling uncontrollably, and I couldn't stop. I literally got hysterical. Much to my amazement, I wasn't spirited off to the nearest collectivistic snake pit; in fact, this fit of hysteria was the best thing that could have happened to me. Suddenly everyone froze and gaped at me; apart from the sound of my laughter, everything was quiet. Maybe they thought I had lost my mind, and for all I knew, I may have been close. In any event, my "losing it" enabled me to take control of the rehearsal, and once I regained my composure, we soldiered on. Just before opening night, the chorus asked to see me, and I came rushing in, anticipating another crisis. Instead, I was showered with hugs, kisses, tears, and gifts. Over and over, I was told how much everyone enjoyed working with me. "If you love me so much," I said with a smile of incredulity, "why did you make me suffer?" Everyone roared with laughter. The Russian sense of humor is decidedly an acquired taste.

At the time, the Maryinsky was divided into opera and ballet fiefdoms. The differences between the two of them were stark. Members of the better-known Kirov Ballet lived like honored guests in a five-star hotel with upholstered armchairs, plush draperies, and fresh food in the canteen. The opera was more like an austere barracks with wooden chairs, bare windows, and thin porridge. Perhaps most ominously, the ballet had toilet paper and the opera didn't. I took to keeping a supply on me at all times.

Our *Ruslan and Lyudmila* was a terrific success, and from here the floodgates opened. Over the following years, we collaborated on productions of Prokofiev's *Ognenny angel* (*The Fiery Angel*) and *Obrucheniye v monastïre* (*Betrothal in a Monastery*), Borodin's *Knyadz Igor* (*Prince Igor*), and Mussorgsky's *Boris Godunov*. In short order, we became known as the opera company spearheading the cause of the Russian repertoire in America.

By 1998, Gergiev's career had begun to skyrocket, as I knew it would. I dearly wanted to continue our relationship, but it was not to be. When the Metropolitan saw what we had, it made him an offer he couldn't refuse, nor could we even begin to match it. The Met paid $7 million to subsidize the Kirov for a three-week residency at Lincoln Center. Next it named Gergiev its principal guest conductor, and at the insistence of Joseph Volpe, the general manager, the contract had an exclusivity clause: Gergiev was prohibited from conducting at any other American opera house. We haven't seen the Kirov and its extraordinary maestro since. But I'll always have the satisfaction of knowing he burst onto the American scene on my watch in San Francisco.

In 1980, when the San Francisco Symphony moved to Davies Symphony Hall, the ballet and opera had been able to expand their offerings. Mr. Adler seized the opportunity to develop a "citywide summer season" anchored by performances at the opera house, but also including numerous other organizations, large and small. For the opera, this meant adding performances in June and July, which, Adler hoped, would ultimately lead to increased exposure, ticket revenues, and contributions. The "full city plan," however, collapsed, leaving Adler holding a fistful of contracts with principal artists as well as the orchestra and chorus; in fact, he had committed the company to a summer season for years to come. And so San Francisco now had two seasons: one that ran from September to December, and another one that ran in June and July. Terry more or less followed the Adler pattern, shuffling a few things around but not really addressing the inherent problems—or potentials.

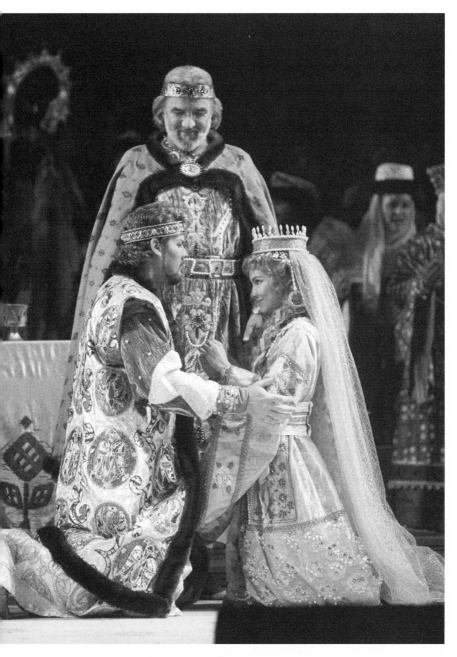

Ruslan and Lyudmila, *with Anna Netrebko as Lyudmila,*
Jeffrey Wells as Ruslan, and Gábor Andrassy as Svetozar.
Larry Merkle, photographer; courtesy of San Francisco Opera.

From the outset, the summer season should have been fully integrated into a season-long slate of events, but instead it became a forlorn, stand-alone, occasional affair. There were artistic successes but no consistent programming and consequently no consistent audience. The board became convinced that the summer season was a money loser and began pressing us to trim or cut it altogether. This didn't make the costs go away. Plans—even half-baked plans—continued to mean signing major stars years in advance. The chorus and orchestra were still under contract, so even if the board demanded the cancellation of the summer season, it would still have to be paid for. This was the primary explanation for something I hadn't expected to find when I arrived: a deficit that had been accumulating for years. No one had even mentioned this, and it certainly wasn't publicly known. In fact, most of the staff had no clue. San Francisco Opera had a major and distinct problem, one I knew couldn't be allowed to continue, certainly not with the major renovation effort looming ever closer on the horizon.

The obvious solution, it seemed to me, was to combine the autumn and summer seasons into a single, if "spread-out" season. This way we could realize savings and efficiencies, for example, with marketing and scheduling, and also generate an increase in ticket revenues by offering full-season subscriptions. But it soon became obvious that the board members could not fit the idea into their preconceived notions of life in their aristocratic world. "A full-season subscription including the summer?" one member inquired in befuddlement. "But that's when we always go to Europe." Another one flatly stated that subscription performances in the summertime couldn't happen because they might interfere with her forays back to the East Coast to pick up her children from college or visit "the lake." I decided that, for the time being, it would be more prudent to concentrate on showing them that, even if it didn't turn out to be a cash cow, the summer season at least need not be a money loser. If we could have a few successful summer seasons, maybe I could convince the board that the spread season was the next logical step.

In the face of massive indifference and more than a little hostility, I managed to program *one* opera in 1989: Philip Glass's *Satyagraha*. In addition to this, two important ballet companies presented programs using our orchestra. In 1990, we did Wagner's *Ring*, something that is only an occasional project for a company, unless you're Seattle Opera. As big as the *Ring* is, I decided to think even bigger for 1991. Adler's idea of a citywide event had merit, but it had failed because of a lack of leadership. In 1991, the year of the bicentennial of Wolfgang Amadeus Mozart's death, I decided to take up the challenge. I organized a Mozart Festival, a citywide program of performances, films, lectures, and all kinds of community events, one of the biggest of its kind anywhere. The participants included San Francisco's "Big Three," the ballet, the opera, and the symphony orchestra, plus the American Conservatory Theater and a slew of smaller groups. Larger organizations contributed $25,000 each, and smaller ones gave $100; regardless of size, every group got equal promotion in 250,000 brochures and other media. It was going very well until the symphony's music director at the time, Herbert Blomstedt, decided in a spasm of Scandinavian gloom that he would take advantage of the historical event being commemorated to open the Festival with Mozart's *Requiem*; that piece was the composer's final work, written feverishly on his deathbed and completed after his untimely demise a few weeks before his thirty-sixth birthday by his pupil Franz Xaver Süssmayr. Imagine launching a joyous festival celebrating the career of one of the most life-affirming composers in history with a funeral mass! Of course, the *Requiem* is an undeniable masterpiece, but I think we would have been wiser to follow the example of Vienna, where the Mozart year was *concluded* with a performance of the mass on December 5, the actual death anniversary, at the majestic Saint Stephen's Cathedral.

At the press conference, I was asked about this oddity, and I somehow managed to keep a straight face when I said, "Actually, it's an excellent idea. We open the Festival with the *Requiem*, and then we do a flashback." Chalk one up for my histrionic talents—I actually came across as enthusiastic.

The Mozart Festival was an unqualified success. Crowds thronged to events put on by Bay Area organizations large and small, from the well known to the unknown. I wanted to prove that summer in San Francisco was ideal for performances, and that's just what I accomplished, but it had cost me a lot of time and energy. I couldn't run a festival and an opera company at the same time. When it ended, I called a meeting of the participating companies. We were now looking at 1992, a Rossini year, celebrating the 200th anniversary of the composer's birth concurrently with his fiftieth birthday, as he had been born on February 29. Everybody expected me to manage the project once again, but I said, "I can't do this two years in a row." I was exhausted. Nobody else stepped up, and the idea of an annual citywide event fizzled out.

I went back to producing stand-alone summer festivals for the company. We celebrated Rossini in 1992, adding a new production of *Guillaume Tell,* and commemorated Richard Strauss in 1993, adding the composer's *Daphne* to the repertoire. All in all, we were achieving increasingly promising results. Finally, summer seasons were being accepted. We were on a roll, or so I thought. For 1994, I planned a French Festival, including Offenbach's popular *Les contes d'Hoffmann,* the Gluck rarity, *Iphigénie en Tauride,* and Berlioz's *La damnation de Faust* featuring Frederica von Stade, Jerry Hadley, and Samuel Ramey. We hoped to culminate the festival with the American premiere of Olivier Messiaen's *Saint François d'Assise,* using the Salzburg production staged by Peter Sellars and conducted by Kent Nagano. And then—just like that—the board members pulled the plug on the whole project. Too expensive, they said. No one wants to come to summer operas, they added. I howled, I cajoled, I reasoned—all to no avail. We had been building audiences and revenue for three years. If we threw that away, we'd have to start again from scratch. The board wouldn't budge. That fabulous French Festival became a desultory series of concerts featuring the singers we had under contract. I offered the symphony our cast for *La damnation de Faust,* and it jumped at the chance; the production was a tremendous success, one that should have been ours.

Part of the reason the board was so intent on canceling the 1994 French Festival was that the national economic downturn that had begun in the early 1990s was slowly becoming a full-blown recession. It was, of course, a totally legitimate concern, but canceling the summer season was not the solution. Once again, it meant a lot of expense with no resultant income. More important, it destroyed the awareness of the summer season as an integral part of our annual program, something we would have to overcome yet again in the future. To be sure, the recession obliged us to make painful cuts; at one point, we made a major reduction in administrative staff. Still, I was adamant that the stage should be the last place to suffer. We continued to contract first-tier artists, and we got very creative with our productions. In 1994, for example, I engaged Gerard Howland to make the sets for virtually every show for the season. It was exciting to have so many new productions, but the real reason we did it was that Gerard essentially created a mammoth

Guillaume Tell, *with Timothy Noble as Tell and Janet Williams as his son, Jemmy. Larry Merkle, photographer; courtesy of San Francisco Opera.*

unit set that could be arranged in different ways for different productions. These weren't always the greatest or the most visually exciting productions, but they were respectable, and more important, they were inexpensive. And our musical standards continued to be high: among the many highlights of that season was Massenet's *Hérodiade* with Plácido Domingo as Jean, Dolora Zajick in the title role, Renée Fleming as

Hérodiade, *with Renée Fleming and Plácido Domingo.*
Larry Merkle, photographer; courtesy of San Francisco Opera.

Salomé, and Gergiev in the pit. Our sets went lean, but our artistic quality remained superb.

In 1995, I returned to the citywide festival format. It meant more work than I had time for, but I simply couldn't turn away from the occasion. The world was celebrating the fiftieth anniversary of the United Nations, which had been founded in San Francisco. In fact, the concluding ceremonies were held at the War Memorial Opera House. I was determined that San Francisco Opera would play a role in making the occasion one to remember. We helped to organize events and performances by all kinds of organizations. Our own program included a single performance of Gluck's *Orphée et Euridice* and touring performances of Prokofiev's *Lyubov k tryom apelsinam* (*The Love of Three Oranges*) and Gershwin's *Porgy and Bess*. It was a good effort, but it wasn't the lengthened opera season I had envisioned.

The special events were something else. We welcomed three presidents of the United States—Bill Clinton, Jimmy Carter, and Gerald Ford—as well as 140 ambassadors to the United Nations. I had our resident artists, the Adler Fellows, sing at the opening ceremony, and while there was a lot of pomp and circumstance, my fondest memories of that evening involved two of the Fellows, a married couple. She was pregnant and just beginning to show, and he had yet to tell his family back home in Serbia. The ceremony was broadcast all over the world, though. His family tuned in and put two and two together. We may have been celebrating the United Nations at the opera house, but one family in Serbia was more interested in its newest member.

Local magnate Walter Shorenstein made a major donation to support the festival and immediately began throwing his weight around. He wanted to make sure he would be rubbing shoulders with the famous and powerful as much as possible, while dealing imperiously with everybody else—an interesting take on the spirit of the United Nations. I had to ensure that the festival would run smoothly, and Walter was in a position to run roughshod over my efforts. He might have succeeded had I not ended up having an unforeseen advantage. As it turned out, the U.N. representative who served as the liaison (and de facto chief of the whole event) just happened to be an Iranian—a cousin of the former shah, in fact. Needless to say, she and I became fast friends. When I needed something, I would sidestep Walter and go straight to her. Walter had to be very cooperative with me, which was a refreshing turn of events.

That's the only explanation I can think of for what he did to me and the opera just a year later, taking flagrant advantage of us at a delicate moment in our history.

In 1988, I thought I was coming to a perfectly organized company, where the only challenge would be to create great art. By 1995, my main challenge was keeping ahead of the crises. Change was hard won, but substantial. We finally had a functioning management team, one that was getting better all the time. I was chipping away at resistance to the idea of expanding our season. Finances were in reasonable shape: our budgets were balanced, or close to it. Donations and ticket income were rising steadily, and the endowment was growing nicely. Relations with the unions had dramatically improved. Performances were of a consistently high quality, and we were doing loads of company premieres as well as numerous new productions. And I had found some allies on the board.

However, one big question loomed over everything we did: what would we do when the opera house closed for renovations and repairs? I didn't exactly know, but I was sure of one thing: how we handled this episode in the company's history would have an impact for years to come.

Our world had changed after the Loma Prieta earthquake. For eight long years, uncertainty hovered over everything: performances, finances, leadership, audiences, our home, our future. The company would not be back to normal until we fully reckoned with the fallout of that fateful day. In a way—and I can say this only from the comfortable perch of retrospection—it was almost a blessing in disguise. "Normal" at San Francisco Opera up to that point carried its own excess baggage. Having to grapple with the consequences of an earthquake might give us an opportunity to jettison some of that superfluous matter—maybe even make us stronger. Again, I can say that now. At the time it was pure hell.

I couldn't have done it without help. In this context, I need to thank a lady who shall remain nameless, because I'm sorry to say I have forgotten her name. In 1990, Tully Friedman threatened to resign as president of the board of directors if she were made a member. She was, and he did. While I no longer had to contend directly with Tully, his immediate successors brought in issues of their own. Tom Tilton, who headed the board from 1990 to 1993, was a dear man, but he was far too congenial for the job. Still, Tom was passionate about the company, beloved by staff and artists, and generous to a fault. When he left this earth far too early, he bequeathed a large gift to our endowment, and it has been used to sponsor several productions. Then came David Chamberlain, who served from 1993 to 1995.

Finally, in 1995, a prominent local attorney named William W. Godward was named president. Here was one of the most incredible instances of *kismet* in my entire professional life. I couldn't have asked for a better partner, ally, or friend. With Bill's help, I would be able to guide San Francisco Opera through the unprecedented, potentially company-killing challenges that lay ahead. Anyone who has any feeling at all for San Francisco Opera should thank the operatic gods that Bill became board president at that critical juncture. I certainly did.

Of course, as planning for the restoration proceeded, most of us on the staff were concerned largely with the refurbishing of our performance facilities, but the issues arising were even greater than that, as Mr. Godward pointed out in a summary of events he kindly provided for this book:

> There were public issues to be considered as well. First of all, air-conditioning. The theater had once had a fairly large but rather antiquated system, which apparently had fallen out of use. Fortunately San Francisco weather much of the time is clement enough without air-conditioning, and so it was decided to air-condition vital areas and hold the rest of it for some future time. Nevertheless, the cost would come to some ten million dollars. Then there were seating arguments. We wanted staggered seating, but an inspection showed that most of it was already staggered, which meant we could ignore this problem. The cost factors for everything, though, were so large that it was determined to do the work that required the total shutdown of the house and then add other improvements in short periods of times or implement them incrementally in between operations and performances.

It's an overstatement to say we began to plan the instant the earth stopped shaking on October 17, 1989, but it's not all that much of an exaggeration. After our five days in the Masonic Auditorium, when we were finally allowed back into the opera house, cosmetic damage was evident everywhere—cracked plaster, broken glass, and so on—but it wasn't immediately clear if the house would have to be closed down. As we gingerly soldiered on in the crippled house, we entered into a delicate balancing act.

When the quake hit, we weren't even halfway through the 1989 autumn season. When it became clear that the opera house wouldn't have to be closed immediately, we did our best to continue according to the plans we had made beforehand, but we still had one conspicuous symbol of our uncertain situation: I'll never forget the day workers screwed a steel net right beneath the theater ceiling to catch chunks of falling plaster. Ungainly, but effective, like a huge Band-Aid, it was a constant reminder that, sooner or later, the patient would have to undergo surgery.

After a lot of wrangling, we hammered out a budget. Of course, the city did hold an insurance policy on the building, to the tune of $60 million, which might have covered the entire restoration had the city taken better care of its property. Public funds would take care of all the work required by law: seismic upgrading, compliance with the Americans with Disabilities Act, and the like, but the ballet and the opera would have to pay for any sorely needed improvements to theater technology and backstage areas: lights, rigging, dressing rooms, that sort of thing. These hadn't been refurbished since the house opened back in 1932! Making these improvements would create an extra financial burden, but it would also be a once-in-a-lifetime opportunity. If we did this work, we would be able to mount better productions and take better care of our artists, which in turn would also benefit the audience. We made a wish list of every possible improvement we wanted, from stem to stern. The price tag came to $65 million, but our consultants told us we could raise only around $30 million, which meant we would have to tighten the belt on our ambitions. Finally, we announced a campaign to raise $28 million, hoping that this more modest goal might be exceeded, something that would make for good press.

As we prepared to close the house at the beginning of 1996, we planned to remain closed for eighteen months, hoping we could open our 1997 autumn season in September, as usual. But we had two last-minute scheduling issues. The contractor needed to begin preliminary work before the end of 1995, so in addition to an opera season, we had to contend with demolition, detours, and workers roaming about the halls. Then came the real shock: at the eleventh hour, the contractor told us the eighteen-month closure we had planned would have to be extended to thirty-six. At a crisis meeting, we determined that we could handle one season out of the house, but two or more would kill us. Bill analyzed the schedule and determined that if the contractor were to use back-to-back shifts, he could complete the work in the envisioned eighteen months with no increase in costs. Fortunately, we were able to put out these flash fires as quickly as they flared up, but it was like having a few minor heart attacks with no time to rest up.

Those six long seasons leading up to our move were turbulent. We had to duct-tape ways around the damage and make adjustments to productions, scheduling, and the like. It was all we could do to stay on top of things, but we did get a lot of goodwill and support. Our solo artists, the chorus and orchestra, stage hands, and staff rolled with the punches. Our audiences and the general public seemed to understand what we were going through, and they continued to fill the house and rally round us. Only one group was conspicuously unsupportive: the local critics, who became even more petty and vicious than before. Apparently they had no idea what we were facing or what was at stake. When we finally vacated the house, they even upgraded the nitpicking.

There was one final surprise. In its sixty years of existence, the opera house had become a repository for thousands of odds and ends stored in every conceivable nook and cranny. Some things belonged to the city, some to the opera, some to the ballet, and others were unaccounted for. There was no time to figure out who owned what. The city and the ballet buried their heads in the sand. We took on the responsibility and the expense and had everything stored in one mammoth warehouse, to be sorted out later. Once again, the opera was assuming full responsibility for something that cried out for cooperation. It was a pattern that could not be allowed to endure.

Nothing could be accomplished without our board. It would have to sign off on any plans, help generate public support, and write some fairly hefty checks. From the outset, I knew that most of the members would never be able to regard the closure as an opportunity. In fact, by that point, I knew them well enough to anticipate their response: "Shut down the company for the duration!" I decided to sneak up on them by doing some research, working out some options, and trying to anticipate every question. The key, I knew, would be to make the board members think they had done all the work and come up with all the answers, and were thus entitled to take the full credit. I might have been away from Tehran for more than a half-century, but when the occasion demanded I could still wheel and deal as deviously as the most cunning rug peddler. I began to do double duty, running an opera company and trying to coordinate a massive project. My only real ally was Bill Godward, who shared my vision and did everything possible to make it happen. It was a case of Bill and me against the rest of the world for a long time.

First off, I began to scour the city for potential temporary venues. Only a very few had the number of seats we would need. The instant I walked into the cavernous Civic Auditorium, I thought, "Wow, this is a real possibility." It was only a block away from the opera house; the environs—parking, restaurants, and so on—were already familiar to our patrons. Of course, there were also some question marks. There was no pit. Because of its size, we would probably need to use some kind of electronic enhancement. The Civic Auditorium had also been damaged in the earthquake, but fortunately the opera had a great friend at city hall. Rudolf Nothenberg, then the chief administrative officer of the city, was in charge of the repair schedule, and he arranged to have the Civic Auditorium work done by the time we needed to move. We couldn't have asked for a greater favor.

Rudy, incidentally, had an intriguing childhood, which ideally suited him for the civic duties he would subsequently assume. He had escaped Nazi Germany with his family via China, finally settling in the huge exile community in Shanghai. He is still fluent in Mandarin and thus able to communicate with San Francisco's huge Chinese community in its own language.

About this time, a lightbulb went on over my head. In recent years, the composer and philanthropist Gordon Getty had been pushing his idea of presenting opera like a Broadway musical, with multiple performances per week, rotating casts, and moderate ticket prices. In theory, ticket revenue would cover the production. He had actually approached the Metropolitan Opera about doing such a production on Broadway. Despite his commitment to covering the entire $15 million cost, the Met's general manager, Joseph Volpe, turned him down, sending him a pages-long, single-spaced letter, which, diplomatically but definitely, said, "Thanks, but no thanks." If I had to guess, I'd say this was simply too complex a task for people at the Met—they would have had to engage a second orchestra, chorus, and crew—or maybe they thought it just wouldn't work. However, a production along those lines would be perfectly suited to our out-of-house period. We already had an orchestra, chorus, and crew under contract. We just needed a way to produce. I approached Mr. Getty, and he agreed to fund two "Broadway-style" productions, one each in 1996 and 1997. This was on top of his generosity to the opera house renovation and his annual contributions to our general operating fund. This would give him an opportunity to test his theory, and we would have at least one production to offer.

Now all we needed was an appropriate Broadway-style theater. Fortunately, there were a few options: the Curran, the Golden Gate, and the Orpheum, all owned by Walter Shorenstein, the same guy who thought his contribution to the U.N. commemoration was a free ticket to hobnob on Mount Olympus while tossing table scraps to the underlings. The Orpheum was the logical choice, as it was just around the corner from the Civic Auditorium. I approached my old friend Walter, and he agreed to rent the Orpheum to us for 1996 and 1997—at a hefty price, of course. There was only one problem: the Orpheum's pit was too small, and expanding it would cost $500,000. Once again, I went to Mr. Getty, and once again he came to our rescue. That got me thinking: if we now had a theater that could accommodate an opera orchestra, why not use it for productions during the regular season? After all, while the Civic Auditorium would be perfect for big arena-style operas, we couldn't do a whole season of those. The cost was prohibitive. The Orpheum could accommodate smaller-scale productions. Having a second venue would also alleviate scheduling and rehearsal issues. One season, two locations.

Things were beginning to shape up. Now for the hard part: getting the board . . . on board. If I had to convince the members all by myself, it would never happen. Their favorite refrain by this time was, "Shut down the company!" I had heard it so often, I could have it set to music. Perhaps the anvil chorus from *Il trovatore*, complete with thwacking hammers, would be the appropriate musical setting:

> Shut down the company,
> That stratagem's a honey!
> Shut down the company
> And save a stack of money!

Very few board members seemed to have the imagination to contemplate keeping the company running. The few who sympathized with me—great civic leaders like Dede Wilsey and Bernard and Barbro Osher —were vastly outnumbered by the naysayers and the "silent majority." Fortunately, Bill Godward was perhaps the only person who held sway with most if not all the members. Everyone knew and trusted Bill. He had never held a grudge, never done anything underhanded. Through-out his years of quiet, dedicated service, he had always put the company first. Even the most jaded board members couldn't ignore him. When Bill talked, everyone listened.

He also anticipated a lot of problems well in advance and implemented plans that helped us evade many snags before they could happen. To quote him again: "One issue—a major one—was to be sure that anything built, purchased, and installed for either of our temporary venues could be ultimately brought back to the restored opera house and used there, as the opera was paying for all of this."

We began to present our ideas, starting out with the area we knew would get the most attention: finances. Yes, producing a season out of the house would cost money—a lot more than an average year. But it would also result in ticket revenue and contributions. Going dark meant no income at all. If we told our ticket purchasers and donors to take a year off, we might lose many of them for good. Then there was the matter of fixed costs: if we shut down, our financial obligations wouldn't magi-cally disappear. We would still have contracts to honor, and these ran into the millions. And what about the staff? Would we lay everyone off? Imagine the bad feelings that would create, the loss of talent and institu-tional memory, and the difficulty in rebuilding it all when the time came. The cost of that alone would be astronomical. Finally, I pulled out my ace in the hole: an analysis showed that if we shut down, our total debts would ultimately exceed the $20 million in the endowment, meaning bankruptcy. It all finally came to a Hobson's choice: either we would try, and perhaps fail, or else we would just curl up and die.

Then there was our obligation to the community. Our subscribers and patrons had stood by us year after year; we owed them our best effort. The opera is San Francisco's largest performing arts organization, draw-ing thousands of tourists who spend dollars at restaurants, hotels, and other attractions, all of which would be affected by a suspended season. Not to mention the fact that San Francisco had justifiably earned the title of "the City That Knows How." We had to do our part to turn those pretty words into action.

It was a Herculean task. As if we didn't have enough problems with the logistics in general, we discovered that our plans for the Orpheum might go up in smoke, as the ballet had smelled a good thing and put a "hold" on the premises behind our backs. Fortunately, the ballet began having second thoughts, finally releasing the place well in time for us to move in as projected. But this was not the only run-in we would have with our twinkle-toed fellow minstrels.

With the issue of the Orpheum resolved in our favor, I began to lay out some options. We had two possible venues, both within a stone's throw of the opera house. Two productions—the "Broadway-style" shows—were funded thanks to Mr. Getty. The unions, already on notice, would make every accommodation for necessary waivers, and principal artists were willing to put up with the inconvenience. The staff was more than willing. Since we would be temporarily freed from the scheduling restrictions of the opera house, we could spread our season to include January and February performances, giving us an opportunity to test whether people would attend opera in those months. And we could ensure a high level of revenue by maintaining our seating policy. Priority was based, in part, on loyalty and contributions, meaning that anyone who wanted good seats in the renovated opera house would be . . . ahem . . . well advised to maintain subscription and contribution levels during our out-of-house period. If this sounds a bit like extortion, let me say in our defense that this was becoming a survive-or-die proposition. If anyone was angry about that bit of coercion, I was hoping to be forgiven once that individual had seen what we had done.

Fund-raising wouldn't exactly be straightforward. We would need to raise money for an opera season—something we were used to doing year after year—as well as procure onetime funding to relocate our administrative offices, make the temporary venues workable, and then move back. The total for this, even minus the projected ticket revenue, was estimated to be $25 million. On top of that, we would need to raise money toward the $28 million goal for the opera house improvements. To avoid having competing campaigns, we decided to make one "save the opera" effort, making it possible for a donor to support the company, the opera house restoration, or both.

We knew the money was there, but we also knew it would take some convincing to get people to swing wide their wallets. Bill and I hosted no fewer than sixty-five cocktail parties (he estimates the figure at eighty) to present our ideas. I engaged Gerard Howland to turn the Civic Auditorium into a viable place for opera, and he made a model of the proposed setup. Over and over, we trotted it out, stating our plans to board members, major donors, civic leaders, and anyone else who would listen.

An early godsend, a major grant from William and Rosemary Hewlett, without which I doubt we would have been able to proceed, was followed by sizable donations from Bernard and Barbro Osher and Richard Goldman, as well as many other contributions, giving us some reason to think some of our major patrons approved of what we were trying to do.

With these major gifts, the options I'd presented, and Bill vouching for everything, slowly but surely board members began to come around. About two-thirds of the way through our series of parties, we started to sense a shift in mood. In particular, the board silenced its "Shut down the company" chorus. At a special dinner, one of the last in the opera house before it closed, two board members not only applauded our efforts, but also wondered out loud, "Why would we do anything other than what we were doing?" I was incredulous.

As 1996 approached, there was a mad rush of activity. Crews cleared the stage, and about one hundred staffers packed up files, furniture, and equipment. In one wild weekend, everything was moved to temporary offices on Market Street, overlooking U.N. Plaza.

While the temporary offices were more than adequate, getting anything done in them became an exercise in pain management for me, as I had to contend with the noise pollution generated by a gentleman of no discernible aptitude, who was exercising his constitutional right of free expression by playing one clinker after another on the saxophone underneath my window for the duration of my eighteen-month stay. To this day, I cannot hear a saxophone solo without my blood pressure going briefly stratospheric.

There was also some unexpected bad news. The $28 million campaign was supposed to have been a joint effort between the opera and the ballet, and as we were the larger organization, we offered to do the lion's share. The opera would raise $18 million and the ballet $10 million. Instead, the ballet concentrated on raising money exclusively for itself and stopped taking our phone calls. We had to pick up the slack; we had neither the time nor the resources, but we had no other choice. That didn't stop the ballet from showing up for all the photo opportunities. It left us holding the bag and then took a bow when the campaign was successfully completed. The ballet was the institutional equivalent of a bad stage colleague who makes himself look good at your expense.

We had two temporary venues, but it wasn't as simple as just turning on the lights and raising the curtain, and from time to time, there were surprises.

Walter Shorenstein was charging us an arm and a leg to use the Orpheum, but we were responsible for making the place opera-ready. With Mr. Getty's funding, work commenced on expanding the pit beneath the Orpheum stage.

First up was our "Broadway-style" production of *La Bohème*. It ran for four weeks and was an unqualified hit. We attracted forty-five thousand patrons, more than 60 percent of whom had never attended an opera before. Ticket sales went through the roof, and the town was buzzing: San Francisco Opera may have been out of the opera house, but it was still alive and kicking. This was exactly the sort of start I had hoped for, and it was probably crucial for convincing some of our hesitant patrons that operas at our temporary venues might be a good thing. As busy as I was, I attended many of those performances, if only for a few minutes here and there. It was simply a pleasure to see so many fresh faces, all trying opera for the first time. During one intermission, a young couple dressed to the nines approached me with big smiles, telling me how much they were enjoying the show. They did have one question: "Is this the original Broadway cast?" I kept a straight face. Their exuberance was touching and emblematic of the run as a whole. We had created a Broadway *Bohème* long before Baz Luhrmann made headlines with his version— and we offered our audiences the original musical score.

My delight with our success was dimmed by Walter. Shortly after we closed, he notified us that we couldn't have the Orpheum for our June 1997 "Broadway-style" production of *Madama Butterfly*. Just like that. Case closed. It didn't seem to concern him in the least that we had a contract and that we had paid half a million dollars to make a good orchestra pit in his theater. I was at my wit's end. We had been moving heaven and earth for months, and this was the last thing we needed. Shorenstein offered us the inferior Golden Gate Theater, located about a quarter-mile away in a decidedly grungier and more crime-prone part of town—for a price, of course.

We had very solid grounds for litigation and seriously considered taking the matter to court, but it would have taken years to settle. Then there was the more delicate matter of the 1996–97 main season, which included three productions at the Orpheum. These were unaffected by Walter's plans, and we had already begun selling subscriptions. If this thing got ugly, he could really screw us over, leaving us without a place for these productions and putting us in the unenviable position of having to refund some $5 million in tickets. Although it galled me, I swallowed my pride and accepted his demands, resigning myself to the Golden Gate instead of the Orpheum we had spent so much money refurbishing. Walter gave me his crooked smile and said, "Fine, let me take you to lunch."

"Walter," I replied grimly, "I'm not hungry. Oh, and by the way, they're doing a remake of *It's a Wonderful Life*, and I'm suggesting you for the role of Mr. Potter." He didn't take offense. He'd never heard of the movie.

Our main season was set to open at the Civic Auditorium in September. In a sense, we were returning home. San Francisco had used the Civic, apart from two years at a place called Winterland, from its first performance in 1923 until the opera house opened in 1932, and now we were back there. Unfortunately, but unsurprisingly, the seismic work was behind schedule, and we weren't able to move into the Civic until a scant eight weeks before opening night. In fact, when we did move in, work was still being done. If that sounds like a lot of time, consider that we had to move everything in, essentially create a theater, and rehearse the first few shows, all with the clock ticking. A great deal of the construction was being done at our scene shop off in an area of the city the locals had dubbed Dogpatch, then assembled at the Civic. For example, there was the new stage with more than six hundred sections, all built at the shop, numbered, trucked over, and pieced together like a gigantic jigsaw puzzle. The house had a big ring of seats, but none in the center (the equivalent of the orchestra section), so we built temporary seating, including "boxes" featuring seats brought over from the opera house. We priced the extra one thousand seats at $15 and $8, attracting a lot of young people.

We had to figure out dressing rooms and the like; as it turned out, these were very far away from the stage, which meant increased lead times for entrances and exits, which in turn meant that production books had to be revised. Finally, there was so much extra room at the Civic that we were able to create a true patron's lounge, something we couldn't do at the opera house. I had it decorated with set pieces from our lavish production of *La Gioconda*, which marked the birth of our Gioconda Lounge. Excited by the possibilities, Bill checked in on our progress often, bringing doughnuts for the crews every time he came.

Opening night in the improvised quarters at the Civic Auditorium while we were out of the War Memorial Opera House. The opera was Prince Igor. *Larry Merkle, photographer; courtesy of San Francisco Opera.*

It seemed as if the hammering, sawing, and painting would never end. Because of the delays, we wouldn't have as much rehearsal time as we had envisioned. I knew some of our directors and designers would bristle at this, and it was clear that I'd have to set an example. I was directing our *Carmen*, and I had technical elements—lights, scene shifts, and so on—completed in just a few days. Now if anyone protested over a short rehearsal period, I could truthfully say, "It can be done. I did it." The flurry of activity belied meticulous planning. Anything used at the Civic was purchased with the thought of bringing it back to the renovated opera house, as Bill had foreseen. And so, while we were buying a lot of new stuff, most of it would be put to long-term use. This took a great deal of planning, but we felt it was the only fair application of the donations we were receiving.

Our opening-night performance of *Prince Igor* was rough—the test drive, so to speak, of many things to come, including the video monitor system installed so that Sergei Leiferkus, Elena Zaremba, Paata Burchuladze, Jeffrey Wells, and the other singers could see conductor Alexander Anissimov, who was actually behind them along with the entire orchestra. The audience was more than understanding, they were downright appreciative. You could sense a special electricity in the house that night. They were willing to go all the way with us on this little adventure. We had built it, and they had come. Word spread, and more wallets opened.

We pulled off a number of coups. The Civic had a thousand more seats than the opera house, so we were able to offer a lot of cheap tickets, and most of the less expensive seats were filled on any given night. Our Gioconda Lounge, with dinner service and room for two hundred people, was extremely popular. While we had to use electronic sound enhancement, our sound designer, Roger Gans, came up with a brilliant and original approach: he wrote out meticulous cues that called for mikes and speakers to be hot only at specific times, thus avoiding a generic overall sound from area microphones. These cues were called from a production book, much like lighting cues. This way the sound had specific direction and came across as more natural. In addition, we were able to avoid embarrassing moments, as had happened a couple of decades before on Broadway, when this sort of technology was still in its infancy and one soprano toddled into a backstage restroom complete with a live body mike, volubly regaling the audience with what is normally regarded as a private moment.

Without any scheduling limitations, we were able to produce for the first time in January and February, and attendance did not appreciably diminish. And whatever anyone might say about our venues and productions, no one could quibble with our casts: Olga Borodina, Jennifer Larmore, Karita Mattila, Ruth Ann Swenson, José Cura, Thomas Hampson, Ben Heppner, and Dmitri Hvorostovsky, to mention a few of the most prominent, are not exactly garage-sale artists.

Whatever we did in our temporary quarters, if they had carped mercilessly at some of the austerity measures necessary in the earthquake-damaged house, the ladies and gentlemen of the press had a field day weighing in on all kinds of problems attributable to the special out-of-house situation, simply taking it for granted that conditions in a fine-tuned opera house could be transferred to any other location without a hitch. Nothing seemed to evade their eagle eyes, no matter how tangential. One critic, for example, flaunted his acuity by complaining that some of the crowd costumes in *Aida* had been seen before and went on to carp about the Ethiopian prisoners looking "too white." The reason for this was simply that there were no showering facilities at the Civic Auditorium, and so we decided to dispense with the body makeup. The alternative would have been to send everybody out in the street, bring in fire trucks, and then sell tickets to that spectacle.

Another critic called attention to the way we handled the swan boat in *Lohengrin*, invariably invoking the classic remark made by the great tenor Leo Slezak when some overzealous stagehands somewhere in Europe pulled the boat past him into the wings on the other side of the stage, whereupon he called out, "What time is the next swan?" Believe it or not, the critics even bellyached about the artists who had to be replaced because of illness. It was that petty.

When the smoke cleared, we had produced a 1996–97 main season of ten shows—seven at the Civic and three at the Orpheum—and lived to tell the tale. I got one last surprise on closing night at the Civic. After the final bows, there was a commotion in the wings, and I saw people moving toward the stage. I had no idea what was going on until I began to recognize faces: makeup artists, costumers, choristers, stagehands, production crew, music staff, more than a hundred people in all—each one carrying a suitcase. I get chills to this day remembering that moment. Soon we would be going home.

Our last out-of-house production was the Broadway *Butterfly*. By this point, we had no spare money to make the Golden Gate suitable for opera, and what little we did have needed to be spent on extra security and shuttle buses. There was no pit, so we made do with an orchestra on the floor in front of the stage. We gave a total of twenty performances, and while they were not as successful as the *Bohème*, we still managed to attract thirty-six thousand patrons. Even in the face of man-made adversity, we were not just surviving—we were surviving with style. Incidentally, the reason Walter had kicked us out of the Orpheum was that he wanted to expand the stage to accommodate a lavish (and lucrative) touring production of *Miss Saigon,* a much-watered-down version of the *Butterfly* story.

Occasionally somebody mentions the time we spent out of the house, complimenting me on all the "planning" and "organization" that must have been involved, but in fact I never actually had the time to make any sort of master plan, and even had the time been available, I wouldn't have had enough support to make a gargantuan effort of this scale work. What I did was keep all the options open, see what could be done, and slog through one day at a time. It was a day-to-day challenge just to get by.

At one point in the restoration process, there was another crisis to confront. A fire had broken out in the box area of the opera house. Fortunately, it was quickly extinguished, but this event, too, threatened to put a crimp in our schedule. After everything we'd been through, I just couldn't conceive of our not moving back in time for a new season. The damage was huge, but any major delay would hurt us financially, and the injury might prove fatal. We had to open.

Then another glitch came about toward the end of construction. The city and the committee had arranged with a bank to finance the restoration and pay the bills to the contractor as they fell due, advancing money based on the city's funds along with signed pledges from donors. Suddenly the committee and the city were informed that the pledges were insufficient to cover the required advance payment to the contractor. In fact, we still needed $2 million, or else the contractor would not be paid and the project would stop. Fortunately, two of our dedicated patrons stepped in, and we were able to guarantee the necessary funds based on their own private promise to guarantee them. In the end, the opera and the committee came up with the funds, and the patrons didn't have to meet that obligation, so what could have been a fatal episode was averted.

Finally in August, less than a month before the opening of the 1997 season, we moved back. There wasn't much time to ooh and aah over how beautiful and new everything seemed. We had a lot of work to do. The offices would be chaotic for a while, but I knew our staff could handle that challenge. I was more concerned with the stage. We needed to be able to handle all our splendid new equipment instantly to get our productions up and running. Unfortunately, our rigging system was undergoing teething problems. We'd click "up" and the sets would descend, or vice versa, that sort of thing. The days passed, and the problems persisted. We were getting dangerously close to the start of the season. I wasn't too worried about opening night—the event was the Seventy-fifth Gala Concert—because as long as the lights and the curtain worked, everything would be fine. But I was concerned about our operas. We had yet to do any technical work on our opening production of *Tosca*, let alone the shows that would follow. One of the major problems was finally exposed. A crew chief pulled me aside to inform me of what he considered

The lineup of stars at the reopening gala, 1997.

a serious situation. All the rigging had been jumbled. Not only did it not work properly, it might pose a danger for anyone onstage. This was supposed to be the responsibility of the renovation coordinator—the "turtle" I had inherited from Terry and Adler—but apparently he had shown no inclination to do anything about it. It turned out the crew chief was absolutely right. When the "turtle" learned what had happened, he cornered the crew chief, who was his subordinate, and yelled at him about "chain of command" and other such drivel. If our conscientious crew chief hadn't blown the whistle on the situation, we might have had some injuries to contend with. The "turtle," however, was more concerned with appearances. After this little explosion, corrections could be made.

Still, we were losing time. I had engaged the great English director John Copley to stage our *Tosca*, which would be a re-creation of the inaugural production staged by Armando Agnini to open the opera house back in 1932. With time running out rapidly, I had to face the possibility, however, that it might not happen. I took John to lunch and laid out the facts: Technical elements were unknown. We might have to give a concert version in costume. Decisions would have to be made, probably at the last possible moment. And all of this was the purview of the general director; I was the only one who, just hours before curtain time, could say, "Bring me some furniture. We're doing a concert." I asked him to

With Leonie Rysanek, at the seventy-fifth anniversary of the San Francisco Opera and reopening of the house, 1997.

With Beverly Sills, our mistress of ceremonies at the reopening of the San Francisco opera house in 1997.

accept another production. He was unhappy and even considered suing the company. But what else could I do? I had a season to open. Our final dress rehearsal was an unmitigated disaster. Nothing worked as it was supposed to. I could only fall back on the old theater adage: bad dress rehearsal, great opening.

I kept an upbeat smile for the public, but in reality I was almost completely worn down from the endless hours, the tension, the uncertainties—and above all, the solitude. Despite the constant support of my wife and the stalwart assistance of Bill Godward, I felt as if I had been facing all the challenges of the past years on my own. It all caught up with me at rehearsals for the Seventy-fifth Gala Concert. As I walked to the podium to run through my speech, I felt overwhelmed. I couldn't breathe. Muttering some kind of excuse, I made my way to the wings, steadied myself on one of the rails, and lost it! Crying, trembling, trying to catch my breath—and then I felt arms wrapped around me. It was one of the wonderful chorus ladies, hugging me from behind. She said nothing, made no fuss. She just knew. I instantly pulled myself together. It was the only moment in the past eight years that I had allowed myself to fall apart.

The Seventy-fifth Gala Concert was the official unveiling of the renovated opera house. Despite the premium prices, it was the hottest ticket in town, so hot, in fact, that we transmitted the performance in full to Symphony Hall so that another large audience could share the occasion with us.

Before it started, I had the house lights turned down as low as possible, and the ushers guided people to their seats by flashlight. In keeping with tradition, the concert began with the National Anthem—but I had arranged a twist. I had a scratchy recording led by Gaetano Merola pulled from the archives. After a few bars, Donald Runnicles brought in the orchestra, and the recording faded. Little by little, I had the house lights brought up, reaching maximum brilliance at "And the rockets' red glare." Only at this point could the audience witness the full splendor of the renovated opera house, the impeccable gilding, the sky-blue ceiling, the glittering chandelier. Everyone went wild with applause, and backstage my heart leaped.

We were home.

12

LEAVING MY HEART

I managed to open *Tosca*—barely. Conductor Nello Santi and our stars, Carol Vaness, Richard Margison, and James Morris, rose to the occasion, and the production introduced a young basso from Canada making his San Francisco debut in the small but important role of Cesare Angelotti. He was one of our Adler Fellows, John Relyea, who would ultimately have a huge impact on the operatic world. In short, we were back in business—and from there, we settled into our season. There were growing pains, countless last-minute crises, and a learning curve when it came to our new equipment, but each day we got more and more comfortable. When all was said and done, our first season back in the house was a technical shakedown period, handled so skillfully that our audience didn't know that we were learning as we moved along.

Even in the glow of our successful return, many board members began to settle back into their old patterns. Now that we were back, they started showing less and less interest in what I had to say, especially when it came to my other plans for the company. Bill Godward remained my only real ally. "Lotfi," Bill told me over and over again, "your problem is that you make it look easy."

Dysfunction, strike, recession—and then an earthquake! It seemed as if a series of plagues were afflicting my first years at San Francisco Opera.

But one problem was entirely of my own making. In addition to running the company, Gaetano Merola and Kurt Herbert Adler had served as conductors. Merola had genuine skill and a total familiarity with the repertoire he conducted. Adler was competent, but exuded a hype that suggested he was Arturo Toscanini and Leonard Bernstein rolled into one. By the time Terence McEwen took over as general director in 1982, it was clear that the company needed an experienced, capable music director, someone able to conduct, hire musicians, consult on repertoire, and advise on casting—in other words, to do what Merola and Adler had done previously.

The man Terry chose was Sir John Pritchard, a distinguished English conductor. I had worked with Sir John in Europe and often joked that he conducted Mozart as if he were weaving a tea doily. He brought a good reputation to the opera house, but Terry had contracted him for only ten weeks per year. That was not enough: a music director has to be in residence for a minimum of five months. I needed to figure out a way to handle this situation so that the company would get what it needed and John received the respect he deserved.

As it happened, circumstances largely took over. Terry had promised John the 1990 *Ring* revival—a mammoth undertaking and, running sixteen hours over four evenings, totally exhausting for any conductor. Wagner was not good for John or for us. I decided to take him to a superb meal, and just as we were getting to the cognac, I said, "John, you don't really want to conduct the *Ring*, do you?" He very sweetly replied, "You know, you're absolutely right, Lotfi! I don't think I should do it." He moved on to his other assignments, but all of a sudden he became severely ill, losing weight rapidly. He was trying hard, but his skills seemed to be evaporating with every passing day. We didn't know it at the time, but he was dying of lung cancer.

John never directly told me about his illness. Not once. I finally figured it out, but played along with the notion that he was just "tired." When he led *Orlando furioso*, I had to engage Randall Behr to stand behind him and do the actual conducting. Some players who didn't know the whole story cruelly started calling them Edgar Bergen and Charlie McCarthy. But I couldn't bring myself to tell John he should stop working. Conducting was all he had left, and he was dying five thousand miles away from home. After the Loma Prieta earthquake, when we performed *Idomeneo* at the Masonic Auditorium, it became obvious to everyone how ill he really was. Nevertheless, he valiantly conducted from his wheelchair, and at the end the audience gave him a tremendous ovation, to which he responded with a gallant salute. When it became clear that he was nearing the end, I arranged for him to return to England, but the day before his scheduled departure, he had to be hospitalized. I was there, holding his hand when he died.

I had lost a great friend and colleague, but I had to focus on the company. We needed a conductor for the *Ring*, not to mention a new music director. Once again, I contacted Ronald A. Wilford at Columbia Artists in New York, who managed the best batons in the world, and once again he proved a sad disappointment. I may have been the general director of the second-largest opera company in the country, and not incidentally, as a stage director, also a long-standing, profit-making client of the agency, who had just made a transcontinental journey to see him. In the throes of self-deception, I thought this might have entitled me to a little better treatment than he would accord a beggar on the corner of 57th Street, but Ron's idea of *noblesse oblige* was to keep me waiting nearly an hour before having me summoned into his office to keep a prearranged appointment. When I was finally ushered into the imperial presence, reminiscent of my audiences with the shah, I flashed my usual Persian smile and said, "Mr. Wilford, do I kiss the ring now?" I then told him that I wanted good conductors in San Francisco, and he barely looked up as he told me, "No, I haven't got anybody." That was pretty much the end of our "meeting."

I now had only about eighteen months to find someone for the *Ring*—a terribly short time period in the world of Wagner. Viennese conductor Peter Schneider, an old friend from Heidelberg, was available for two of the four cycles, and so I engaged him. We needed somebody to second him, and Peter suggested a young Scottish musician named Donald Runnicles, who had just assumed the post of general music director at the opera house in Freiburg, Germany. Hildegard Behrens spoke highly of him. With those recommendations, and not many options, I decided to engage him for the other two *Ring* cycles.

It is always stressful to bring in an unknown, especially to lead something as unforgiving as the *Ring*. The first thing I noticed about Donald was actually the most elemental: he worked lefthanded, one of the very few professional conductors to do so. This requires some adjustment by the orchestra and the singers; for a time, everything looks a little like a mirror image. I might have taken this as an omen: in many respects, my whole relationship with Donald would be topsy-turvy, but that wasn't obvious at the beginning. Donald made an excellent impression with the *Ring*. He knew the music well and got a potent sound out of the orchestra. Critics and audiences loved him. Since he had played a major role in the success of the *Ring*, I began to wonder if he was the right man to be

our new music director. He was young and skillful and seemed to be con-
structively ambitious. I offered him the position, to begin in 1992, and
he accepted. The arrangement was for him to conduct three productions
per year, as well as assist with casting, orchestra relations, and shaping a
distinctive sound for the company.

Donald's first few seasons had highs and lows, which is to be expected
with anyone starting a new job. When he was on, his performances were
very, very good, even electrifying. But when he was off, he was way off.
Sometimes he didn't seem familiar with a score, as if he were sight-reading
it, even in performance. He also had a habit of letting the orchestra over-
power the voices. Ensemble and balance suffered. I began to get the impression that he cared about some operas but not about others, and this
seemed to be turning into a pattern. This was odd, considering he always
had his choice of whatever three operas he wanted each season.

He was inconsistent about his other responsibilities. Sometimes he was
hard-nosed with the chorus, hovering over auditions, putting this one or
that one on probation (then failing to attend the required follow-up hearing). And sometimes it was if he didn't know the chorus existed. It put
a lot of people on edge. He almost never sat through guest conductors'
performances, something a music director must do to evaluate talent and
ensure that musical values are upheld.

Donald's behavior became so weirdly insecure that I couldn't help
thinking back to my college psychology courses (which focused on children with special needs). Guest conductors should be a boon to any opera
house, but Donald was more than reluctant to put out the welcome mat.
He refused to share, giving himself eight orchestra readings and allot-
ting only one or two to guest conductors. I took Donald to lunch one day
and told him, "You are the music director of a house that has excellent
conductors, like Gergiev, Dohnányi, Schneider, Santi, and Pappano. You
should be proud."

But he wasn't. He was jealous, especially of anyone he suspected might
be better than he was. He showed absolutely no intellectual ambition.
Other conductors, like Patrick Summers and Christian Thielemann,
are voracious readers, but I never saw Donald pick up a book. When I
worked with him on an incredibly profound piece, such as *Death in Venice*, we couldn't discuss the deeper aspects. At the same time, he began
making demands: more money, more time off to travel, and funding for
special projects (such as recordings featuring himself).

The relationship between a general director and a music director should be like a good marriage. You need to respect one another, and you must believe you're both working for the same goal: the success of the company paying your salary. If you can't trust your partner, you're up a creek. Unfortunately, some music directors start well, but when they don't get their way, they start working behind the general director's back. This is what happened to me. I should have moved much, much faster to correct the problems. In fact, I should have hit the brakes when things started going downhill. I'm not trying to make excuses, but it was an extremely stressful time, and I had so many other priorities that dealing with Donald was not on top of my list. It should have been.

Our chorus director, Ian Robertson, provided a sorely needed counterweight in the music department, dispelling some of the nastiness with his skill, scholarship, and good nature. I loved his jokes. He kept everyone around him loose, and that is a priceless trait in an opera house. Chorus directors are often better musicians than conductors are. When you have a good one, it's important to provide opportunities to lead performances, and that's what I did with Ian. I should have gone farther. If I had it to do all over again, I would have made Ian responsible directly to me rather than subordinate to Donald. It was my mistake, and I hope he will accept my apology.

I was also blessed with a magnificent principal guest conductor, the legendary Sir Charles Mackerras. Here was an elder statesman to complement our young music director.

I tried hard to secure the services of guest conductors on Sir Charles's level. One of the most interesting possibilities worked right next door. I thought it would be fabulous if the conductor of the San Francisco Symphony, Michael Tilson Thomas, would also work at the opera. I tried to get him many, many times. We would sit and talk about quite a few projects, but I finally came to realize that he was afraid of opera. Or rather, he can do opera only on his own terms. He said he wanted to conduct *Don Giovanni*, for example. I said wonderful, then he said no. Instead, he wanted to do *Tristan und Isolde*. Finally, he settled on *La damnation de Faust* with Thomas Hampson, but the minute it was announced that Hampson was doing this work in Salzburg as well, Michael said he had lost interest. After that I gave up. We had so many 8:00 A.M. coffees at his house, but it was all a waste of time.

As I worked my way through one crisis after another, I had hoped

Donald Runnicles would be more supportive, but no such luck. I had made a great mistake signing him to a five-year contract. It should have been three years, with the first two as a kind of probation period. After five years, it was too late. I had my hands full keeping the company alive, and I didn't have the time or the energy to counter him. By the time his contract expired, there was no way I could get rid of him. He was already signed to another five-year term.

Fortunately, my chain of command had me reporting to my friend Bill Godward, the president of our board, who oversaw the running of the company, while the board chairman acted, in Bill's words, as the "conduit to the public," chairing board meetings and recruiting well-to-do donors. This probably explains why Donald decided to drive in a wedge by currying favor with Reid Dennis, the long-term chairman, and, on his retirement, with his successor, Franklin Pitcher ("Pitch") Johnson. Soon the board had polarized into factions: Bill and I plus a few well-meaning trustees were on one side, while the chairmen and Donald formed a junta on the other.

Once he had solidified his position, Donald's behavior became even more erratic and self-serving. It was everything I had seen before, only worse. I could only close my eyes. The company had overcome so much, and we were making so many positive strides toward being a better, more functional organization. I knew Donald would hang like a dark cloud over everything. It turned out that his cloud was parked largely right over my head. My contract was set to expire, and Donald began pushing for a new general director.

I had been planning to retire anyway. It had been a hell of a ten-year ride, and I was ready for a rest, but Donald wanted to make sure he had a hook into determining my successor. It was a bold move, but by this point the chairman and the junta were under Donald's spell. There was one last thing, however, I wanted to accomplish at San Francisco Opera: the transition to the spread-season format. I had been working on this project ever since my arrival, and I was in a unique position to make sure it got done. The board, pushed by the junta, began spending all its time talking about the next general director, forgetting about the critical issues before it, especially the spread season, as well as long-term fund-raising and budget control. As the discussion over the new leadership heated up, the board began spending all its time discussing "what was wrong" with the company. This distressed Bill Godward no end, considering how well we had handled so many complex problems over the past few years, with him as the voice of reason. Donald convinced the junta that Bill, as honorable and selfless a leader as San Francisco Opera has ever had, was merely Lotfi Mansouri's puppet. And the junta disgracefully took Donald at his word. It began overriding Bill and launched a campaign for a new general director—but with one small victory for Bill. My contract was extended by two years, specifically so we could address the issues of the spread season and long-term funding.

After that, I would be more than ready to retire.

The climax of my relationship with Donald came when I was scheduling our 2000–2001 season—my last, as it turned out. I was planning *Der Rosenkavalier*, a work very close to my heart and one of the most complicated scores ever composed, with myriad melodic subtleties along with intricate harmonic and rhythmic progressions that call for the ultimate in virtuoso conducting, from the first downbeat to the final cutoff. I knew from the outset of the planning stage that Donald would simply ruin it with his indifference and lack of preparation. Instead, I engaged Charles Mackerras; as it turned out, this would be his final appearance with the company. Donald was livid, but I held firm. "I just don't think you and I are a good match," I told him. The next thing I knew, his agent had gone to the chairman of the board, who in turn came ranting and raving into my office. A reasoned, adult conversation was not going to work, so I decided to furnish evidence. I had my media guy pull tape from the conductor's monitor to show three different conductors in action: Valery Gergiev in *The Fiery Angel*, Patrick Summers in *Louise*, and Donald. It was evident when you compared the three that Valery was dynamic, Patrick had total, cool control, and Donald was a cipher. I showed the chairman the tape, but he didn't understand what he was looking at.

Donald was one enemy I had seen coming. There would be one more, who appeared at the last minute. Patrick Markle, my production director, began to sniff opportunity with the coming regime change, and he immediately began pushing for more power and influence. He had been pressuring me for a while to have Jenny Green, our costume director, report to him rather than directly to me. I knew this was because he was jealous of her skill and popularity. I refused to give in to this suggestion. He also began to press the company to replace our supertitle technology with Met Titles—conveniently, as it turned out, as he owned a major stake in Met Titles.

There is an old adage to the effect that the most important journeys are determined by the destination, not the route. We had survived innumerable problems, ones that probably should have capsized us, but we had made it through to our goal with a bit of élan, and that gave us the momentum to continue moving forward. The level of professionalism and cooperation among the staff had improved dramatically. Relations with our unions were much better. And with our sparkling opera house, we were able to focus on the best possible productions. Finances, despite all we had been through, were in decent shape—no more duct tape. Our years of struggle had made us stronger.

The capstone of our institutional makeover was the spread season. At the Civic, with our performances in January and February, we had proved that we could have a successful subscription season beyond the confines of the traditional September to December format. I wanted that to continue. We had to contend with the ballet, which moved into the opera house in December for the inevitable stream of *Nutcracker* performances, and then, after a brief period at the beginning of the year when the house was closed for maintenance, the ballet presented a season from late January to May. As I looked at the calendar, I saw that we could extend our season at least into early January if the maintenance could be done later in the year. I worked with the War Memorial to move the maintenance period to July, when neither the ballet nor the opera was producing. After a lot of discussion, the people at War Memorial agreed to the change, and San Francisco Opera's main stage season moved into January.

It wasn't as easy as saying, "Okay, presto, change-o, the January and summer operas are now part of the subscription season." Every department in the company would have to adapt to a new way of doing things so that we could produce, promote, and fund productions through a unified organization. What had been an off-and-on operation would have to become a single, yearlong effort. The board finally approved this plan, beginning in the 1999–2000 season. Twelve years had elapsed since I had first suggested a spread season.

Like any general director, I have had my share of regrets: the productions and artists that got away and so on. But there is one production I should go out of my way to mention: *Arshak II*. In 1997, Gerard Svazlian, a member of the opera orchestra, asked me about scheduling an opera by an Armenian composer. I had never heard of any, so I remained noncommittal; after all, I was constantly being asked to program this or that work. Gerald, however, was as persistent as they come. He wanted an Armenian opera at San Francisco to coincide with the 1,700th anniversary of Armenia's conversion to Christianity, which was rapidly approaching. The more I demurred, the more insistent he became. It got to the point where I was nervous just walking down the hallway for fear he might be lurking around the next corner, ready to spring at me and buttonhole me with yet more of the glories of Armenian opera. Finally, I did something rash. I said, "Gerard, go raise me a million bucks, and I'll do your opera." I should have remembered from my boyhood in Tehran how close-knit Armenians can be, and how resolute they are when they want something.

Much to my shocked amazement, Gerard actually raised that princely sum, and then I was stuck. A cultural advisory committee was organized, consisting of authorities on Armenian history, literature, art, and culture. In due course, that committee proposed *Arshak II*, an opera by one Tigran Chukhadjian, written in 1868 to an Italian libretto by the Armenian poet Tovmas R. Terzian. The plot, based on historical events from the fourth century A.D., concerned "the violent struggles waged by King Arshak for national unification during a period of bitter internal revolts and external hostilities with Persia and Byzantium." The obscurity of the theme was matched only by the obscurity of the composer.

We used a newly constructed version of the original score, mounted a fine production by the ultra-professional Francesca Zambello, issued flowery press releases trumpeting our glorious discovery, threw a gala opening, promoted it as a major company premiere—and harvested the ridicule of almost everyone whose surname didn't end in "ian." Chukdakjian was called the Armenian Verdi, and *Arshak II* was touted as something similar to *Nabucco*. In reality, it was nothing short of a total flop, and the single worst repertoire choice I ever made. I still cringe at the flak I took for that fiasco.

Now the board had a new refrain: "Change the company." This was what the members said they wanted the general director to do. When they announced that I would be succeeded by Pamela Rosenberg, they would get their wish and then some.

Our tenures were scheduled to overlap a full eighteen months, from early 2000 to the start of the season in 2001. When Pamela arrived, I cordially welcomed her, arranged for office space, and assigned one of my best staffers to assist her. Her appointment was the board's doing, and whatever feelings I might have had about it, I certainly had nothing against her personally. She was a fellow professional doing her job. During the entire eighteen months, she didn't solicit my opinion about budget matters, repertoire choices, board members, fund-raising plans, or donors. And eager not to exert any pressure on her, I never attempted to offer her any advice she might regard as unwelcome. I think I might have helped her avoid some mistakes. For example, I could have shown her that the last time we had done *Così fan tutte*, we had lost $500,000 on six performances; when she programmed *Così* in 2004–5, she scheduled thirteen performances and lost a fortune.

Terry had left me a list of people to watch out for, and I should have done the same thing for Pamela. At the top would have been Donald Runnicles and Patrick Markle, who, the instant she arrived, stopped talking to me and spent all their time getting chummy with her—as if she and I were somehow competing! Both of them had been instrumental in her appointment, and it soon became clear that both thought they could control her and push their own agendas. I also should have warned her about the board junta, describing in lurid detail my own experiences with those people, but I didn't want to be regarded as meddlesome.

I began to see changes in my plans for seasons beyond 2001. This is normal during a transition period, but what shocked me was the sheer volume. Pamela canceled one contract after another, costing the company millions. Then there was the matter of *Silk*, an opera I had commissioned from André Previn. Although nobody had heard one note of it, she simply canceled it, costing the company hundreds of thousands of dollars, a sum that was taken out of the budget for my final season.

By this point, I had been shut out of the process completely. I had a very telling luncheon with Pitch Johnson. He told me that he was covering the cost of buying out all those contracts, blithely adding, "You know, Lotfi, I also considered buying out your contract."

I had poured my soul into that company for forty years, but Pitch understood the world only from his point of view as an investment banker accustomed to bullying CEOs. With my Persian smile firmly in place, I said, "Pitch, that would have cost you a bundle!" I meant it.

I never made my concerns publicly known. Instead, I concentrated on my last season, working with some of my best-loved artists and producing some of my favorite works, including the world premiere of *Dead*

Man Walking and a lavish production of Rimsky-Korsakov's *Tsarskaya nevesta* (*The Tsar's Bride*) starring such international luminaries as Anna Netrebko, Olga Borodina, and Dmitri Hvorostovsky. The last months of my tenure consisted of starting rehearsals for the 2001–2 season and tying up loose ends. On my last day, I walked out of the opera house with decidedly mixed feelings, but happy that I was leaving the company in far better shape than I had found it. San Francisco Opera was a much more professional operation, the season structure had been resolved, finances were stable, and the city's beloved opera house was iridescent. Despite everything, we had maintained an enviable level of artistry, producing dozens of company premieres and featuring first-rate talent, while introducing a phalanx of handpicked young artists who wasted no time making international names for themselves. The company's annual budget had increased from $28 million to $54 million, and along with that, contributed income had risen from about $7 million to $24 million. The day I arrived, the endowment stood at $12.7 million, and the day I left, it was $45 million. Everyone was more interested in what Pamela would do than what I had done, but that was fine with me. I had nothing to be ashamed of, and more than a little to feel proud of.

One modest little marketing tool my team and I came up with was a source of particular pride and perhaps best summarizes my attitude toward serving the theater by serving the community. Taking advantage of San Francisco's status as perhaps second only to New York as a major international tourist magnet, we decided to establish a link with our many visitors by inviting hotel concierges, taxi drivers, and other members of the hospitality industry to our dress rehearsals. They showed up in droves, they departed wreathed in smiles, and they praised San Francisco Opera to the skies when tourists asked them what there was to do in this radiant gem of a city. This way we showed San Francisco's best side to all those out-of-towners while providing a genuine cash cow for the company.

In many ways, Pamela turned out to be like Terry when it came to leadership and management: a power vacuum developed, and certain managers started jockeying for position. The second I retired, Donald leaped into action. Among his first orders of business was to cancel the position of principal guest conductor, which was then held by Patrick Summers. Patrick went on to become music director of Houston Grand Opera, then headed by David Gockley. Donald also began to assign more

Ann Panagulias and Hans Hotter in Lulu. *Marty Sohl, photographer; courtesy San Francisco Opera.*

and more operas to himself, far more than the three per year called for by his contract. As he was getting paid by the performance above and beyond his salary as music director, his compensation suddenly went through the roof, which shocked the union. For other productions, he began bringing in second-rate conductors with depressing regularity, continuing to assign several staging rehearsals to himself while leaving just one or two to the others. If I had to guess, I would say he was intent on making sure no one would look better than he did—that weird insecurity again. As for Patrick Markle, he carved out a realm for himself. I had shielded Jenny Green from him for years, but Pamela quickly acquiesced to his demand to have Jenny report to him. Jenny immediately quit and went to Los Angeles Opera, a great gain for that company and a huge

The Tsar's Bride, *with Anna Netrebko and Dimitri Hvorostovsky.*
Larry Merkle, photographer; courtesy of San Francisco Opera.

loss for San Francisco. With all of Pamela's ambitious new productions,
Patrick would have the budget of a king for at least a couple of seasons.

I knew when Pamela arrived my stock would plummet, and indeed
I was accused of running secret deficits, promoting mediocre programming, and avoiding the fashionable trends of *Regietheater* that were all
the rage in large parts of Europe while nonetheless being decried with

the somewhat less than flattering term of "Eurotrash" in much of the rest of the world. One Saturday, Pamela called me out of a clear blue sky to say that she was just sick about a story that was about to be published in the *Wall Street Journal*. Before I read it, she wanted to explain and apologize. The article, she said, misquoted her as having said I had left San Francisco Opera in a terrible financial state.

"Pamela," I replied, "isn't that what you've been telling people all over town anyway?" I tried to say this with my tongue firmly implanted in my cheek, but it was the truth. As San Francisco Opera's financial woes increased, Pamela had taken to saying that I had nearly run the company into the ground. Maybe she was just parroting a story that was being fed to her by the board, but by this point, I had run out of patience and good-will. I had my lawyer send a letter to the board of directors essentially saying that if there was any more of this kind of slander in print, they could look forward to a major libel suit.

I had been contracted to return to the house to direct three productions in Pamela's first season, but after all the ill feeling that had arisen, I decided to drop out of two of those productions. I did, though, come back to direct a gala production of Franz Lehár's *Merry Widow* because the sets and costumes had already been made. Apart from the premiere of that production, I did not attend a single performance at San Francisco Opera during Pamela's tenure.

At the same time, I did have some compassion for her. She may have arrived to waving palm fronds, but I knew how fickle and finicky our board could be, and from the news filtering from the opera house, I knew she wouldn't last. Whatever one might think of her artistic choices, and the jury will probably be out forever on that issue, the numbers tell the tale during her tenure. San Francisco Opera lost twenty thousand subscribers. She canceled Western Opera Theater, the last remaining opera tour in the country and a valuable training ground for the company's young artists. The January performances I had worked so hard to get into our spread season were cut. Perhaps most seriously, she had much of the company's inventory of productions destroyed, I presume in anticipation of creating all new productions, which didn't happen. She did have a few impressive productions built, but apart from a *Barbiere di Siviglia*, the company hasn't revived any of them, and there doesn't seem to be much interest on the part of other companies to rent them. The result was ultimately a financial double whammy: today the company has to rent most of its productions, which costs money, but it doesn't have much of an inventory to rent out, meaning it brings in very little rental income.

Pamela had good motives, and her artistic taste was unique—certainly for North America—but asking her to run San Francisco Opera was like engaging a baritone to sing Norma. The fit was fundamentally wrong. She may have been a native Californian, but she had never really worked here, and her European experience did not prepare her for the social and fund-raising aspects of the job. I found her to be a shy, introverted person, and the larger-than-life demands of the general director's job must have taken a terrible toll on her. I believe she had been set up by Donald, who imagined he could manipulate her, and by the board of directors, which made promises it had no way of keeping.

In some ways, the board was as naïve as Pamela. Those people really didn't understand that she had *no* experience in fund-raising and no temperament for it either. Nevertheless, they promised to back her, totally unaware of how expensive this promise would prove to be. Pitch Johnson put in something like $15 million of his own money, but even with that, the deficit ballooned. I remember once reading a board member's claim that the deficit was only $200,000 and laughing out loud. In Pamela's final year, the deficit was a crippling $7 million.

Ultimately, her allies behaved like rats on a sinking ship. At least I had always been able to count on Bill Godward. Pamela had no one at all. When the board finally woke up to the writing on the wall, a huge sum was put up to buy her out. When her "retirement" was announced, I sent her a note congratulating her on her artistic efforts and expressing sympathy for the situation in which she found herself. She had been misled by self-serving individuals, I wrote, and I meant that with all sincerity.

Tides turn. When Pamela was forced out, many people suddenly started remembering me with a good deal of fondness. Someday, Pamela will find herself "rehabilitated" as well. That's how it is in our business.

As the search for a new general director began, Donald Runnicles and Patrick Markle, true to form, suggested themselves as a team to succeed her, with Donald serving as artistic director and Patrick as general manager. Their offer was turned down, but, oddly enough, they were offered spots on the search committee. This must have led to some awkwardness. Surely both of them knew that if a capable successor were to be named, there would be no more room for them at San Francisco Opera, and that's exactly what happened. Patrick is now heading a seat-back titling company in Santa Fe. Donald did manage to hold out until the end of his contract in 2009. He is being replaced in San Francisco by a conductor of truly international format, Nicola Luisotti. I can't help reflecting on the irony of the gala honoring Donald on his departure, featuring the massed forces of the opera house in a grand performance of the Verdi *Requiem*—a magnificent work but symbolically, like Herbert Blomstedt's Mozart commemoration, a mass for the dead.

Pamela has been succeeded by David Gockley, with whom I have been friends for well over forty years. In fact, back when we were all at the Santa Fe Opera, Midge and I gave a party to celebrate David's twenty-first birthday. In the course of his administration, he has invited me to stage some revivals of my old productions; one of these was *Der Rosenkavalier*, but I turned that down when I found out who would be conducting. As far as other productions were concerned, there comes a time when it is more satisfying to enjoy the memories of past successes, and heaven knows, there were plenty of them.

During my time at San Francisco Opera, I experienced the highest highs and the lowest lows of my entire career. One moment, I would be euphoric over a company premiere, a commission, or a debut artist. The next minute, I would be crushed by intractable management woes or the board's antipathy. I found myself blessed with the greatest of friends and hounded by the bitterest foes. Never in my life had I been on such an emotional roller coaster. In fact, I think I have yet to grapple with my nearly forty-year relationship. It's still coursing through my heart.

13

AN OPERATIC VOICE FOR
NORTH AMERICA

At some point in almost every published recollection of an operatic career, there is a chapter taking a position on modern developments in operatic production. I'd like to skip that chapter in my book: being a stage director myself, still active in a long career with roots in a number of cultures, I'd rather allow my own body of work, much of it fortunately documented on film and video (see Appendix A), to stand as my own operatic credo rather than taking issue with the work of my colleagues. That said, there is one point I would like to raise in defense of some members of the staging craft, whatever else I may think of their work. In response to the challenges raised by what might be called the departures in which they have indulged, many of them make what I consider a valid point by stating that, given the dearth of new material and the constant requirement to reinterpret great classics that have been subject to a thousand diverse readings since their inception, often hundreds of years ago, there seems to be nowhere else to take these older works than—to paraphrase The Mamas and the Papas—somewhere they've never been before, with directors adding elements of their own political or aesthetic agendas in the process. The responses to this attitude usually vary from rhapsodic approval of new and challenging interpretations to the comment that, if these people think they have something to say, let them write their own operas and see if anybody buys a ticket.

As I see it, this challenge should be addressed more to the opera companies themselves in their capacity as articulators of the cultural thrust of a society. Rather than try to capture transitory headlines with yet another deconstruction of a masterpiece, let them challenge imaginative directors, conductors, singers, and musicians with new and interesting works that reflect the spirit of a given time and place, thus giving the community that supports them the enrichment of an operatic voice to which they can relate directly, in a language and idiom they readily understand. Since the inception of my long career, this has been an effort that has captured my imagination. When it fell to my lot to be entrusted with the leadership of two major theaters, both in cultural capitals on my adopted continent, I felt one of the most important contributions I could make would be to leave behind a legacy of new operas as a meaningful expression of the culture from which they emerged.

In the history of any major European opera house, the chronicler invariably pays the highest tribute to the significant works that first saw the light of day on that theater's stage. Over the years, for a number of complicated reasons, both financial and societal, the contribution of most American opera houses to this nourishing culture has been fairly sparse, with the possible exception of the pieces that emanated from a Ford Foundation grant to the New York City Opera back in the 1950s. This enabled that theater to produce 100 percent American seasons, introducing new works and providing major New York productions to a number of other fine operas by great composers like Douglas Moore, Kurt Weill, Marc Blitzstein, Robert Ward, Carlisle Floyd, and Gian Carlo Menotti.

Some twenty years later, as regional opera began to flourish in North America, new audiences expressed a keen interest in new works, and the burgeoning companies have provided them, often in excellent productions. Many of these have traveled well, so that audiences in one city have a chance to witness works first presented elsewhere and benefit from the hands-on involvement of the creators in the realization of their brain children.

After more than a half-century of involvement in the operatic craft, though I am thankful for the fact that I continue to teach and direct, I have given more than a little thought to the heritage I will leave behind. Certainly a major part of that heritage will be formed by the seven operas it has been my privilege to bring to audiences in Toronto and San Francisco, many of which have gone on to enjoy vibrant lives of their own on other stages. If I am remembered for nothing else, I think these works will endure as long as opera is presented; I refer especially to *A Streetcar Named Desire*, with a score by the eminent composer, conductor, and pianist André Previn, and *Dead Man Walking*, composed by a man whom nobody had heard of but who became a household name as a result of this deeply moving score: Jake Heggie.

One of the great stumbling blocks to presenting new opera today is the fact that most composers throughout the world are no longer the participatory theater pragmatists Mozart, Verdi, and Wagner were in their time, but rather emerge from the academic world. There, experimentation and new ideas are the order of the day, and all the clichés about the ivory tower apply. This is a fine thing in its way, but sometimes it is a good idea to leave the experimentation in the lab, and instead of writing to challenge fellow academics with one new compositional idea after another, it makes sense, with as large scale a proposition as an opera is, to make sure the music can communicate with telling immediacy to an audience. This is not pandering—it is common sense.

Commissioning an opera is like raising a child: you never have any idea how it is going to turn out. A living company *must* create new opera, dealing with the themes of our era and advancing its music and personalities. But it's a real crapshoot, from beginning to end. You can cast the greatest singing and musical talent of the day, and the power and poetry of the libretto and its source can be anticipated, but the music is another matter altogether, no matter how prominent and skilled the composer.

Even when you workshop the new pieces, you cannot know how the music will sound until it is almost too late to change it. By then, the critics may already have killed you. The same critics forget (or never knew) that many famous operas had disastrous opening nights, for a thousand different reasons. Many were later rewritten and perfected: *Il barbiere di Siviglia, Carmen, La traviata, Madama Butterfly, Antony and Cleopatra*—the list goes on and on.

The gestation period for a new opera is a long one; the process begins as many as three or four years before opening night. Lord knows how many things can go awry in the interim, and how many anxious weeks and months one can spend waiting for manuscripts that seem never to show up on time.

Even when a commission goes extremely well, it is always an expensive proposition. It has become necessary to spread the risk among several companies, getting a share of the credit and sharing a load of the costs. Even when a general director takes these precautions, however, sometimes the project just falls on its head, and there's no escape. Only once did I cancel a composition. We had tried workshops, but no repairs were possible. I knew it would flop, and although many of the critics had expressed somewhat reserved enthusiasm, it did flop when it was picked up in New York.

With all the others, I took my chances. Posterity will have to judge, and in a couple of cases, as I said before, it already has, with more than encouraging results.

In my twelve years in Toronto, I commissioned three operas for public performance, and another three were given in special workshops we organized at the Tanenbaum Opera Centre. The workshops were part of the Canadian Composers' Program (see Chapter 9). Although by no means secret events, they were intended primarily to hone the skills of rising Canadian composers and librettists in a small setting.

The public operas in Toronto were different. Two of them were written for children and given in collaboration with "Prologue to Performing Arts," a group that performed for the schools in metropolitan Toronto. "Prologue" was founded in 1966. From the beginning it partnered with the Canadian Opera Company, the National Ballet of Canada, and Young People's Theatre to give shows for youngsters in grades seven through nine. These were important contributions to young people, a first for our company, and perhaps a first for all of Canada. Our third public production was a full-scale "adult" opera, written by one of Canada's most distinguished musicians, Harry Somers.

My first commission, *The Magic of Mozart*, which premiered in 1978, featured the talents of an even more eminent composer. Although I certainly cannot claim to have secured Mozart's services, I did enlist the talents of Mavor Moore, a well-known Canadian writer, producer, and educator and the perfect partner for devising an in-school introduction to Mozart's music. He came from a prominent family in Canadian arts and literature, and in his career he wrote more than a hundred plays, documentaries, musicals, and other theater pieces. Mavor was also well regarded as the creator of CBC National News, an institution not unlike "Hockey Night in Canada." Everyone watches it. Many thousands of Toronto schoolchildren enjoyed his charming introduction to the great Mozart, and I was proud of our contribution to their understanding of art and music theater.

Unlike *The Magic of Mozart*, the next children's opera, *A Rose Is a Rose*, first performed in 1987, had an original libretto and score, written and composed by Ann Mortifee, who was young and just launching her career when we were introduced. Born in Zululand, South Africa, she came to Vancouver as a child. As a teenager, she began singing in coffee-houses, where she came to the attention of playwright George Tyga. Ann has an unusual charisma and honesty, and Tyga hired her as a singer for his powerful 1967 drama, *The Ecstasy of Rita Joe*. Four years later, Ann worked with the Royal Winnipeg Ballet on a dance version of *Ecstasy*. After that, she wrote four more ballet scores, a musical, and more than ten albums and appeared in shows with Harry Belafonte, Ramsey Lewis, Michel Legrand, Bobby McFerrin, and John Denver. *A Rose Is a Rose*, about the travails of early adolescence, was well received, instantly accessible, sincere, and true.

Toward the end of my tenure in Toronto, everyone was talking about Harry Somers and his opera *Louis Riel*, written in 1966–67 at the behest of the Canadian Opera Company and sponsored by the Floyd S. Chalmers Foundation. I took Harry to lunch one day, eager to see if he and the Canadian Opera Company might again be a good fit. After the success of our chamber and children's operas, we felt we were ready to commission a major work for our subscription audience.

I initially asked Harry if he could reduce *Louis Riel* to a one-hour piano version for presentation in schools. We wanted to get the story, the music, and its composer into a public arena. It didn't work. He simply couldn't condense the historical events into that short a time span. I then asked him to compose a new opera. He had a Thomas Mann story in mind, and his was the last contract I signed before leaving. *Mario and the Magician* was produced a year and a half later.

The libretto was by Rod Anderson, a past president of our board, an economist, a charming gentleman partially responsible for bringing me to Canada, and a genius. He composes piano rags, which I used to call "Wagnerian rags." But Rod's libretto was rather windy, a problem compounded by the fact that Harry wasn't really up to the challenge.

The production, which premiered in 1992, was very expensive and unfortunately very unsuccessful. Walter Stothers, a major patron and onetime president of the board, apparently went into the bar at the end of the first act and said, "Well, that's a million dollars for a piece of shit!" Nobody remembered that I had commissioned it, and *Mario* has also faded from memory. I got off scot-free. By then I was already in San Francisco.

Terry McEwen, my predecessor, loved the nineteenth century. He was a great fancier of *bel canto* and owned one of the most comprehensive record collections anywhere in the world. He crafted Pavarotti's recording career, and his closest friends were operatic legends, like Renata Tebaldi, Régine Crespin, and Joan Sutherland. Their voices were the sounds he heard in his imagination. During the six years Terry was general director in San Francisco, he was able to commission one opera, *Esther* by Hugo Weisgall. When he made the commission, he told Weisgall, "I want an opera in the style of Meyerbeer with double choruses and ballets."

Having directed three Meyerbeer operas, two of them twice, I knew where Terry was coming from and consequently had my doubts from the outset. Meyerbeer's lavish nineteenth-century operas were the talk of Paris when he wrote them, but they tend to go on forever, more or less pandering to the well-heeled operagoers of the day. Some members of the audience frequently wandered in and out of the auditorium during performances and spent time chatting or playing cards in the lounges, where a servant would summon them to their boxes when Madame So and So was about to sing her big aria or the ballet girls were getting ready to add sparkle to the evening. After the star turns, they would file back to the lounges and continue their social evening, leaving the connecting tissue of the works, much of which was accompanied by some fairly inspired music, to the people in the cheaper seats. While this superb music has caused many of the works to be reinstated for brief runs in the repertoire, usually in truncated versions, they hardly serve as role models for twentieth- or twenty-first-century compositions, but Terry was calling the shots, apparently oblivious to the fact that a work of these proportions was certainly not the right vehicle for as dissonant and challenging a composer as Hugo Weisgall.

Esther was taken from the Old Testament story, detailing the title character's courage and her successful efforts to prevent a massacre of the Jews in ancient Persia, where she was the wife of King Ahasuerus, whom the Greeks called Xerxes. It was Weisgall's tenth opera. *Six Characters in Search of an Author* had been a big success in 1959, but *Nine Rivers from Jordan* was a fiasco a decade later. By the time he received Terry's commission, Weisgall's reputation was very mixed. Although Terry had commissioned the opera, it had not been decided who would direct it. The Persian setting might perhaps have made it ideal for me, but I couldn't warm up to the libretto, and so I passed on shepherding the project myself, still unacquainted with the music. Frankly, I was tempted to cancel the whole thing outright, but I decided it was only fair to the creators at least to workshop the one act that had already been written and see how it went in that setting.

I engaged two brilliant young Americans, Francesca Zambello to serve as director/dramaturge and Bruce Ferden to conduct, and recruited the young professional singers of the San Francisco Opera Center (the Adler Fellows) for the cast. When everything was ready, we had Weisgall fly out from New York in July 1989. We invited a small audience. I felt obligated to do all this because it was slated to be the first company commission (and world premiere) in years.

Esther was first performed with piano upstairs at the opera. We had a critical session with Weisgall, Zambello, Ferden, librettist Charles Kondek, my music administrator Kip Cranna, artistic administrator Sarah Billinghurst, and a few others. We felt the libretto needed a bit of fine-tuning, but when we made this suggestion, Mr. Kondek became defensive.

After that session, we held a private meeting. I said to one of my key artistic staff members that, after the first act, I just didn't know where the piece was going. No one did. *Esther* was supposed to be a grand opera in three acts, but it was already off the rails.

I decided to workshop the second act as well. In March 1990, we did Acts I and II in our rehearsal building, again staged by Francesca Zambello, with the singers working from memory but without costumes or scenery. I had a few donors and board members attend, mainly because we might need their money.

For this second workshop, we cast outside singers in some of the roles and used Adler Fellows from the Opera Center for the others. This cast included two major names, Patricia Racette and Elaine Bonazzi, along with such fine singers as Roy Steverns, Ross Halper, Randall Wong, LeRoy Villanueva, and Catherine Keene. All of this cost even more money, and at the time, company finances were fairly tight. This production would entail a major financial commitment, requiring a chorus of 110, a ballet, a very large cast, and sets and costumes of de Mille proportions. Terry had made no provision for any of these expenses; only the basic fees had been set: $80,000 for Hugo Weisgall and half that sum for Charles Kondek.

So we did the second workshop, at greater expense than we could really afford, around $55,000, and had another meeting. The artistic team was not happy, although very diplomatic. No one was enthusiastic —except for Weisgall and Kondek, of course. *They* had no misgivings whatsoever. It was their baby, and while I couldn't blame them for feeling parental, I couldn't help but recollect the amount of fine-tuning composers like Verdi and Puccini lavished on their compositions even after their premieres.

Sarah, Kip, and I tried to estimate a budget; when we finished our calculations, it came to $1 million or so. By the second workshop, I knew the music was academic and unexciting. Even though it had some good moments, all in all it lacked the sweep necessary for such an epic story. The drama didn't register. During our meetings, I watched the others, and they just sat there with their shoulders slumped. The buck, however, stopped at my desk. If I was going to raise money, I would have to believe in *Esther*, and frankly I didn't. It didn't help that the company's financial situation was fairly weak and we couldn't find much foundation support to underwrite a production. In one comment we received, the project was declared "a dead opera in a dead style."

World premieres can be very glamorous and good for the name and health of a company. However, doing a piece just for the sake of claiming a premiere is not an adequate motivation. The work has to be of optimum quality, and this simply wasn't. It would have been cowardly to blame it on Terry McEwen. I could have produced what I knew was a weak opera, but that wouldn't have been professional. In fact, I consulted Terry only after I had resolved the issue in my own mind.

I had an extremely bad night after the second workshop. I had to make a decision, and by the morning I had come to the conclusion there was no way to save *Esther*—I just didn't feel it could hold an audience. The project would have to be canceled. I don't remember anyone trying to change my mind. I ran the decision by Kip, Sarah, Francesca, and Bruce and thanked them all for their hard work. Then we informed the board, and I called Hugo. The major reason I gave was financial: "Terry wanted a grand opera, and we just can't afford it." If Weisgall had offered to cut it down, I would have had to find another reason. I'm sure Hugo saw through me. We paid him the full amount of his contract, all $80,000 of it, thus avoiding a lawsuit, but he was understandably offended and hurt. He was a nice man who was musically fairly locked in the strictures of the early atonal movement and worked in that generally inaccessible style that never really draws large audiences, whatever the intellectual merits of the score might be. But he was also an old man, over eighty, and he knew this would be his final major work. It came as no surprise when he bad-mouthed me all over the place, claiming I had no taste.

I gave his librettist the same excuse. We also paid him every cent we owed him for an opera we never produced. The only public statement we made was about the company's financial limitations. I said nothing about the work's artistic shortfalls. Fortunately for its creators, the opera was picked up by the New York City Opera and premiered there on October 8, 1993, in a semi-staged production with a unit set and an excellent cast featuring the superb Lauren Flanigan in the title role. The response was generally negative. In one of the more generous reviews, Edward Rothstein wrote in the *New York Times*, "Mr. Weisgall's uncompromising modernism, his acidic melancholy and muscular dissonances make a compelling case for difficult music used for difficult purposes . . . there were times when the score could have been less unrelenting. But its power is unmistakable." In a review published in London's *OPERA* magazine, Martin Mayer said, "*Esther* is a much stronger piece than Weisgall's long, worthy, self-centered career would lead anyone to expect." Damning with faint praise.

As I write this, *Esther* is slated for a revival in 2009, again starring Flanigan, and I wish it well, even though I still honestly doubt if the piece has the goods to enter the repertoire.

I had never before been in such a spot, and it put a very dark cloud over my head with the New York crowd, especially writers like Patrick J. Smith, who wrote in *Opera News*: "Mansouri's action is hardly a worthy recognition of Weisgall's stature as an opera composer, and hardly an appropriate politeness to his predecessor's wishes. We'll see if Lotfi Mansouri replaces *Esther* with an American work, or Bizet's *Les pêcheurs de perles*."

While we couldn't find an American work to replace *Esther*, we did substitute a very modern European piece, Hans Werner Henze's *Das verratene Meer* (*The Betrayed Sea*) with a libretto by Hans-Ulrich Treichel based on Yukio Mishima's novel *The Sailor Who Fell from Grace with the Sea*. Our leads included Ashley Putnam, Tom Fox, and Craig Estep, and the production was led by Markus Stenz, who had conducted the world premiere at Berlin's Deutsche Oper only months before, and directed by Christopher Alden.

Two years later, I was invited to give the West Coast premiere of John Adams's *The Death of Klinghoffer*, detailing the murder of wheelchair-bound Jewish American tourist Leon Klinghoffer, thrown overboard from the Italian cruise ship *Achille Lauro* during a hijack attempt by Palestinian terrorists. The proposal was for a coproduction with the Théâtre Royal de la Monnaie in Brussels, where the opera had been originally commissioned by the theater's director at the time, Gérard Mortier.

I used to meet Mortier at conferences in Europe. He had been an assistant to Rolf Liebermann, a Swiss composer who ran the opera companies in Hamburg and Paris. Gérard is a real *provocateur*. He headed the Salzburg Festival for almost ten years and would hold a press conference every week, making it as controversial as he could. The last production he did there was a frantically salacious *Die Fledermaus*, which he blatantly heralded as his "gift" to the Austrians, whose occasional lapses into sentimentality he found revolting. Gérard is a Napoleon type, rather short and compact. Born in Flanders, he speaks a number of languages perfectly. He's a doctrinaire advocate of in-your-face conceptual theater and a champion of anything far-out and challenging to the audience, and although he's self-important, I like him because he's such an original personality.

When Gérard took over Brussels, he swept everything out, including Maurice Béjart, the brilliant choreographer who had been there for years and brought much distinction to the house with his brilliant conceptions of often ultra-modern dance ideas, ballet, if you will, for people who do not like ballet. I think Gérard wanted him out of the place because he couldn't stand the idea of two *enfants terribles* under the same roof.

Gérard Mortier will not win any gold medals for diplomacy or discretion. When asked why he never brought artists of the stature of Luciano Pavarotti and Jessye Norman to the Monnaie, he bluntly replied, "Unfortunately our corridors are not wide enough."

Way down deep, I believe Gérard does not really like opera. He brought in people like Ursel and Karl-Ernst Hermann, who created a nonsensical production of Mozart's *La clemenza di Tito* in which the main character was depicted as a rich Jew rather than a Roman emperor, with the result that Riccardo Muti refused to conduct it.

Needless to say, Gérard is crazy about Peter Sellars. After the murder aboard the *Achille Lauro*, he got the idea of asking Sellars, composer John Adams, and librettist Alice Goodman to depict this tragedy in operatic form. Once the project got rolling, Gérard called me in San Francisco, asking me to be his partner and promote it worldwide. I was intrigued, and it was affordable. Adams was to be paid $150,000 and Goodman $50,000.

I like John Adams. He lives in the San Francisco Bay Area, and opera as an art form can deal with any subject matter. The notion of an opera about the eternal conflict between Israelis and Palestinians was wholly contemporary—that appealed to me. John's first opera, *Nixon in China*, had originally been workshopped in San Francisco with two pianos at the Herbst Theater. Legend has it that Terry McEwen heard it and walked out, so David Gockley took it for Houston. I was sorry that we had never done *Nixon*, although we did get close. We were going to offer it in our June 2001 series, in cooperation with Robert Cole of Cal Performances at the University of California, Berkeley. It was going to be a major production, in close collaboration with both Bob and the English National Opera in London. We *almost* made it. One of the reasons we took *Klinghoffer* was because *Nixon* never happened.

Gérard asked me to see *Klinghoffer*. I flew to Brussels, watched rehearsals, and attended opening night. It was very American. Even the conductor, Kent Nagano, was American. He was born in Morro Bay in central California, studied at San Francisco State University, and even sang in the San Francisco Opera Chorus for two seasons. He was just then launching what would become an international career. Today he works all over the world and has succeeded Charles Dutoit as the music director of the Montreal Symphony and Zubin Mehta as general music director of the Bavarian State Opera in Munich.

I knew Peter Sellars from Chicago, where he had directed Wagner's *Tannhäuser*, basing it on the career of Jimmy Swaggart, one of a long line of disgraced televangelists. I was not impressed with his work but decided to go along with Mortier.

After I weighed all the issues, I told Gérard, "Yes, we'll take it." The production was supposed to go on to Los Angeles, Lyon (where Nagano recorded it), and Glyndebourne. General director Peter Hemmings canceled it in Los Angeles, but it eventually made it to Vienna and the Brooklyn Academy of Music in New York.

Our stage was bigger, but otherwise the production was the same as the Brussels original. The work itself aroused a lot of controversy wherever it was performed, many critics claiming it was far too sympathetic to the Palestinian cause, others contending it was unfairly predisposed toward Israel. Because of my own origins, people thought I might take a biased position, and I got letters, 50 percent of which claimed I was pro-Israel and the other 50 percent of which called me pro-Palestine. Somebody even sent me a book about terrorism. I didn't read it, but I wrote a nice letter, pointing out that I had been raised in the Middle East and thus was not exactly unfamiliar with the issue.

The interesting thing about *Klinghoffer* is that it deals with both sides. The audience has to think for itself and realize that both sides have legitimate grievances. But in the opera, there was one problem I could not resolve. The librettist, poet Alice Goodman, is a real intellectual snob. Among other things, she insisted on not having titles translating quotes from the Koran. I told her, "I was raised studying the Koran, and I can't say I always know what it means." Her libretto was such a frantic attempt to be ultra-literary that it overshot the mark. It should have been heartrending, but it wound up sounding like a Hallmark card written by a Ph.D. candidate. In the final analysis, it reminded me of a Händel oratorio: now the Israelis sing something, now it's the Palestinians' turn, and back and forth it goes. The actual hijacking became tangential. I certainly would have staged it differently, and without dancers, for heaven's sake! How artificial can you get? It meant Peter didn't know what to do with the chorus. It could have been like *Turandot*: the chorus as protagonist, whether Arab *or* Israeli. Instead, despite the wonderful Mark Morris Dancers, the choreographic insertions were meaningless. John Adams conducted himself, so the audience thought it was getting the authentic article, and the San Francisco chorus under Ian Robertson was terrific.

I felt, and John agreed, that our opening night was even stronger than the one in Brussels. I believe it was because of the power of the chorus, but in San Francisco we didn't have the big success we had hoped for. The audience just didn't get involved, which I attribute to the weakness of the libretto. The conflict was not adequately articulated, and so the audience did not feel the personal tragedy of Klinghoffer's death or the symbolic tragedy of his being a Jew. All in all, the reaction was rather lukewarm. We didn't sell many tickets, but I don't regret it. I wanted to do John Adams. He is an important American composer and has earned a place in our best houses.

Despite this cool reception, the opera has proved to have a good shelf life. As of this writing it has had sixteen productions, two of them concert performances. In 2003 it was produced as a film, directed by Penny Woolcock. Perhaps the best thing about *Klinghoffer* was that it put San Francisco back on the world stage for new work, which made it much easier for me to commission opera intended for our company from the outset, as was the case with the next project.

Years ago, I had seen a wonderful French movie made by Roger Vadim in 1959 and starring Jeanne Moreau, Gérard Philippe, and Jean-Louis Trintignant. The film was called *Les liaisons dangéreuses*, based on the eponymous raunchy novel by Pierre Choderlos de Laclos, which was considered wildly scandalous when it came out in the eighteenth century but has meanwhile reappeared as a classic of its time and spawned a number of metamorphoses. Among these are the Vadim film, a period version in English with Glenn Close and John Malkovich, a 1987 Royal Shakespeare Company stage version by Christopher Hampton, starring Alan Rickman, Lindsay Duncan, and Juliet Stevenson, and a couple of made-for-television versions both in period and updated. When it was presented at the Music Box Theater on Broadway, I sat there, riveted. Everything was in white, with a horrible decadence under that surface. It was about the manipulation of human relationships and the concept of love, but when the protagonist, Valmont, actually does fall in love, truth destroys the game. In its focus on the manipulation of human relationships, it strongly reminded me of *Così fan tutte*, only darker, toying with human feelings and identities in a devastating whirlpool of malign seductions and intrigues. I thought it would be a powerful subject for an opera.

From the outset of the commissioning process, my partner was Kip Cranna. We contacted Christopher Hampton, flew him to San Francisco, had a wonderful meeting, and asked him to work for us. However, he wasn't available at the time, and we would have had to wait two or three years. We started looking elsewhere.

Kip gave me tapes and CDs of composers like Charles Wuorinen and his circle. None of them worked. I was searching for a modern-day Mozart. Composer Conrad Susa had done a couple of things I listened to, and he seemed very good. Because he lived in the Bay Area and taught at the San Francisco Conservatory of Music, I thought he might be our best choice. When we finally met, I found him to be a very cool cucumber. There's a wonderful line in Myfanwy Piper's libretto to Benjamin Britten's *The Turn of the Screw*, when the Governess says to Mrs. Grose, "I tell you, they are not with us, but with the others." I came to realize that was our Conrad.

My dream choice for librettist had been Terrence McNally, but he was also unavailable. Then we found Philip Littell in Los Angeles, a young actor-writer, who seemed like a good guy. We organized a meeting between Philip and Conrad, and they got along very well. I asked Philip to look at Hampton's play, the way he had streamlined the novel, which was a fairly convoluted series of interlocking letters. The drama has to be distilled from within them. I wanted him to use the Hampton play simply as a guide. We didn't want any accusations of plagiarism, and I definitely didn't want a play set to music. It was to be an original work from start to finish, and Conrad and Philip were in accord with this.

I had actually chosen the voices before I chose Conrad. I envisioned Valmont as a baritone, a kind of Don Giovanni character, Madame de Tourvel as a soprano, and the Marquise de Merteuil as a mezzo-soprano. Before a note was written, I had already cast the opera in my imagination: Thomas Hampson would be ideal as the rake Valmont; Renée Fleming would be superb as the saintly Madame de Tourvel. For the scheming Marquise de Merteuil, I thought of Frederica von Stade. My choice surprised her. Over lunch one day, she said, "Can I ask you a rather personal question? What made you think of me as the Marquise?"

I said, "Look, Flicka, I have learned you never cast a bitch to play a bitch. They always try to be so nice and gracious. It just doesn't work. You cast somebody who has been around bitches. Think of some of the Fiordiligis and Marschallins you've had to work with. Draw from them." It became one of the best things Flicka ever did.

When I saw Australian tenor David Hobson in Baz Luhrman's famous *La Bohème* production in Sydney, I knew I had to have him. He was so good, and so handsome. He's also a composer, and he had done a rock *Macbeth*. I wanted Canadian mezzo Judith Forst, too, of course. She is unparalleled. I was flattered that these singers trusted me, because none of them knew anything about Conrad's work.

I told Conrad and Philip that was the package. For a composer and librettist, a cast of this caliber is like a gift from heaven. They offered no resistance. I didn't give them a running time or a set number of acts. We wouldn't be doing the *Ring*, but it was to be a full-length opera. We did agree that the chorus would not have a major function, and so it appears onstage only in the last scene.

Frederica von Stade as the Marquise de Merteuil, and
Thomas Hampson as Valmont in Dangerous Liaisons.
Bonnie Kamin, photographer; courtesy San Francisco Opera.

Dangerous Liaisons was my first major commission. Although I was hovering, I did not exercise any kind of control, although I did reserve the right of first refusal, and the *Esther* cancellation was still fresh in everyone's memory.

After I put Philip and Conrad together, we needed a director who could also serve as a dramaturge. This is an authority figure, arising from the German theater, who works for a company adapting plays and librettos to the specific needs of stage performance. In our time, a dramaturge has become an essential midwife to new opera, and we wanted the best. That was Colin Graham, who would also direct *Liaisons*. Colin had worked with Benjamin Britten and definitely belonged in the top league. I sent Philip to Colin, and the two of them worked very closely

LOTFI MANSOURI

together. Colin became a super-editor and a very imaginative factor in that equation. Kip was also with us every step of the way. He is a refreshingly objective person who never forces his opinions, yet exercises artistic influence. He became Conrad's tamer. I came to believe Conrad must have come from the Deep South. He was so laid back—I imagined him on the front porch with a julep in his hand, while he scratched a beagle's ear with the other. Kip was the one who kept pushing him, going over to his place and pressing him to finish. Kip was Conrad's conscience, and very hands-on about it.

Just before the sets were to be built, in March 1994, we had still not received much music from Mr. Susa. I had all these artists under contract, so I needed a contingency plan in case Conrad failed to deliver. If worse came to worst, I could put Renée in *Werther* and so on. I called Conrad into my office one day, along with Kip, and tried to keep my emotions under control. I reminded Conrad where we were and who was in the cast, and pointed out that in two weeks, the designs were going to the workshop. I told him, "Before I spend all this money . . ." and gave a thirty-minute oration. He just sat there like a buddha. Finally, when I was finished, panting and perspiring, he casually looked over at me and mumbled, "You know, Lotfi, you're making me nervous." I had given him *two years* to write his score, and I had received nothing more than a couple of pages. Ultimately Conrad agreed to my demand that he get help with the orchestrations, so that the piece would have a fighting chance of being ready on time. The work was completed by Donald Ontriveros with assistance from Manley Romero.

We went ahead and built the sets and costumes. Moments before the open dress rehearsal, we finally got the orchestrations for the last scene. We had to hold the curtain and keep our guests in the lobby while Donald Runnicles read through the score with the orchestra. This was the only scene involving the chorus, and they had to wait, too.

Kip had made a schedule for Conrad and Philip, specifying when we had to have Act I, Act II, and so on, but it had to be reworked to accommodate Mr. Susa's casual approach to creativity. Conrad had been paid $135,000 for his labors, and Philip received $25,000 for his. The orchestrations cost even more. Fortunately, Philip was always on time, and Colin proved a wonderful dramaturge, who never missed a deadline.

When *Liaisons* first went to the board of trustees, I don't think too many of the members knew anything about the story or the source, although they doubtless knew the all-star singers we were getting. A lot of them are capable financiers, but they are not all that familiar with the day-to-day operations of an opera house. Very few understand the art form or the company that brings it to the audience. I went to the finance committee for extra money, but I had to do most of the fund-raising myself, appealing to people who, like the extraordinarily generous Bay Area arts patron Phyllis Wattis, were really excited by the new work. Once it had gone through the finance committee, I could take it as a fait accompli to the full board. I never had to ask permission, so long as it was in the budget the committee had approved. We did nine productions that year, and fortunately there was no summer season to worry about. I did cushion the extra costs of *Liaisons* by doing revivals with casts that were not all that expensive.

All of this was undertaken in the context of "Pacific Visions," a series of commissions that I announced in 1993 and that would ultimately include *Dangerous Liaisons* (1994), *Harvey Milk* (1996), *A Streetcar Named Desire* (1998), and *Dead Man Walking* (2000). This was the longest sustained series of commissions in the history of our company, and not one was a failure. Mr. Adler had commissioned exactly two operas in his twenty-eight years at the opera. I was deeply proud of our track record and believed that our mission included creating work that would eventually join the standard repertoire.

As a general director, you have to sell this sort of thing. You have to make it sound like the most important thing in town. My dream was to do a commission every year. It didn't have to be huge. It could be a chamber opera, or something just for the company. For example, in 1995, for the U.N.'s fiftieth anniversary celebrations, I commissioned William Bolcom to compose a symphonic poem based on Walt Whitman's antiwar poems, which was sung by Marilyn Horne. I sold the board on that dream, and the members came to understand how a company of our stature had to be a torchbearer, especially for American opera.

We weren't in competition with the Met, which I have always regarded as a lavishly financed museum, although things seem to be undergoing some changes under the leadership of Peter Gelb. In the final analysis, it makes no sense whatsoever to try to compete with anyone. Every community and every company must have its own profile. Chicago has always been a singers' company, for instance. There, Carol Fox would go to the record companies and say, "Get me the singers in your *Tristan* recording," and that's how she cast. She wanted the best of everything— from records.

I did it differently, by starting with the budget. I had a simple formula, and *Liaisons* was part of it. I would categorize operas as "A," "B," or "C." *Liaisons* was a "B," with a small chorus and no ballet. It was an excellent but expensive cast. To devise the particulars, we would count heads, then measure how big the individual heads were. We counted unit costs, for set, props, rehearsals, and so on. We had sixty-nine regular orchestra members, already in the budget. We gave ourselves a bit of working room, too, as *Liaisons* was a period show with special costs.

I wish the music had evidenced more penetrating psychological understanding. Some of it was a little facile, but I don't pretend to be a composer. I never lost confidence, but I was never a hundred percent excited. I think it worked, but musically it couldn't stand without the libretto. That said, one of the most exciting scenes was the one in which Madame de Tourvel discovers that she has been used by Valmont. Renée did a fantastic job. When she realized that she had completely given in to his machinations, as Colin staged it, she *gradually* awakened to the horror. It was chilling and very moving. Here Conrad's music had all of the impact I had hoped for, and it was one of the highlights of the opera. The combination of the dramatic situations, the staging, Conrad's atmospherics, and Renée's acting made it deeply memorable.

Colin, as a director and dramaturge, exerted a strong artistic influence. He played a major role in marshaling all these talents, and everybody cooperated willingly with him. He was the shepherd and contributed his vast experience and knowledge to the project. His death in April 2007 was a tragic loss to the opera world.

The company got together for the first time for a sing-through. Even though the orchestrations weren't complete, the work was basically finished. I welcomed everybody, and then Colin took over. Everybody was enthusiastic and excited, and I felt as though I were in the tenth month of a pregnancy. We had wanted to do workshops throughout the process, but Conrad never met any deadlines, and so we couldn't do even one. Nonetheless, Conrad was very pleased with himself. Why wouldn't he be, with Renée, Thomas, and Flicka singing his music? The cast was stellar right down the line: although I hadn't been able to get Marilyn Horne for the role of the Aunt, Johanna Meier was superb in the role, and Judith Forst and Mary Mills were also major artists who lent special prowess to important supporting roles.

The only casting problem was Conrad himself. I don't know if he has any nerves at all. He never seemed aware of how incredibly significant his task was. He seemed to be working on the end of a long catalogue of operas rather than doing his very first score for this medium. Donald and Colin made excellent musical suggestions, and they all worked hard to make Conrad look good.

Was Mr. Susa ever a prima donna? Never—I don't think he has the energy.

When all was said and done, I got the funniest card from Philip Littell. He wrote, "Lotfi, you have my ass." This was the highest compliment he could pay. Renée genuinely liked her role, and Thomas Hampson loved his part, too. I told him, "Tom, this is you."

There are two Thomas Hampsons. One was born in Elkhart, Indiana, and raised in Spokane, Washington, and he still has a kind of irrepressible "gee whiz" American provinciality about him. The other Hampson is very grand. He has a bit of the noble Valmont in his own personality, so the role came easily to him.

Flicka was crazy about her role and wanted to be given music for her final scene—the last line in the opera. The line has since become famous: "I'm *hungry*." I think that was Colin's suggestion.

Word of mouth for *Liaisons* was very good. We sold out the run, and that was the acceptance we wanted. Although successful, it was not the triumph *I* wanted. I had hoped it would become standard American repertoire, but it hasn't. Three performances were videotaped, and PBS later broadcast the best of them. Perhaps a repeat telecast may lead to other productions. The work has been produced at college workshops but has received only one professional production to date: in 1998, the Washington Opera performed a substantially revised version with new orchestrations by the composer.

Credit for bringing the tragic story of Harvey Milk to the operatic stage belongs to David Gockley, then general director of the Houston Grand Opera, who now holds my former position in San Francisco. We are longtime friends and colleagues, and I had directed a number of productions for him in Houston. In 1994, he called to ask if I would be interested in sharing a production about the late Harvey Milk. This seemed a natural for our company, since Milk was an elected—and murdered—supervisor in San Francisco and the first openly gay man to hold that office. The mayor of San Francisco at the time, George Moscone, fell victim to the same murderer: former supervisor Dan White, an ex-cop no less.

David had chosen librettist Michael Korie and composer Stewart Wallace, who in 1989 had done *Where's Dick?* for him in Houston. David wanted us to go to New York to meet them and listen to some of the work they had already finished. Their original treatment attempted a history of gay rights, but got lost in indignation. At my request, Kip Cranna traveled to Houston to meet with David and his team. Kip expressed my concern that we could not commit to the piece unless it was dramatically worthwhile, coherent, and succinct. At the beginning, *Harvey Milk* was none of these things. The creators did make several cuts and changes we had asked for, including the addition of a love scene for Harvey and his partner, Scott Smith, which had been missing in the original plotline. Opera is not very good at politics, but it does very well with love scenes.

Satisfied with these changes, Sarah Billinghurst, Kip Cranna, and I went to Stewart's apartment in New York. My first impression of these gentlemen was not positive. I found them pretentious, pseudo-intellectual East Coasters and self-satisfied. There was an aura of mirthless superficiality about them.

However, the topic was absolutely right for San Francisco. I never met Harvey Milk, but I was very much aware of him. I liked the revised libretto; it was honest speech. My real concern was the music: it just wasn't good enough. When I said so to David, he told me he thought they could develop it further. They never did.

David is very clever about budgeting. He got his partners to assume the capital costs, and Houston Grand Opera itself ended up putting a lower sum into it. Our share of *Harvey Milk* was $164,000. New York City Opera, Houston, and San Francisco were to be the partners, but the people at City Opera were a problem. When we did *The Ballad of Baby Doe* with them, we had to sue to recover costs. They wanted to get everything for free.

Houston had first performance rights because *Harvey Milk* had been David's idea. We decided to stage it at the Orpheum as a theater piece, and I put it in our subscription series to guarantee an audience.

Donald Runnicles helped a lot, because the original orchestration was very weak. Fortunately, we had more than a year to work on our version of the piece, following the Houston world premiere in January 1995 and the New York performance after that. To his immense credit, Donald worked very closely with Stewart Wallace, analyzing every bar toward improving the orchestration, clarity, and sound. Other people on our musical staff, including the brilliant pianist and coach Peter Grunberg, worked to simplify and clarify the overcomplicated orchestrations and the needlessly difficult rhythmic notation. As a result, we had to create an entirely new vocal score and set of orchestral parts at a cost of several thousand dollars. The "San Francisco version" is now considered definitive, and it is certainly a wholesale improvement on the original.

Luckily the director, Christopher Alden, was very good and required no help from us. Like the creators of the piece, he is gay himself, deeply understood the subject matter, and addressed it without reservation.

There was a major problem with the Houston costumes. By the time they got here, they were in tatters, and Jenny Green, the head of our costume shop, was furious. They were so cheaply and poorly made that we had to redo most of them, which gave Jenny the opportunity to improve the look of the show completely. The production quality was far better, dramatically and musically, than the one in Houston.

Just before rehearsals began, I got a call from Moscone's successor as mayor of San Francisco, Dianne Feinstein, now the senior senator from California. She said, "Lotfi, I understand I'm in this opera. How am I being portrayed?"

I answered, "Dianne, you're being done by a soprano."

That phone call, and my truthful reply (albeit a non sequitur), set me worrying about local response in the Bay Area. I invited Dianne to the opening night, but she didn't come. A lot of other local personalities depicted in the opera *did* come, apparently to see themselves. The amazing thing was that the gay community didn't swarm in to see the show. We even timed one of the performances so that the candlelight march marking the anniversary of Harvey's murder would end at the Orpheum right before curtain time, so that everyone could come in after Mayor Willie Brown made a speech and handed out awards. But the support we expected never materialized. We couldn't get a penny from James Hormel, a well-known gay philanthropist, and the rest of the gay community didn't back our production. This was disappointing to me and made me wonder if the real Harvey Milk might have been more a popular cause than a popular person. At least we got a recording out of it. Attendance was in the 70 percent range; we usually drew in the 80s.

Dramatically, the piece was excellent. The chorus was superb, and Robert Orth was spectacular in the title role. Some scenes were very touching, but the production, the staging, and the cast saved it from its second-rate music. I've never even listened to the recording. There was an authenticity about the story that we did not compromise, but overall it was not a great success. It was an appropriate piece for and about our city. But that was that. Apart from those in Houston, San Francisco, and New York, the only other performances were given in a completely different (and Euro-weird) production in Dortmund, sung in German and presented prior to our local premiere in San Francisco.

I am a great fan of the 1951 film version of *A Streetcar Named Desire* and have a tape of the original 1947 Broadway production with Marlon Brando and Jessica Tandy. I never saw Brando onstage, but I did meet Tennessee Williams, and I have always found his dramatic voice profoundly stirring. He understood the human heart. We met in 1972 when I was doing *La fille du Régiment* in Philadelphia with Beverly Sills, and he was in the city for the out-of-town tryout of his play *Out Cry* starring Michael York. One evening, I saw him having dinner at Bookbinder's, a wonderful seafood restaurant, and while I generally don't bother celebrities, I said to myself, "When will I ever have a chance to meet him again?" So I walked over to his table, apologized for the intrusion, and told him how much I admired his writing. He promptly turned on the southern charm and couldn't have been more gracious, asking what I was doing in town. I told him I was directing an opera, and we chatted for about five minutes. He was just as I had imagined him to be: well mannered and relaxed.

That meeting reinforced a desire I had held for years: to make an opera of *Streetcar*. From the outset, I was convinced it had the ingredients of a great opera. The conflict between Blanche's vulnerability and the animal force of Kowalski is very operatic and very real. It is an eternal conflict. Gentle poetic souls are so often crushed by insensitivity and jungle behavior, and yet we all have animal impulses within us. The creative, sensitive element must be developed and learned. When you starve any of us, we invariably resort to animal behavior, just to survive, no matter how sophisticated we might be otherwise. I identify with Blanche in terms of the beauty she saw and the family dysfunction she suffered. I also recognize the brutal, volatile side of humanity: Stanley is capable of love, but only in carnal guise. His wooing is physical. He is our animal within. He could placate Stella only with sex, and when he screams for her at the end like a wounded beast, he reveals that, when deprived, he can be just as vulnerable in his way as Blanche is in hers.

In the hands of the right composer, Blanche could rival Norma or Lucia. She is a great character. Her flights of fancy, her spoken monologues lend themselves perfectly to musical treatment.

It was years earlier, when I was still working in Geneva, that I first got the idea *Streetcar* could be a great opera. Although it is anchored in American consciousness, I thought it could be effectively done in Switzerland, and Dr. Graf was supportive.

The first composer I approached was Leonard Bernstein. I was directing a German-language production of *Showboat* at the Vienna Volksoper in March 1971, and he was in the Austrian capital conducting the Philharmonic. He used to come to our rehearsals to watch a friend of his in the cast. One day I saw him on the street, chain-smoking as usual and looking hopelessly lonely and forlorn. Perhaps, subliminally, I related that view of him to my perception of Blanche and her injured personality. Lenny, who had probably achieved more than any other musician of his generation, always seemed to be yearning hopelessly for something beyond his reach.

We spent a lot of time together in those days. One night, while we were drinking wine in a restaurant, I told Lenny I had always dreamed of doing *Streetcar* as an opera, and I said he would be the ideal composer. At first, he was quite excited about the project. He knew Tennessee Williams, he had a marvelous background in jazz, and he understood the special flavor of New Orleans, but he also had a dozen different irons in the fire, and he was a hero in Vienna, which kept him busy in that city for much of the year. That night he said, "We'll talk." But we never did. I still think Bernstein could have written the Great American Opera on a subject like that.

The next time I tried to move ahead with *Streetcar* was years later when I was general director in Toronto. The composer I approached was Stephen Sondheim. I had wanted to start a commissioning program, and *Streetcar* was on the back burner throughout my Toronto years. I kept alert to news of anyone else trying to make an opera of it, but no one ever did. I checked out Canadian composers, of course, but most of them were academic navel-gazers, and they never could have handled material with that directness. My composer had to understand smoky jazz and genteel decay. With all respect, Toronto could never inspire that kind of music—Canadians are too hygienic.

One year we organized an Opera America Conference, and because I was on the board at the time, we hosted it in Toronto. We invited Sondheim to do a talk on music theater. I cornered him because at that time I had fallen in love with his *Company*, and one of my all-time favorites, *Follies*, is incredibly brilliant, almost Felliniesque. The octet of the two couples, in the present and the past, is overwhelming.

Sondheim could have been an American Mozart, but he's afraid of opera and says he doesn't like it. I thought he would have been ideal for *Streetcar*. He told me it was such a wonderful play it didn't need music. I replied that one might say the same thing about *Othello* and the Falstaff plays. He just wasn't interested. The project returned to the back burner, but over time I was getting more and more afraid someone else would take it. And then I found a way of securing the rights, without which there would have been no way to proceed on the project.

On a visit to New York during my early career, I had met a wonderful gentleman named Herman Krawitz, who was on the administrative staff at the Metropolitan Opera. Herman's wife, Rhoda, is a psychiatrist. She was doing a book on the children Freud had analyzed and asked me to help her set up an interview with Dr. Graf. The Krawitzes had a wonderful apartment on East 57th Street, full of great art and culture. We talked, and I got to know them both quite well. Later, Herman was involved in an important project to record American composers on his own label, New World Records.

By 1988 I was general director in San Francisco. One day, I had lunch at the Krawitz home, where I told them my hope was to do one commission a year. I told them about *Streetcar*, and all of a sudden Herman perked up, "Franco Zeffirelli has been dreaming about this for years and years. I've got to get you two together."

I knew Franco from my European days. Early on, he was brilliant. His *Bohème* staging at La Scala in 1962 with Karajan conducting was one of the greatest nights in all opera. Sadly, he began losing the marvelous delicacy he had at the beginning, and his productions became bloated.

If he were to produce *Streetcar*, there would probably be a dozen real streetcars rolling back and forth across the stage.

Tennessee Williams died in 1983. A dragon lady in London by the name of Lady Maria St. Just was one of the trustees of his estate and became like Fafner sitting on the gold. Anybody who wanted to do anything with Williams's work had to go through her. Luckily, she was great pals with Zeffirelli. Herman said my only hope of getting the rights was through him. So against my better judgment, I began work with Franco. Herman got us together in New York, Los Angeles, and Europe. We had three or four conversations over a couple of years about our shared dream. Franco had worked on the first Italian production of *Streetcar* in 1949 in Rome under the guidance of the author, whom he met through Luchino Visconti, whose assistant he had been.

When we first discussed the project, he was gung ho, suggesting he write the libretto and direct it. He envisioned the project with a huge chorus, whereupon I swallowed hard and told him I hadn't contemplated having any chorus at all, nor did I think it should be a "grand" opera in any case. Fortunately, I was able to win him over, and he finally agreed. He then went on to tell me he had the perfect composer for the project. I swallowed again. Then he mentioned David Grusin.

Grusin is a very talented Hollywood composer, who did Franco's 1979 film *The Champ* and scored *Mulholland Falls*, *Bonfire of the Vanities*, *Tootsie*, and many others, winning a huge collection of awards, including six Oscars. He also has a good background in jazz. As I didn't know him personally, I thought it would be a good idea to invite him to San Francisco. Before he arrived, I listened to his CDs, mostly piano music. I found his melodies fairly sentimental. Some were very good, but not what I had in mind: I wanted something more acerbic, with greater depth. When he came to San Francisco, I asked him how much work he had done for voices. It wasn't much. You need a composer who understands voices, who knows how to use musical approaches to dramatize the differences between Blanche and Stella. Even though he came from a little town in Colorado, he is the essential casual Hollywood type and wasn't the least bit intimidated by the prospect of composing music for an American classic. For him, it was just another assignment, not all that exciting. His apparent diffidence made me uncomfortable.

I told Franco, as diplomatically as I could, that I wasn't convinced about Grusin, but Zeffirelli had made up his mind that this was the man for the job, and I didn't want to lose the project. Franco is a very determined individual, and he was determined to have Grusin. But I don't give up that easily. As there was no way I could get the rights without Zeffirelli, I tried to appease him. I kept telling him it was a chamber piece, but he wanted a blockbuster. For a while I delayed things and deliberately wasted time. I couldn't tell Herman and Rhoda anything about this, because they were so close to Zeffirelli. I just had to play for time to see how things would evolve. The adagio dance went on for months, but while I was doing *Satyagraha* and *Klinghoffer* and the rest of my projects, I kept thinking about this quintessential American classic. Then fate intervened on my side: the dragon lady died.

Control over *Streetcar* passed to the estate's other trustee, John Eastman. Behind Franco's back, I asked Kip Cranna to acquire the operatic rights to *Streetcar*. I wanted to be in the driver's seat, yet keep the information away from Franco. I didn't breathe a word to him, Herman, or Rhoda, and that's how San Francisco got the license.

The publisher imposed certain conditions. The libretto would be thoroughly checked, and no change of characters would be allowed, so as to guarantee the integrity of the property. In 1970, Lee Hoiby had composed an operatic version of Williams's *Summer and Smoke* with a libretto by Lanford Wilson. It's a very good piece and provided a useful role model for us.

I wanted an American composer. I knew that Samuel Barber had briefly considered it, but then turned to *Vanessa* instead. Kip acquired CDs of various composers, and most of them sounded learned and lifeless. I went to see John Corigliano's *The Ghosts of Versailles* and found it a pastiche. John Adams would be wrong for it, and Sondheim had turned me down. I didn't want a Broadway-style piece either. It had to have the personality of an opera, not a sung play. Frank Loesser's *The Most Happy Fella* came close to what I had in mind. It's a wonderful show, one I know quite well, having once understudied the part of Tony, but it was also a little off the mark for what I envisioned.

Getting desperate, I even started looking abroad. I thought about Hans Werner Henze, whom I had met in Zurich in 1961 when he brought his *Elegy for Young Lovers* to us, starring Dietrich Fischer-Dieskau. I also knew his ballet score, *Undine*, and thought it was brilliant. And I had done the North American premiere of *Das verratene Meer* when we had to find a substitute work for *Esther*. I admired Henze very much and started courting him on a visit to London. The only problem was that by then he, like Pollini and Visconti, had committed himself to Communism, although he continued his champagne and caviar lifestyle—some Communist. He wasn't interested.

I talked to English composer Harrison Birtwhistle, who had written *Punch and Judy* and *Mask of Orpheus*. He's a bit long-winded and needed an hour and a half to tell me that "you people" didn't understand his work. A woman in Los Angeles said she would underwrite anything Birtwhistle wrote, but he wasn't interested. This was probably a blessing in disguise; his score would probably have appealed to seven people.

Our search went on for months with frequent discussions between Kip and me about almost every composer in the English-speaking world, and a few beyond it. Finally, I decided to sound out André Previn. At first he declined, saying he didn't feel up to the play's demands, but on December 19, 1994, we received word from his agent, Jonathan Brill, that he had changed his mind and wanted to do *Streetcar* after all. Once André was on board, that was it.

André had started making music at MGM while still very young. Though born in Berlin, he was totally American and had been involved in just about every phase of music, from playing in jazz combos, to writing film scores, playing concertos, and conducting just about every major symphony orchestra in the world. I listened to his music and felt good about it right away. Jazz was always part of the idea. I was looking for the mind-set of a Bernstein and found somebody very close. André had the jazz element along with a solid classical background.

Meanwhile, having Previn's name attached to the project seemed to be a plus point in Kip's negotiations. The attorney for the estate, Michael Remer, said he would work out the final details with Previn's lawyer, Paul Baumgarten.

The more prominent André became, the more he started working through his assistant, Ellyn Kusman, another dragon lady in London. In spite of her, we worked out our terms. Now we had to find the right librettist.

Again, I wanted Terrence McNally. He's a passionate opera lover and a superb asset to the Met broadcasts. I called him, and he was interested. We had settled on a time frame with André, and I wanted to get Terrence on board right away, but out of the blue his *Ragtime* project was picked up by producer Garth Drabinsky in Toronto. Because of his prior commitment to *Ragtime*, he had to pull out.

Then André suggested the Nobel Prize–winning author Toni Morrison. They had worked together, and he admired her very much. She is known largely as a novelist, but later in her career she did the libretto for Richard Danielpour's opera *Margaret Garner*, drawn from her own book *Beloved* and produced in 2005 in Detroit with Denyce Graves in the title role. Opera had always interested her. But she was a tough bargainer! She wanted the moon. We finally settled on a fee of $80,000, which I agreed to pay only because of André and because she was a big name and a writer who knew the South. *Streetcar* was finally on track—or so I thought. Three months later, I got a call from André: "Oh, Lotfi, I can't stand her. She doesn't have any time. She can't do anything for a year!"

This was a terrible setback. I said, "André, baby, you tell her." I reminded him that she had been *his* first choice, that I had acquired her services for him, and that this was one problem he was going to have to solve, because I wasn't about to call her and say, "Sorry, Ms. Morrison, Mr. Previn doesn't want you after all." Although André agreed, behind my back he got Christina Scheppelman, my artistic administrator at the time, to make the call. So Toni Morrison was out. We didn't pay her, because she hadn't submitted one line. André works very fast, and obviously she doesn't. He scheduled his time, down to the minute, for composition. If she couldn't keep up, he couldn't work. He had also declined conducting engagements in order to compose within a very tight window.

I then proposed Philip Littell as librettist. Previn knew his work from *Dangerous Liaisons*, said yes, and we made the deal.

No one would envy Littell's task of adapting a world-famous drama with the Williams estate looking over his shoulder, but the estate granted fairly broad terms, insisting only that the libretto "shall in all events be substantially similar to the play in respect to language, plot, characters, tone and structure, shall be faithful to the spirit of the play, and shall contain no nudity." Littell's real problems came when he conceived words that Williams never wrote. His first attempt to give Mitch an aria met with disapproval. Mitch was too shy to express those deeply personal feelings, the estate argued, and the words had to be considerably toned down. The estate also objected to Littell's deletion of Blanche's "ape" speech, in which she tells her sister Stella (with Stanley overhearing) that her husband is a primitive brute. Littell duly reinserted the speech, but at a different place in the story.

We did have occasional disputes. Littell wanted to depict Blanche as a calculating liar, thus losing the poetry and sadness of her character. André and the rest of us objected. It was pretty tense for a while, but we finally settled in favor of Williams's original concept.

Long before Previn came aboard, I had envisioned Renée Fleming as Blanche. I felt that Blanche had to be a soprano because of her flights of fancy, and I thought of Stella as a lyric mezzo, with which André agreed. I moved to secure Renée's services. I had engaged her in San Francisco for *Arabella* in 1998 and now asked her to do *Streetcar* that season as well. She said yes.

Then André called. He was courting soprano Sylvia McNair at the time and felt she would be the perfect choice for Blanche. Feeling awkward, I went along: I let Renée out as Blanche and put Sylvia in. Then I started negotiating with Sylvia's agent, and months went by. By then, she and André started having problems. Sylvia went to Santa Fe, partly to make up with her husband. All of a sudden she refused to commit to the project until she had seen the finished score. When André heard about it, he exploded. I told Sylvia's agent that if she did not sign her contract by the end of June, I would regard it as a rejection. I flew to Bayreuth to try to mend fences with Renée, taking a couple of André's CDs with me and prepared to grovel.

She was gracious and understanding, but told me she couldn't do both *Arabella* and *Streetcar* in the same season. I had foreseen that possibility and approached the fine British soprano, Janice Watson, who agreed to do all seven performances of the Strauss opera. Now we had our company, our composer, our librettist, and the leading lady I had wanted in the first place.

Initially, I had offered the role of Stanley to Bryn Terfel. I loved his acting and singing, and he has a remarkable way with words, but he wasn't interested. Then I thought of Rodney Gilfrey, a handsome, all-American guy, who is not exactly a warm performer. You want implicit brutality, and Rodney is tough. He always shows up at rehearsals in T-shirts and blue jeans. I arranged for him to meet Previn, and after the Morrison and McNair debacles, I didn't think André was going to say too much. But Rodney made a mistake. He got all dressed up. André phoned me and said he was wrong for the part—too uptight. I called Rodney and

Renée Fleming as Blanche duBois in Streetcar Named Desire.
Marty Sohl, photographer; courtesy San Francisco Opera.

told him to put on his usual outfit and pay another visit to André. He did, sang the "Soliloquy" from *Carousel*, and André was sold.

From the beginning, I also wanted tenor Anthony Dean Griffey for Mitch. He's a wonderful singer and a sweet person. He worked out perfectly. Because we couldn't find the right mezzo for Stella, we turned the part into a soprano. Elizabeth Futral became available, and she was excellent in the role. I also wanted the great Judith Forst as Eunice, and she was brilliant, as usual.

In my heart, I was dying to direct *Streetcar* myself, but I felt too close to the project to do it justice. If I got involved in it creatively, people might think this was just an ego trip. It was a necessary decision, but a hard one to make. I considered many fine directors, including Jack O'Brian, artistic director at the Globe Theater in San Diego. This is one of America's finest companies, and I had long hoped to bring Jack to San Francisco, but he was doing a tour of *Damn Yankees* with Jerry Lewis and had to pass. I ultimately decided to engage Colin Graham as the dramaturge and stage director. Colin knew music so well that André was sold on him immediately. Colin deeply understood the importance of the work and made a tremendous contribution to its success. Because André is such a consummate professional, we had to pair him with someone who was equally flexible, well prepared, and serious. That was Colin Graham.

Workshopping a new opera has become essential. We had an early play-through of the vocal score just with pianists. Then, during the week of November 18–25, 1997, we worked through the structure and the narrative and tested their demands. During those eight days, we used some of the singers from the San Francisco Opera Center, including Alison Buchanan, Peggy Kriha Dye, David Okerlund, Jay Hunter Morris, Mary Philips, John Autry, and Raymond Very. Cast members Rodney Gilfrey and Anthony Dean Griffey were able to join us for short periods. André came over, as did Philip and Colin. Notes were taken, and tapes were played. It was an extremely useful exercise and helped us realize how great the final show was going to be.

André, by now slated to conduct his own work, and associate conductor Patrick Summers listened very closely, making minor changes, noting concerns, then making more changes. André was totally collaborative throughout the workshop process. The workshop was intended to hone the drama and the music, and it succeeded. No modern company should ever consider commissioning an opera without including an early workshop in the process—and in the budget.

There are, of course, certain practical difficulties, which need to be spotted and corrected. Sometimes, they even have musical implications. At one of the final rehearsals, we realized we had a problem with a rotating set. It kept squeaking. This was the setup for Blanche's famous last line about being dependent on the kindness of strangers, and the rodent noises were guaranteed to crack up any audience. What to do? André had the best answer: he simply added a few bars of music to cover the squeak, and no one ever noticed.

Meanwhile, the outstanding question of Franco Zeffirelli was still hanging in the air. I hadn't exchanged a word with him since the Fafner lady died. In the summer of 1995, I was doing the opening of the Arena di Verona Festival with a new production of *Rigoletto*, to be followed by Franco's new production of *Carmen*. I looked at the rehearsal schedule and saw that Franco had fifteen evenings on the stage for his usual gargantuan spectacle, complete with the entire city of Seville onstage along with a sizable mountain range in Act III, and I had three. Gargantua notwithstanding, that was ridiculous. So I took him to lunch. When he appeared with his usual entourage, I showed him the schedule. He was very accommodating and gave me two of his fifteen rehearsals, so now I had five. That settled, he said, "By the way, how's the *Streetcar* project going?" I had been afraid he might bring it up.

"Oh, Franco, I'm still working on it. A lot of obstacles you know . . ." I stuttered on and on, and that was it. He never asked about David Grusin.

The world premiere of *Streetcar* cost a great deal of money. We paid Previn $180,000, Littell got $45,000, and the estate received $20,000, but of course that was just the beginning. There are always onetime costs, those associated with orchestral arrangements and part-sets, phone calls and personal visits, travel from distant places, workshops, extra rehearsal time, revisions, special publicity and promotion, and so on, ad infinitum. It isn't like doing the forty-ninth production of *Aida*, as costly as that opera is. When raising the money, I found André's name very helpful. I obtained much of it, again, from Phyllis Wattis, one of San Francisco's great ladies, as well as several others who respect new music. André Previn himself is a wealthy man, but it never occurred to me to ask him to invest in the opera personally. That was something that should never be done. He was delighted to have the commission. He worked extremely hard, sent us scenes as they were completed, and talked about instrumentation, and we never had anything like the drama we had endured with Conrad Susa. Once on track, everything just rolled.

The first time we worked the production in rehearsal, I was touched. I had told André I usually don't tell creative people anything but would love it if he made an aria out of Blanche saying, "I want magic." Today, I hear singers do that piece in auditions. Previn had understood immediately.

The rehearsal process was a delight, especially with Colin Graham at the helm. He was happy glue bonding together all the artists. They understood what an important work we were dealing with and gave it their best shot. The first great thrill was the *Sitzprobe*, when the singers and orchestra first joined forces. Before that, it was all piano accompaniment. I said, "Oh, my God, we have a production." It was something I had dreamed of for more than twenty years.

André got Brian Culbertson, one of his Hollywood collaborators, to help with the orchestrations. These arrangers never get much credit, but they do get money. I also had the wonderful Patrick Summers share the conducting chores with André, who conducted the first four performances and then stayed on for the first of Patrick's. That night, the piece ran twenty minutes shorter than usual. André rushed onstage, hugged Patrick, and the audience gave them a standing ovation. He said, "Patrick, why didn't you tell me I was so slow?"

Opening night was the usual mass of contradictions. I was in seventh heaven, and I was in solitary. I had done all the work putting the package together, securing the rights, finding the librettist and composer, recruiting the artistic and production teams, figuring out the budget and the schedule, the whole nine yards. Then, on opening night, I became the invisible man. All the artists wanted to concentrate on their work. Nobody needed me any more—the child was walking under its own power.

But opening night was also a gala. Everybody who was anybody attended, including Joseph Volpe, the general manager of the Metropolitan, and CAMI's Ronald Wilford.

Opening nights of new works make you fly. Every fiber of your being makes you overactive. Reality doesn't exist. Midge is the only one who understands this. She never says a word. We didn't talk until we got home, then she asked me simply, "Are you satisfied?"

I was and I wasn't. Personally, I wished the *Streetcar* music had been a little more complex, halfway between Previn and Henze. It needed more texture. I think of *Lulu* or *Wozzeck* and wish it had reached those levels, but I know it didn't. I wish André had been more artistically ambitious. There were nice moments, but I wanted the music to make stronger points.

The following morning, Columbia Artists gave a brunch at the Ritz Carlton Hotel and invited all the stars. It was an elite gathering. During dessert, Ron stood and offered a toast to "the greatest impresario in North America, Lotfi Mansouri." I didn't say a word, but it was quite a compliment, especially considering the source—the same man who had refused to help me find a music director only a few years previously.

The reviews were generally favorable. In *USA Today*, David Patrick Stearns wrote, "In the opening moments, the music establishes the tawdriness and mental instability behind Blanche's pretensions with big, brassy chords that sound like bluesy bebop falling apart. There also are a half-dozen touching, psychologically eloquent arias in a harmonically lush, post-Richard Strauss style."

In the *London Sunday Telegraph*, critic Michael Kennedy wrote, "Previn has composed tuneful, dramatic and essentially American arias for the main characters. One of these, Blanche's 'I want magic' brought the first night to a halt with applause. . . . Where Previn's musicianship shows most clearly is in his writing for voices—every word of the text was audible."

Finally, in the *Los Angeles Times*, Mark Swed commented, "The love music . . . does exactly what music should do for an opera. It reveals why people feel the way they do. No explanation is necessary."

For the company, it was a huge success. It sold out every night and put San Francisco back on the operatic map. In its first eight years, it had twenty-one productions, including outings in such far-flung locations as Los Angeles, Turin, Eisenach, Tokyo, Washington, Strasbourg, San Diego, and New Orleans, and it was also given in concert. PBS telecast it in December 1998, and it was seen by thousands. *Streetcar* was recorded on CD and made available on home video, where many thousands more have enjoyed it.

I am very proud I helped make it happen, and rejoice in all the approval. But you can never satisfy everybody.

Shortly before we opened, we held a press conference, and one of the journalists asked why I didn't imagine Stanley Kowalski as a tenor. I said it was because I didn't know one tenor who looked as good as Gilfrey in a torn T-shirt. That was a sight Tennessee Williams would have savored, and I flatter myself that he would have taken great pride in the work as a whole.

After the success of *Streetcar*, I looked at numerous other projects. John Corigliano was the first composer I approached, but he wanted me to do his opera *The Ghosts of Versailles* before he would accept a commission. I like John's romanticism—his soundtrack for *The Red Violin* and his orchestral music—but I had my problems with *Ghosts*. It was a collage. In many ways, the work's greatest merit is also the greatest impediment to other productions. Commissioned for the Metropolitan Opera's hundredth anniversary, with the specific proviso that it make full use of that house's vast resources, it opened with a lavish and prohibitively expensive Colin Graham production, conducted by James Levine. It featured one star turn after another by an enormous cast of the best artists the opera world had to offer, including stellar performances by Teresa Stratas, Renée Fleming, Håkan Hagegård, Marilyn Horne, Graham Clark, and Gino Quilico, to mention only the best known. But *Ghosts* requires forces of that caliber to make its impact, and with all respect, I don't think it makes sense to embark on a work of such proportions if you have reservations about it.

We then contacted John Guare, a very good playwright, who had written *Six Degrees of Separation*. He recommended an Italian novella, a kind of extended poem called *Silk* by Alessandro Baricco. It's a beautiful story set in Provence and China.

We talked to André Previn again about a second commission and thought *Silk* would make a good subject. The interludes, the voyage from France to China, the Eastern and Western worlds contrasted in the music—it could be ideal, and, of course, we also hoped it would prove attractive to San Francisco's mammoth Chinese community. It would also be highly visual. André loved it. I proposed Colin Graham as the librettist and engaged both of them. We made a verbal agreement with André, a fee was settled, and the opera was scheduled for June 2002. I engaged baritone Bo Skovhus for the leading role. I didn't want to hire anyone else until we had received the score, although André and I did agree about the voice types for the secondary roles.

Then Pamela Rosenberg scuttled the whole project. I was naïve: I had thought Pamela would allow my last year's plans to go ahead and, if they flopped, blame them on me. I had no idea she was going to jettison them in the nearest dumpster. We had never exchanged a single word about *Silk*, but she had seen *Streetcar* on television, I was told, and thought it was "schlock." In many ways, her attitude pointed up the differences between her fundamentally Euro-modern attitude and my somewhat more traditionally based approach in which emotion is a crucial part of the equation. In her school of thought, emotional involvement in a creative work seems to impede a scholarly approach to the intellectual challenges, the structural intricacies, multilevel expressive devices, cross-references to other creative forms, philosophical and sociopolitical statements, that sort of thing. In contrast, I tend to feel that an emotionally gripping work spurs the beholders to seek a greater understanding of how the creators took hold of their emotions in the first place.

Ron Wilford, André's manager, called me in high dudgeon. I told Ron to take the matter to our board, and he asked the company for $300,000 to compensate André not only for the canceled commission, but also for conducting engagements he had dropped to make time for the composition. In the end, André settled for $175,000, in addition to which he was allowed to retain the rights to *Silk*, which San Francisco Opera had purchased on his behalf. Colin Graham was paid another $50,000. He had already written and delivered the libretto and deserved the compensation. And so I was called upon to find $225,000 in "my" budget to settle the costs for Pamela's cancellation of *Silk*.

Pitch Johnson had said he would subsidize all of Pamela's cancellations, but the actual funding came from his general pledge. He had guaranteed $500,000 in the form of stocks as a gift to the company. By the time these stocks were sold, the share value had fallen to $350,000. I had counted on his $500,000 in the master budget for the whole company, and so this was a double loss on my side of the ledger. We lost $150,000 in the value of his stocks and $225,000 in the disappearance of *Silk*. And so Pamela's cancellation came out of my budget *and* the income I had been counting on—a very bitter pill for me to swallow.

Pamela couldn't have read the *Silk* score, because it didn't exist. She could have been patient, but she wanted to marshal the company's full resources for her own production of Olivier Messaien's magnum opus, *Saint François d'Assise*, a daunting work replete with enormous intellectual challenges but not exactly one that meets a large and diverse audience halfway.

In the meantime, my staff and I also talked about doing Arthur Miller's play *All My Sons* or Sinclair Lewis's novel *Elmer Gantry*. We felt the revival meetings in the latter work could make for a great American opera, and Thomas Hampson was dying to portray Gantry. However, another team, Robert Aldridge and Herschel Garfein, had started a *Gantry* project in Boston. They came to San Francisco at our invitation and presented a video and CD of what they had done, but they reminded me of the problems we had faced with the team we had for *Harvey Milk*, so we decided to pass.

Another play I loved was arguably Miller's greatest masterwork, *Death of a Salesman*. It's like an American *King Lear*, but I never found the right composer for it. As we considered all of these possibilities, we were approaching the end of the year 2000.

I wanted an opera that belittled the idea of the millennium. Whose millennium? The Iranians'? That was only 1,300 years. The Chinese? Theirs was 4,000. All of this millennium talk was so narrow, so provincial. It betrayed how little we know about the rest of the world. In 1997, I went to Gérard Philippe's grave in the south of France, above Saint-Tropez. Philippe had starred, along with Gina Lollobrigida, in René Clair's dazzling 1952 film, *Les belles de la nuit* (*The Beauties of the Night*), concerning a discontented music teacher who fantasizes about romances with beautiful women from different historical periods. In each period, an old man appears, complaining that things nowadays are terrible—it was all so much better in the old days. I realized this would make a fabulous *opera comique* and thought once more about asking Terrence McNally to do the text.

At that time we had a young man in the public relations department by the name of Jake Heggie, a trained pianist and composer, who had written some very nice songs for Carol Vaness, Renée Fleming, Frederica von Stade, and Jennifer Larmore. I felt he had a great gift for vocal composition and that it might be worthwhile to have our own in-house composer. Jake is an incredibly good self-promoter, relentless, and charming. All of a sudden, it was like having a son—he couldn't do enough for me. At first, I thought he could do *Belles de nuit* with McNally. We brought Terrence to California, and the two of them hit it off. They came to my office and said they would like to collaborate. I had given the film to Jake, and he liked it, but Terrence said he didn't think he was the right librettist for *Belles*. Although nobody had done that sort of elegant comedy for a long time and it could have been magnificent caviar, Terrence said it wasn't to his taste.

The team was more important than the story, and I wouldn't force them to do anything they didn't believe in. Terrence proposed a project based on the 1993 chronicle by Sister Helen Préjean, *Dead Man Walking*. He thought it would make a good opera. I said, "Terrence, this sounds wonderful! We'll do it!" I hadn't read the book yet, but I had seen the Oscar-winning movie by Tim Robbins starring Susan Sarandon and Sean Penn. It was tremendous and very American in its themes. Terrence was flabbergasted that I had agreed so quickly.

Jake was in line with Terrence. I think the two of them had cooked things up beforehand anyway. Terrence is a born theater cat. He has an innate awareness of what works onstage. I sent Jake to New York to work on the music with him. Terrence offered Jake a room, and so it began.

Terrence's libretto would be based on the book, not on the film screenplay. We negotiated with Sister Helen's order, the Congregation of Sisters of St. Joseph of Medaille, for the rights to turn the book into an opera. Sister Helen, a determined woman, was extremely happy to see her anti-death-penalty message put forward in yet another medium.

Terrence sent me the libretto a few months later. When Midge read it, she started to cry.

I organized a meeting in San Francisco to discuss casting. Sister Helen had to be a lyric mezzo, of course. You couldn't have a conventionally romantic voice in the part. The killer had to be a menacing baritone. It would all lead to the transforming admission of guilt, a unique and incredible journey.

I thought of the tall, imposing, and highly intelligent Susan Graham for the role of Sister Helen. I found out from her agent that at the time we would be producing *Dead Man*, she was scheduled to be in Paris preparing to sing Dulcinée in Massenet's *Don Quichotte* for Hugues Gall at the Opéra Bastille. I flew over to see Hugues, a good colleague and friend. As it happened, Susan was also there, and when we attended a performance together at the Bastille, I told her about the role. She was familiar with the film, and I convinced her to consider singing the pivotal role. In real life, Sister Helen is a smart woman with a deeply rooted faith. I have no idea what Susan's personal beliefs are, and don't care. She is a first-class actress without a trace of false glamour, convincingly honest in anything she portrays.

She would, however, have to ask Hugues to let her out of her Paris commitment, as we were heading into production. Hugues graciously consented. I invited him to the premiere, of course, but he was unfortunately unable to attend.

Once we had Susan, we started to look for the baritone. I'm enormously fond of Simon Keenlyside's work. He seemed ideal for the role, because he is a complicated man and a brilliant, somewhat tormented artist. I took Simon to lunch and schmoozed him, but he turned me down.

Meanhile, Jake had endeared himself to Frederica von Stade, which is not hard to do. Flicka is an incredibly generous person, who even gave him one of her pianos. He told Flicka he wanted her to be the mother of the murdered girl, but Flicka wanted to be the mother of the murderer, and that is how we cast her. She was an important artist to have in the world premiere, and Jake would write the music especially for her, most pivotally in the interrogation scenes.

I began auditioning baritones, but I didn't want European elegance. The voice had to be a bit rough; it had to credibly belong to a Southern sharecropper type. It couldn't be the voice of an Italian doing an American. I auditioned thirty or forty baritones, but none of them came close. I wrote agents, describing the type I wanted, and always gave Sean Penn as a point of reference. I was in Merkin Hall in Manhattan, auditioning one baritone after another. All of a sudden, a guy came onstage. Before he even opened his mouth, I said, "He looks like just what I want. I hope he can sing." He could. I didn't even know his name. I called Terrence and arranged for him to hear the guy. Terrence said yes, and then Jake heard him and said yes. And that's how we got John Packard.

We also had to have covers. We cast Christine Jepsen to understudy Susan Graham, and she proved a major asset to the rehearsal period. I brought a tall, good-looking baritone, Teddy Tahu Rhodes, from New Zealand to try out as a cover for Joe, Packard's role. I gave him the monologue to learn, and when he did it, he was absolutely mesmerizing. Teddy is now making a big international career, and he is a highly gifted actor-singer. He is destined to be a major star. I wasn't worried about rivalry between him and John. They are both intelligent artists. Whenever Teddy did the push-up sequence in his underwear, all the secretaries and members of the music staff came to the wings to watch—he has an impressive physique.

Terrence suggested Joe Mantello as director and Michael Yeargan as designer. While I had worked with Michael many times, Joe had never done an opera before, but I accepted both recommendations without hesitation. Conductor Patrick Summers was already on our staff, and he, too, brought his immense talent to the production.

There was just one problem. Patrick and Jake began campaigning for Donita Volkwijn, a young singer from South Africa who had done the role in workshop, to sing Sister Helen's associate, Sister Rose. After I said no, they appealed to Donald Runnicles. In our business, very little surprises me anymore, but this came as a shock. They felt Theresa Hamm-Smith, whom I had cast in the role, was not vocally right, although she was later singled out for praise. Theresa was also a good match for Susan, with a lyric, strong top.

Donald called me, even though he had nothing whatsoever to do with the production. That didn't bother me. I went through the motions with Donald, and that was that, but I was disappointed with Patrick. I had made him principal guest conductor, given him *Streetcar*, and moved his career miles forward. And I had dug Jake out of the PR department and given him a Tony-winning playwright as his collaborator. Going behind my back to Donald, of all people, knowing of my strained relationship with him—that wasn't just disloyal, it was plain dumb. Donald was the last person in the world likely to change my mind. Although Patrick's involvement came as a surprise, considering his great intelligence, I already had Jake's number: he is a charmer. He even tried to seduce three thousand strangers in a single shot: he took a curtain call at all eight performances, although in fairness to him, I must admit he's not the only composer to have taken that many curtain calls.

When I left as general director, Donald promptly eliminated Patrick's position as principal guest conductor—so much for loyalty.

We did a first-act workshop in August 1999 with Terrence, Jake, Joe Mantello, and Patrick Summers, along with the singers Kristen Clayton, John Packard, Elena Bocharova, Donita Volkwijn, and several invited audience members. Revisions resulted. Patrick was wonderful in this process, because he knows so much about orchestration, the voice, everything. He was an incredible guide to Jake, and Jake ate out of his hand. Patrick was the real engineer of this music.

The libretto was so solidly crafted that very little needed to be rewritten. There were a few changes initiated by Joe, who was concerned that Sister Helen not appear too uncertain or indecisive. He wanted her more

Opening night of Dead Man Walking, *2000,*
with Terrence McNally and Jake Heggie.

resolute and determined, more like the real person. Most of the changes involved her monologue as she drives to meet the condemned man for the first time.

Ultimately the libretto was the foundation of our success. It is brilliant and moving. The use of the car radio at the beginning and the dead silence at the end were both Terrence's ideas. His understanding of theater is incisive, and like Tennessee Williams, he also knows the human heart.

Director Joe Mantello also did a wonderful job. He shaved away the operatic mannerisms and brought in reality. Together with Michael Yeargan, he produced the tremendous set. Michael is a superb designer and went on to win a Tony Award for *The Light in the Piazza*.

For all his meaningful contributions, Joe's ignorance of operatic practice made him a bit hard to work with. In drama, as a director you wander around with a script in your hand and sort of make it up as you go along. In opera, you arrange the lighting and the rehearsal sequences first, before you do anything else. Everything is planned day by day, minute by minute. Hundreds of people take their cues from this scheduling. Joe Mantello was always asking for more rehearsals. I had to tell him,

"Look, Joe, this is the very last piano rehearsal you have. After that, there is *nothing* else. Whatever else you've got to do has got to be done by then. After that you give notes. *There's no more time.*" He sometimes forgot that San Francisco Opera was running another nine productions at the same time, and he would grouse and use four-letter words. There is a certain arrogance about him, but he backs it up with talent. I have no problem with a little arrogance when it comes from somebody as gifted as Joe Mantello.

After our huge success, I noticed that, in every interview, Jake would take personal credit for the casting—all of it. At first I was peeved, and then I was amused. Now that I'm not general director any more, he has stopped currying favor with me. Lotfi who?

Along with a few shorter stage works, he wrote another opera, *End of the Affair*, for Houston, and it was then substantially revised for Seattle, but it just didn't work. He is now working on an operatic version of *Moby Dick* for Dallas, with San Francisco also participating in the commission. I hope he has the same success he did with *Dead Man Walking*, which worked so well because all the elements came together perfectly and because we surrounded him with the A team.

Susan Graham had a sensational success, and she deserved it. She was everything I had hoped she would be. There was a wonderful scene in which Robert Orth, as the father of the murdered girl, erupted in a shattering outburst. In reply, Flicka was even more heart wrenching when she asked, "Will killing my child bring back your children?" I wept. Everyone wept. It was one of the greatest nights I have ever experienced in music theater, and the deep intimacy of text and music made it possible.

On opening night of *Dead Man Walking*, there was a candlelight procession outside the opera house of people opposing capital punishment. Sister Helen went out to talk to the participants. The guests in my box included Sean Penn, Susan Sarandon, and Tim Robbins. Their friends Robin Williams, Garry Marshall, and Julie Andrews also attended. It was quite an opening.

Terrence was very pleased, although he has a poker face and never shows much emotion. Jake thanked him before the curtain went up, but once the production triumphed it was all his doing. I hope Pitch Johnson is aware that, had he bought out my contract, as he had threatened to do, *Dead Man* would never have happened.

The reviews from all over the world could not have been more enthusiastic. Writing in the *Guardian* in London, Martin Kettle said the piece "makes the most concentrated impact of any piece of American music since *West Side Story* more than 40 years ago." And a local critic, Joshua Kosman, in the *San Francisco Chronicle* stated that the opera "must be reckoned as something of a masterpiece—a gripping, enormously skillful marriage of words and music to tell a story of love, suffering and spiritual redemption." David Littlejohn in the *Wall Street Journal* called the opera "the most compelling piece of musical theater I encountered this season" and kindly went on to comment, "I regard *Dead Man Walking* as one of the triumphs of the retiring general director, Lotfi Mansouri."

Perhaps the most meaningful tribute came from an unexpected source. *Dead Man Walking* would not have happened without the generosity of Phyllis Wattis. At the outset of the project, I had given her, along with Terrence McNally, the film and the book. For two or three months I didn't hear from her. I got nervous and called her up. She asked me to come see her.

"Lotfi, I watched and read everything. I want to let you know that I am in favor of capital punishment." I told her that I'm not involved in politics. I don't want to do productions to tell people what to think, nor do I believe this is the function of theater anyway; its purpose is, rather, to give people something to reflect on so that they can make up their own minds. In this sense, opera can deal honestly with any issue. Let the audience decide.

She gave me *2 million dollars*! At the party after the premiere, Phyllis told me in that lovely direct way of hers, "You know, Lotfi, about the issue of capital punishment—I'm not so sure any more."

Most important, Sister Helen was thrilled. She felt that we had conveyed the message, without sermonizing. The opera, like her story, was about faith and forgiveness and love, but it was also an intensely personal experience for the audience.

The show went beyond my expectations, especially because of the audience. Among professionals, our former principal guest conductor, Sir Charles Mackerras and his wife, Judy, were stunned by the evening. *Dead Man* assumed a life of its own, and we had to add two extra performances. Since then, many other companies have picked it up. By the end of 2007, it had already been performed in fourteen cities in six different countries. Its moral arguments are universal. So long as the United

States, as well other countries such as China, Bangladesh, Iran, Iraq, Nigeria, Pakistan, Saudi Arabia, and Yemen, continues the savage practice of capital punishment, this opera will endure.

When the members of Pamela Rosenberg's creative team for *Saint François* came to the opera house, they attended a performance of *Dead Man*, and the next day Patrick Markle, our technical director, brought them on a courtesy call to my office. I already knew what their reaction would be. In most Central European theatrical circles, the two most damning insults are "Das ist so amerikanisch!" and, worse, "Das ist so Hollywood."

I courteously asked them in German, "Na, wie hat es Ihnen gefallen [Well, how did you like it]?"

They stared at one another for a long moment in embarrassed silence. Finally, they looked over at their stage director, Nicolas Brieger, who, true to form, stammered, "Herr Mansouri, das ist . . . das ist so amerikanisch."

I was happy to confirm their statement with gratitude, adding helpfully, "The writer, the librettist, the composer, the stage director, the designer, the cast, the story—all *amerikanisch*."

They sat there wide-eyed, confused because I had taken their condemnation as a compliment. The irony went right over their heads.

LORDS AND LADIES OF THE LARYNX, POTENTATES OF THE PODIUM

Mansouri's Gallery of Illustrious Colleagues

Yes, many of the singers and conductors I have had the privilege of collaborating with over the years are pretty eccentric. Considering the challenges they have to face, they almost have to be. Beyond the actual rigors of performance, any singer with a major career is expected to carry a large repertory of roles in his or her head, develop a fair degree of fluency in a variety of languages, and be ready to give convincing portrayals of this vast array of characterizations often at a moment's notice. Stories about an artist being pushed onstage or sent into the pit without rehearsal, sometimes racing from the airport while the theater holds the curtain—with radically varying results—have almost become a cliché. This would fray anybody's nerves, and any artist who meets these challenges over and over again without seeming to be under any strain, giving a discerning audience all it bargained for, and then some, is worthy of tribute.

I'd like to offer my readers some memories of the best of the best, along with one or two portraits of some genuine oddballs, who required some endurance on my part as they strutted and fretted through their professional lives but who, in the final analysis, proved more than worth the effort it took to put up with their shenanigans.

Let me begin with one of the best. When I came to Canada, I met mezzo-soprano Judith Forst, who inspired everyone not just with her sunny nature, but also with her consummate professionalism. Gifted with a glorious, solidly focused voice and exceptional musicianship, as well as acting ability that breathes life into every character she delineates, she has given definitive performances in an enormously wide range of characterizations, including such diverse parts as Rosina and Cenerentola and ranging all the way to Augusta Tabor in *The Ballad of Baby Doe*, Kabanicha in *Kat'a Kabanová*, and Klytämnestra in *Elektra*, plus all the stops along the way. Yet she is self-aware in the best sense: she knows her limits. She is objective, pulling signals out of the air and knowing how to discard the useless ones. She has the gift of watching, listening, and experimenting. She asks pertinent questions and demands to be convinced on an intellectual level.

She continues to seek out new challenges and goes on setting an example for colleagues eager to have a solid professional basis, free of illusions and other nonsense. In this, she joins a very few others who derive their artistic satisfaction exclusively from the art.

Dame Joan Sutherland is one of these. Her historic partnership with Richard Bonynge was magical. It remains a beacon to others, a glowing example of personal realism, and demonstrates a willingness on Joan's part to collaborate. Richard placed very high demands on her work and told her in no uncertain terms when she failed to reach the standards he set for her. I recall one orchestra dress rehearsal of *Traviata* in which he called her down with such vehemence that she walked off the stage, leaving me to mark the title role.

Joan Sutherland had a long and glorious career because she took advice, sought a partner who could provide it, and never lost her infectious, earthy sense of humor and self-irony.

This was a far cry from the highly gifted Maria Ewing. She failed to follow the example of Sutherland or Forst and wound up paying a terrible price for her illusory approach. She started as an alluring mezzo who could convince audiences possibly better than anyone else that her enchantingly sung Cherubino was really a boy, while countering this performance with a frothily feminine Dorabella. But she started to become enormously complicated as she drifted into the leading soprano repertoire.

My last experience with her was a nightmare. I engaged her as Salome for our Strauss Festival at San Francisco in the summer of 1993. She became difficult, stubborn, and wrongheaded. In the easier sections, she would drag the rhythms, then rush like crazy in the more difficult parts. To his credit, Donald Runnicles did his best to cope with her.

Married to Sir Peter Hall at the time, she expected to be addressed as

"Lady Hall," then put a sign on her dressing room saying that she was not to be spoken to at all. Of course, people called her a few other names behind her back.

There are so many demeaning remarks about dumb tenors, including the one about the tenor who was so stupid that another tenor noticed it. But I can mention a quartet of great tenors, who prove the exact opposite.

Plácido Domingo is a unique and spectacular artist—arguably the most versatile tenor in operatic history. I've had the pleasure of directing him in quite a few productions, and I've always said I'd rather have a day with Plácido than weeks with many others. His artistic curiosity is limitless, and he constantly challenges himself in a wide variety of repertoire, styles, and languages. He's indefatigable in rehearsals and continues to have an ongoing drive for growth. Beyond his artistic and musical gifts, he is one of the most generous, compassionate, giving colleagues I've ever had the pleasure to know. He truly sets a standard we should all aspire to.

The late James McCracken was a special artist and a great human being. He was, in a way, a giant in our world. Generous to a fault, he would give his all onstage—and to his friends. I had the privilege of directing him in his signature roles. His Otello, in particular, spoiled me for many others. He lived every note of the role. As Samson, Canio, and other characters, he would get so involved in the role that he would often threaten to upset his own equilibrium. In addition to being a tremendous colleague, he had a wonderful sense of humor. Rehearsals with him and Gobbi number among the most treasured memories of my career. His untimely death left a terrible void, and I still miss him.

Siegfried Jerusalem started out as an orchestra musician, playing both violin and bassoon, and he is also an excellent pianist. As his mother and brother both live in Canada, I had the good fortune to bring him to the Canadian Opera Company. He even forgave me for saddling him with a lousy director and a wacko conductor for *Lohengrin*, as detailed in Chapter 9. I then reengaged him for the title role in *Idomeneo*, and he was equally splendid. At the end of a long, creditable career, he now teaches, does character roles, and excels as a recitalist.

Jon Vickers was colossally intelligent, although his many eccentricities certainly could be worrisome. On the plus side, he remains unmatched as a total artist in the heroic repertoire. He brought a special power to every role he sang and a wonderful spontaneity that meant no two of his performances were ever exactly alike. This quality had to be taken into consideration by anyone who was staging him. In a certain sense, you did not "direct" Jon Vickers.

He excelled in characterizations that did not draw life from interaction with other characters, such as Florestan, Siegmund, Peter Grimes, and Handel's Samson. His problems in relating to others in real life carried over to the stage.

Just as Jon's isolation could be a stirring experience, the great Italian bass-baritone Paolo Montarsolo exuded a sense of interactive participation that gripped audiences like an embrace. Paolo was connected to everyone and everything around him, and it showed in the rightness of ensemble he always inspired. His buffo roles had the timing of a Charlie Chaplin, but I also directed him as the Doctor in an Italian-language production of *Wozzeck* in Palermo, and he was chilling. He also had an incredible flexibility, adjusting both to the production and to the audience. One day, in rehearsal at La Scala, he told me, "Please don't expect me to give you everything I gave you in San Francisco; people here concentrate more on the singing."

He loved literature and was always reading to expand his cultural horizon, constantly learning and developing. This wealth of background resulted in our not needing to talk much: his receptiveness was instantly transformed into dramatic action without much having to be said.

This quality also applied to his fellow basso, Nicola Rossi-Lemeni. He was obsessed with acquiring new and meaningful experiences. He was part Russian, part Italian, born in Turkey, raised in Rome, and infused with genuine sophistication. His elegance was so pronounced that when served champagne at a party, he would extract a sterling silver cocktail stirrer from his pocket. He courted quite a few women in his life, including Renata Tebaldi and the daughter of the great conductor Tullio Serafin, finally marrying the fabulous soprano Virginia Zeani, who is now retired from the faculty of Indiana University.

Rossi-Lemeni was a staggering Wozzeck, and equally gripping as Don Quichotte and the Father in *Louise*. He portrayed a definitive Boris Godunov, always drawing from his profound understanding of obsession. He was a born stage animal, with enormous emotional revelations he could instantly turn into stage action, yet he was always in full intellectual control of his impulses.

Many of Rossi-Lemeni's qualities also stand out in the personality of tenor Nicolai Gedda, a remarkable linguist with an international background and an enormous range of definitive portrayals. He lent new dimensions to Auber's lightweight but vocally demanding comedy *Fra Diavolo*, which I staged in an English-language production in San Francisco. In rehearsal, I hit him with a huge challenge, asking him to change his clothes, from the attire of a dandy to that of the character's real self, while singing an aria loaded with high Cs. He agreed, on condition that he be given an hour each day with whomever he was playing opposite to practice handling the clothes and props. The result was breathtaking. He practiced and practiced, and on opening night it looked like the easiest thing in the world.

The only artist I ever encountered who could outdo him in the language department was his Swedish compatriot Elisabeth Söderström, who enjoys a major position in my personal pantheon. She is fluent in ten languages, with a partly Russian background like Nicolai's. Elisabeth is incapable of superficiality. She has an incisive intelligence and a keen knowledge of the human heart—and the human mind. She always worked her characterizations from the inside out, never relying on mere choreography to create a role. Her characters ranged from the Mozart roles of her early career all the way to the roles of her mature period, when she became an expert on the works of Leoš Janáček. She is also one of the very few artists who excelled in all three leading roles in Strauss's *Der Rosenkavalier*.

She always understood her own limitations, selecting her roles judiciously and never overtaxing her beautiful but not very large voice. Vanity has never clouded her judgment. Like , she is a devoted wife and mother. While her sons were growing up, she spent as much time as she could at home, restricting her overseas appearances to recitals, but what recitals they were!

In contrast to this attitude, career seemed to come first for Carol Vaness, who has no fear at all of pushing the envelope, hurling herself body and soul into such go-for-broke characterizations as Donna Anna and Elettra in *Idomeneo*. Carol is an indefatigable researcher, giving her material a lot of thought, playing everything at the keyboard, overflowing with intellectual ambition. We first met at the twenty-fifth anniversary gala for Mr. Adler, and shortly afterward, I began inviting her to Toronto. She gave an incredible performance as Madame Lidoine, the new

*With Elisabeth
Söderström in
Geneva, ca. 1971.*

prioress in *Les dialogues des Carmélites*. This role has often led to fame for its most inspired performers, and Carol was no exception. As a colleague, she can sometimes be fairly high maintenance, and we have had a few run-ins, but at the end of the day she is really worth it.

There is one artist whose career I helped guide from its inception, when I was starting out with Dr. Graf in Zurich. Dr. Graf had an uncanny ear for voices, and when he heard a young Welsh mezzo named Gwyneth Jones, he knew he had found the genuine article. A glutton for hard work, she learned the enormous role of Fidès in Meyerbeer's *Le prophète* in the incredible space of forty-eight hours and absolutely nailed it. That was ambition brought to bear at the right place.

When she switched to soprano, urged on by Nello Santi, I had the privilege of directing her first Desdemona, in which she held her own with James McCracken as Otello, and Tito Gobbi alternating with Ramón Vinay as Jago, then gave her full support to Vinay when, brilliant colleague that he was, he briefly returned to the tenor range to replace the indisposed McCracken on short notice.

With Carol Vaness, ca. 2000.

I also directed her first Tosca and watched her get a little carried away in one performance. We had rehearsed the scene in which Scarpia tries to seduce her by improvising the subtext, what Tosca is thinking during the scene, speaking it in English. Then in performance she got so into it that I actually heard her say something to the effect of "not with me you son of a bitch." I had to take her aside and remind her that, if she *was* going to externalize those feelings she would have to do it in Italian. Would that she had known when the time had come to retire, but singing is her life.

In a far more tragic way, Tatiana Troyanos never wanted to stop living. She was one of the greatest artists I ever knew, but she had a rather complicated personality. We worked together in Europe, Canada, and the United States. She had a major triumph in Aix-en-Provence as the Composer in Strauss's *Ariadne auf Naxos*. We met when I directed her as Carmen. She had a rich mezzo voice with a tremendous extension that allowed her even to sing roles like Donna Elvira with enormous dramatic energy. People tried to push her into the soprano repertoire, but she was wise enough never to go any farther than was natural. Her energy and commitment were contagious. The price Tatiana paid for all of this was heart palpitations and other physical problems. She developed an unfortunate habit of canceling. One evening before a performance of *Don Carlo*, in which she was cast as Princess Eboli, I found her on the floor of her dressing room, shaking with anxiety. She said she couldn't go on, and I said, "Okay, honey. Don't worry about it. Your cover is in costume and ready to go." Then she paused and said, "Just give me ten minutes," and wound up giving a magnificent performance.

In the mid-1980s she developed cancer, and when it recurred, her friends thought she had abandoned hope. Her final performance was again Strauss—this time Clairon in *Capriccio*. She was already very ill. I went to her dressing room on opening night and said, "Remember, your character is very sexy, a superstar." She took out her lipstick and wrote on the mirror, "SEXY! SUPERSTAR!" In the face of her own death, she remained an astounding artist. We never discussed her condition, nor did the audience ever find out how ill she was.

Tito Gobbi gave me some of the highlights of my career. He was not only a great singer but also a great actor, intellect, writer, and painter. Directing him as Simon Boccanegra, I learned the opera as I never had before, even the minute detail of the difference between a Genoese and a Roman cross. He was a brilliant, insidious Jago, a lascivious, truly evil Scarpia, and a delicious Gianni Schicchi. What an artist!

A similar great Italian artist is Ferruccio Furlanetto. Rehearsals with him are always exciting, challenging, and rewarding. It's like doing a *pas de deux* with a great partner. His Shakespearean characterization of Philip in *Don Carlo* and his Boris are music theater magic. Then there is his delightfully seedy Don Basilio in *Il barbiere di Siviglia*.

Birgit Nilsson knew instinctively that she was a superstar, yet she had the humility to regard her great gifts as just that: gifts, not attributes to be touted but qualities to be developed and nurtured. This common-sense approach made her one of the easiest artists to work with, as I discovered when Mr. Adler asked me to direct her in *Turandot*, which I did in 1964. The scene in Act III where the heroine finally succumbs to Calaf's kiss is very difficult to stage. I've always done it like a kind of dance, tightly timed to the music, so that the kiss finally happens on a specific chord. We talked about how Calaf's passion is so magnetic it

*Birgit Nilsson,
backstage at
San Francisco
Opera, 1981.*

actually helps her overcome her terror of men. After the kiss, her rigidity and resistance melt away, and she emerges from the embrace as a more complete human being, shy and vulnerable. She was very happy with what we did, and told everybody in the house about it, whereupon people began saying to me, "Lotfi, we've heard your kiss is the best."

One afternoon, I thanked her for her hard work and great insight, to which she replied, "Hard work? Turandot is my vacation role. I've only got about seventy-six bars to sing, as compared to Isolde's twelve hundred and twenty-five bars—and I get the same fee." Fees meant a lot to Birgit, but she was never obsessed with them. The fact that she got good money for good work just meant that she was on the right track and kept her firmly grounded. As one sign of how smart she was, she never dropped Mozart from her repertoire, saying she thought of that music as real medicine for her voice.

Another smart soprano with talent to match is Renata Scotto, but on one occasion her Italian impulsiveness almost got her into hot water with the San Francisco audience before she even arrived in the country. She was due in California to partner Luciano Pavarotti in the title role of *La Gioconda,* and I had been assigned to direct. This production meant a great deal to all of us, because it would be the very first opera performance to be telecast worldwide from America. Unfortunately, shortly before leaving Italy, Renata came out for a curtain call after a performance of *Un ballo in maschera* at La Scala, and some of the audience booed her, to which she responded with an unmistakable hand gesture,

Renata Scotto, skeptically listening as I give her notes after a Gioconda
rehearsal. Ira Nowinski, photographer; courtesy San Francisco Opera.

in a sense telling the ingrates what they could do with their disapproval.
As a consequence, several of them decided to repeat their catcalls at the
stage door, to which she replied by calling them "finocchi di Milano!"
(Milanese faggots).

The slur made all the papers and actually preceded her to San Francisco, which is just about the last city in the United States where you can
get away with a remark like that, as we discovered when the production
opened. This indiscretion was only one reason our *Gioconda* laid a huge
egg. Unfortunately, Renata's diligence came up against Luciano's lassi-
tude, and the result of the contact deep-sixed the production before the
curtain rose. Luciano, as intelligently and meticulously as he produced
his voice, was not the world's most studious of singers, and he often failed
to learn the whole opera until the last minute. This infuriated Renata at
rehearsals, and she would sit down in a corner and refuse to take part, so
I was forced to sing the title role in order to feed Luciano the cues.

As beautiful as her singing was, she was never much of an actress. She was a bit old-fashioned and often unwilling to stand beside anyone who made her look chubby or short, both of which she was. In our doomed production, even the curtain calls were a problem. We had agreed that no one would take a solo call until the very end of the evening, but Luciano got so excited he jumped out by himself after an earlier act. Renata was so furious she refused to take a bow at all, and the documentary shows me on my knees vainly begging her to respond to the applause.

It was the last time we worked together. Unfortunately, as her career continued, she made some very poor repertoire decisions, taking on unsuitable roles like Norma and Lady Macbeth, which may have prematurely truncated what could have been a longer career.

Beverly Sills never made those mistakes. She had enormous wisdom about what was right for her and why, and she knew instinctively when it was time to call it a day and continue on to other pursuits, accruing great benefit to opera all along the way, as both a singer and a company manager. Perhaps one of her greatest virtues right from the beginning was patience. Rather than trying to work her way up through provincial theaters in Europe, she remained in the United States and built a modest but solid career, largely concentrated on magnificent performances at the New York City Opera, honing her acting skills to match her rock-solid vocal production, which kept her sounding appealingly creamy all the way to the top of her sizable register. Passed over by Rudolf Bing at the Metropolitan, who had the effrontery to suggest in his memoirs that he saw no reason to favor her over the international artists he engaged "just because" Sills was a Jewish girl from Brooklyn, she built her talents, waited her turn, then took the Metropolitan and the biggest European theaters by storm at the height of her ability.

Beverly and I worked together on a production of *La fille du régiment* in which her sense of humor lent a zany note of "I Love Lucy" comedy to her tremendous vocal prowess. The production traveled all over the place. Throughout her singing and managing career, her frequent appearances on television talk shows and the straightforward, effervescent manner she revealed during all these exposures did a lot of good for the way average Americans perceived opera and the people who make it happen.

In a very different way, Leontyne Price also became an American icon with a magnificent international career. Starting out as a solidly grounded girl from Mississippi, after completing her studies as a scholarship student at Juilliard she did some of her initial coaching with a man named Jack Metz, with whom I had also worked. Jack had a long list of students, including Kathryn Grayson, Leona Mitchell, and Eileen Farrell. He was an expert in the Italian repertoire, and she learned a lot from him; like all of the top artists in the field, for all her string of triumphs, she never stopped learning.

She also had an incisive sense of humor. When asked in a film documentary about Kurt Herbert Adler which of his attributes she would best remember, she shot back, "His charming deviousness." That line tells you a lot about both of them.

Another great singer with a long and well-managed career is Marilyn Horne. She and I go back to the 1950s in Los Angeles. Everybody called her "Jackie" even then. She started her professional life at the age of eighteen, singing solos with the Roger Wagner Chorale, while studying, as I did, with the Zweigs and Lotte Lehmann. Back then, she also recorded the sound track voice for Dorothy Dandridge in Otto Preminger's 1954 movie version of *Carmen Jones*. Jackie has a fabulous personality and an infectious laugh.

Her career went stratospheric when Sutherland and Bonynge drew her to the *bel canto* style. Jackie first performed with Joan in a concert version of Vincenzo Bellini's *Beatrice di Tenda* at Carnegie Hall in February 1961. In 1965, they joined forces again for a performance of Rossini's *Semiramide* with the Opera Company of Boston. Director Irving Guttman brought them back together in *Semiramide* and *Norma* productions in Vancouver—and other operas. These great triumphs cemented a close friendship that they enjoy to this day.

Carol Fox, the head of the Chicago Lyric Opera, engaged me to stage a production of *L'italiana in Algeri* for Jackie there, and it was a marvelous experience. That's when we really connected professionally and personally. Our next contact was *Norma* in San Francisco. By then I had worked a great deal with Joan Sutherland, and I felt right at home with *bel canto*. In rehearsal I kept urging Jackie to appear more and more vulnerable. She's a very staunch woman, and I needed to remind her that she had to come across with a plausible characterization of a virginal Druid priestess. After we opened, she sent me a review describing her "touching vulnerability." She circled that line in red.

Once I became general director of San Francisco Opera, we collaborated frequently, and we gave her a big gala on the fortieth anniversary of her first appearance there. In 1995, she became director of opera studies at the Music Academy of the West, where we had both studied with Lehmann and where she invited me to direct *Albert Herring*. Since then, I have returned often to work with the very gifted students she handpicks for her summer courses.

Jackie has a unique voice, a fantastic technique, and a magnificent sound—all combined with the intelligence of a mathematics professor, which has had a definitive impact on her choice of roles and the other music she sings so splendidly. Like all great artists, she knows where to seek the best advice, and she takes it, benefiting enormously from her interaction not only with the Bonynges but with collaborating artists such as Marvin Hamlisch, who often accompanies her performance of Broadway selections. Part of her legacy is the Marilyn Horne Foundation, which she founded on her retirement to encourage recital singing. Many major artists have emerged from that foundation, including such rising stars as sopranos Isabel Bayrakdarian, Heidi Grant-Murphy, Jennifer Aylmer, Nicole Cabell, and Susanna Phillips, mezzo-sopranos Stephanie Blythe, Michelle de Young, and Isabel Leonard, counter-tenors David Daniels and Bejun Mehta, tenors Bruce Ford, Lawrence Brownlee, and Alek Shrader, and baritones Russell Braun, Rodney Gilfry, and Earle Patriarco, to mention but a few of the most prominent and promising. The list goes on and on.

Throughout the history of opera, many have competed in the "If you've got it, flaunt it" sweepstakes, but no one ever matched the panache of my former fellow student in the Lehmann master classes, Grace Bumbry, an immensely talented artist with a magnetic personality, who wore her success occasionally on her sleeve, but why not? She put in plenty of hard work to achieve it.

While Grace is flashy on- and offstage, many an artist who is dynamite in performance can be fairly diffident in private life. Samuel Ramey is a prime example. When I first met him in 1966, he was a young apprentice at Santa Fe. I was directing *La Cenerentola* there, and he had a walk-on in that production. I first directed him as a star in the title role of Verdi's *Attila*, a historical figure who was no shy, shrinking violet, and he threw himself into the flamboyant role with great seriousness.

Sometimes an explosive career can lead to a devastating ending. I must admit I was not altogether surprised by Jerry Hadley's suicide in July 2007. He was a sweet man, but he also made some poor choices. A good-looking guy and remarkable linguist, an intelligent musician, and a convincing actor, he refused to be limited by the fact that his voice was best suited for Mozartian roles and tried to exploit a vocal versatility he just didn't have, egged on by the wrong advisers. The result was that his voice began to fail; in a way he was trying to turn a clarinet into a trumpet. If anything positive can come of his harrowing death, it is that other singers might not make the same mistakes.

One artist who let her own colossal intelligence be her guide was Regina Resnik. She was in her early twenties when she debuted with the New Opera Company of New York in the daunting role of Lady Macbeth with the great Fritz Busch on the podium. After a promising Met debut as Leonora in *Il trovatore*, she was soon appearing as Aida and Santuzza and in the title role of a legendary production of *Fidelio* led by Bruno Walter. In 1955, after having pursued an international soprano career for fourteen years, it became clear to her that she was really a mezzo, and she made the switch over the heated objections of many who sought to advise her at the time. They were wrong; she was right. Her Carmen redefined the role, and she excelled in one part after another, running the gamut from the captivating Marina in *Boris Godunov*, sung in the perfect Russian she had spoken with her parents as a child, all the way to a bouncy Dame Quickly in *Falstaff* and the forbidding Old Countess in Samuel Barber's *Vanessa*, a role she created at the Metropolitan.

We first became associated in the autumn of 1963, when she came to San Francisco to sing the Prioress in my production of *Les dialogues des Carmélites*. She asked Mr. Adler who I was, and when he told her, she suggested we meet. She was a charming luncheon partner, and when we finished our dessert, I asked her if I had passed my audition. She laughed.

I'm not sure I ever passed my audition with Sherill Milnes. He was a terrific baritone but seemed somehow locked in his persona as an all-American hunk. I first directed him as Rodrigo in *Don Carlo* at the Chicago Lyric Opera. He was always very studious, but unfortunately he thought working things out intellectually was acting. The audience should never be aware of technique, but his technique was so apparent it got in his way. He was never a problem; he worked very hard to respond to what I was trying to give him, but he invariably let the machinery show. Despite his flawless vocal technique, his performances never quite got beyond the "stand and deliver" stage. I hope he had better success with other directors, because I feel I never really got through to him.

When the Russians came to America, they brought along a bundle of energy who soon skyrocketed to international renown thanks to a velvety voice and total identification with a wide variety of roles. Of course, this was Anna Netrebko, and I am proud to say that she first came to America to sing in San Francisco. She could steal a show as Musetta, and when she moved on to Mimì, she owned the stage. Only once in a lifetime does this level of talent come along. She breathes a special air, and I am reassured by the way she has handled her career with discretion and wisdom.

The case of another Russian frankly has me worried. I first saw and heard Dmitri Hvorostovsky when he won the 1989 BBC Cardiff Singer of the World Competition. I immediately tried to sign him up for Prince Andrei in our *War and Peace* production, but he turned me down.

Dmitri is an enormous talent with a rather quirky personality and a somewhat childish way of reacting to things. He was wonderful in our *Tsar's Bride*, even though he was a bit jealous of Anna's success, but he never got along with Olga Borodina. Although they were supposedly playing lovers, they always exuded negative vibes, which I did my best to ignore. I later cast Hvorostovsky as Don Giovanni in a very good production, but he seemed to be having trouble in rehearsals. I talked to him about the seducer as chameleon, always finding the right idiom to feign sincerity toward whatever woman he is after. Nothing he says is real, but Dmitri argued with me, saying, "No, I am a strong magnet, and women are drawn to *me*." So I gave him an Errol Flynn movie and told him to watch the past master of screen seduction. It apparently didn't communicate anything to him: his performance never quite made it, and he said he would never do it again. I don't think he has.

In the many years of my career, I've had the pleasure of working with some of the greatest artists in the world of opera. Well at the top of the list is Italian soprano Graziella Sciutti. We met when she was singing Susanna in Dr. Graf's production of *Le nozze di Figaro* in Geneva. She identified totally with the character and succeeded splendidly in making one of the longest roles in the repertoire seem short. Seemingly delicate onstage, she could reveal a spine of steel when confronted by stupidity and arrogance. This was the case when she took Susanna to Salzburg and found herself confronted by a director determined to set new and higher standards of self-importance. Before starting a rehearsal for the second act, Graziella, true to form, came out onstage to check the many props her

*With Graziella
Sciutti in San
Francisco, 1998.*

character has to handle in that act. While doing this, she looked around the stage and discovered there were only two openings in the set for entrances and exits, and the action calls for a minimum of three with all the drawing-room-comedy comings and goings. She courteously pointed this out to the director, who responded with a tirade against "conventional" singers who had not kept up with the tremendous metaphysical growth of Central European theater, whatever that meant. Graziella kept her own counsel. Staging began, and everything went smoothly until the Count knocked on the locked door, whereupon Cherubino hid in the closet, and Susanna escaped to . . . er, there was nowhere for her to escape. Everything ground to a halt, and the director suggested that they continue work on the act the following day, seeing to it that a third escape route had been inserted. How this guy kept his job I will never know.

I first worked with Graziella in *Così fan tutte*. Having directed it many times, I thought I knew the opera inside and out, but I never really understood Despina until I learned it from her. I used to joke that she had cornered the market on the "na-na" roles—Susanna, Despina, Zerlina, Norina, Rosina, and Adina—but Graziella was far more than the reigning soubrette of her generation. She was a theater animal through and through, and I was proud to have helped her launch her directing career.

Here's what happened. She had been engaged to do Francis Poulenc's *La voix humaine* at the Glyndebourne Festival and called me to ask if I thought she was right for the part. I said I thought she was perfect and went on to suggest that as the opera is a solo monologue, a director was superfluous with an artist of her intelligence. She should direct it herself. She rose to the challenge, and she was heartbreaking in the role.

Soon afterward, I invited her to Toronto to direct a new *Nozze di Figaro* production with three different casts. That was her first outing as a full-fledged stage director. She was wonderful with artists, whether they were established performers or newcomers, winning them over with her knowledge, sensitivity, discipline, and good humor. She also cooked just about the best pasta I ever tasted, and I will never forget the view of her petite figure behind the wheel of her Rolls-Royce.

A few opera singers have had successful careers as actors, usually after their retirement from the opera stage, but I can think of only one who ever crossed that bridge in the other direction, albeit for a single production. One evening in the late 1950s I was sitting at home in Los Angeles when the phone rang, and a voice on the other end said, "Mr. José Ferrer would like to talk to you."

Frankly, I thought it was a joke, and I didn't believe it was Ferrer until he got on the phone and told me in his unique voice that he had been engaged to appear in Puccini's *Gianni Schicchi* in the 1960 Santa Fe season. At first, I thought he'd been asked to do a silent cameo as Buoso Donati, the rich man who dies seconds before the curtain goes up, then lies there as a corpse for the rest of the evening, but he assured me he was planning to do the title role and asked me to help him prepare it.

He invited me to come to his home, the former Ira Gershwin estate, equipped with some of the most sophisticated sound equipment I had ever seen. When I discovered he was just as nervous as I was about the encounter, this cemented the relationship. In the course of our work together, I discovered he was better prepared for the task than I had originally envisioned. A Princeton graduate, he could read music and was a great lover of opera. While he was playing Iago to Paul Robeson's legendary Othello on Broadway back in 1943, with his wife at the time, Uta Hagen, as Desdemona, he and Uta were introduced to Robeson's voice teacher, Jerome Swinford, and both of them started taking lessons with him.

Our lessons went on for three months. I taught him how to dramatize the music and sang all the other roles for him, so he could play with each

LOTFI MANSOURI

one of them. José took direction like a sponge, always yearning for more. He also had a great sense of humor, which contributed to his great success as Schicchi. The Santa Fe production went so well it was later taken to the Brooklyn Academy of Music in New York. I can't help wondering what might have happened if Ferrer had lent his special talents to some other operatic challenges.

It isn't hard to recognize when an immortal has entered the room in cases like José Ferrer, but sometimes a first encounter with a total unknown rings the same bell in your head. I had that sensation in the mid-1980s while I was directing in Houston and a young soprano flew in to audition for me. The minute she started singing "Dove sono," I knew Renée Fleming was an artist destined for greatness. She was attractive, musical, communicative, and intelligent, yet presented the music in a disarmingly straightforward, unaffected way.

In one phase, she sometimes let the hype being spread about her by her media consultants go to her head, as witness her interview with the late Ed Bradley on CBS's *60 Minutes*, when her naturalness and originality were overwhelmed by her determination to appear glamorous. After wonderfully cross-pollinating collaborations on her early assignments with us, especially the new operas she had helped introduce to the world, her new obsession with her image caused some problems when we worked together on Charpentier's *Louise*. Vocal mannerisms began creeping in, and the lady in the Fifth Avenue gowns radiated through the characterization of the oppressed girl on the wrong side of Paris discovering love for the first time. Her singing was magnificent, but everything else about the performance was a bit false, and she never really threw herself into the last act, when Louise becomes hysterical.

To her credit, she knew how to read the unmistakable signs. At opening night, Sam Ramey and Felicity Palmer as Louise's parents brought the house down in their curtain calls, while the applause for Renée, though enthusiastic, was somewhat more subdued. I took advantage of the opportunity to tell her gently that she was being too careful, too studied, and she got the message. From then on, she went for broke, realizing that you can never fool the audience. When she came back for the Marschallin in *Der Rosenkavalier*, the last production I would do in San Francisco, her performance was pure glory.

Some day, I hope I'll be able to thank her personally for all the trouble she went through to take part in my Farewell Gala. When push came to shove, she proved she was still the real trouper I had met when she started out.

Another true immortal is that great Welshman Bryn Terfel. The first time he sang for us in San Francisco was in the title role of *Le nozze di Figaro*, in which his great intelligence and insight, plus his uncanny sense of words, left an indelible mark on the role, as they do with whatever he sings, and his selections are made with great self-awareness and discrimination. I just hope he continues to choose to work with me.

His Nick Shadow in Stravinsky's *The Rake's Progress* was a particularly great success. Bryn knows how effectively understatement can communicate, which makes the audience even more aware of the enormous resources he has at his command when he wants to use them. He even develops a special walk for each character, adding to the indelible imprint he leaves on all his characterizations. His loyalty to family, friends, and colleagues is ironclad: he still retains the services of Doreen O'Neill in Cardiff, the same manager he has worked with since the beginning of his career.

Another great baritone was Giuseppe Taddei, a Genoese darling and a great talent. He started out as a Verdi baritone, and I directed him in Chicago as Mustafá in *L'italiana in Algeri* with Marilyn Horne. I later took him to Tehran as Falstaff. He had an uncanny way with a text, bringing such sophistication to comedy. He was not a buffo—he drew the comedy out of the situation. He knew what Shakespeare meant when he gave this grotesque character a noble title: he was always *Sir* John.

Taddei had both intelligence and instinct. He could portray such dignity in the face of insult and chaos. He externalized everything he could glean from the text, at the same level as Callas and Gobbi. Nowadays, with mediocre artists you can hear the cerebral machinery going "clickety-click," while the great ones simply become the character. Taddei's skill in that respect was a benchmark.

Dorothy Kirsten was another artist who grasped inner meanings instinctively. I met her in the 1950s in Los Angeles when I was dramatic director at the UCLA Opera Workshop. On Saturday afternoons we often did a scene from the repertoire of a major star, and then that star would come in to critique our work. For Dorothy Kirsten we did the last act of *Manon Lescaut* with two students. She was very kind to the singers, telling the soprano, "Now raise your hand and look at the sun rising."

I stupidly interrupted her and said, "But Miss Kirsten, this is a sunset."

She replied, "Mr. Mansouri, the music says sunrise."

I later directed her in two productions in San Francisco, including *Manon Lescaut* and *Tosca*. We also did *La fanciulla del West* at the Vancouver Festival. She really owned the role of Minnie. During rehearsals for that production, our daughter, Shireen, was born two weeks early in Santa Fe, and Dorothy graciously toasted the new arrival by treating everyone to champagne. She suggested we name the child "Minnie," but I replied, "Do you really want my daughter to go through life as Minnie Mansouri?"

Dorothy was dying to sing Desdemona, but no one ever asked her to do it. It was the only dream in her long career that never came true. She went on to become a successful crossover artist, as wonderful singing the hits of the day as she was in opera.

Another artist who stayed true to his principles throughout a long career was the Spanish Austrian tenor from the Canary Islands, Alfredo Kraus. He had a focus and repose onstage that were magnificent to behold, and he had the wisdom to stick to his core repertoire all the way, continuing to give top-class performances into his seventies. He always said no to offers to sing Don José and Radames. I directed him in *I Puritani* in Dallas early in my career. We also did a *Werther* in Chicago with Tatiana Troyanos. His French was superb, and he had internalized the French style. Werther was one of his great roles. Although he had a roving eye, he handled his rather complicated private life with such discretion that not a breath of scandal ever emerged in the outside world.

There is fortunately room and recognition aplenty in our profession for artists who combine talent with charm, decency, wisdom, and high principles. One such person lives right here in San Francisco. I have never heard an unkind word about Frederica von Stade. For years I admired and adored her work all over the world and finally managed to get together with her professionally in San Francisco. She and her husband, Michael Gorman, have a home on Alameda Island in the Bay. Flicka is a very generous human being, on- and offstage. When the earthquake hit, she became a mascot for the opera house renovations. She does occasionally pay a price for her good heart. She is too smart not to know when she is being taken, but she would rather be naively generous than see someone of value devoid of crucial support.

She joins the others in the top echelons of my personal Valhalla, but that didn't stop me from bringing what might have become a mawkish event down to earth. When she was honored in the Bay Area, a film was made about her many accomplishments, and the many witnesses to her career tried to outdo themselves heaping praises on her. When it was my turn, I put on a sour face and said, "I am so fed up with that goody-goody Flicka von Stade. Flicka this, Flicka that, but damn it! It's all true!"

Of course, singers walk a perilous tightrope every time they step on-stage, and we can be eternally grateful that they rise so gloriously to the challenge. Putting up with the occasional eccentricity is more than worth it at the end of the day. Yet nobody has a greater obstacle course to surmount than the gentleman—and sometimes the highly gifted lady —on the podium. I'd like to conclude this gallery with portraits of a few conductors whose work has enriched, and sometimes complicated, my life.

It's quite a parade—from the likes of Otto Klemperer, Ernest Anser-met, and Nello Santi at the dawn of my career, all the way to Valery Ger-giev, Charles Mackerras, André Previn, and Patrick Summers in more recent times.

Most conductors are—or can be—fairly flamboyant characters. In one remarkable case the conductor was so agonizingly introverted that it is amazing he accomplished all that he did, but his was perhaps the most unique career in the history of American operatic performance.

John Crosby invented the Santa Fe summer Opera Festival and led it for forty-three years, an unmatched tenure anywhere in the world. During this period, he commissioned eleven world premieres, including Carlisle Floyd's *Wuthering Heights* and Tobias Picker's *Emmeline*. He created a superb apprentice program that gave early opportunities to Samuel Ramey, Rita Shane, Frederica von Stade, Neil Shicoff, Tatyana Troyanos, and James Morris, as well as a young baritone named David Gockley, who now serves as general director at the San Francisco Opera. John gave Kiri te Kanawa and Bryn Terfel their American debuts. He was a magnificent organizer, a first-class manager and fund-raiser, and an indifferent conductor who gradually got worse. His emotional prob-lems were crippling.

I worked in Santa Fe for eight summers, starting in 1965, when the Festival was still small. Over the years, I directed thirteen operas that John conducted. He had a vision of bringing great singers to this beauti-ful desert location, just outside the city, and building an opera house for them. His father was a New York attorney who loaned John the initial

Preparing Tosca *at Santa Fe Opera, 1969, with John Crosby and Mirna Lacambra.*

$200,000 to get things started. His brother was my guitar teacher, a very nice guy, married with kids and all that goes with a conventional middle-class family. This certainly wasn't true of John.

During World War II he was stationed in Germany, playing several instruments in the army band and entertaining his fellow soldiers at the piano in bars during off-hours. When he was discharged, he studied at Yale, then cast about for a career. A bout of asthma in his youth had sent him to New Mexico, and in the course of his school years he fell in love with the place. He set out to create the Santa Fe Opera Festival from whole cloth as a kind of American Bayreuth, becoming one of the great visionaries in American opera. He was an incredible fund-raiser and knew just how to present his vision to the wealthy people of Santa Fe. He was also a very solid, penny-conscious manager. He knew where every paper clip was and how much it cost. He even had a tractor. He would dig up the garden with it and water the flowers. It might as well have been called the John Crosby Festival, because there was little John didn't do personally.

Regrettably his people skills were nowhere near his managing talents. He hated physical contact. When he visited us in Geneva, he was charming with Midge, then didn't recognize her when we arrived in Santa Fe. Whenever we had parties in our temporary quarters there, he would wind up alone in the kitchen. The price he paid for his fear of human contact was the coldness of his conducting. There has to be some joy of communication, but he was so emotionally restricted the best he could do was beat time. He was a wonderfully studious musician with a keen analytical mind, and he knew every note. He loved music and would talk about it all the time, but because he was so tight on the podium, his vision never really came across.

Ultimately, he betrayed almost all of his friends. He brought wonderful singers and musicians to New Mexico, including Stravinsky and Hindemith, Penderecki and Henze, but if anyone ever bought a home there, that was the end of his or her association with the Festival.

At the beginning, I did almost all of his productions, and I was proud of our collaboration, but I soon realized that anybody higher in his favor would get the best he had to offer, the best accommodations, the best car, everything. We were given an empty house and had to furnish and equip it ourselves. In the summer of 1971, I discovered I would need to be in San Francisco earlier than usual, and he felt betrayed. He considered my schedule his personal property, and he didn't invite me back the following season.

Four years later he sent a handwritten letter to me in Geneva, saying that the American Bicentennial and his own fiftieth birthday were coming up, and he couldn't imagine doing Puccini's *La fanciulla del West* with anyone else. Midge told me not to fall for his blandishments, but I accepted his offer anyway, whereupon he hired somebody else. Midge was right: he just wanted to dangle a carrot in front of our noses for the pleasure of pulling it away. Fortunately, we were able to do one final production together, *Lucia* in 1978.

For all his problems, John Crosby should be remembered for what he created and the people he presented. When he finally stepped down in 2000, he retired to Rancho Mirage, California, where he died two years later, sad and alone.

Not every shy individual is an uncommunicative musician. Many of the greatest first come to life when they step into a rehearsal room and come into contact with their colleagues. In one case, a conductor with whom I worked early in both of our careers was so unimpressive in personal contact I didn't recognize his enormous gifts until I saw him in action.

His name was Carlos Kleiber, and we were both protégés of Dr. Graf in Zurich. We did a French-language *Fledermaus* together in Geneva in 1965. We were both young and had a lot to learn, and neither of us was quite certain how to treat the other. He would come to my rehearsals, and I to his, both of us taking notes and making suggestions. Then he stepped onto the podium and underwent a remarkable metamorphosis. It is to his credit that he managed to conquer his shyness and make a colossal impact on the musical world, although that diffidence probably caused him to cancel as many performances as he did. When he died, the chroniclers outdid themselves with praise, all of it richly deserved. I regret that I didn't recognize at the outset that this reserved young man sitting by himself in the back of the rehearsal room was on his way to becoming, arguably, the greatest conducting genius of the past fifty years.

Unlike many of his contemporaries, Carlos excelled in both the concert hall and the opera house. So many fine symphonic conductors fail to recognize that their contribution to the dramatic event is as important as, if not more so than, the stage director's. A first-class opera conductor is always a total collaborator. Karl Richter understood this. Largely a specialist in Bach, trained as an organist, he rose to the occasion when he worked on an opera. When we worked together on Mozart's *Idomeneo*, he would listen carefully to my conversations with the singers, as I would to his. It certainly made the singers' lives easier to know we were all on the same team.

The finest conductors are always the finest accompanists. In the early 1960s, Hans Hotter was performing and teaching in Aspen, and he loved to tell the story of the curly-headed seventeen-year old kid from Cincinnati who begged him to let him play for some of the singers in his master classes. His name was James Levine, and he is as gifted a pianist and accompanist as he is a conductor. During his long, brilliant career, his immense knowledge of when to breathe, when to push ahead, when to hold back was crucial to the success of many singers. Luciano Pavarotti always made a special impact when Jimmy was on the podium, carrying him right through the performance.

Jimmy is perhaps one of the most versatile conductors in the business, capable of leading authentic performances of Mozart, Verdi, Wagner, Berlioz, Corigliano, you name it, often working with orchestras and singers who specialize in those works, as he did in Vienna, Salzburg, and Bayreuth. But by and large, apart from his duties at the Met and as the music director at the Boston Symphony, he remains pretty close to home, preferring to build the forces he works with rather than fly somewhere on a jet plane, do a quick guest shot, and then head back to the sky. This is probably why I could never get him to work with us in San Francisco, though I certainly tried hard enough. Gracious as he is, he always courteously declined, and this graciousness manifested itself in the very thoughtful message he sent me at the beginning of every season. Singers tell me he still likes accompanying his own coaching sessions.

Many people on the music staff of opera houses never move from their positions as staff pianist, rehearsal accompanist, coach, or prompter, and opera couldn't happen without them. In some cases, the right mentor has made all the difference. Probably the best-known example is Robert Craft, but I often wondered what he was doing on the podium.

He earned his fame as the amanuensis to Igor Stravinsky for the last thirty years of the great composer's life. When Stravinsky celebrated his eightieth birthday in 1961, Zurich Opera offered a double bill of *Rossignol* and *L'histoire du soldat*. I was involved in preparing *Rossignol* for Dr. Graf. As always, Robert did all the preparatory work for the maestro, who arrived at the last minute to conduct the performance. The audience was never the wiser. Yet this time, the usual procedure didn't work. The day after the dress rehearsal, Stravinsky announced he would conduct only *L'histoire*, because he could do it one beat to the bar. We had to bring in another conductor for *Rossignol*, much to the displeasure of the audience.

In 1966, I directed a new English-language production of *Wozzeck* in Santa Fe with Robert Craft conducting. He brought some severe emotional shortfalls to the podium, seeming to be afraid of any musical freedom, a disastrous way to approach a work as theatrical as this one. He was so cautious he would subdivide every beat. It was impossible to stage the piece, because the singers' eyes were all glued to the conductor, trying to follow what every finger, elbow, and shoulder move was communicating. It killed my attempts to get the artists involved in their characters and wrecked the scene where Marie reads the Bible. Finally I got so fed up I went to town and bought a slide rule, putting it on his music stand without saying a word.

The current generation has produced one or two women whose talents can stand up to anything our gender has to offer. Simone Young, the brilliant Australian conductor and head of the Hamburg State Opera, is one of these.

Sarah Caldwell did not fare as well. She served magnificently as the head of the Boston Opera for many years and was a fine stage director, but her conducting talents left much to be desired. She owed her Met debut to Beverly Sills, who was not all that fond of having a dominant force on the podium, and Sarah was anything but that. Her stewardship in Boston was a little like John Crosby's in Santa Fe: totally dedicated to creating and running a strong company, offering innovative productions of great repertoire with magnificent casts. If only she had kept her hands off the baton. Rumor has it she sometimes fell asleep in the pit.

Given the choice between an irascible conductor who occasionally lends a note of genius to a performance and a craftsman with a solid routine, I'll take the latter every time. Franceso Molinari-Pradelli could be both, but he was never less than a consummate *routinier*. He was fun, charming, volatile, and knew every note of the score so well that he could conduct any opera in his vast repertoire blindfolded. He was totally practical and knew just how to cooperate with the stars. If only he hadn't fallen in love so often. Whenever we had a break, he would invariably cry on my shoulder about some woman who was not responding to his blandishments. It was always about a different lady—I could never keep track of his roster.

Another superb *routinier* was Leopold Ludwig, who kindly kept whatever private life he may have had to himself. He could make something meaningful out of very little, especially when I worked with him in San Francisco. He was highly proficient and could work with total competence under the limited circumstances Mr. Adler provided. Because there was no time to cultivate nuance, we had to work hard and fast, and he always rose to that challenge with flying colors, a *Kapellmeister* of the first order, constant and effective.

Georges Prêtre is another conductor for whom I have the highest regard. I directed his American debut in 1963: *Samson et Dalila* in San Francisco with James McCracken. Georges is *très sportif*, like a rubber ball, and has remained vibrant and exciting into his mid-eighties. We got along splendidly. The opera poses all kinds of problems. The first act is an oratorio, the second *verismo*, and in the third the two are combined. It calls for a courageous conductor, and Georges was that.

We later did Massenet's *Hérodiade* together in Nice. It was to be recorded and filmed, built around José Carerras, but that was the terrible year he was diagnosed with leukemia. It became a nightmare. We kept looking for tenors and other leading artists who would blend with them, but nobody worked out. We tried Plácido with Jessye Norman. I got Grace Bumbry and Leona Mitchell. It was all a little like the stateroom scene in the Marx Brothers' *Night at the Opera* with people wandering in and out of all the doors.

Getting the production ready was pure chaos: at one point, one tenor walked in from stage right and the other from the left, nobody sure who would actually do the rehearsal. Pierre Médecin, the director of the theater, was getting more and more frustrated, and one night Leona Mitchell, who had already been rehearsing for eight hours, decided to mark in order to protect her voice.

Prêtre stopped and said, "Madame, I have to hear what you are doing."

Leona replied, "Excuse me, Maestro, but I've been singing all day, and I don't have anything left."

Pierre cholerically called from the house, "Madame, if you're not going to sing this rehearsal, I don't need you," whereupon she walked off the stage. Grace saw what had happened and walked off in solidarity—we were scheduled to open in six days. A meeting was called, and it was decided that Leona was out of the production.

I went to see her and said, "Leona, honey, go to your hotel and don't *dare* leave town. Just stay there—I'll get back to you." She was wonderful, in glorious voice, she had the role down cold—and who else knew Salomé in *Hérodiade*? I had to find a way to keep her.

The final dress rehearsal was scheduled for the next day, followed by opening night. The company was sleepwalking. No one had any idea what was going on. Every time the singers went onstage, there was another singer. They just wanted to get it over with. After one very demoralizing rehearsal, I went to Georges' room and asked, "You are not content?"

"Oh, no. But what can we do? We don't have anyone else."

"Non, Maître, Madame Mitchell has not left town."

Georges blinked. I said I could ask her to come back. He blinked again. Then I phoned her at the hotel and said, "Leona, get over to the theater as fast as you can." They were soon kissy-kissy, huggy-huggy, and she sang the role like the champion she is. Even Pierre was diplomatic for a change, while Leona acted like a lady, teaching both of them how to behave.

Meanwhile, Georges had given an interview to a major newspaper, in which he told the reporter he didn't do much opera because he didn't care for stage directors. When I went back to wish him luck before the first curtain, I put on a sad face and told him I was disconsolate because of his comment in the interview.

He replied, "Ah, non, mon cher ami, I wasn't talking about you." I kept on my best verge-of-martyrdom face, and unfortunately that was the last time we worked together.

Georges Prêtre brings wonderful energy to everything he touches. His tone colors are marvelous, detailed, and brilliant. Unfortunately, he was too European to fit into an American lifestyle, where conductors are more or less expected to schmooze the more influential members of the audience. Otherwise, I would have had him over here in a flash—and maybe, over time, he might even have started liking stage directors.

Another conductor very much like Georges Prêtre in temperament and talent was Gianandrea Gavazzeni. When Dr. Graf took me to Salzburg to assist him on Verdi's *Simon Boccanegra*, he conducted a cast featuring Tito Gobbi, Leyla Gencer, and Giorgio Tozzi. When I directed the revival the following year, I found Gavazzeni to be a marvelous gentleman. He was on the Toscanini wavelength. In fact, he and Toscanini were the only conductors ever made honorary citizens of the composer's hometown in Bussetto. He was as clean as Toscanini, but not as driven. He was more intellectual, more scholarly, and perhaps more insightful. He had a great ear and helped the singers a lot, especially in the ensembles. His sense of balance was superb. He was a specialist and stuck with the Italian repertoire, of which he was a past master.

He was always impeccably clad, with salt and pepper hair. His Rossini was wonderful, but I discovered that he didn't like rain to be simulated with actual water, and I had planned it for the storm in *Cenerentola*. I didn't show it to him until the first piano rehearsal, and when he saw water descending, he turned around, without missing a beat, and said, "Mansouri, if you had read my book about Rossini's storms, you would never have done this."

I replied, "Maestro, if you had sent me a copy, I would have read it."

He went back to conducting, shaking his head. Teresa Berganza, who was singing the title role, loved the rain and thanked me for the shower.

She said it was good for her voice. Although Maestro Gavazzeni was the senior partner, he was very generous and said he liked what I was doing. I still regret that I never read any of his books.

One of the greatest talents I ever worked with was Giuseppe Patané. He was immensely musical and openhearted and understood the essential nature of opera as drama. Not only was he in total control of the customary Italian repertoire, he could conduct anything. He even spoke fluent German, an aptitude that James King once described as "quite a feat for a Neapolitan."

Like Carlos Kleiber, Thomas Sanderling, Mariss Jansons, and the Järvi brothers, he was the son of a well-known conductor, Franco Patané, but in his case, the son was the greater talent. After his initial studies in his hometown, he debuted at the Teatro San Carlo there at the age of nineteen. Then, following a period as assistant conductor at San Carlo, he quickly established a pan-European career that took him to Munich, New York, and London and that included a position as resident conductor at the Deutsche Oper in Berlin. He made his La Scala debut in 1969, returning two years later for *L'elisir d'amore* with Pavarotti, which also marked our first collaboration, followed by other productions in San Francisco. He was a very kind man. We had apartments together at San Francisco's Inn at the Opera, and his wife used to cook for us all the time. Having started out together, we were on an equal footing. We were planning other productions together when he succumbed to a heart attack in the middle of a *Barbiere di Siviglia* performance in Munich in May 1989. It was a catastrophic loss for the craft and for all his friends. He was only fifty-seven.

There were quite a few terrific conductors from my early career who remained with me over the years. Franco Capuana, Fausto Cleva, and Nicola Rescigno were all past masters of the Italian singing line, with total control over their orchestral and vocal resources, and they all knew music theater inside and out. Maybe we didn't realize it at the time, but working with them was like taking a master class in the grand style: they sometimes taught directly and always by example.

Franco Capuana and I did *Werther* together in Geneva in 1962, featuring Giuseppe di Stefano in the title role. Maestro Capuana was extremely generous, loyal, and professional. He premiered a lot of works that have since been forgotten, conducted at La Scala from 1937 until the war, then became music director there in 1949. He was especially fine in *verismo* because he knew just how to tell the truth in sound, and he was so well versed in Italian culture and tradition that the music flowed in and out of him like the air he breathed.

Fausto Cleva was totally different, yet he achieved very similar results. Having studied in Italy, he came to the United States in 1920 and soon picked up some of the American qualities of high energy and instinct. He conducted more than 650 performances at the Metropolitan and also enjoyed great success in Cincinnati, San Francisco, and Chicago. Many younger colleagues learned a lot from him. He conducted my production of *La fanciulla del West* in Vancouver as if he had composed it, but he had one or two odd personality traits, including the fact that when he lost his temper, he would swear like a longshoreman—invariably in Italian. He thought nobody would understand him, but this misapprehension misfired more than once.

On one occasion he was letting the orchestra have it in no uncertain terms, when one of the players pointed urgently to the auditorium, where Cleva suddenly realized that a group of Italian nuns, attending the rehearsal on his invitation while visiting the United States, had picked up on every word and were sitting in the auditorium with their heads lowered. He apologized abjectly for his indiscretion, but none of them raised their heads, until one of the older nuns, clearly the leader of this delegation, looked up, smiled faintly, and said, "It's all right, Maestro, the sisters are praying for you."

In our *Fanciulla* production, an excellent Canadian mezzo-soprano named Lyn Vernon sang the role of Wowkle, Minnie's Indian maid. According to the score, most of Wowkle's dialogue consisted of "Ugh, ugh, ugh!" A lesser conductor would have let it go at that, but not Fausto Cleva. Stopping the rehearsal precipitously, he looked sternly up at Lyn and exclaimed, "No, not 'ugh, ugh, ugh'—it is written 'oogh, oogh, oogh!'" Lyn was nonplused. A farm girl in her childhood, she had probably grown up surrounded by Native Americans, but I reassured her the maestro's word was law, and she would simply have to switch to "oogh, oogh, oogh!"

The third member of this triumvirate was Nicola Rescigno. He may be the most underrated of the three, but in many ways, he had the most refined taste of them all. A New Yorker who grew up in an Italian family, he combined his Mediterranean cultural background with his Big Apple savvy to help found two of the finest companies in the United States, the Chicago Lyric Opera and the Dallas Opera. He was the collaborator of choice for Maria Callas, Alfredo Kraus, and Mirella Freni, who entrusted him with important performances and recordings. He also brought some of the finest artists of their generation to this country, including Joan Sutherland, Jon Vickers, Teresa Berganza, Gwyneth Jones, and Montserrat Caballé. He discovered a twenty-year-old Spanish tenor living in Mexico by the name of Plácido Domingo and gave him his U.S. debut regardless of his tender age. He also first presented American audiences with the visionary productions of Peter Hall and Franco Zeffirelli at a period when Dallas was bidding fair to become a major operatic capital, referred to by many a local patron as "La Scala West." This was where he gave the American premieres of Handel's *Alcina* and Monteverdi's *L'incoronazione di Poppea* back in the 1960s, when nobody had ever heard of those masterpieces.

Following his retirement from Dallas in 1990, he continued a bustling career all over the world almost until he died in his adopted city of Rome in 2008 at the age of ninety-two. Throughout his musical life, he was the ultimate singers' conductor. His 1958 and 1962 concert films with Callas from Hamburg reveal just what a subtle and self-effacing conductor can do in the service of high art. His interviews in the 1998 BBC documentary *The Art of Singing—Golden Voices of the Century* reveal his singular expertise in this very complicated craft. Only conductors of his caliber know when to lead, when to follow, and how to honor the difference. I had the pleasure of collaborating with him on several productions in Dallas, including *I Puritani* and *Don Carlo*. I also brought him to Canada to conduct my *Turandot* production.

Some conductors devote themselves almost entirely to a single house for many years, and their devotion is rewarded. This was the case with Bruno Bartoletti. He made his U.S. debut in 1956 at the Chicago Lyric Opera as a last-minute replacement recommended by Tito Gobbi. He ultimately joined the company as artistic director and principal conductor in 1964. He also served in a parallel function, as artistic director of the Maggio Musicale Fiorentino, the May Music Festival in his native Florence, which he headed from 1986 to 1991. In 2006, he concluded his fiftieth season with the Chicago company by conducting the same opera he had led at his debut, *Il trovatore*, on which occasion the theater's podium was named for him. He returned to Florence at the end of the following season at the age of eighty-one, stating his plans to remain for the rest of his life in the home he built there and named Villa Fox for Chicago's Carol Fox.

He was another one of those maestros who couldn't care less what was happening on the stage. I was doing *Don Carlo* in Chicago with a wonderful cast and Bartoletti conducting. He would sit in my rehearsals reading the Milan newspaper *Corriere della Sera*. The paper was printed on onion skin, so every time he turned a page, it would crackle throughout the auditorium. I suggested he need not necessarily attend my rehearsals, to which he replied that he needed to see what I was doing. Then he went back to his paper. Go figure.

One man who never quite got his career together anywhere was Swiss conductor Peter Maag. He could have been another Karajan, but he was too blunt and direct, and he made a lot of noise, which I could always hear through the paper-thin walls of the hotels we stayed in. He was a fantastic, incredibly knowledgeable musician, detailed without a hint of preciousness. And he was a delightful colleague with a great sense of humor and a keen eye for the ladies. He certainly knew his stuff, in particular when it came to Mozart, although he could get a bit carried away accompanying the recitatives at the harpsichord.

One night, in a performance of *Così fan tutte*, his flights of fancy at the keyboard reached the point where nobody onstage had the vaguest notion of where he was. It brought the drama to a standstill. He finally realized he had hit a dead end and looked pleadingly up at the stage.

Gabriel Bacquier as Don Alfonso walked downstage and inquired, "Cher Maître, avez-vous fini?"

Peter replied, "Oui."

Then Bacquier asked, "Alors, je continue?"

Peter nodded yes.

Everybody thought I had come up with the gag and laughed hysterically.

During my general director years in San Francisco, I had the pleasure of introducing many fine conductors—many of whom have already been mentioned in this chronicle—to that theater's discriminating audience. The list includes Christoph von Dohnányi, who joined us in 1989, and Yuri Simonov, in 1990. The year 1991 heralded the San Francisco debuts of Valery Gergiev, Peter Schneider, and Markus Stenz, as well as two young men, one a Berliner, the other an English conductor of Italian descent, who grew up in the United States. Both of them have since become household names worldwide.

Christian Thielemann, whose North American debut with *Elektra* I arranged that year, has it all: intellectual understanding, emotional power, and superb technique. Having served with distinction at the Deutsche Oper Berlin, where he was general music director, he now holds the same position with the Munich Philharmonic, where he succeeded James Levine in 2004. The other first-rate younger conductor is Antonio Pappano, who had been my rehearsal pianist for *Attila* at the New York City Opera. After he launched his conducting career, I brought him to San Francisco for Bellini's *I Capuletti ed i Montecchi*. He currently serves as music director at the Royal Opera House Covent Garden in London.

Composer John Adams conducted for us in 1992, as did Kent Nagano, and 1993 brought Sir Andrew Davis, who is now music director of the Chicago Lyric Opera, while 1997 marked the debut of Yuri Temirkanov. All of them made significant contributions to musical life on the West Coast.

Were anyone to ask, of all the renowned artists it has been my privilege to work with, who is my favorite conductor, the answer would have to be that he is the one I have saved for last in this gallery of greatness: Sir Charles Mackerras brings just about everything to the table, even though his total lack of self-promotion may not have vouchsafed him the level of public acclaim lesser colleagues imagine they are entitled to. Nevertheless, I suspect that in years to come, as real quality rises to the surface, it will be general knowledged that Mackerras was a uniquely gifted conductor, incapable of giving a bad performance. He can do anything, from Handel to Strauss, and although he has one or two areas of expertise, particularly in the Czech repertoire, including a remarkable fluency in that complicated language, he has never fallen victim to overspecialization. His Mozart is as beautiful, idiomatic, and downright stunning as his Janáček. He has a vast repertoire and an innate sense of tempi. And although the designation "maestro" should be reserved for the likes of Sir Charles, he distinguishes himself by his down-to-earth modesty, never seeking personal glory, never traveling with a retinue, and never playing politics to leapfrog to important positions. He does what he does for the joy and the glory of the music.

Every production, every rehearsal, and every community event with him was golden. He is such a great scholar, so penetrating, and yet generous to a fault. Any disagreements that I had with him were intellectual and never personal. Suffice it to say that we never received anything but compliments from our artists, staff, and audiences whenever Sir Charles came to town. The gala we organized for him on his seventy-fifth birthday in 1995 was one of the company's finest moments.

Having admired him since my days in Switzerland, when I would travel to Britain with his performances at the old Sadler's Wells Opera at the top of my must-see list, I had always wanted him to be involved with my work in whatever capacity he deemed appropriate. Although I never persuaded him to come to Toronto, I got him to return to San Francisco, where he had previously conducted for Mr. Adler, to lead the 1989 production of *Lohengrin* and then asked him to join the company as principal guest conductor doing two productions a year. He served in that capacity from 1993 to 2002, and his years with us were among our very best. The orchestra adored him, the singers revered him, and he returned their affection without ever losing an ounce of his authority.

If he has a secret weapon, it is his wife, Judy. As Judy Wilkins, she was a first-rate oboist, having finally surrendered her career to his many years ago. She is both his kite and his anchor, always smoothing his path. People like Sir Charles need space to do their work, and I have never imposed on him in any way—Judy wouldn't allow it.

As I wander through this gallery of memories, recollecting the zanies and the geniuses, and all the fascinating individuals in between, I cannot help but marvel at the remarkable personalities who have added such a wealth of new and meaningful perceptions to my own life and made my experience in this most interactive art such a joy.

In his play, *Huis clos* (*No Exit*), the French author-philosopher Jean-Paul Sartre comes to the remarkable conclusion that "l'enfer, c'est les autres" (hell is other people); I disagree: in my life, both personal and artistic, for all the eccentricities and quirks I have had to put up with, my dealings with these enriching colleagues have been like a passport to heaven.

EPILOGUE

STILL IN PROGRESS

What an incredible half-century! Over these years, I have helped make opera happen in nearly five hundred productions—in the United States, Canada, Great Britain, France, the Netherlands, Germany, Brazil, Austria, Russia, Italy, Switzerland, Turkey, Argentina, Yugoslavia, Iran, Australia, and Japan—in all those countries and in many, many languages. As I write these words, plans are now under way for a new project in Mexico.

What a journey, and what a cast of characters! I have been blessed by saints and locked horns with devils. I have experienced the gamut of everything life has to offer and sustain: joy, sorrow, love, hate, friendship, betrayal, success, failure, intrigue, cabal, and hostility; rave reviews and devastating pans, opportunities offered, missed, and denied. And like everything else in my life, this book is just a way station.

I could never have made it this far without a sense of humor. No matter how bad things may get—and I have experienced some barely endurable low points—if you can find the funny side, you've conquered challenge. Come to think of it, my own pretensions may have been the most ridiculous part of it all.

Starting off as a kid in a dysfunctional family in Persia, and moving on to a career in opera that took me all over the world, demanded all my energy and ambition. Over the years, I may have turned my back on my Persian culture, but I never jettisoned one of its most important teachings: *kismet*. My name is Mansouri; I believe in *kismet*.

But of course I could never have done as much as I did by sitting back and waiting for fate to take a hand in my life; on the contrary, I have tried to walk hand in hand with destiny, as an equal partner. In the final analysis, the most important events are determined by *kismet*—what we do with them is up to us.

I have tried to make good on whatever was destined for me and to take things as far as I could. When Midge and I met, it was *kismet*. She has been a partner throughout this half-century, with all its ups and downs, in different cities and countries, giving me our daughter and compensating for everything I may have lost in Tehran. We were destined to meet. But we were not destined to succeed—we made that happen.

Destiny determined a career in opera for me, then brought me together with the Zweigs, who gave me whatever taste I have in music, with Jan Popper at UCLA and with Herbert Graf, who took me to Europe and gave me every opportunity a young man could ask for. Destiny sparked my encounter with Herman Geiger-Torel, who suggested my candidacy for the post of general director in Toronto, and with Terry McEwen, who recommended me for the same position in San Francisco. When these remarkable strokes of fate came about, I took over from there and did my best to make a career.

And because so much has happened in the art during my lifetime, I continue to believe in it as an ongoing, vibrant form with a glorious future. New artistic visions and technological developments offer us an amazing array of production options, unknown at the beginning of my professional life. Of course, like any other gift of the gods, it can be used to obfuscate or to add profundity and significance. The bottom line here is never losing sight of the continuum and respectfully honoring the spirit of the creators in our interpretations. From there on, the sky is the limit.

I hope I will be around to witness some of this progress, and I am grateful for the opportunity to make my own contributions. In this spirit, I continue to pursue my career, knowing that all action is ultimately interaction. If in this volume I have succeeded in thanking the wonderful people who have nourished my life with their interaction, I will be happier yet.

In this spirit, I greet them all with these thoughts from the final words written by the greatest author the world has ever known, William Shakespeare, in his epilogue to *The Tempest*:

> Gentle breath of yours my sails
> Must fill, or else my project fails,
> Which was to please. Now I want

Still in Progress

Spirits to enforce, art to enchant:
And my ending is despair
Unless I be relieved by prayer,
Which pierces so, that it assaults
Mercy itself and frees all faults
As you from crimes would pardoned be
Let your indulgence set me free.

APPENDIX A
FILMS AND DVDS

"The Day I Met Caruso" (television)
September 5, 1956 (broadcast)
Produced by NBC Television
Directed by Frank Borzage
Caruso played by Lotfi Mansouri

The Daughter of the Regiment (DVD)
1974
Produced by Wolf Trap Opera
Directed by Lotfi Mansouri
Distributed by VAI
Starring Beverly Sills

Norma (DVD)
1981
Produced by CBC Canada and
    Canadian Opera Company
Directed by Lotfi Mansouri
Distributed by CBC, VAI
Starring Joan Sutherland

Yes, Giorgio (film)
1981
Produced by Alain Bernheim
Directed by Franklin J. Schaffner
Distributed by MGM
Starring Luciano Pavarotti; opera
    scene directed by Lotfi Mansouri

Anna Bolena (DVD)
1984
Produced by CBC Canada and
    Canadian Opera Company
Directed by Lotfi Mansouri
Distributed by CBC, Video Artists
    International
Starring Joan Sutherland

Moonstruck (film)
1987
Produced by Patrick Palmer and
    Norman Jewison
Directed by Norman Jewison
Distributed by MGM
Starring Cher and Nicolas Cage;
    opera scene directed by
    Lotfi Mansouri

L'Africaine (DVD)
1988
Produced by WNET, KQED, RM Arts,
    Bayerischer Rundfunk, and ORF
Directed by Lotfi Mansouri
Distributed by RM Associates, ORF
Starring Plácido Domingo and
    Shirley Verret

The Merry Widow (DVD)
1988
Produced by Australian Opera
Directed by Lotfi Mansouri
Distributed by Kultur
Starring Joan Sutherland

The Makropulos Case (VHS)
1989
Produced by CBC Canada and
    Canadian Opera Company
Directed by Lotfi Mansouri
Distributed by VAI
Starring Stephanie Sundine

Les Huguenots (DVD)
1990
Produced by Australian Opera
Directed by Lotfi Mansouri
Distributed by Kultur
Starring Joan Sutherland

La Bohème (DVD)
1990
Produced by San Francisco Opera
Directed by Francesca Zambelo
Distributed by RM Arts Associates
Starring Luciano Pavarotti,
    Mirella Freni

Orlando (DVD)
1990
Directed by Pier-Luigi Pizzi
Distributed by RM Arts Associates
Starring Marilyn Horne

Mefistofele (DVD)
1991
Produced by RM Arts,
    Channel 13/WNET, KQED,
    San Francisco Opera
Directed by Robert Carsen
Distributed by Kultur
Starring Samuel Ramey

Capriccio (DVD)
1993
Produced by Judy Flannery and
    San Francisco Opera
Directed by Stephen Lawless
Distributed by Kultur
Starring Kiri Te Kanawa

Turandot (DVD)
1994
Produced by San Francisco Opera
    and RM Arts
Directed by David Hockney and
    Peter McClintock
Distributed by RM Associates
Starring Eva Marton

Ruslan and Lyudmila (DVD)
1995
Produced by Jane Seymour,
    Colin Wilson
Directed by Lotfi Mansouri
Distributed by RM Arts Associates
Conducted by Valery Gergiev

A Streetcar Named Desire (DVD)
1998
Produced by John Walker,
    Judy Flannery, Cate Gateley
Directed by Colin Graham
Distributed by San Francisco Opera,
    Channel 13/WNET-RM
    Associates, and Deutsche
    Grammophon
Starring Renée Fleming; a
    San Francisco Opera production;
    world premiere

The Merry Widow (DVD)
2001
Produced by Judy Flannery and
    John Walker
Directed by Lotfi Mansouri
Distributed by BBC, Opus Arts
Starring Yvonne Kenney

SWISS-GERMAN TELEVISION
BROADCASTS, DIRECTED BY
LOTFI MANSOURI

Documentary about Salzburg Festival
    (1962) Jupiter Films, Hamburg
How to Strangle Desdemona
    (documentary), 1971
Schule der Frauen (opera by
    Rolf Liebermann), 1972

CANADIAN OPERA COMPANY
TELEVISION BROADCASTS,
ALL PRODUCED BY NORMAN
CAMPBELL FOR CBC CANADA

Joan of Arc, Canadian Opera
    Company at National Arts Centre,
    Ottawa, 1978
Norma, with Joan Sutherland and
    Tatiana Troyanos, 1981
Anna Bolena, with Joan Sutherland
    and Judith Forst, 1984
The Rake's Progress, 1986
Les dialogues des Carmélites, 1987
La forza del destino and
    Don Giovanni, 1988
Tosca, Makropoulos Case, La Bohème,
    1989

NEW YORK CITY OPERA TELECASTS
OF MANSOURI PRODUCTIONS

La rondine, 1985
Magic Flute, 1987

Productions Directed by Mansouri

The list is organized geographically, by country, city, and/or company,
with productions listed chronologically within each category.
Dates are given wherever available.

ARGENTINA
Buenos Aires
  Die lustige Witwe (*The Merry
    Widow*) (in German), 2002

AUSTRALIA
Sydney, Melbourne, Adelaide Festival
  Die lustige Witwe (*The Merry
    Widow*), 1978
  Les Huguenots, 1981
  Hamlet, 1982

AUSTRIA
Salzburg Festival
  Simon Boccanegra, 1962
Vienna State Opera
  La fanciulla del West, 1976
Vienna Volksoper
  Showboat (in German), 1971

CANADA
Edmonton
  Edmonton Opera Association
  La fanciulla del West, 1983

Montreal
  Opéra Montréal
  Les dialogues des Carmélites
    (*The Dialogues of the
    Carmelites*), 1989
Ottawa
  National Arts Centre
  Le nozze di Figaro, 1976
  Orleanskaya dyeva (*Joan of Arc*),
    1978
  La fille du régiment (*The Daughter
    of the Regiment*), 1980
Stratford, Ontario
  Stratford Festival
  Candide, 1978
Toronto
  Canadian Opera Company
  Don Carlo, 1977
  Wozzeck, 1977
  Il barbiere di Siviglia (Canadian
    Opera Company on tour),
    1977–78
  Il barbiere di Siviglia, 1978
    Spring Season, Royal
    Alexandria Theatre
  Orleanskaya dyeva (*Joan of Arc*),
    1978

Don Giovanni, 1978

Der Rosenkavalier, 1978

Carmen, 1979 Spring Season,
    Royal Alexandria Theatre

Simon Boccanegra, 1979

Tristan und Isolde, 1979

Peter Grimes, 1980

Otello, 1980

Lulu, 1980

Die lustige Witwe (*The Merry
    Widow*), 1981

Norma, 1981

Un ballo in maschera, 1981

Les contes d'Hoffmann, 1981

Jenůfa, 1982

La belle Hélène, 1983

Elektra, 1983

Turandot, 1983

La fanciulla del West, 1983

L'incoronazione di Poppea, 1983

Carmen, 1984

Anna Bolena, 1984

Death in Venice, 1984

Il trovatore, 1984

Faust, 1985

Così fan tutte, 1985

Die Meistersinger von Nürnberg,
    1985

Hamlet, 1985

The Mikado, 1986

Salome, 1986

Boris Godunov, 1986

Die Fledermaus, 1987

Idomeneo, 1987

Ledi Makbet Mtsenskovo uyezda
    (*Lady Macbeth of Mtsensk*), 1988

The Turn of the Screw, 1988

Ariadne auf Naxos, 1988

Věc Makropulos (*The Makropulos
    Case*), 1989

Andrea Chénier, 1989

Die Zauberflöte, 1989

La rondine, 1990

Vancouver

Vancouver Opera Association

La fanciulla del West, 1967

Faust, 1968

Die lustige Witwe (*The Merry
    Widow*), 1976

Jenůfa, 1994

Věc Makropulos (*The Makropulos
    Case*), 1996

Elektra, 2003

FRANCE

Festival of Divonne

La canterina, with *Trouble
    in Tahiti*, 1972

Das kleine Mahagonny, 1973

Festival of Orange (outdoor Roman
    arena)

Hérodiade, 1987

Nice

Falstaff (in the Opera House)

Hérodiade (in the Acropolis), 1987

Paris

Chatelet Theatre

"Viardot and Friends," 2006

GERMANY

Dortmund

Der Bettlestudent (in the Opera
    House, as well as a version
    on an open-air stage on a lake),
    1963

Freiburg im Breisgau

Salome, 1963

Don Giovanni, 1964

Carmen (in German), 1964

Heidelberg
  L'incoronazione di Poppea
    (in Italian)
Kassel
  Aida, 1974
  Ariadne auf Naxos, 1975
Nuremberg
  Lucrezia Borgia (in Italian), 1970

GREAT BRITAIN
London
  Royal Opera House Covent Garden
  Esclarmonde, 1983
  Wigmore Hall
  "Viardot and Friends" (an evening
    of music by Pauline Viardot),
    2006

IRAN
Tehran
  Carmen, 1971
  A Kékszakállu herceg vára
    (Duke Bluebeard's Castle), with
    L'heure espagnole, 1972
  Les contes d'Hoffmann, 1973
  Aida, 1974

ITALY
Genoa
  Le nozze di Figaro
  Werther
  Die Fledermaus (in Italian), 1967
Milan
  La Scala
  L'elisir d'amore, 1970
Naples
  Fra Diavolo (in Italian), 1961
Palermo
  Wozzeck, 1965
  Otello, 1966
  Così fan tutte, 1967

Elektra, 1973
Faust, 1974
Perugia
  Festival Sacra Musica
  Řecké pašije (The Greek Passion)
    (Bohuslav Martinů), 1962
Rome
  Die Zauberflöte, 1966
Turin
  Don Pasquale, 1967
Venice
  Così fan tutte
Verona
  Arena de Verona
  Rigoletto, 1995

JAPAN
Tokyo, Osaka, Nagoya
  La Bohème (on Western Opera
    Theater tour)

NETHERLANDS
Nederlandse Opera
  L'heure espagnole, 1969
  Tosca, 1969 and (new production)
    1978
  Ariadne auf Naxos, 1972
  Capriccio, 1975
  La belle Hélène, 1976
  Gianni Schicchi/Il tabarro
    (Holland Festival), 1977
  La vie parisienne (in Dutch), 1978
  Carmen, 1979
  Arabella, 1983

SOVIET UNION/RUSSIA
Saint Petersburg
  Maryinsky Theater
  Ruslan I Lyudmila (Ruslan
    and Lyudmila), 1993

SWITZERLAND

Bern

Queen of Spades (in German)

Geneva

Die Fledermaus, 1965

Don Pasquale, 1965

Wozzeck, 1965

Louise, 1966

Otello, 1966

Simon Boccanegra, 1966

Werther, 1966

La tempête, 1967

La Bohéme, 1968

Così fan tutte, 1968

Don Quichotte, 1968

Macbeth (Ernest Bloch), 1968

Die lustige Witwe (The Merry
Widow) (in French), 1968

Pelléas et Mélisande, 1968

Les dialogues des Carmélites, 1969

Die Entführung aus dem Serail,
1969

Tosca, 1969

Albert Herring, 1970

Carmen, 1970

La Cenerentola, 1970

Das Land des Lächelns (The Land
of Smiles) (in French), 1970

L'étoile, 1971

Lulu, 1971

Manon, 1971

Faust, 1972

Lucia di Lammermoor, 1972

Showboat (in French), 1972

Turandot, 1972

L'elisir d'amore, 1973

Idomeneo, 1973

Der Rosenkavalier, 1973

Zurich

Amahl and the Night Visitors
(in German; European
premiere), 1960

Don Pasquale, 1961

La traviata, 1961

Samson et Dalila, 1961

Fidelio, 1962

Trouble in Tahiti (Leonard
Bernstein; in English), 1962

Carnival! (Bob Merrill; European
premiere, in German), 1962

Hin und zurück, 1962

Il barbiere di Siviglia, 1962

Blackwood und Co. (Hermann
Schiebler; world premiere),
1962

Le prophète, 1962

Albert Herring, 1963

The Turn of the Screw, 1963

Pagliacci, 1963

L'incoronazione di Poppea, 1963

Die lustigen Weiber von Windsor,
1964

Carmen, 1965

L'elisir d'amore, 1965

Il trovatore, 1966

Faust, 1967

Wozzeck, 1968

Cleopatra (operetta, music of
Johann and Josef Strauss;
world premiere), 1969

Ernani, 1971

UNITED STATES

Chicago

Lyric Opera

L'italiana in Algeri, 1970

Werther, 1971

Don Carlo, 1971

Die lustige Witwe (*Merry Widow*), 1981

Die Fledermaus (in English), 1982

Anna Bolena

Dallas

I Puritani, 1974

Samson (Handel), 1976

Der Rosenkavalier, 1982

Così fan tutte, 1984

Don Carlos, 1988

Die lustige Witwe (*The Merry Widow*), 1989, 2007

La rondine, 2007

Houston

Houston Grand Opera

La fille du régiment (*The Daughter of the Regiment*), 1973

Lucrezia Borgia, 1975

La fanciulla del West, 1976

Andrea Chénier, 1977

Anna Bolena, 1986

Boris Godunov, 1986

La rondine, 1988

Los Angeles

Los Angeles City College

Così fan tutte, 1956

Boris Godunov, 1957

Suor Angelica, 1957

Los Angeles Grand Opera

Tosca, 1960

La traviata, 1960

Le nozze di Figaro, 1960

Los Angeles Opera Company

Die lustige Witwe (*The Merry Widow*), 2007

UCLA Opera Workshop

Les malheurs d'Orfe/Fiesta (double bill; Darius Milhaud), 1958

Pelléas et Mélisande, 1959

Vanessa, 1960

Les Huguenots, 1973

Miami

La fanciulla del West, 1977

Boris Godunov, 2002

New Orleans

Elektra, 1967

New York City

Metropolitan Opera

Esclarmonde, 1976

New York City Opera

La fille du régiment (*The Daughter of the Regiment*), 1975

Attila, 1980

Il barbiere di Siviglia

The Mikado, 1983

La rondine, 1984

Werther, 1986

Die Zauberflöte, 1987

Philadelphia

La fille du régiment (*The Daughter of the Regiment*), 1975

San Diego

Die Fledermaus (two productions), 1976, 2005

Giovanna d'Arco (Verdi Festival), 1980

Otello

Idomeneo, 2001

Turandot, 2004

Don Carlo, 2005

Il barbiere di Siviglia, 2006

Boris Godunov, 2006

Samson et Dalila, 2007

San Francisco

Mefistofele, 1963

La sonnambula, 1963

Samson et Dalila, 1963

Die Walküre, 1963

Les dialogues des Carmélites (*The Dialogues of the Carmelites*), 1963

La traviata, 1963
Il trovatore, 1964
Gianni Schicchi, 1964
*Prodaná nevěsta (The Bartered
    Bride),* 1964
Turandot, 1964
Pagliacci, 1964
La traviata, 1964
Andrea Chénier, 1965
La Bohème, 1965
La fanciulla del West, 1965
La Gioconda, 1967
Manon Lescaut, 1967
L'elisir d'amore, 1967
Un ballo in maschera, 1967
Fra Diavolo, 1968
L'elisir d'amore, 1969
Tosca, 1970
Carmen, 1970
L'africaine, 1972
Die Fledermaus, 1973
Esclarmonde, 1974
*La fille du régiment (The Daughter
    of the Regiment),* 1974
L'elisir d'amore, 1975
Werther, 1975
Andrea Chénier, 1975
La Gioconda, 1979
Don Pasquale, 1980
*Die lustige Witwe (The Merry
    Widow),* 1981
Il trovatore, 1981
Norma, 1982
La Gioconda, 1983
Anna Bolena, 1984
Adriana Lecouvreur, 1985
Manon, 1986
Les contes d'Hoffmann, 1987
L'africaine, 1988
Lulu, 1989

Wozzeck, 1990
Die Fledermaus, 1990
Tristan und Isolde, 1991
Attila, 1991
Andrea Chénier, 1992
Christophe Colomb (Darius
    Milhaud), 1992
Guillaume Tell, 1992
Der Rosenkavalier, 1993
*Věc Makropulos (The Makropulos
    Case),* 1993
Die Meistersinger von Nürnberg,
    1993
Macbeth, 1994
Tannhäuser, 1994
Hérodiade, 1994
*Ruslan i Lyudmila (Ruslan
    and Lyudmila),* 1995
Don Giovanni, 1995
Carmen, 1996
Die Fledermaus, 1996
Salome, 1996
Tosca, 1997
Death in Venice, 1997
Guillaume Tell, 1997
Lulu, 1998
Carmen, 1998
Louise, 1999
Wozzeck, 1999
Nabucco, 1999
Don Giovanni, 2000
*Tsarskaya nevesta (The Tsar's
    Bride),* 2000
Der Rosenkavalier, 2000
L'elisir d'amore, 2001
Tosca, 2001
*Die lustige Witwe (The Merry
    Widow),* 2001

Santa Barbara
Music Academy of the West
Albert Herring, 2002
Santa Fe
Il barbiere di Siviglia, 1965
Tosca (two productions), 1966, 1969
Wozzeck, 1966
La traviata (two productions), 1968, 1970
Lucia di Lammermoor (two productions)
La Cenerentola, 1966
Carmen, 1967
Rigoletto, 1967
Salome, 1967
Der Rosenkavalier, 1968
Help, Help the Globolinks! (Gian Carlo Menotti), 1969

Anna Bolena, 1970
Don Carlos, 1971
Seattle
Black Widow (Thomas Pasatieri, world premiere)
Anna Bolena, 1991
Tulsa
Andrea Chénier, 1981
Die lustige Witwe (*The Merry Widow*)
Washington, D.C.
Washington Opera
Turandot, 2001
Tristan und Isolde
Die Fledermaus, 2003
Wolf Trap
La fille du régiment (*The Daughter of the Regiment*), 1975

INDEX

Abravanel, Maurice, 46–47

Adams, John, 225–27, 241, 292

Adams, Sam, 41

"Addio senza rancor" (aria from *La Bohème*), 129

Adler, Kurt Herbert, 40, 197, 264, 285, 293; as conductor, 201–2; death of, 157; operas commissioned, 232; and San Francisco Opera, 149–53, 155, 159–60, 174; and *Turandot*, 267; and *Yes, Giorgio*, 125–26, 128

Adler, Nancy M., 153

Adriana Lecouvreur (Fernando Cilea), 45, 139

Aghayan, Ray, 24, 27

Agnew, Spiro, 83

Agnini, Armando, 197

Aida (Giuseppe Verdi), 42, 96–97, 141, 143, 155, 167, 247

Aitken, Robert, 135

Akins, Zoë, 42

Albanese, Licia, 62

Albert Herring (Benjamin Britten), 69, 82, 141

Alcina (Georg Friedrich Händel), 290

Alden, Christopher, 224, 236

All My Sons (Arthur Miller), 252

Allyson, June, 40

Altmeyer, Jeanine, 44

Amahl and the Night Visitors (Gian Carlo Menotti), 68, 77

Ambassador Hotel, Los Angeles, 40, 150

American Conservatory Theater, San Francisco, 177

American Enterprise Institute, 160

American Federation of Musicians, 169

Americans with Disabilities Act, 184

Ames, John, 9

Analysis of a Phobia in a 5-year-old Boy (Sigmund Freud), 61

Ančerl, Karel, 130

Anderson, Rod, 110–11, 114, 220

Andrassy, Gábor, 175

Andrews, Julie, 257

Anglo-Persian Oil Company, 14

Anissimov, Alexander, 193

Anna and the King of Siam (motion picture), 40

Anna Bolena (Gaetano Donizetti), 7, 117, 139

Anna Karenina (motion picture), 22

Ansermet, Ernest, 82, 132, 280

Antoinette Perry Award, 65

Antony and Cleopatra (Samuel Barber), 218

Appelbaum, Lou, 136

Arabella (Richard Strauss), 44, 46, 244

Arcop Associates, 121

Arena di Verona, 102, 247

Ariadne auf Naxos (Richard Strauss), 37, 266

Armenian, Raffi, 132, 134

Arroyo, Martina, 79–80

Arshak II (Tigran Chukhadjian), 207–8

Art Gallery of Ontario, 121

Art of Singing-Golden Voices of the Century, The (TV feature), 290

Arts Council of Great Britain, 112

Ashkenazi, Danny, 50

Attila (Giuseppe Verdi), 291

Auber, Daniel-François Esprit, 70, 264

Auto Club of Southern California, 51

Autry, John, 246

Aylmer, Jennifer, 272

Ayres, Lew, 41

Bacquier, Gabriel, 291

Balanchine, George, 77, 82

Ballad of Baby Doe, The (Douglas Moore), 261

Ballet/Opera House Corporation, Toronto, 121, 142

Ballo in Maschera, Un (Giuseppe Verdi), 268

Barber, Samuel, 46, 48, 241, 273

Barbiere di Siviglia, Il, 68, 72, 116–17, 137, 213, 218, 267, 288

Baricco, Alessandro, 250

Bartók, Béla, 96

Bartoletti, Bruno, 290–91

Bastianini, Ettore, 73

Baumgarten, Paul, 242

Bay Bridge, San Francisco–Oakland, 166

Bayerische Staatsoper, 226

Bayrakdarian, Isabel, 119, 272

Bayreuther Festspiele, 54, 56, 70, 134, 144, 281, 284

Beatrice di Tenda (Vincenzo Bellini), 271

Beethoven, Ludwig van, 76–77, 95

Behr, Randall, 201

Behrens, Hildegard, 202

Belafonte, Harry, 220

Bell, Donald, 130

Belles de la nuit, Les (*The Beauties of the Night*) (motion picture), 252

Bellini, Vincenzo, 271, 292

Benny, Joan, 36

Berg, Alban, 49, 139

Berganza, Teresa, 287, 290

Bergen, Candice, 36

Bergen, Edgar, 201

Bergman, Ingmar, 155

Bergman, Ingrid, 35

Bergonzi, Carlo, 129, 138

Berlin, Irving, 25

Berlioz, Hector, 283

Bernard, Annabelle, 53

Bernardi, Mario, 133–34

Bernheim, Alain, 123

Bernheimer, Martin, 148, 152–53

Bernstein, Leonard, 65–66, 69, 97, 104, 200, 238, 242

Bertolucci, Bernardo, 135

Betrayed Sea, The. See *Verratene Meer, Das*

Betrothal in a Monastery. See *Obrucheniye v monastire*

Billinghurst, Sarah, 5, 222–23, 235

Bing, Rudolf, 50–51, 53, 63, 153, 270

Birch, Ruth, 42

Birtwhistle, Harrison, 242

Bisset, Jacqueline, 124

Bizet, Georges, 224

Blackwood & Co. (Hermann Schiebler), 68

Index

Blomstedt, Herbert, 177, 215
Blythe, Stephanie, 272
Boboli Gardens, Florence, 59
Bocharova, Elena, 9, 255
Bohème, La (Giacomo Puccini), 31, 42, 53, 65, 128, 161, 191, 195, 239
Böhm, Karl, 155
Boito, Arrigo, 1
Bolcom, William, 232
Bonazzi, Elaine, 222
Bonfire of the Vanities, The, 240
Bonynge, Richard, 3, 8, 68, 261, 271
Borge, Victor, 130
Boris Godunov (Modest Mussorgsky), 40, 174, 273
Bornemann, Fritz, 85
Borodin, Alexander Porfiryevitch, 116, 174
Borodina, Olga, 4, 210, 274
Borzage, Frank, 41–42
Bosquet, Thierry, 172
Boston Symphony Orchestra, 284
Boswell, Philip, 113
Boulez, Pierre, 132
Boyer, Charles, 42
Bradley, Ed, 277
Bradshaw, Richard, 141, 143
Brando, Marlon, 237
Braun, Russell, 272
Braun, Victor, 130, 137
Brecht, Bertolt, 33, 120
Brecht Festival, Toronto, 120
Brégent, Michel-Georges, 113, 136
Bregman + Hamann Architects, 12
Brentano, Felix, 109
Breslin, Herbert H., 125
Bride and the Wolf, The (film project), 128
Brieger, Nicolas, 259
Brill, Jonathan, 242

Britten, Benjamin, 34, 82, 140, 228, 230
Brook, Peter, 95
Brooklyn Academy of Music, 226, 277
Brown, Debria, 53
Brown, Willie, 4, 236
Brownlee, Lawrence, 272
Bruckner, Anton, 61
Buchanan, Alison, 246
Büchner, Georg, 140
Buckley, Emerson, 126
Bumbry, Grace, 44, 53, 272, 286
Burchuladze, Paata, 193
Burnett, Carol, 7–9, 34
Burrowes, Norma, 133
Busch, Fritz, 62, 273

Caballé, Montserrat, 290
Cabell, Nicole, 272
Cagney & Lacey (TV series), 41
Caldwell, Sarah, 285
Callas, Maria, 48, 278, 290
Cal Performances, 226
CAMI. *See* Columbia Artists Management
Campbell, Elaine, 9
Campbell, Norman, 9, 10, 117
Canada Council, 112, 135, 137
Canadian Broadcasting Corporation (CBC), 137
Canadian Opera Company, 105, 148, 158, 262; development of, 105, 108–10, 113, 117–20, 122; and Dr. Geiger-Torel, 105, 108–10; and new orchestra, 130–35; performing venues, 115, 140–43; and supertitles, 146; and Toronto Symphony, 130–31; tours, 137–38; and works commissioned, 219–21
Canadian Opera Company Orchestra, 131

Canadian Opera Composer's Program, 136, 138, 143, 219

Canadian Opera Ensemble, 119, 135

Candide (Leonard Bernstein), 66

Cantatrice, La (Franz Joseph Haydn), 104

Capriccio (Richard Strauss), 121, 267

Capuana, Franco, 288

Capuletti ed i Montecchi, I (Vincenzo Bellini), 292

Cardiff Singer of the World Competition, 274

Carmen (Georges Bizet), 53, 78, 83, 87, 100, 116, 153, 193, 218, 247

Carmen Jones (motion picture), 271

Carnegie Hall, New York, 271

Carnival! (musical), 68

Carreras, José, 286

Carson, John, 147

Carter, James Earl (Jimmy), 181

Caruso, Enrico, 9, 41–42, 165–66

Cass Timberlane (motion picture), 29

CBC. *See* Canadian Broadcasting Corporation

CBC Talent Festival, 119

Cenerentola, La (Gioachino Rossini), 287

Centre Lyrique, Geneva, 104

Cerha, Friedrich, 140

Chagall, Marc, 36

Chaliapin, Fyodor, Jr., 129

Chamberlain, David, 183

Champ, The (motion picture), 240

Champion, Gower, 41

Chaplin, Charles (Charlie), 263

Charpentier, Gustave, 277

"Che gelida manina" (aria from *La Bohème*), 31

Cher (Cheryl Sarkisian), 128–29

Chéreau, Patrice, 144

Chicago Lyric Opera, 271, 273, 289–90, 292

Chocolate Soldier, The (motion picture), 23

Chopin, Frédéric, 17, 23

Chukhadjian, Tigran, 208

Cimarosa, Domenico, 141

Civic Auditorium, San Francisco, 186, 189, 192–95

Clair, René, 252

Clark, Graham, 250

Clayburgh, Jill, 124

Clayton, Kristen, 255

Clemens, Samuel. *See* Twain, Mark

Cleopatra (Johann Strauss, Jr., Josef Strauss), 69

Cleva, Fausto, 288, 289

Cliff Hotel, San Francisco, 163

Clinton, William Jefferson (Bill), 3, 181

Close, Glenn, 228

Coates, Edith, 143

Coffin, William Sloane, 36

Cohan, George M., 42

Cole, Robert, 226

Collins, Martha, 129

Colman, Ronald, 26

Columbia Artists Management, 171, 202, 248–49

Company (Stephen Sondheim), 239

Congregation of Sisters of St. Joseph of Medaille, 253

Contes d'Hoffmann, Les (Jacques Offenbach), 96, 157, 178

Cook, Jean, 63–64, 75

Copley, John, 197–98

Coq d'or, Le. See Zolotoy petushok

Corelli, Franco, 45, 73, 156

Corigliano, John, 241, 250, 283

Corriere della sera, Milan, 291

Così fan tutte (Wolfgang Amadeus

Mozart), 39, 102, 141, 208, 228, 275, 291

Covent Garden. *See* Royal Opera House Covent Garden

Cowan, Ruth, 46

Craft, Robert, 284

Cranna, Clifford (Kip), 6–7, 161, 222–23, 228, 231, 236, 241

Crespin, Régine, 55, 153, 221

Crosby, John, 280–81, 285

Crouse, Russell, 37

Cuccaro, Costanzo, 117

Culbertson, Brian, 248

Cunning Little Vixen, The. See *Příhody Lišky Bystroušky*

Curran Theater, San Francisco, 187

Dallas Opera, 289–90

Damnation de Faust, Le (Hector Berlioz), 178, 204

Damn Yankees (musical), 246

Dandridge, Dorothy, 271

Dangerous Liaisons (Conrad Susa), 230–33, 243–44

Danielpour, Richard, 243

Daniels, David, 272

Daphne (Richard Strauss), 178

Darnell, Linda, 29

Daudet, Alphonse, 17

Davenport, Mary, 64

Davis, Andrew, 130, 292

Davis, Bette, 24

Day I Met Caruso, The (TV film), 41–43

Dead Man Walking (Jake Heggie), 209–10, 217, 232, 253, 257–59

Death in Venice (Benjamin Britten), 140, 203

Death of Klinghoffer, The (John Adams), 225–28, 241

Decca Records, 156

de Garmo, Tilly, 33, 39, 44–46, 54, 73, 295

della Casa, Lisa, 46

Del Monaco, Mario, 59

de los Angeles, Victoria, 130

Dennis, Reid, 162–63, 205

Denver, John, 220

Descher, Sandy, 42

Désilets, Richard, 113, 136

Deutsche Oper Berlin, 85, 224, 288, 292

de Young, Michelle, 272

Dialogues des Carmélites (Francis Poulenc), 117, 140, 265, 273

Diamond, Jack, 141

Diba, Farah, Empress of Iran, 83, 88, 93–94, 99

Dippel, Andreas, 165

Disneyland, 48

Distel, Sacha, 88

Divonne Festival, 104

Dohnányi, Christoph von, 203, 291

Domingo, Plácido, 1, 48, 139, 148, 157, 179–80, 262, 286, 290

Don Carlos (Giuseppe Verdi), 140, 267, 273, 290–91

Don Giovanni (Wolfgang Amadeus Mozart), 5, 62, 77

Donizetti, Gaetano, 7, 73, 141

Don Pasquale (Gaetano Donizetti), 68

Don Quichotte (Jules Massenet), 253

Dortmund Opera. *See* Theater Dortmund

Drabinsky, Garth, 243

Dreamplay (Timothy Sullivan), 136

Ducloux, Walter, 49

Dukakis, Olympia, 129

Duke Bluebeard's Castle. See *Kékszakállu Herceg vára, A*

Duncan, Lindsay, 228

Dunne, Irene, 40

Durbin, Deanna, 22–23

Dutoit, Charles, 226

Duval, Pierre, 117

Dye, Peggy Kriha, 246

Eastman, John, 241

Eastman School of Music, Rochester, N.Y., 65

Ecstasy of Rita Joe, The (George Tyga), 220

Eddy, Nelson, 23

Elegie für junge Liebende (Hans Werner Henze), 241

Elektra (Richard Strauss), 145, 261, 292

Elias, Rosalind, 48

Elisir d'amore, L' (Gaetano Donizetti), 288

Ellington, Edward Kennedy (Duke), 130

Elmer Gantry (Sinclair Lewis), 252

Emmeline (Tobias Picker), 280

End of the Affair (Jake Heggie), 257

English National Opera, 226

Ernani (Giuseppe Verdi), 68

Ernster, Dezső, 75

Escalero, Katja, 9

Esfandiary, Soraya, Empress of Iran, 93

Estep, Craig, 224

Esther (Hugo Weisgall), 221, 223–24, 241

Evgeny Onegin (Pyotr Ilyitch Tchaikovsky), 82

Ewing, Maria, 261

Falstaff (Giuseppe Verdi), 96, 273, 278

Fanciulla del West, La (Giacomo Puccini), 100, 114, 279, 282, 289

Farouk, King of Egypt, 32

Farrell, Eileen, 271

Fawzia Binte Fuad, Empress of Iran, 32, 92–93

Feinstein, Dianne, 3, 236

Feldman, Laurie, 152

Felsenstein, Walter, 56–58

Ferden, Bruce, 222

Ferrer, José, 276–77

Ferrier, Kathleen, 130

Fidelio (Ludwig van Beethoven), 73–76, 273

Fiery Angel, The. See *Ognenny angel*

Fille du Régiment, La (Gaetano Donizetti), 133, 141, 237, 270

First Love, 22

Fischer-Dieskau, Dietrich, 46, 241

Fitzgerald, Edward, 20

Flanigan, Lauren, 224

Fleck, Paul, 117

Fledermaus, Die (Johann Strauss, Jr.), 225, 283

Fleischmann, Ernest, 157

Fleming, Renée, 5, 7, 179–80, 229, 231, 233, 244–45, 250, 252, 277

Floyd, Carlisle, 49, 136, 217, 280

Floyd S. Chalmers Foundation, 210

Flynn, Errol, 25, 41, 274

Ford, Bruce, 272

Ford, Gerald, 181

Ford, Glenn, 36

Ford, John, 41

Forever Amber (motion picture), 29

Forrest, Robert, 116

Forrester, Maureen, 117, 119, 140, 146

Forst, Judith, 117, 229, 234, 260–61

Foss, Lukas, 35

Foster, Lawrence, 33

Four Seasons Centre for the Performing Arts, 141

Fox, Carol, 232, 271, 290

Index

Fox, Tom, 224
Fra Diavolo (Daniel-François Esprit
  Auber), 70, 264
Frankfurt Opera. *See* Oper Frankfurt
Frau ohne Schatten, Die (Richard
  Strauss), 4, 44, 153, 155
Fremstad, Olive, 165
Freni, Mirella, 290
Freud, Sigmund, 61, 239
Friedman, Tully M., 158, 160, 163,
  169, 182
Friedrich, Götz, 134
Fuller, Jim, 145, 147
Furlanetto, Feruccio, 267
Furtwängler, Herbert, 44, 48, 62
Futral, Elizabeth, 246

Gábor, Zsá Zsá (Zsuzsanna), 32
Gaitley, Kate, 8
Gall, Hugues, 253–54
Gallantry (Douglas Moore), 118
Garbo, Greta, 22
Gardelli, Lamberto, 82
Garland, Judy, 50
Gasparian, Harmik, 24
Gavazzeni, Gianandrea, 287–88
Gayer, Catherine, 50
Gedda, Nicolai, 70, 264
Geer, Todd, 9
Geiger-Kullmann, Rosy, 108
Geiger-Torel, Herman, 108–11, 295
Gelb, Peter, 232
Gencer, Leyla, 287
General Electric, 146
Geneva Opera. *See* Grand Théâtre de
  Genève
Genovese, Margaret, 113–14
Genovese-Vanderhoof Associates, 114
Gergiev, Valery, 171–72, 174, 203,
  206, 280
Gershwin, George, 181

Getty, Gordon, 6, 186–87, 189, 191
Ghitescu-Mohnbatt, Anca, 139
Ghosts of Versailles, The (John
  Corigliano), 241, 250
Gianni Schicchi (Giacomo Puccini),
  276
Gielen, Michael, 2
Gilfrey, Rodney, 244, 272
Gioconda, La (Amilcare Ponchielli),
  124, 192, 268–69
Giordani, Marcello, 9
Giselle (ballet), 88
Glass, Philip, 176
Glinka, Mikhail Ivanovitch, 6
Globe and Mail, Toronto, 140
Globe Theatre, San Diego, 246
Gluck, Christoph Willibald von, 178,
  181
Glyndebourne Festival, 226
Gobbi, Tito, 59, 81, 96, 265, 267, 278,
  287, 290
Gockley, David, 157, 210, 215,
  234–35, 280
Godward, William W. (Bill), 3,
  182–84, 187–89, 192–93, 198, 200,
  205–6, 214
Golden Gate Park, San Francisco, 153
Golden Gate Theater, San Francisco,
  187, 191–92, 195
Goldman, Richard, 190
Goldmark, Karl, 165
Gone With the Wind (motion picture),
  22
Goodman, Alice, 225–27
Gorbachev, Mikhail, 171
Gordoni, Virginia, 63–64, 74
Gorman, Michael, 279
Götterdämmerung (Richard Wag-
  ner), 138
Gould, Glenn, 119, 130
Graf, Ann-Kathrin, 101, 103

Graf, Herbert, 265, 274, 287, 295; and Adler, 149–51; death of, 102–3; and Freud, 61–62; and Geneva Opera, 81–84; master classes, 46–48; personal life, 94, 100–101, 103; and *Streetcar*, 238–39; and Venice, 59–60; and Zurich Opera, 50–51, 62–65, 72–78

Graf, Lieselotte, 48, 60, 77, 100, 101

Graf, Max, 61

Graf, Werner, 77, 103

Graham, Colin, 230–31, 233, 246, 248, 250–51

Graham, Susan, 9, 248, 253–55, 257

Grand Théâtre de Genève, 81, 84, 101–3, 107

Graves, Denyce, 243

Grayson, Kathryn, 271

Green, Jenny, 161, 206, 211, 236

Green, Johnny, 33

Griffey, Anthony Dean, 246

Grist, Reri, 53, 63–64, 152

Grunberg, Peter, 236

Grusin, David, 240–41, 247

Guadagno, Anton, 50

Guardian, 258

Guare, John, 250

Guererro, Alberto, 119

Guillaume Tell (Gioachino Rossini), 178–79

Gulliver's Travels (Jonathan Swift), 124

Gunsmoke (TV series), 41

Gustafson, Nancy, 166

Guth, Otto, 152

Guttman, Irving, 137

Guttman, Robert, 55

Hadley, Jerry, 272–73

Hafez, 20–21

Hagegård, Hakan, 250

Hagen, Uta, 276

Hager, Paul, 151

Hall, Peter, 261, 290

Halper, Ross, 222

Hal Roach Studio, 41

Hamburgische Staatsoper, 285

Hamilton, Stuart, 119

Hamlet (Ambroise Thomas), 139

Hamm-Smith, Theresa, 255

Hampson, Thomas, 204, 229–30, 233

Hampton, Christopher, 228–29

Handel, Georg Friedrich, 227, 263, 290, 292

Hanslick, Eduard, 61

Harbourfront Festival, Toronto, 118, 120

Hardy, Oliver, 70

Harrold, Katherine, 124

Hartmann, Rudolf, 46

Harvey Milk (Stewart Wallace), 232, 234–36, 252

Hawlata, Franz, 4

Haydn, Franz Joseph, 104

Heggie, Jake, 218, 252–56

Hellyer, Paul, 121

Hemmings, Peter, 110, 226

Henze, Hans Werner, 224, 241–42, 248, 282

Hepburn, Audrey, 37

Heppner, Ben, 119, 146

Herbst Theater, San Francisco, 226

Herman, Robert, 50

Hermann, Karl-Ernst, 225

Hermann, Ursel, 225

Hérodiade (Jules Massenet), 179–80, 286

Heure espagnole, L' (Maurice Ravel), 96

Hewlett, Rosemary, 190

Hewlett, William, 190

Hindemith, Paul, 74, 282
His Butler's Sister (motion picture), 23
Histoire du soldat, L' (Igor Stravinsky), 284
Hitler, Adolf, 55
Hobson, David, 229
Hockney, David, 117
Hoffman, Grace, 53–54
Hofmannsthal, Hugo von, 44, 146
Hoiby, Lee, 241
Holmes, Eugene, 53
Homburger, Walter, 130–31
Hope, Bob, 40
Hopf, Hans, 144
Hormel, James, 236
Horne, Marilyn (Jackie), 1, 44, 53, 153, 156, 232–33, 250, 271–72, 278
Horst, Philip, 9
Hotter, Hans, 45, 62, 211, 283
Houston Grand Opera, 3, 210, 234, 236–37
Howland, Gerard, 178, 189
Huis-Clos (Jean-Paul Sartre), 293
Hummingbird Centre, Toronto, 141
Hunter, Kim, 41
Hvorostovsky, Dmitri, 9, 210, 212, 274

Idomeneo, re di Creta (Wolfgang Amadeus Mozart), 166, 201, 283
I Love Lucy (TV series), 270
Imperial Oil Opera Theatre, Toronto, 122
Incoronazione di Poppea, L' (Claudio Monteverdi), 69, 144, 146, 290
Indiana University, 69, 263
Intermezzo (Richard Strauss), 44
Internal Revenue Service, 138
International Opera Studio, Zurich, 69, 81

Iphigénie en Tauride (Christoph Willibald von Gluck), 178
Ironside, Edmund, 15
Italiana in Algeri, L' (Gioachino Rossini), 271, 278
It Pays to Be Ignorant (radio program), 24
It's a Wonderful Life (motion picture), 192

Jackson, Kate, 124
Jalili, Jahangir (uncle of L.M.), 17, 18
Jalili, Mehrangiz. *See* Mansouri, Mehrangiz
Janáček, Leoš, 34, 74, 140, 264, 292
Jane Eyre (Charlotte Brontë), 39
Janovsky, Judy, 171
Jansons, Mariss, 288
Järvi, Kristian, 288
Järvi, Paavo, 288
Jenůfa (Leoš Janáček), 34, 49, 140
Jepson, Christine, 254
Jerusalem, Siegfried, 134, 262
Jewison, Norman, 128–29
Joan of Arc. See Orleanskaya dyeva
Johnson, Franklin Pitcher (Pitch), 205, 208, 214, 251, 257
Jolson, Al, 9, 114
Jones, Gwyneth, 5, 69, 81, 265–66, 290
Journal of Canadian Studies, 136
Journet, Marcel, 165
Juch, Hermann, 78–81
Jucker, Emil, 78
Juilliard School of Music, New York, 65, 271
Juliana, Queen of the Netherlands, 32
Jumping Frog of Calaveras County, The (Lukas Foss), 35, 36
Jurinac, Sena, 74–75

Kafka, Franz, 94

Kanawa, Kiri te, 280

Karajan, Herbert von, 62, 76, 78, 96, 239, 291

Kaťa Kabanova (Leoš Janáček), 261

Keaton, Buster, 41

Keene, Catherine, 222

Keenlyside, Simon, 254

Kékszakállu Herceg vára, A (Béla Bartók), 96

Kennedy, Jacqueline, 79–80

Kennedy, Michael, 249

Kern, Jerome, 40

Kerns, Robert, 63–64, 67

Kerr, Deborah. 37

Kettle, Martin, 258

Khalsoum, Oum, 23

Khayyam, Omar, 20

Khomeini, Ayatolla Ruholla, 95, 105–6

King, James, 53, 153, 288

King and I, The (motion picture), 37, 40

Kirov Ballet, St. Petersburg, 171, 174

Kirov Opera, St. Petersburg, 6, 171–74

Kirsten, Dorothy, 278–79

Kismet (musical), 116

Kleiber, Carlos, 283, 288

Kleiber, Erich, 109

Kleine Mahagonny, Das (Kurt Weill), 104, 120

Klemperer, Otto, 33, 44–45, 54, 73–77, 280

Klinghoffer, Leon, 225, 227

Knyadz Igor (Alexander Borodin), 174, 193

Kodak Carousels, 147

Komische Oper, 56

Kondek, Charles, 222–23

Königin von Saba, Die (Karl Goldmark), 165

Kónya, Sándor, 150

Korie, Michael, 235

Korngold, Erich Wolfgang, 42, 44

Kosman, Joshua, 258

Krachmalnik, Samuel, 63, 65, 126

Kraus, Alfredo, 279, 290

Krawitz, Herman, 239–41

Krawitz, Rhoda, 239, 241

Krips, Josef, 77

Krolloper, Berlin, 33, 74

Kusman, Ellyn, 242

Kyu Won-Han, 9

Laclos, Pierre Choderlos de, 228

Ladd, Alan, 22

Lady Macbeth of Mtsensk. See *Ledi Makbet Mtsenskovo Uyezda*

Lafayette Park, San Francisco, 166

La Fenice. *See* Teatro La Fenice

Lalive, Jean Flavin, 102

Land des Lächelns, Das (Franz Lehár), 105

Landry, Rosemary, 119

Lansbury, Angela, 41

Lanza, Mario, 41

Laperrière, Gaetan, 113

Larmore, Jennifer, 252

La Scala. See Teatro alla Scala

Last Tango in Paris (motion picture), 135

Laurel, Stan, 70

Lawford, Peter, 41

Lear, Evelyn, 53

Leberg, John, 113, 131, 145–47, 161, 163

Ledi Makbet Mtsenskovo Uyezda (Dmitry Dmitrievitch Shostakovich), 140, 153

Lee, Ella, 54

Legge, Walter, 76

Lehár, Franz (Ferenc), 105, 213

Lehmann, Lotte, 42, 44–46, 109, 130, 271–72

Leiferkus, Sergei, 193

Leigh, Vivien, 22

Leinsdorf, Erich, 150

Leonard, Isabel, 272

Levine, James, 283–84, 292

Lewis, Henry, 34

Lewis, Jerry, 246

Lewis, Ramsey, 220

Liaisons dangéreuses, Les (film), 228

Liebermann, Rolf, 225

Light in the Piazza, The (Tennessee Williams), 258

Lili (motion picture), 68

Limonick, Natalie, 48

Lincoln Center, New York, 6, 128, 174

Lindsay, Howard, 37

Littell, Philip, 229–31, 234, 243, 246–47

Little Foxes, The (play), 39

Liszt, Ferenc (Franz), 23

Lloyd's, 139

Locambra, Mirna, 281

Loesser, Frank, 241

Lohengrin (Richard Wagner), 134, 193, 262, 293

Lollobrigida, Gina, 252

Loma Prieta earthquake, 166, 182, 201

London, George, 53

London Records, 156

Los Angeles City College, 39

Los Angeles Civic Grand Opera, 49

Los Angeles Opera, 48–50, 211

Los Angeles Philharmonic Orchestra, 49, 157

Los Angeles Times, 152, 249

Louise (Gustave Charpentier), 206, 263, 277

Louise M. Davies Symphony Hall, 167, 174

Louis Riel (Harry Somers), 220

Lubitsch, Ernst, 39

Lucia di Lammermoor (Gaetano Donizetti), 282

Ludwig, Christa, 104

Ludwig, Leopold, 285

Luhrman, Baz, 229

Luisotti, Nicola, 215

Lulu (Alban Berg), 140, 249

Lustigen Weiber von Windsor, Die (Otto Nicolai), 68

Lustige Witwe, Die (Franz Lehár), 213

Lyubov k triam apelsinam (Sergei Sergeievitch Prokofiev), 181

Maag, Peter, 291

Macbeth (Giuseppe Verdi), 229

MacDonald, Jeanette, 23

Mackerras, Charles, 132, 204, 206, 258, 280, 292–93

Mackerras, Judy Wilkins, 258, 293

MacMullen, Bruce, 145–46

Madama Butterfly (Giacomo Puccini), 22, 149, 191, 195

Maggio Musicale Fiorentino, 290

Magic Flute, The. See *Zauberflöte, Die*

Magic of Mozart (Mavor Moore), 219

Mahler, Alma, 54

Mahler, Gustav, 62

Malkovich, John, 228

Mambro, Joseph di, 134

Mann, Heinrich, 33

Mann, Thomas, 33, 210

Manon Lescaut (Giacomo Puccini), 66, 278

Mansouri, Hassan (father of L.M.), 13–19, 23, 25–28, 31–32, 73, 85, 89–92, 96–98, 106

Mansouri, Marjorie (Midge, wife of
L.M.), 6, 37, 68, 72, 81, 100, 158,
198, 248, 253, 282, 295; and San
Francisco, 149–51; and Toronto,
110–13; and Wagner, 144–45
Mansouri, Mehrangiz (Mehri,
mother of L.M.), 13–20, 23, 25–28,
30, 98
Mansouri, Saltnat (grandmother of
L.M.), 13, 21, 26, 85, 90–91
Mansouri, Shireen (daughter of
L.M.), 100, 105–6, 154
Mantello, Joe, 254–57
Maple Leaf Gardens, Toronto, 139
March, Fredric, 22
Marcos, Imelda, 83
Margaret Garner (Richard Daniel-
pour), 243
Margison, Richard, 9, 200
Maria Golovin (Gian Carlo Menotti),
46
Marilyn Horne Foundation, 272
Marino, Amerigo, 50
Mario and the Magician (Harry
Somers), 210
Markle, Patrick, 206, 209, 211,
214–15, 259
Mark Morris Dancers, 227
Marriage of Figaro, The. See *Nozze di
Figaro, Le*
Marshall, Gary, 257
Marshall, Lois, 119
Martin, Wolfgang, 50
Marx Brothers, 12, 286
Maryinsky Theater, St. Petersburg,
171, 173
Mask of Orpheus, The (Harrison
Birtwhistle), 242
Maslin, Janet, 127
Masonic Auditorium, San Francisco,
167–68, 183, 201

Massenet, Jules, 179, 253, 286
Massey Hall, Toronto, 135
Mattila, Karita, 166
Mayer, Martin, 224
McCarthy, Charlie, 201
McCracken, James, 53, 63–65, 68, 75,
81, 156, 262, 265, 285
McEwen, Terence A. (Terry), 155–57,
159–60, 174, 197, 200, 221, 223,
295
McFerrin, Bobby, 220
McLaglen, Victor, 26
McNair, Sylvia, 244
McNally, Terrence, 229, 242, 252–58
Médecin, Pierre, 286
Mehta, Bejun, 272
Mehta, Zubin, 135, 226
Meier, Johanna, 234
Meistersinger von Nürnberg, Die
(Richard Wagner), 119, 139
Menotti, Gian Carlo, 33, 46, 48–49,
68, 217
Merkin Hall, New York, 254
Merola, Gaetano, 49, 149, 150,
199–201
Merola Program, 154
Merry Widow, The. See *Lustige
Witwe, Die*
Merry Wives of Windsor, The. See
Lustigen Weiber von Windsor, Die
Messiaen, Olivier, 178, 251
Metro-Goldwyn-Mayer, 242
Metro International Caravan, 117–18,
120
Metropolitan Opera, New York (the
Met), 53, 118, 124, 126, 128, 170,
186, 232, 248; and Beverly Sills,
270; commissions, 221–59; and
Donald Runnicles, 202–6; and
Fausto Cleva, 289; first telecast,
62; and Herbert Graf, 46; and

James Levine, 283; and James McCracken, 63, 65; labor negotiations, 169–70; and L.A. tours, 49; and L.M.'s farewell gala, 1, 5; and Lothar Wallenstein, 109; and Lotte Lehmann, 44; and 1906 tour to San Francisco, 165; and Pamela Rosenberg, 208–15; première of *Vanessa*, 48; and Regina Resnik, 273; and Russian repertoire, 171–75; and Sarah Caldwell, 285; schedules, 124, 176–80; and supertitles (Met Titles), 148; and U.N. commemoration, 181–82; and Valery Gergiev, 174

Met Titles, 206

Metz, Jack 271

Meyerbeer, Giacomo, 150, 221, 265

MGM. *See* Metro-Goldwyn-Mayer

Milk, Harvey, 235–37

Miller, Arthur, 252

Miller, Glenn, 24

Miller, Nancy. *See* Adler, Nancy M.

Milnes, Sherill, 273

Mineo, Sal, 41

Miranda, Carmen, 22

Mirvish, Anne, 116

Mirvish, David, 116

Mirvish, Edwin, 114–16

Miss Saigon (musical), 195

Mr. Imperium (motion picture), 32

Mitchell, Leona, 125, 271, 286–87

Moby Dick (Jake Heggie), 257

Molinari-Pradelli, Francesco, 285

Moll, Mariquita, 49

Montarsolo, Paolo, 263

Monteverdi, Claudio, 34, 144, 290

Montgomery, Kenneth, 133, 138, 145

Montreal Symphony, 226

Moonstruck (motion picture), 128

Moore, Ann, 120

Moore, Douglas, 118, 217

Moore, Mavor, 219

Moorefield, Olive, 53

Moreau, Jeanne, 228

Morel, Jean, 65

Morgenthaler, Ernst, 72

Morgenthaler, Fritz, 72–73, 82

Morris, James, 157–58, 200, 280

Morris, Jay Hunter, 246

Morrison, Toni, 243–44

Mortier, Gérard, 225–26

Mortifee, Ann, 220

Moscone, George, 235

Moses und Aron (Arnold Schoenberg), 132

Most Happy Fella, The (Frank Loesser), 241

Mozart, Wolfgang Amadeus, 95, 131, 177, 215, 218–19, 228, 239, 264, 283, 291–92

Mulholland Falls, 240

Münchner Philharmoniker, 292

Murphy, Heidi Gran, 272

Music Academy of the West, 44, 46–47, 272

Music Box Theatre, New York, 228

Mussorgsky, Modest Petrovich, 174

Muti, Riccardo, 225

My Fair Lady (motion picture), 37

NAC Orchestra, Ottawa, 133

Nagano, Kent, 178, 226, 292

National Arts Centre, Ottawa, 117, 133

National Ballet of Canada, 130, 142, 219

National Public Radio, 137

Nazli, Queen of Egypt, 32, 92

Neidlinger, Gustav, 75

"Nessun dorma!" (aria from *Turandot*), 126

Netrebko, Anna, 6–7, 175, 210, 212, 274

New Opera Company of New York, 273

Newsom, Gavin, 107

Newton, Christopher, 135

New World Records, 239

New York City Opera, 50, 146, 224, 236

New York Times, The, 127, 224

Nicolai, Otto, 68

Night at the Opera, A (motion picture), 286

Nilsson, Birgit, 135, 138–39, 150, 267–68

Nine Rivers from Jordan (Hugo Weisgall), 221–22

Niska, Maralin, 40, 50

Nixon, Marni, 37, 50

Nixon, Richard Milhous, 34

Nixon in China (John Adams), 226

Noble, Timothy, 179

No Exit. See Huis-clos

Nono, Nuria, 33

Norma (Vincenzo Bellini), 117, 271

Norman, Jessye, 225, 286

Nothenberg, Rudolf, 185

Nozze di Figaro, Le (Wolfgang Amadeus Mozart), 49–50, 116, 133, 276, 278

Nutcracker (ballet), 207

Oberon (Carl Maria von Weber), 48

Objective Burma (motion picture), 25

O'Brian, Jack, 246

Obrucheniye v monastire (Sergei Sergeievitch Prokofiev), 174

Ochman, Wiesław, 166

Offenbach, Jacques, 96, 178

Ognenny angel (Sergei Sergeievitch Prokofiev), 174, 206

Oistrakh, David, 130

O'Keefe Centre for the Performing Arts, 116, 131–32, 138, 141, 145

Okerlund, David, 246

Old Vic Theatre, London, 115

Olivero, Magda, 45

O'Neill, Doreen, 278

Ontario College of Art, 117

Ontriveros, Donald, 231

Opera America, 147, 161, 239

Opéra Bastille, Paris, 253

Opera Company of Boston, 271

OPERA Magazine, 224

Opera News Magazine, 224

Oper Frankfurt, 2, 3

Opernhaus Zürich, 5, 50–51, 63–64, 68–69, 78, 81, 284

Opthof, Cornelius, 137

Orchestre de la Suisse Romande, 81

Order of Canada, 119

Orfeo (Claudio Monteverdi), 34

Orfeo ed Euridice (Christoph Willibald von Gluck), 109

Orlando furioso (Antonio Vivaldi), 201

Orleanskaya dyeva (Pyotr Ilyitch Tchaikovsky), 117

Orphée et Euridice (Christoph Willibald von Gluck), 181

Orpheum Theater, San Francisco, 187–89, 191–92, 195, 235–36

Orth, Robert, 237, 257

Osher, Barbro, 156, 187, 190

Osher, Bernard, 156, 187, 190

Othello (Shakespeare), 1, 239

Otello (Giuseppe Verdi), 1, 35, 58–60, 62–63, 65, 81, 156, 167

Out Cry (Tennessee Williams), 237

"Over There" (song), 42

Pace, Francesco, 49–50

Pacific Visions, 232

Packard, John, 254–55
Pagliacci (Ruggiero Leoncavallo), 42
Pahlavi, Ashraf, 82
Pahlavi, Fatemeh, 20, 82
Pahlavi, Mohammed Reza Shah, 14, 19–20, 24, 26, 32, 82–84, 87, 93–94, 99–100
Pahlavi, Reza Khan Shah, 14–16
Palace Hotel, San Francisco, 165–66
Palestrina (Hans Pfitzner), 45
Palmer, Felicity, 277
Panagulias, Ann, 172, 211
Pantages Theatre, Toronto, 115
Pappano, Antonio, 203, 292
Parker, Eleanor, 32
Parsifal (Richard Wagner), 55
Patané, Franco, 288
Patané, Giuseppe, 288
Patriarco, Earle, 272
Patria II: Characteristics of Man (R. Murray Schafer), 135
Pavarotti, Luciano, 123–26, 138, 152, 155–56, 162, 221, 225, 268–70, 283, 288
Pears, Peter, 82
Pêcheurs de perles, Les (Georges Bizet), 224
Pelléas et Mélisande (Claude Debussy), 50, 132
Penderecki, Krzysztof, 282
Penn, Sean, 253–54, 257
Peter Grimes (Benjamin Britten), 34
Peterson, David, 158
Peterson, Glade, 63–64
Pfitzner, Hans, 45
Philippe, Gérard, 228, 252
Philips, Mary, 246
Phillips, Susanna, 272
Picasso, Pablo, 36
Picker, Tobias, 280

Pikovaya dama (Pyotr Ilyitch Tchaikovsky), 148
Pinza, Ezio, 32
Piper, Myfanwy, 228
Pique Dame. See *Pikovaya dama*
Planet of the Apes (motion picture), 124
Plishka, Paul, 172
Poliuto (Gaetano Donizetti), 73
Pollini, Maurizio, 242
Popper, Jan, 34, 37–38, 48, 50, 295
Porgy and Bess (George Gershwin), 181
Post, Ted, 41
Poulenc, Francis, 140, 276
Powell, Dick, 40
Powell, Eleanor, 36
Préjean, Sister Helen, 253, 255, 258
Preminger, Otto, 271
Prêtre, Georges, 151, 285–87
Previn, André, 4, 218, 242–44, 246–48, 250, 280
Price, Leontyne, 150, 155, 270
Price, Margaret, 150, 155
Příhody Lišky Bystroušky (Leoš Janáček), 56
Prince Igor. See *Knyadz Igor*
Prince of Wales Theatre, Toronto, 115
Pritchard, John, 82, 201
Prokofiev, Sergei Sergeievitch, 171, 174, 181
Prophète, Le (Giacomo Meyerbeer), 150, 265
Puccini, Giacomo, 114, 128, 223, 276, 282
Punch and Judy (Harrison Birtwhistle), 242
Puritani, I (Vincenzo Bellini), 279, 290
Putnam, Ashley, 224

Qajars, 14–15

Queen of Sheba, The. See *Königin von Saba, Die*

Queen of Spades, The. See *Pikovaya dama*

"Questa o quella" (aria from *Rigoletto*), 67

Quilico, Gino, 250

Racette, Patricia, 6, 222

Rake's Progress, The (Igor Stravinsky), 117, 278

Ramey, Samuel, 272, 277, 280

Ramo, Suzanne, 9

Rappold, Marie, 165

Rathbone, Basil, 22

Rattle, Simon, 132

Ravel, Maurice, 96

Reader's Digest, The, 41

Realitillusion (Michel-Georges Brégent), 136

Redlands University, 37

Red Rocks Amphitheater, Colorado, 59

Red Violin, The (John Corigliano), 250

Reinhardt, Max, 33, 149–50

Relyea, John, 200

Remer, Michael, 242

Renée, Madelyn, 125

Requiem (Wolfgang Amadeus Mozart), 177

Requiem (Giuseppe Verdi), 215

Rescigno, Nicola, 288–89

Resnik, Regina, 53, 273

Rhodes, Teddy Tahu, 254

Riber, Jean-Claude, 103–4, 106

Richter, Karl, 283

Rickman, Alan, 228

Riel, Christiane, 113

Rigoletto (Giuseppe Verdi), 49, 67, 247

Rimsky-Korsakov, Nikolai Andrei-evitch, 21

Ring des Nibelungen, Der (Richard Wagner), 104, 152, 176, 201–2, 229

Ritz Carlton Hotel, San Francisco, 249

Robbins, Tim, 253, 257

Roberta (musical), 40

Robertson, Ian, 204, 227

Robeson, Paul, 276

Robinson, Edward G., 49

Robinson, Twyla, 7, 9

Roger Wagner Chorale, 271

Romero, Manley, 231

Rooney, Mickey, 50

Roosevelt, Franklin Delano, 24

Roosevelt, Theodore, 166

Rose Is a Rose, A (Ann Mortifee), 219

Rosenberg, Pamela, 2–4, 208, 209–15, 250, 258

Rosenberg, Philip, 128

Rosenkavalier, Der (Richard Strauss), 6, 33, 44–45, 66, 206, 215, 264, 277

Rossignol, Le (Igor Stravinsky), 284

Rossi-Lemeni, Nicola, 263

Rossini, Gioachino, 177–78, 271, 287

Rostropovich, Mstislav, 171

Rothenberger, Anneliese, 46

Royal Alexandra Theatre, Toronto, 115–16

Royal Conservatory, Toronto, 109

Royal Ontario Museum, 121

Royal Opera House Covent Garden, London, 74, 292

Royal Shakespeare Company, 228

Roy Thomson Symphony Hall, 121

Rubinstein, Arthur, 35–36

Rubinstein, Eva, 35–36

Runnicles, Donald, 3, 202–6, 209–10, 214–15, 231, 234, 236, 255, 261

Index

Ruslan i Lyudmila (Mikhail Ivano-
vitch Glinka), 6, 172, 174–75
Russell, Anna, 141
Russian Community Center, San
Francisco, 172
Rysanek, Leonie, 198

Sabu, 26
Sacramento Philharmonic, 161
Sadler's Wells Opera, London, 133,
293
Safdie, Moshe, 143
*Sailor Who Fell from Grace with the
Sea, The* (Yukio Mishima), 224
Saint François d'Assise (Olivier Mes-
siaen), 178, 251, 259
St. Just, Maria, 240
Saint of Bleecker Street, The (Gian
Carlo Menotti), 49
Saint Stephen's Cathedral, Vienna,
177
Salome (Richard Strauss), 100
Salzurger Festspiele, 62, 73, 109, 150,
178, 284, 287
Samson et Dalila (Camille Saint-
Saëns), 151, 285
San Carlo. *See* Teatro San Carlo
San Carlo Opera, 49
Sanderling, Thomas, 288
Sandlin, Dorothy, 40
San Francisco Ballet, 167, 174
San Francisco Chronicle, 258
San Francisco Conservatory of
Music, 228
San Francisco Opera: and *Arshak II*,
207–8; and Charles Mackerras,
291–92; and Kurt Herbert Adler,
40, 125, 156–59; and Loma Prieta
earthquake, 165–68, 183–201;
and L.M., 1, 4–5, 8, 12, 34–35,
80, 149–53, 161, 163; and Lotte

Lehmann, 44; and Marilyn Horne,
271–72; and supertitles, 146; and
Terrence McEwen, 156–59
San Francisco Opera Chorus, 226
San Francisco State University, 226
San Francisco Symphony Orchestra,
167, 174, 204
San Francisco War Memorial and
Performing Arts Center, 167
Santa Fe Opera, 80, 83, 118, 215,
276–77, 280–81, 285
Santi, Nello, 66, 82, 203, 265, 280
Sarandon, Susan, 253, 257
Sarfaty, Regina, 63
Saroyan, William, 41
Sartre, Jean-Paul, 293
Satyagraha (Philip Glass), 176, 241
Schafer, R. Murray, 135, 136
Schaffner, Franklin J., 123–28
Schaller, Linda, 7
Schellen, Nando, 134
Scheppelman, Christina, 243
Schiebler, Hermann, 68
Schneider, Peter, 202–3, 291
Schoenberg, Arnold, 33, 54, 61, 74,
132
Schoenberg, Nuria. *See* Nono, Nuria
Schuricht, Carl, 108
Schwarzkopf, Elisabeth, 150
Schweigsame Frau, Die (Richard
Strauss), 33
Sciutti, Graziella, 274–75
Scotto, Renata, 92, 138, 268–70
Screen Actors' Guild, 129
Screen Directors' Playhouse (TV
series), 41
Seattle Opera, 176
Sellars, Peter, 178, 225–27
Semiramide (Gioachino Rossini), 271
"Sempre libera" (aria from *La travi-
ata*), 74

Serafin, Tullio, 263

Seventh Heaven (motion picture), 42

Shakespeare, William, 1, 58, 73, 278, 295

Shane, Rita, 280

Shanley, John Patrick, 129

Shaw, Artie, 24

Shicoff, Neil, 280

Shorenstein, Walter, 181, 187, 191–92, 195

Shostakovich, Dmitry Dmitrievitch, 140, 210

Showboat (Jerome Kern), 238

Shrader, Alek, 272

Shrine Auditorium, Los Angeles, 49, 149

Silk (poem by Alessandro Baricco), 250

Silk (opera project for André Previn), 208, 250–51

Sills, Beverly, 92, 96, 146, 198, 237, 270, 285

Simionato, Giulietta, 45, 150

Simmons, Calvin, 132

Simon, Joanna, 69

Simon, Richard, 69

Simon & Schuster, 69

Simon Boccanegra (Giuseppe Verdi), 73, 287

Simonov, Yuri, 291

Six Characters in Search of an Author (Hugo Weisgall), 221

Six Degrees of Separation (John Guare), 250

60 Minutes (TV program), 277

Skovhus, Boje (Bo), 4, 250

Slezak, Leo, 195

Sloan, Douglas (Doug), 110–11

Smith, Patrick J., 224

Smith, Scott, 235

Söderström, Elisabeth, 82, 264–65

Solar Temple, 134

Solti, Georg, 150

Somers, Harry, 219–20

Sondheim, Stephen, 238–39, 241

Sonnambula, La (Vincenzo Bellini), 8

Southam, G. Hamilton, 133–34

Spring Opera Theatre, 154

Staatsoper Stuttgart, 4

Stalin, Joseph Vissarionovitch, 24

Stanford University, 34, 163

Stade, Frederica von (Flicka), 229–30, 233, 252, 254, 257, 279–80

Stapp, Olivia, 146

State of the Union (play), 37

Stearns, David Patrick, 249

Steber, Eleanor, 48

Stefano, Giuseppe di, 288

Steiger, Rod, 41

Stenz, Markus, 224, 291

Stevens, Risë, 23

Stevens, Roy, 222

Stevens, Mr. and Mrs. Thomas, 30

Stevenson, Juliet, 228

Stewart, John, 117

Stewart, Thomas, 53, 55

Stich-Randall, Theresa, 53

Stockhausen, Karl-Heinz, 95

Stothers, Walter, 114, 210

Stratas, Teresa, 128, 138, 250

Straus, Oscar, 23

Strauss, Johann, Jr., 69, 104

Strauss, Josef, 69

Strauss, Richard, 6, 33, 44–45, 145, 155, 178, 264, 266–67, 292

Stravinsky, Igor, 74, 77, 278, 282, 284

Streep, Meryl, 124

Streetcar Named Desire, A (André Previn), 7, 217, 232, 237–38, 240–41, 243–45, 247–51

Strelitzer, Hugo, 39–40

Index

Strindberg, August, 136

Stubbs, Janet, 117

Stuttgart State Opera. *See* Staatsoper Stuttgart

Sullivan, Timothy, 136

Summer and Smoke (Lee Hoiby), 241

Summers, Patrick, 3, 9–10, 203, 206, 210, 246, 248, 255, 280

Sunday Telegraph, London, 249

Suor Angelica (Giacomo Puccini), 40

Susa, Conrad, 228–31, 233–34

Susannah (Carlisle Floyd), 49

Süssmayr, Franz Xaver, 177

Sutherland, Joan, 8, 68, 117, 124, 138–39, 156, 221, 261, 271, 289

Svazlian, Gerald, 207–8

Swed, Mark, 249

Swenson, Ruth Ann, 8–9

Swift, Page, 35

Swinford, Jerome, 276

Tabachnik, Michel, 134

Tabarro, Il (Giacomo Puccini), 40, 150

Taddei, Giuseppe, 96, 150, 278

Tales of Hoffmann, The. See *Contes d'Hoffmann, Les*

Tandy, Jessica, 237

Tanenbaum, Joey, 120–22, 142

Tanenbaum, Toby, 121

Tanenbaum Centre, Toronto, 120, 219

Tanenbaum Courtyard Gardens, 122

Tanglewood Festival, Lenox, Mass., 65

Tannhäuser (Richard Wagner), 23, 226

Tchaikovsky, Pyotr Ilyitch, 117

Teatro alla Scala, Milan, 45, 73, 138, 239, 263, 268, 288, 290

Teatro Colón, Buenos Aires, 109

Teatro la Fenice, Venice, 68

Teatro San Carlo, Naples, 70, 288

Tebaldi, Renata, 92, 129, 152, 221, 263

Tehran Opera House, 94

Telaria, 146–47

Telephone, The (Gian Carlo Menotti), 32

Temirkanov, Yuri, 292

Tempest, The (William Shakespeare), 295

Terfel, Bryn, 244, 278, 280

Terzian, Tovmas R., 208

Theater Dortmund, 237

Théâtre André Dussolier, Divonne, France, 104

Théâtre Royal de la Monnaie, Brussels, 225

Thielemann, Christian, 203, 292

This Is the Army (musical review), 25

Thomas, Ambroise, 139

Thomas, Jess, 53

Thomas, Michael Tilson, 204

Thomas, Robert, 49–50, 63–64

Thomas, Viviane, 146

Thompson, Glenn, 37

Thompson, Marjorie Ann. *See* Mansouri, Marjorie

Thomson, Ulf, 152

Time Magazine, 44

Tony Award. *See* Antoinette Perry Award

Tony Beaver (Josef Marais), 37

Tootsie (motion picture), 240

Toronto Symphony Orchestra, 130, 135, 139

Tosca (Giacomo Puccini), 42, 49, 147, 196–97, 279, 281

Toscanini, Arturo, 44, 48, 62, 150, 200, 287

Tozzi, Giorgio, 287

Tracy, Spencer, 29

Trans-Canada Pipelines, Ltd., 136

Traviata, La (Giuseppe Verdi), 49–50, 64, 68, 116, 137, 143, 218, 261

Trintignant, Jean-Louis, 228

Tristan und Isolde (Richard Wagner), 204, 233

Trittico, Il (Giacomo Puccini), 40

Trouble in Tahini (Leonard Bernstein), 69, 104

Trovatore, Il (Giuseppe Verdi), 68, 79, 155, 187, 273, 290

Troyanos, Tatiana, 117, 266–67, 279–80

Troyens, Les (Hector Berlioz), 104, 153

Tsarskoye nevesta (Nikolai Andreievitch Rimsky-Korsakov), 210

Tucker, Richard, 41

Turandot (Giacomo Puccini), 5, 124, 126, 267–68, 290

Turgeon, Bernard, 118

Turner, Lana, 29

Turn of the Screw, The (Benjamin Britten), 49, 228

Twain, Mark (Samuel Clemens), 35

Twentieth Century Fox, 40

Tyga, George, 220

Tynes, Margeret, 53

Ullrich, Allan, 158

"Un bel dì" (aria from *Madama Butterfly*), 149

Undine (Hans Werner Henze), 241

United Nations, 180

University of British Columbia, 119

University of California at Berkeley, 50, 226

University of California at Los Angeles (UCLA), 27, 30, 34–35, 40, 49–50, 278, 295

University of Southern California (USC), 30

USA Today, 249

Vadim, Roger, 228

Valdengo, Giuseppe, 70

Valente, Bettina, 44

Vancouver Festival, 279

van Dam, José, 82

Vanderhoof, Dory, 114

Vaness, Carol, 9, 117, 200, 252, 264–66

Vanessa (Samuel Barber), 46, 48–49, 241, 273

Van Rooy, Anton, 165

Varnay, Astrid, 53, 144

Verdi, Giuseppe, 1, 58, 63, 96, 140, 156, 215, 218, 223, 283, 287, 292

Vernon, Lyn, 117, 289

Verona Arena. *See* Arena di Verona

Verratene Meer, Das (Hans Werner Henze), 224, 241

Vickers, David, 135

Vickers, Jon, 74, 135, 153, 262–63, 290

Vienna Philharmonic. *See* Wiener Philharmoniker

Vienna State Opera. *See* Wiener Staatsoper

Vienna Volksoper. *See* Wiener Volksoper

Vilar, Alberto, 5

Villanueva, LeRoy, 222

Vinay, Ramón, 35, 62, 81, 265

Visconti, Luchino, 73, 240, 242

Vishnevskaya, Galina, 171

Voina i Mir (Sergei Sergeievitch Prokofiev), 171–72

Volkwijn, Donita, 9, 255

Volpe, Joseph, 174, 186, 248

Von heute auf morgen (Arnold Schoenberg), 61

Wagner, Friedelind, 54–56, 59
Wagner, Richard, 23, 40, 54–55, 119, 135, 144, 176, 218, 226, 283
Wagner, Roger, 40
Wagner, Siegfried, 55
Wagner, Wieland, 55–56
Wagner, Winifred, 55
Wagner, Wolfgang, 56
Wahnfried, 55
Walker, Edyth, 165
Walküre, Die (Richard Wagner), 40, 59, 135, 144
Wallace, Stewart, 235–36
Wallerstein, Lothar, 109
Wall Street Journal, 213
Walter, Bruno, 33, 44, 273
Walters, Jess, 144
War and Peace. See Voina i Mir
Ward, Robert, 217
Warfield, Sandra, 63–64, 68
War Memorial Opera House, 158, 167, 181, 193
Warren, Leonard, 62
War Requiem (Benjamin Britten), 82
Washington Opera, 234
Watson, Claire, 53, 150
Watson, Janice, 244
Wattis, Phyllis, 232, 247, 258
Wayne, John, 41
Weathers, Felicia, 54, 69
Weber, Carl Maria von, 48
Weber, Irene, 32
Weill, Kurt, 104, 120, 217
Weisgall, Hugo, 221–24
Welch, Raquel, 95
Wells, Jeffrey, 175, 193
Welsh National Opera, 132

Werfel, Franz, 33
Werther (Jules Massenet), 231, 279, 288
West Side Story (Leonard Bernstein), 64
West Side Story (motion picture), 37
Westways magazine, 51
Where's Dick? (Stewart Wallace), 235
White, Dan, 235
Whitfield, Michael, 146
Whitman, Walt, 232
Wiener Philharmoniker, 131, 238
Wiener Staatsoper, 62, 131
Wiener Volksoper, 150, 238
Wilde, Cornel, 17, 29
Wilder, Samuel (Billy), 39
Wilford, Ronald A. 171, 202, 248, 251
Wilkins, Judy. *See* Mackerras, Judy
Williams, Janet, 179
Williams, Robin, 257
Williams, Thomas Lanier (Tennessee), 237–38, 240, 244, 250
Wilsey, Diane B. (Dede), 3, 187
Wilshire Ebell Theater, 48–49
Wilson, Lanford, 241
Windward, Irwin, 31
Winters, Lawrence, 54
Wong, Randall, 222
Wood, Cynthia, 155
Wood, Natalie, 37
Woods, Gordon, 142
Woolcock, Penny, 228
Wozzeck (Alban Berg), 49, 68, 130, 132, 134, 140, 249, 263, 284
Wright, George, 116
Wuorinen, Charles, 228
Wuthering Heights (Carlisle Floyd), 280
Wyatt, Carol, 117
Wyler, William, 39

Yeargan, Michael, 254–56
Yes, Giorgio (motion picture), 124, 127
Yoelson, Moshe Reuben, 114
York, Michael, 237
Young, Loretta, 32
Young, Simone, 285

Zajick, Dolora, 179
Zambello, Francesca, 208, 222–23
Zaremba, Elena, 193
Zauberflöte, Die (Wolfgang Amadeus
    Mozart), 47, 57
Zeani, Virginia, 263

Zeffirelli, Franco, 128, 239–41, 247,
    290
Zigeunerbaron, Der (Johann Strauss,
    Jr.), 104
Zoé (Richard Désilets), 136
Zolotoy petushok (Sergei Sergeievitch
    Prokofiev), 4
Zoroastrians, 20
Zurich Opera. *See* Opernhaus Zürich
Zweig, Fritz, 33, 39–40, 44–46, 54,
    62, 73, 295
Zweig, Stefan, 33
Zweig, Tilly. *See* de Garmo, Tilly